What was the effect of the Reformation movement on the parishioners of the German countryside? This book examines the reform movement at the level of its implementation – the rural parish.

Investigation of the Reformation and the sixteenth-century parish reveals the strength of tradition and custom in village life and how this parish culture obstructed and frustrated the efforts of the Lutheran reformers. The Reformation was not passively adopted by the rural inhabitants. On the contrary, the parishioners manipulated the reform movement to serve their own ends. Parish documentation reveals that the system of parish rule diffused the disciplinary aims of the church and rendered the pastors impotent. A look at parish beliefs suggests that the nature of parish thought worked to undermine the main tenets of the Lutheran faith, and that the legacy of the Reformation was a dialogue between these two realms of experience.

CAMBRIDGE STUDIES IN EARLY MODERN HISTORY

The Reformation and rural society

CAMBRIDGE STUDIES IN EARLY MODERN HISTORY

Edited by Professor Sir John Elliott, University of Oxford, Professor Olwen Hufton, Harvard University, and Professor H. G. Koenigsberger

The idea of an 'early modern' period of European history from the fifteenth to the late eighteenth century is now widely accepted among historians. The purpose of Cambridge Studies in Early Modern History is to publish monographs and studies which illuminate the character of the period as a whole, and in particular focus attention on a dominant theme within it, the interplay of continuity and change as they are presented by the continuity of medieval ideas, political and social organisation, and by the impact of new ideas, new methods and new demands on the traditional structure.

For a list of titles published in the series, please see end of book

The Reformation and rural society

The parishes of Brandenburg-Ansbach-Kulmbach, 1528–1603

C. SCOTT DIXON

The Queen's University of Belfast

CAMBRIDGE
UNIVERSITY PRESS

Published by the Press Syndicate of the University of Cambridge
The Pitt Building, Trumpington Street, Cambridge CB2 1RP
40 West 20th Street, New York, NY 10011–4211, USA
10 Stamford Road, Oakleigh, Melbourne 3166, Australia

© Cambridge University Press 1996

First published 1996

Printed in Great Britain at the University Press, Cambridge

A catalogue record for this book is available from the British Library

Library of Congress cataloguing in publication data applied for

ISBN 0 521 48311 5 hardback

CE

For my Mother

Contents

Contents

Preface

The present book is an edited version of my doctoral thesis, which I submitted to Cambridge University in the Autumn of 1992. During the course of my initial research and subsequent revision I have received financial support from a number of funds and institutions, and I would like to thank them here: The Cambridge Commonwealth Trust, who were kind enough to offer me an *ex gratia* grant from my Cambridge Canada Scholarship to help with my stay in Nuremberg; the German Historical Institute, which supported the bulk of my research costs; Clare College, Cambridge; the Worts Travelling Scholars Fund; the Cambridge Historical Society; the Prince Consort and Thirlwall Fund; and the Institut für Europäische Geschichte, Mainz, where I was able to add some finishing touches to the work.

Over the years I have received help from a great many people, only a few of whom I can mention here. Andrew Pettegree has offered me guidance and support since my days as an undergraduate at the University of St Andrews. I hope I grow to be as useful to my own students. I owe a tremendous debt to my supervisor, Bob Scribner. Without the example of his scholarship, I would not have approached the archives to investigate this issue; and without the benefit of his extensive knowledge and judicious supervision, I would still be there. Henry Cohn and Tom Scott were very approachable examiners; where I have incorporated their advice, the book has profited. The staff and scholars in the libraries and archives in Nuremberg, Bamberg, Munich, and Mainz have helped me every step of the way. It was a privilege to work in such a friendly environment. I would like to reserve a special note of thanks for the staff at the Landeskirchliches Archiv, Nuremberg, who made my stay in the archives a daily pleasure. Marion Tonke and Annemarie Müller, in particular, were very helpful. Gerhard and Waltraud Köstler gave me a home when I was in desperate need of one and became my good friends. I am grateful to them all.

My greatest debt is recorded in the dedication.

Abbreviations

ARG	*Archiv für Reformationsgeschichte*
LKAN	Landeskirchliches Archiv Nürnberg
MKA	Markgräfliches Konsistorium Ansbach
MDB	Markgräfliches Dekanat Baiersdorf
MDF	Markgräfliches Dekanat Feuchtwangen
MDG	Markgräfliches Dekanat Gunzenhausen
MDH	Markgräfliches Dekanat Hof
MDK	Markgräfliches Dekanat Kitzingen
MDLz	Markgräfliches Dekanat Langenzenn
MDL	Markgräfliches Dekanat Leutershausen
MDN	Markgräfliches Dekanat Neustadt an der Aisch
MDS	Markgräfliches Dekanat Schwabach
MDU	Markgräfliches Dekanat Uffenheim
MDW	Markgräfliches Dekanat Wassertrüdingen
MDWz	Markgräfliches Dekanat Wülzburg
MSK	Markgräfliches Dekanat (Superintendentur) Kulmbach
MSB	Superintendentur Bayreuth
Sehling	Emil Sehling (ed.), *Die evangelischen Kirchenordnungen des XVI.* *Jahrhunderts*. Tübingen, 1961, 11 (Bayern: Franken), part 1.
StaN	Staatsarchiv Nürnberg
StaB	Staatsarchiv Bamberg
ZbKG	*Zeitschrift für bayerische Kirchengeschichte*

Introduction

Writing in 1526, the Ansbach clergyman Johann Rurer encouraged his prince, margrave Casimir of Brandenburg-Ansbach-Kulmbach, to view the widespread support for the evangelical faith as proof of its divine provenance:

Your princely grace can witness [the truth of the faith] therein, that now the people everywhere want to have the Word of God preached to them, that they are so eager and anxious, stream and press with such frequency and urgency [*gewalt*] – often from great distances – to hear the Word preached, regardless of the fact that they are called Lutheran, heretical, or in other ways scolded and fiercely punished.[1]

As they hunger for bread, Rurer continued, now the people hunger for the Word of God, the teaching of the Gospel 'clear and pure'. But was Rurer correct in his assumption that the margrave's subjects longed to hear the Word of God, or was this just the hopeful projection of a pious man looking to convert an indifferent ruler to the faith? What was the reaction of the subject population to the religious movement radiating from Wittenberg? Did the margrave's rural subjects in Ansbach and Kulmbach show an interest in the evangelical movement? Did they eventually embrace the Lutheran faith once it was officially introduced? And if Rurer's judgement rings true – that the people hungered for the Word – what was the ultimate effect of Lutheranism in the years following Casimir's death in 1527, when margrave Georg the Pious assumed rule and introduced the Reformation into Brandenburg-Ansbach-Kulmbach? Did religious reform extend to the rural parishes? Did it affect the lives of those in the smaller towns, in the villages and the forest hamlets? Western Christendom, scholars have long claimed, was deeply impressed by the religious upheavals of the sixteenth century. But how was confessional change experienced by the subject population? What was the relationship between the Reformation and the long-term development of rural society? The following work is an attempt to answer these fundamental historical questions.

This study investigates the implementation of the Reformation in the German principality of Brandenburg-Ansbach-Kulmbach and the implications of this event

---

[1] Johann Rurer, *Cristliche unterrichtung eins Pfarhern an seinen herrn/ein fursten des heyligen Reychs/ auff viertzig Artickel und puncten gestelt/was eins rechten/waren/ Evangelischen Pfarhern oder Predigers/Predigen und lere sein soll/mit einfürung etlicher sprüch in heiliger geschrifft gegründt/das solch lere/das ware wort Gottes sey/Auch ableynung viler vermeinten einreden/ fast nützlich un[d] trostlich zu lesen unnd zuhoren* (1526), Dii.

for the rural populace. The object of this investigation is the rural parishioner, the men and women who lived in the outlying towns, villages, and hamlets during the first century of reform. Unlike the 'articulate minorities', people who shaped the course of the Reformation either through their published works or their recorded actions, the rural parishioners have left little or no testimony behind. It is not possible, therefore, to analyse the effects of the Reformation on the rural populace as a historian of ideas might trace the development of an intellectual movement or as an anthropologist might observe the many subtle gestures behind a cultural disposition. The role played by the rural parishioner in the reform movement must be reconstructed out of source materials which portray, rather than directly represent, the thoughts and actions of the parishioners themselves (tithe disputes, parish visitation returns, parish litigation, feuds between the pastor and his congregation, witchcraft trials). Respecting the limitations, however, the historian can recreate the process of reform and intuit its effect on rural society. The Reformation in the rural parishes has its own story to tell.

A social history of the Reformation movement in its rural setting can make no claims to methodological innovation. Over the last thirty years scholars have grown sensitive to the charge that Reformation studies had become too ahistorical, too concerned with doctrine and rhetoric at the expense of the social milieu. Since the publication of Bernd Moeller's *Imperial Cities and the Reformation* (1962) there has been an outpouring of works devoted to the social history of the Reformation, works concerned less with the development of theology or the clash of confessional politics in the Empire than the fate of the Reformation movement in specific social and temporal contexts. The Reformation has been placed in a much more complex dynamic; religious reform was frequently manipulated by the interests of different social classes and hostage to a type of religiosity bound up in, and inseparable from, the secular realm. No longer determined solely by the tracts and directives flowing out of Wittenberg, the Reformation movement, as it is described by social historians, followed different paths and separate destinies, so that no two models of its unfolding were exactly alike. Only one thing ties all of this scholarship together. Up to this point, the vast majority of this work has situated reform in urban centres.[2] The

---

[2] See the overviews by Euan Cameron, *The European Reformation* (Oxford, 1991), pp. 213–66, 475–87; Hans-Christoph Rublack, 'Forschungsbericht Stadt und Reformation', in Bernd Moeller (ed.), *Stadt und Kirche im 16. Jahrhundert* (Gütersloh, 1978), pp. 9–26; Kaspar von Greyerz, 'Stadt und Reformation: Stand und Aufgaben der Forschung', *ARG* 76 (1985), 6–64. The more significant works would include: Bernd Moeller, trans. H. C. Erik Midelfort and Mark U. Edwards, *Imperial Cities and the Reformation* (Durham, 1982); Hans-Christoph Rublack, *Die Einführung der Reformation in Konstanz von den Anfängen bis zum Abschluß 1531* (Gütersloh, 1971); Steven Ozment, *The Reformation in the Cities* (London, 1975); Hans-Christoph Rublack, *Eine bürgerliche Reformation: Nördlingen* (Gütersloh, 1982); Lorna Jane Abray, *The People's Reformation: Magistrates, Clergy and Commons in Strasbourg 1500–1598* (Oxford, 1985); Thomas A. Brady, *Ruling Class, Regime and Reformation at Strasbourg 1520–1555* (Leiden, 1978); Kaspar von Greyerz, *The Late City Reformation in Germany: The Case of Colmar 1522–1628* (Wiesbaden, 1980); R. Po-Chia Hsia, *Society and Religion in Münster 1535–1618* (New Haven, 1984).

Introduction

detailed social histories of the Reformation and the patient investigations of religious change and its consequences have been studies of the Reformation in the cities. In contrast to our understanding of the process of urban reform, the course of the Reformation in the countryside remains relatively unknown. The standard rejoinder to the preoccupation with the cities has been the interest in the Peasants' War of 1525.[3] But the 1525 uprising was an event located in a crosscurrent of unique circumstances, many peculiar to the war itself; the war was not necessarily representative of the relationship between the Reformation and rural society. Only quite recently, in response to this gap in Reformation scholarship, have scholars begun to pay more attention to the dynamic of religious change as it occurred in the countryside. The focus is still on the first decade of the movement, however, with the Peasants' War looming over events. There have been few systematic attempts (for the German lands) to analyse the influence of the Reformation in a rural environment using an approach that is sensitive to parish-level changes over the long term.[4] This need was made evident after the publication of Gerald Strauss's *Luther's House of Learning* (1978), a work which challenged the very essence of Lutheran claims to success (the realisation of their educational goals and the indoctrination of the faith) yet suffered the weight of very little

---

[3] See the overview by Tom Scott, 'The Peasants' War: A Historiographical Review', *The Historical Journal*, 22, 3 (1979), 693–720, 953–74.

[4] Most modern studies of the Reformation in the countryside still focus on the growth of the church and the extension of the state without paying much heed to events in the outlying parishes. See, for instance, Heinz Schilling, *Konfessionskonflikt und Staatsbildung. Eine Fallstudie über das Verhältnis von religiösem und sozialem Wandel in der Frühneuzeit am Beispiel der Grafschaft Lippe* (Gütersloh, 1981); Günther Wartenberg, *Landesherrschaft und Reformation. Moritz von Sachsen und die albertinische Kirchenpolitik bis 1546* (Gütersloh, 1988). Recent works focusing on the reception of the Reformation in the rural parishes include: Peter Blickle, *Gemeindereformation. Die Menschen des 16. Jahrhunderts auf dem Weg zum Heil* (Munich, 1987); Franziska Conrad, *Reformation in der bäuerlichen Gesellschaft. Zur Rezeption reformatorischer Theologie im Elsass* (Stuttgart, 1984); Peter Blickle (ed.), *Zugänge zur bäuerlichen Reformation* (Zürich, 1987); Hans von Rütte (ed.), *Bäuerliche Frömmigkeit und kommunale Reformation. Referate, gehalten am Schweizerischen Historikertag vom 23. Oktober 1987 in Bern* (*Itinera*), 8, 1988; Peter Blickle (ed.), *Landgemeinde und Stadtgemeinde in Mitteleuropa. Ein struktureller Vergleich* (Munich, 1991). All of these studies are limited in focus to the first few decades of the movement. See the overview by Tom Scott, 'The Common People in the German Reformation', *The Historical Journal*, 34, (1991), 183–91. The English Reformation has been rather better served in this respect. See the literature cited in Christopher Haigh, *English Reformations* (Oxford, 1993), pp. 339–42; Ronald Hutton, 'The Local Impact of the Tudor Reformations', in Christopher Haigh (ed.) *The English Reformation Revised* (Cambridge, 1987), p. 114, n. 1; Rosemary O'Day, *The Debate on the English Reformation* (London, 1986), pp. 133–65. The effect of the Counter-Reformation in the countryside has been examined by Marc R. Forster, *The Counter-Reformation in the Villages* (Ithaca, 1992). My own work went to press before I was able to consult Bruce Tolley, *Pastors and Parishioners in Württemberg during the Late Reformation, 1581–1621* (Stanford, 1995). I have, however, consulted Tolley's Stanford doctoral dissertation, which formed the basis of his book.

counter-evidence in return.[5] Our knowledge of events at the parish level during this century of religious change remains slight, even though this was the level at which the Reformation was experienced by the vast majority of the population. Local studies of the Reformation in the outlying parishes are crucial for a broader understanding of confessional change in the sixteenth century.

This book sets out to analyse the progress of religious reform in the former German margravate of Brandenburg-Ansbach-Kulmbach. Though it was of relatively modest dimensions, the margravate proved to be one of the most important territories in the Empire for the spread and consolidation of the Lutheran faith. Situated in south-west Germany, the northern principality of Kulmbach (Bayreuth) was the less developed of the two territories in the mid sixteenth century and was home to *circa* 60,000 subjects. Ansbach, to the south, was marginally larger than Kulmbach and more densely populated. (It is difficult to offer exact calculations, as both sections of the principality were beaded with multi-jurisdictional enclaves and lines of territorial interweave.) To the east of Ansbach were the lands of Nuremberg, to the south the dukedom of Pappenheim and the principality of Oettingen along with the Eichstätt bishopric, to the west Hohenlohe and the two imperial cities Schwäbisch Hall and Rothenburg. The bishopric of Würzburg sat to the north-west.[6] Kulmbach bordered the bishoprics of Bamberg and Würzburg to the west, while the imperial city of Nuremberg lay to the south. Nuremberg sat in the middle of the margravate and thus separated Ansbach and Kulmbach, precluding unification and extending its boundaries – up to twenty-five square miles – while it defended its jurisdictional claims.[7] Relations between the two powers were always strained, even in the early sixteenth century when the margravate and the imperial city worked together to effect religious change. Only a common devotion to Lutheranism gave cause for cooperation; and even during the period of their collaboration Nuremberg

---

[5] Gerald Strauss, *Luther's House of Learning: Indoctrination of the Young in the German Reformation* (London, 1978); Gerald Strauss, 'Success and Failure in the German Reformation', *Past & Present*, 67 (1975), 30–63. For a critique of Strauss's work, see James Kittelson, 'Successes and Failures in the German Reformation: The Report from Strasbourg', *ARG* 73 (1982), 153–74; James Kittelson, 'Visitations and Popular Religious Culture: Further Reports from Strasbourg', in Kyle C. Sessions and Phillip N. Bebb (eds.) *Pietas and Societas: New Trends in Social History* (Kirksville, 1985), pp. 89–102. For the latest overview of the 'success or failure' debate, see Geoffrey Parker, 'Success and Failure During the First Century of the Reformation', *Past and Present*, 136 (1992), 43–82.

[6] Rudolf Endres, 'Die Markgraftümer,' in M. Spindler (ed.), *Handbuch der bayerischen Geschichte* (Munich, 1971), III, part 1, pp. 398–9; Gottfried Stieber, *Historische und Topographische Nachricht von dem Fürstenthum Brandenburg-Onolzbach, aus zuverläßigen archivalischen Documenten, und andern glaubwürdigen Schrifften verfaßet* (Schwabach, 1761), pp. 5–16; Johann Bernhard Fischer, *Stätistische und topographische Beschreibung des Burggraftums Nürnberg unterhalb des Gebürgs; oder des Fürstentums Brandenburg-Anspach* (Ansbach, 1790), First Part, pp. 111–19.

[7] Heinz Dannenbauer, 'Die Entstehung des Territoriums der Reichsstadt Nürnberg', *Arbeiten zur deutschen Rechts- und Verfassungsgeschichte*, 7 (1928), 1–258; G. Pfeiffer, 'Der Aufstieg der Reichsstadt Nürnberg im 13. Jahrhundert', *Mitteilungen des Vereins für Geschichte der Stadt Nürnberg*, 44 (1953).

remained suspect and fearful of its powerful neighbour. And not without good reason: Brandenburg-Ansbach-Kulmbach was not a marginal territory, nor its rulers inconsequential lords.

As in other lands in the Holy Roman Empire, the Reformation in Brandenburg-Ansbach-Kulmbach was introduced in stages, periods of progress followed by terms of regression lasting the entire sixteenth century. When Luther first posted his theses in 1517, margrave Casimir (1515–1527) ruled over both Ansbach and Kulmbach. Thus the evangelical movement first penetrated the Franconian lands during Casimir's reign; but as will be shown, Casimir did little to promote the Reformation. True to the Hohenzollern philosophy of rule – that policy which had raised the Zollern castellans of Nuremberg to princes of the realm, margraves over the Franconian lands of Ansbach and Kulmbach, and ultimately Electors of the Mark Brandenburg – Casimir remained a devoted servant of the imperial cause. He died, as his son observed, in the service of the Empire, true to the Catholic faith.[8]

Not until margrave Georg the Pious (1527–1543) returned to his Franconian inheritance in 1528 was the reform movement actually introduced in the principality. Famous above all for his gesture before Charles V at Augsburg (1530), where he vowed he would sooner lose his head than forgo the Word of God, Georg's belief was always the final logic of his public actions. 'A man must render greater obedience to God than man', was how he answered those who would question this policy.[9] Immediately upon his return to Ansbach in 1528 he began preparing his domain for a full conversion to the evangelical faith, and he remained committed to the movement until his death in 1543. His work was not in vain. The son of Georg the Pious, Georg Friedrich (1556–1603), consolidated the work begun by his father in the religious realm. Ansbach and Kulmbach were divided up into a system of chapters ruled by a clerical elite. Annual synods monitored ecclesiastical affairs, while a consistory enforced the margrave's directives. Together with the clergyman Georg Karg, Georg Friedrich built an order for the church in the principality which has remained valid to this day. The reigns of Georg the Pious and Georg Friedrich – the period from 1528 to 1603 – witnessed the introduction and the consolidation of the Lutheran church in Brandenburg-Ansbach-Kulmbach and therefore provide the timescale for this study.[10]

---

[8] Christian Meyer, *Geschichte der Burggrafschaft Nürnberg und der späteren Markgrafschaften Ansbach and Bayreuth* (Tübingen, 1908), p. 106, n. 3.

[9] M. J. H. Schülin, *Leben und Geschichte des weyland Durchlauchtigsten Marggraff Georgens, zugenannt des Frommen* (Frankfurt, 1729), p. 108; Wilhelm Löhe, *Erinnerungen aus der Reformationsgeschichte von Franken, insonderheit der Stadt und dem Burggraftum Nürnberg ober und unterhalb des Gebirgs* (Nuremberg, 1847), pp. 112, 115.

[10] Individual histories of the margraves are provided by Günther Schuhmann, *Die Markgrafen von Brandenburg Ansbach. Eine Bilddokumentation zur Geschichte der Hohenzollern in Franken* (Ansbach, 1980).

Introduction

This work is divided into five main sections. The first chapter offers a narrative summary of the introduction of the Lutheran religion into Ansbach and Kulmbach. In order for the faith to take root the prince had to supply the appropriate guidance and support, while his subjects had to be receptive enough to allow the movement to take hold. Chapter 1 examines the Reformation's spread and reception in the principality. The second chapter traces the development of the Lutheran church in Brandenburg-Ansbach-Kulmbach; it outlines the emergence of a Lutheran clerical estate, the offices, the territory of the new church, the ordinances and mandates issued to define the structure of the church, the emergence of the consistory, and the significance of the visitation process for the implementation of reform. Chapter 3 investigates the quality of the Lutheran clergy and the nature of anticlericalism in Ansbach and Kulmbach. This chapter examines the state of clerical maintenance – often a motive for grievances against the clergy – especially the changes in income and wealth distribution introduced by the process of reform. Parish-level resistance to changes in income and distribution is explored in a final section. The fourth chapter looks at the impact of the Reformation on village culture. A survey of parish customs and pastimes illustrates the extent to which religious change actually affected village life and whether it is fitting to claim that the Reformation represented a 'disciplining' activity at the level of the parish. The Reformation is thus addressed at the point where injunction and practice met: the problems confronting reform are revealed in a detailed study of the political dynamic between the parish and the pastor. The final chapter addresses parish religion – or popular religion – and whether the outlook of the average parishioner was in fact modified by the Reformation process. Popular beliefs and customs are placed in two categories: Those thought to represent the continuance of a Catholic mentality are dealt with in a section on sacraments and sacramentals; the second section investigates popular magic, popular religion, witchcraft, and the local traditions of parish beliefs that continued to thrive throughout the century, despite the intervention of the Lutheran authorities. A concluding look at a witchcraft trial assesses the influence of the Lutheran faith on the parish mind during the first century of reform and thus offers some answers to the question uniting the work: how was the Reformation experienced in the rural parishes?

The emergence and reception of the evangelical movement, 1521–1533

THE REFORMATION IN THE TOWNS

In *A Dialogue Concerning Heresies* Thomas More made two observations that have since become commonplace in modern histories of the Reformation movement. More reasoned that the urban environment first gave the movement scope for development, while the strength of popular support ensured the movement's success:

> And yet in dyverse other partyes of Almayne and Swycherlande, thys vngracyous secte [Lutheranism] by the neglygence of the governours in great cytyes, ys so ferforth grown, that fynally the commune people have compelled the rulers to folow them, whom yf they had take hede in tyme, they myght have ruled and led.[1]

Recent scholarship has supported More's observations. The urban environment was very important for the reception and survival of the evangelical faith in the Empire.[2] The teaching of the reformers seems to have found a vast and eager audience among the 'commune people'. But these two points have to be qualified. The urban environment in sixteenth-century Germany was far from a uniform setting. Cities adopted the Reformation for different reasons to different ends; there was no fixed pattern to the Reformation in the cities, even if the coincidence of interests or the rationale behind reform may have honoured certain similarities from place to place. The same can be said for the role of the common man. The spread of the Reformation in the countryside was often encouraged and facilitated by the peasantry; but, like their urban counterparts, the rural parishioners acted out of complex motives. And yet More's assumption is fundamentally correct: the reform movement first took root in the cities; the initial strength of support at the parish level was dynamic enough to elevate the movement to a trans-parochial event. The Reformation in Brandenburg-Ansbach-Kulmbach bears witness to the truth of More's insights.

[1] Thomas More, 'A Dialogue Concerning Heresies', in Thomas M. C. Lawler, Germain Marchadour, and Richard C. Marius (eds.), *The Complete Works of St Thomas More* (London, 1981), vol. 6, part 1, p. 369, lines 31–5.

[2] On the 'urban Reformation', see Cameron, *The European Reformation*, pp. 213–63, 475–87.

The evangelical movement

Nuremberg

In its central location, dividing the territories of Ansbach and Kulmbach and spreading its jurisdictional claims deeper and deeper into the margravial lands, Nuremberg had always acted as a deterrent to the Hohenzollern quest for territorial unity. There is thus some irony in the fact that the Reformation in Brandenburg-Ansbach-Kulmbach was very much reliant upon the guidance and support offered by the free imperial city. The consolidation of the evangelical faith in the margravate, seen by both contemporaries and modern scholars as a major step on the path towards the centralisation of power in the early modern state, was in no small measure encouraged and mediated by the reform-minded inhabitants of this 'outpost of Wittenberg in southern Germany'.

Luther's message was first championed by the Nuremberg Humanist sodalities; Christoph Scheurl, once on the faculty at Wittenberg, Anton Tucher, Hieronymus Ebner, Kaspar Nützel, Wenceslaus Linck, Lazarus Spengler, and Willibald Pirckheimer were among the more prominent members. (Pirckheimer and Spengler were named in *Exsurge, Domine* (1520), Luther's bull of excommunication.) But religious reform was a concern not just of the academic elite. The Nuremberg magistracy had long been at work extending the reach of the city council's powers into the realm of ecclesiastical affairs. On the eve of the Reformation, there was little the bishop of Bamberg could do in the face of Nuremberg's considerable ecclesiastical leverage. Right of presentation to both city churches, St Sebald and St Lorenz, had been conferred upon the council in 1474 and further extended in 1513; all of the religious houses were governed by the council to some degree; the majority of private mass foundations had devolved into the council's hands. Nuremberg was the classic example of a free-imperial city prospecting for exclusive powers of jurisdiction within its city walls. Luther's call to reform held a certain appeal to an urban magistracy looking to limit the influence of the Catholic church.

There was also a depth of popular support for the faith in the city, manifesting itself in verbal battles in the streets, anonymous slander sheets, songs, and mock processions. Evangelical sermons by the clergymen Andreas Osiander and Dominikus Schleupner fell on eager ears. Luther's appeal in Nuremberg was wide. As Christoph Scheurl wrote in 1520: 'the patriciate, the multitude of the other citizens and all scholars stand on Luther's side.'[3] An official at the 1524 Diet in Nuremberg estimated that the majority of Nuremberg residents had been 'infected' by the teachings of 'la secte

---

[3]   Gottfried Seebass, 'The Reformation in Nürnberg', in Jonathan W. Zophy and Lawrence P. Buck, [eds.] *The Social History of the Reformation* (Columbus, 1972), pp. 22; 17–39; Günther Vogler, 'Imperial City Nuremberg, 1524–1525: The Reform Movement in Transition', in R. Po-Chia Hsia (ed.) *The German People and the Reformation.* (London, 1988), pp. 33–49.

Luthériane'.[4] By mid-decade, Nuremberg made its sympathy for the evangelical faith public. In March 1525 a religious colloquy ended in a victory for the Lutheran faction.

The path of reform in Nuremberg has been well researched and is well known; it would be an unnecessary digression to trace the process in any detail here.[5] For the analysis of the spread of the Reformation in Brandenburg-Ansbach-Kulmbach one point should, however, be stressed: Nuremberg helped to facilitate reform in the margravate, not only when the two powers worked together to implement religious change in the late 1520s, but at the very outset of the evangelical movement. Nuremberg's scholars and printers published the works defending the faith; Nuremberg's councillors advised the margraves as events unfolded; Nuremberg's merchants, burghers, tradesmen, colporteurs, and subject peasantry carried the message into the principality; and Nuremberg's clergy, Osiander premier among them, guided less certain consciences along the path to reform. The larger towns in the margravate – Kitzingen, Schwabach, and Ansbach – had an exemplar for their conduct.

Kitzingen

Once in the possession of the prince-bishops of Würzburg, Kitzingen fell under the control of the margraves of Brandenburg Ansbach in 1443. Unlike the imperial town of Nuremberg, Kitzingen was not fully self-governing. The margrave was represented in the town by a host of higher officials, though local polity was managed for the most part by members of the town council. Kitzingen was governed by a council of twenty-four members. Twelve of these men, the High Council (*Inneren Rat*), also functioned as a town court. There was no popular representation in urban polity; members of the commune did not have an appreciable role in governance. This exclusion of the town commune from rule was not left unchallenged. In 1430, and again in 1511–12, the commune pressed for greater involvement. In fact, using the increased war demands of the margrave as leverage, the commune was able to wrest some concessions from the ruling elite (involvement, for instance, in the yearly accountancy). But town government, despite the efforts of the communal leaders, remained a closed oligarchy of elite council members.[6]

The town council was also in contest with the neighbouring ecclesiastical foundation. Kitzingen's local abbey had long been at odds with the town

---

[4] Adolf Wrede (ed.), *Deutsche Reichstagsakten.* (Göttingen, 1963), vol. 4, p. 742; Heinrich Richard Schmidt, *Reichsstädte, Reich und Reformation* (Stuttgart, 1986), pp. 45–8; 152–80.

[5] See the works cited in Vogler, 'Imperial City Nuremberg, 1524–1525,'; Schmidt, *Reichsstädte, Reich and Reformation*, 342–55.

[6] Dieter Demandt and Hans-Christoph Rublack, *Stadt und Kirche in Kitzingen* (Stuttgart, 1978), pp. 9–12; Ingrid Bátori and Erdmann Weyrauch, *Die bürgerliche Elite der Stadt Kitzingen* (Stuttgart, 1982).

authorities. The resident abbess claimed the right to dictate affairs at the local markets – including the collection of dues, the supervision of weights and measures, and the supervision of the quality of wares – and was thus able to influence the local economy. Throughout the fifteenth century the town council worked to deprive the female superior of these rights; and gradually, as in other German cities, the council extended its efforts into the realm of ecclesiastical affairs. As early as the 1480s the council was embroiled in a quarrel with the abbess over the sequence of masses in the parish church. Although the abbey maintained patronage, the council was able to influence the nature of the service through its resistance to the abbey's plans. And as the council opposed the will of the abbey, it extended its own powers over church affairs in Kitzingen. By 1534, the council had rights of patronage to eight foundations, the abbess to three. The church of Saint Johann remained in the abbey's gift, but this did not stop the councillors from interfering in local ecclesiastical affairs. Incensed by the absence of the pastor and the run-down state of the incumbent's dwelling in 1515, for instance, the council directed a letter of complaint to the procurator. Nothing came of it. Another letter was sent to Würzburg, but the bishop's officials did not react to the complaint. Finally, in 1516, the council took a step that it viewed as 'extraordinary' when it forwarded its grievances about the state of the Kitzingen church to the margrave. This petition to the margrave represented the fusion of interests that would transport the Reformation to the towns and cities in the margravate: magisterial reform under the guidance of a territorial prince.[7]

When the Kitzingen council submitted its letter of grievance to the margrave in 1516, mention was made of the preaching of the Word and how the parishioners were deprived of this service when the incumbent was absent or the vicar incompetent. In 1522 this complaint was repeated, but with an added emphasis: the need for the *evangelical teaching* and the Word of God.[8] Luther's call for reform had found a following in Kitzingen. Inhabitants of the town, eager to hear the new faith proclaimed, invited the noted preacher Diepold Beringer, the Peasant of Wöhrd, to discourse in the open air from a purpose-built podium. Beringer is said to have lectured before 8,000 people in Kitzingen in single sessions on such matters as the inefficacy of the saints and the deceptive wiles of the Catholic church.[9] Beringer's sermons were suspended by the margrave, despite the council's efforts to defend his actions, but not before the strength of support had been demonstrated. By 1523 the Kitzingen council was openly supporting the reform movement.

Two crucial initiatives, it might be said, won the supporters of reform their cause. First, the council was still in mitigation with Johann von Wirsberg over

---

[7]   Demandt and Rublack, *Stadt und Kirche*, pp. 20–34.
[8]   Demandt and Rublack, *Stadt und Kirche*, pp, 189, 203–5.
[9]   Ozment, *The Reformation in the Cities*, pp. 66–7; Demandt and Rublack, *Stadt und Kirche*, pp. 58–9.

the installation of a suitable vicar in the parish church. The Kitzingen magistrates went so far as to claim that unless a worthy man was appointed soon the council – with the margrave's approval – would use its 'evangelical freedom' to elect a pastor itself. The strength of its claims should not be overestimated: Würzburg was still recognised as a court of appeal; no steps were taken without the intervention of the margrave. None the less, the council had made its support for the evangelical movement clear and this action had the intended result. On 23 February 1523 a new candidate was placed into office, Johannes Schenk von Sunau, a former Franciscan who suspended many of the Catholic ceremonies after he assumed office. Reform initiative was in place. Secondly, the council was able to secure the most lucrative mass foundation in the town when the absent incumbent Jörg Bracheim died in 1522 while in Rome. Protesting that the mass priest, to that point, had failed to reside, the council confiscated the foundation. When Würzburg objected, the council, supported by the margrave, reminded the bishop that the foundation duties had never been fulfilled; rather than squander the wealth on absent clerics, it would use the income for more appropriate ends. This was a first step in the centralisation of parish funds, a reform of parish income which culminated with the placing of a common chest in the church in 1523. The Kitzingen council had made its intentions clear: It was determined to administer the local church in line with the directives of the evangelical movement.

Schwabach

In the town of Schwabach events took a similar turn. Schwabach was situated near important trade routes along the river Pegnitz and soon came into contact with the ideas emerging from Wittenberg via Nuremberg.[10] The parish was well-served by ecclesiastical institutions. The town church had up to twelve altars, two of which were guild foundations. In Schwabach, as had been the case in Kitzingen, there was a strong lay interest in the regulation of local religious affairs. The burghers often found themselves in conflict with the Cistercian monastery of Ebrach, especially when the monastery, which had the right of presentation and the task of tithe collection, withheld tithes from the pastor. This sequestering of the parish income gave rise to a strong anti-clerical sentiment in the town, a sentiment much in evidence throughout the fifteenth century and up to the early years of the evangelical movement. On the eve of the Reformation, Casimir was intervening in Schwabach in order to settle disputes between the town and the monastery over clerical income. As the evangelical faith took hold in the town, the Ansbach officials were forced to

[10] Luther may have travelled through Schwabach on his way to Augsburg to meet with Cajetan. See Herbert Reber, 'War Luther in Schwabach? Ein Beitrag zu den Itineraren von Luthers Romreise 1510/11 und der Augsburger Reise 1518', *ZbKG*, 37 (1968), 19–36.

issue statements to the Schwabach magistracy in an effort to suppress religious disquiet.[11]

In spite of Casimir's attempts to prevent religious innovation, the reform movement took hold in Schwabach. In 1523, before the feast of Saint Michael in the town church, a renegade monk, dressed as a weaver, usurped the pulpit and handed a copy of Urbanus Rhegius's tract against indulgences, *Der Hymelisch Ablaßbrieff* (1523), to the preacher. The man was imprisoned; but the parishioners, in particular the artisans, petitioned the regional official for his release. Fearing unrest, the town officials freed him from prison. Threats against the clergy now grew more vocal. On 10 October 1523, the Catholic priest Johann Linck complained to the margrave that he and his clergy were not safe in the town; death threats had been directed their way. The following year the secular officials observed that neither Linck nor his chaplains were secure against the risk of an artisan class (*das gemain handtwercks volck*) eager for the Word of God. (This may have been true, though the secular officials, who were determined to secure the evangelical faith, may have exaggerated.) In February 1524 the council established a common chest in the church, an event orchestrated from the pulpit by a Lutheran sympathiser, Johann Dorsch. When Dorsch was chased out of town by order of Casimir, two like-minded men, Johann Feyelmayer and Burkard Leykam, were placed into office by the town officials and told to preach the Gospel. Ultimately, in reaction to the intervention of the Eichstätt bishop, both Feyelmayer and Leykam were dismissed. By the year 1524, however, the movement had taken root in the town, and Casimir's efforts to contain reform were proving ineffective.

The Reformation in Schwabach was both encouraged and directed by the Schwabach *Stadtrichter* and part-time pamphleteer Hans Herbst. Steps taken to introduce reform were defended by Herbst in print. Herbst's *Discussion of the Schwabach Common Chest* (1524), for instance, reads as a conversation in a woollen mill over the establishment of the common chest. After addressing the problems associated with the common chest, and the solutions so near at hand, Herbst has his evangelical sympathisers ultimately win all hearts for their cause. (Even the steadfast Catholic antagonist – she who would like to see Luther borne off 'body and soul' – is converted to the cause.) In an effort to hasten the process of reform, Herbst published a poem during the Shrovetide carnival and directed it, quite clearly, at the local magistrates, who were commended for the steps they had taken. Dressed in the guise of a fool, the voice of Reform approaches the town officials and praises the common chest. But the common chest was not enough; the parishioners needed:

> An evangelical man,
> Who can preach to us from God's word
> How man, with meetness, should honour and serve
> Our Lord God and the authorities.

[11] Heinrich Wilhelm Bensen, *Geschichte des Bauernkriegs in Ostfranken* (Erlangen, 1840), p. 385.

Not content to let reform follow a gradual course, Herbst then directed a pamphlet against the Catholic priest Johann Linck. Published on 4 March 1524, *A Brotherly and Christian Admonition, grounded in Holy Scripture* was, in effect, a call to Linck to account for his sins and recognise the truth of the new faith.

The spread of evangelical propaganda, together with the strength of conviction shared by the higher officials in the town, eventually persuaded the margrave to comply with their wishes. Casimir allowed the council the right to appoint an evangelical man to office. The Schwabach magistracy, in an effort to secure an appropriate preacher, wrote to Luther and Andreas Osiander in the hope that they might recommend suitable candidates. Schwabach sent its own candidate, Burkard Leykam, to Wittenberg in March, 1524, for examination. In the end Leykam was not appointed to the post, but the town was successful in its bid to secure an evangelical sympathiser. In 1524 Casimir approved the appointment of the Lutheran sympathiser Hans Hoffmann.[12]

Ansbach

In Ansbach, home to the margrave's court, religious change was slow to take shape, in spite of the strength of support for the faith shared by the margrave's councillors. Ansbach was home to two men of substantial importance who were also early followers of Luther: chancellor Georg Vogler and the clergyman Johann Rurer. Vogler and Rurer did much to encourage the spread of Luther's ideas. During the Council of Worms (1521), as the margrave's court advisors and the town patricians followed events with interest, Vogler wrote to the Ansbach councillors praising Luther and openly supporting him. Evangelical clergymen were soon at work in the town. In 1523 the Catholic town priest resigned his post and Rurer, until that point the foundation preacher, assumed his office and began to give evangelical sermons.[13] On 9 April 1525 Rurer celebrated an evangelical service in the town church of St Johannis for the first time.[14] Support for the faith was also demonstrated by the town inhabitants. In 1524, following a lecture by the Catholic clergyman Dr Johann Weinhardt, a local tailor, Michael Zieckh, suggested to Weinhardt that he had misrepresented Luther's view of the Eucharist. The tailor offered Dr Weinhardt some Lutheran tracts so that he might understand his error.[15] Despite this depth of support, however, reform could not

---

12   Heinrich Schlüpfinger, *Die Stadtpfarrei Schwabach vom Mittelalter bis zur Neuzeit* (Schwabach, 1975); Herman Clauβ, *Die Einführung der Reformation in Schwabach 1521–1530* (Leipzig, 1917); C. Scott Dixon, 'The German Reformation and the Territorial Town: Reform Initiatives in Schwabach, 1523–1527', *German History* (1996, forthcoming).

13   Georg Kuhr, 'Der katholische Pfarrer Johannes Mendel und die Anfänge der Reformation in Ansbach', in *Festgabe Matthias Simon: Zeitschrift für bayerische Kirchengeschichte*, 32 (1963), 74–82.

14   Karl Schornbaum, 'Wann wurde in Ansbach der erste evangelische Gottesdienst gehalten?', *Beiträge zur bayerischen Kirchengeschichte*, 9 (1903), 26–29.

15   Karl Schornbaum, 'Zur religiösen Haltung der Stadt Ansbach in den ersten Jahren der Reformation', *Beiträge zur bayerischen Kirchengeschichte*, 7 (1901), 147.

take root. The city remained under the sway of the margrave and the powerful anti-evangelical factions (chief among them Casimir's wife). Ansbach was not securely reformed until margrave Georg arrived in 1528; and even then the authorities were reluctant to abolish the Catholic mass without the margrave's explicit instructions.[16]

The uneven progress of reform in Ansbach is mirrored in the dispute between the Catholic archdeacon Weinhardt and the fervent evangelical Rurer. Weinhardt opposed Rurer's reform efforts at every turn, ultimately sending a letter of complaint about Rurer's conduct to margrave Casimir in 1525 (in his capacity as adjudicator of clerical discipline). Rurer drafted his own apology and defended himself in the face of Weinhardt's claims. Weinhardt maintained that Rurer preached the 'malicious, unchristian, and Lutheran learning' during a time of unrest. Weinhardt stated openly from the pulpit, 'dear Ansbachers, I regret that you are being deceived!' and he expressed his concern that the townsfolk should be so easily led astray. Rurer answered with the appropriate theological justification for his sermons – *sola fides, sola gratia* – and insisted that he preached nothing but the words of Christ. It was not the evangelical sermons, countered Rurer, but rather Weinhardt's attacks against the evangelical faith that were the cause of unrest in the town.

The Ansbach parishioners were caught in the middle of this dispute. When Weinhardt's maid wanted to attend Rurer's sermon, he asked of her: 'will you go to the heretical sermon as well?' On occasion Rurer's sermons would be disrupted by the Catholic clergy. Speaking aloud and admonishing the congregation to turn away from the pulpit, the Catholic chaplains would insult Rurer from the back of the church. There can be little doubt that this quarrel, though very much a skirmish between theologians, affected the Ansbach parishioner in this time of troubled consciences. 'With these and similar words,' observed Johann Rurer, 'he [Weinhardt] had offended and reviled not only me, but rather the Christian honour of my audience, noble and non-noble, learned and unlearned, those of high and low estate. For if I am an unchristian preacher, so too must my listeners be unchristian as well.'[17] Rurer was correct to imply that this period of religious confusion cast a broad shadow of doubt.

MARGRAVE CASIMIR AND THE REFORMATION

Most of the other towns in the principality shared Ansbach's dilemma. As Casimir did not take a resolute stand in confessional matters, as will be shown

---

[16] StaN, *Ansbacher Religionsakten*, III, Tom. viii, fasc. ii, fos. 124–5.
[17] Walter Brandmüller, ' "Herrn Johannsen Ruerer Pfarhern zu Onolzbach antwurt uff Doctor Weinharts clage." Eine Verteidigungsschrift des Ansbacher Reformators Johann Rurer aus dem Jahre 1525', in Walter Brandmüller, Herbert Immen Kötter, and Erwin Iserloh (eds.) , *Ecclesia Militans: Studien zur Konzilien- und Reformationsgeschichte: Remigius Bäumer zum 70. Geburtstag gewidmet* (Paderborn, 1988), vol. 2, pp. 235–79.

in greater detail below, town magistrates could not implement and consolidate reform. Only scattered references to local reforming attempts exist. A historian has suggested that Martin Helffer was preaching the Gospel in Hof as early as 1517.[18] Both Johann Wildeneuer and Johann Eck (no relation to the Ingolstadt professor) championed the evangelical faith in Kulmbach in the early 1520s, thus spreading the reform message first planted in the town when Luther spent a night at the Augustinian monastery on his way to Augsburg (1518).[19] Georg Schmalzing of Bayreuth had read 'a book or four of Doctor Martin and others' and did not shy away from preaching. In Wunsiedel the church ceremonies began to change in 1523. That same year Kaspar Hedio congratulated Adam Weiß of Crailsheim for residing in a land where the Word of God was so loudly proclaimed.[20] In 1525 Schwabach, Uffenheim, Kitzingen, Ansbach, Gunzenhausen, and Bayreuth sent supplications to the margrave asking for the elimination of the Catholic mass and the establishment of the evangelical alternative.[21]

Even in the neighbouring dioceses the reform movement took hold. In Würzburg the bishop Lorenz von Bibra opened the town gates to Luther while the reformer was on his way to his Heidelberg defence (1518). After von Bibra's death, and the election of a less indulgent prelate, Lutheran sympathisers were not as vocal, but the evangelical movement survived. Paul Speratus, for instance, a Cathedral preacher, gave public lectures on the evangelical faith until 1521. His words, it was claimed, served to incite 'dissent and unrest'. Clergymen took wives; indeed, two married canons in Würzburg were imprisoned. (In response, a defence of clerical marriage, directed at the bishop of Würzburg, was published in Bamberg.) A Lutheran community survived in Würzburg well into the final decades of the century; in 1583 the Lutheran community was confident enough to begin construction of a separate gravesite. But there was little scope for development, and little hope that Würzburg would develop into a biconfessional city, especially after the election of the Counter-Reformation bishop Julius Echter (1573–1617). A similar situation existed in the other major diocese of Bamberg. In Bamberg at least two clergymen, one of whom was a Carmelite, preached the Gospel in public until bishop Weigand von Redwitz put an end to all independent reforming efforts.

---

[18] Schülin, *Leben und Geschichte*, p. 27.

[19] Erwin Herrmann, *Geschichte der Stadt Kulmbach* (Kulmbach, 1985), pp. 174–5; Caspar von Lilien, *Gottseeliger Glauben- und Religions-Eifer der Durchleüchtigsten Herren Marggrafen zu Brandenburg* (Bayreuth, 1672), p. 16.

[20] Matthias Simon, *Evangelische Kirchengeschichte Bayerns.* (Nuremberg, 1952), pp. 149–73.

[21] StaN, *Ansbacher Religionsakten*, III, Tom. II, Schwabach fos. 25–28; Uffenheim fos. 29–32; Kitzingen fos. 33–35; Gunzenhausen fos. 37–40; Ansbach fos. 42–47. The Bayreuth Supplication is in StaB, C3, 1554, fos. 1–4. All of these supplications are a standard form and follow an original draft, written perhaps by Vogler or Rurer.

Nevertheless, it is symptomatic of events that evangelical pamphlets were still being dedicated to the bishop in 1523.[22]

The spread of the evangelical movement in the rural parishes cannot be recreated in any great detail. Parish documentation does not record junctures or upheavals in local ecclesiopolitical affairs with the same detail or sense of destiny as the records of independent cities. The historian of rural Germany is forced to posit possibilities and predispositions; a narrative account of local events is rare. This lack of testimony should not eclipse the role played by local reformers, where such is known, or the fact that events in the countryside often equalled urban intensity. The Reformation in the countryside advanced, to a certain extent, independent of events at the centre. But in Ansbach and Kulmbach the process can at best be approximated. Up to the year of the Peasants' War (1525), the strength of rural support can only be inferred from the mandates and resolutions designed to contain religious discourse. In October 1524, for example, the Ansbach meeting of the estates (*Landtag*) ordered the margrave's subjects, whether secular or spiritual, to refrain from discussing contentious religious issues and abusing people of dissimilar views, whether in the church, the street, or the local ale houses.[23] The nobleman and court steward Hans von Schwarzenberg advised against as much when he addressed the territorial estates assembled in Ansbach on 1 October 1524: 'Our gracious Lord [has been informed that] there are some people [in the country] who preach and talk in such a fashion that it causes strife.'[24] The spread of the evangelical movement in the rural parishes was often represented by the authorities as a form of unrest.

Casimir was concerned with the 'strife' incited by these itinerant preachers and he made his feelings of unease known. Until the outbreak of the Peasants' War the unfolding of the Reformation in the rural parishes was viewed, and recorded, by fearful eyes. It is therefore difficult to establish where and when the rural parishioners were acting in the name of religion. On occasion the parishioners would reveal behaviour that might have been encouraged by Luther's ideas. A primary concern of the Bamberg clergy was the great danger facing the bishop's officials whenever they entered the margrave's principality and encountered the resistance of Casimir's servants and subjects.[25] The spirit of reform may have been behind this behaviour. Even more explicit was the manner in which the villagers of Wendelstein greeted their new incumbent in 1524. In the *Wendelstein Church*

---

[22] Walter Scherzer, 'Die Protestanten in Würzburg', *ZbKG*, 54 (1985), 97–117; Ernst Schubert, 'Protestantisches Bürgertum in Würzburg am Vorabend der Gegenreformation', *ZbKG*, 40 (1971), 69–82; Löhe, *Erinnerungen*, pp. 58–62; Hans-Christoph Rublack, 'Reformatorische Bewegungen in Würzburg und Bamberg', in Moeller (ed.), *Stadt und Kirche im 16. Jahrhundert*, pp. 109–24.

[23] Sehling, pp. 80–1.

[24] Gottfried G. Krodel, 'State and Church in Brandenburg-Ansbach-Kulmbach 1524–1526', *Studies in Medieval and Renaissance History*, 5 (1968), p. 171.

[25] StaB, C2 1814, fos. 30–1. This document has no date. Casimir offered a response in 1524, so it must be in or close to this year.

Ordinance the parishioners claimed that it was their right to appoint and dismiss the clergyman; the pastor was in effect their servant. He was to preach the Gospel, minister the sacraments as defined by Scripture, and serve as a faithful worker for the Lord. Eichstätt was no longer his court of appeal; henceforth he was to refer to the margrave Casimir.[26] Isolated examples such as these suggest that there was a mode of behaviour and action in the rural parishes provoked by the evangelical movement. But there is no faithful record of the progress of reform or the scale of support. Only when the state intervened did parish activities come to light, and then indirectly, as a foil to the margrave's will. And it is one measure of margrave Casimir's indecision in the face of the evangelical movement – and one reason for the relative lack of reform testimony in the rural sources – that the margrave's will in the early 1520s was rarely in evidence.

Luther's reform proposals were slow to win official approval in Brandenburg-Ansbach-Kulmbach. Margrave Casimir did not endorse Lutheranism, thus limiting its implementation; but neither did he legislate against it. The course of action he chose was determined by the context of political events. Following the April 1524 Diet of Nuremberg, Casimir, along with other Franconian estates (almost exclusively secular princes), sat at Windsheim to draw up a theological statement or abstract for the pending imperial Diet at Speyer. This course of action was in response to the resolution of the 1524 Nuremberg Diet, which curtailed the radical nature of confessional dialogue and ordered the estates of the Empire to meet and draft proposals on how to deal with the 'Luther affair'. Casimir wanted to use the Windsheim gathering to form a coalition against the strength of the Franconian bishops, the cities, and, if only indirectly, the Swabian League.[27] Religious concerns, however, soon took centre stage.

At the Windsheim meeting a list of twenty-three articles summing up the position of the reformers was presented to the margrave and the estates. Johann Rurer had drafted the articles, citing the supposed Catholic error and following it with the evangelical correction. The sacraments were reduced from seven to two, communion was to be extended *sub utraque*, the power of the bishops was restricted, the mass and the Gospel should be read in German – on the whole it was a statement of early Lutheranism, including the unsure footing in matters relating to free will and images in the church.[28] Discussion was then tabled until the estates met in Ansbach on 25 September 1524. Casimir sent out a notice to the

---

[26] 'Erstlich so werden wir dich für kain herren, sunder allain für ein knecht und diener der gemaind erkennen..' Sehling, p. 78; Krodel, 'State and Church', p. 152. See also the analysis of the document by Blickle, *Gemeindereformation*, pp. 27–8.

[27] Karl Schornbaum, *Die Stellung des Markgrafen Kasimir von Brandenburg zur reformatorischen Bewegung in den Jahren 1524–1527* (Nuremberg, 1900), pp. 30–5.

[28] Lorenz Kraußold, *Geschichte der evangelischen Kirche im ehemaligen Fürstenthum Bayreuth* (Erlangen, 1860), pp. 26–30. Both Schornbaum and Götz saw the influence of Zwingli in the articles and the subsequent *Ratschläge*. The Wittenberg theologians also felt that the article over the use of pictures in the church was questionable.

clergy to prepare preliminary reports on the faith and to send them to Ansbach before the meeting and, if possible, to attend in person 'so that on the set day the matter may be dealt with all the more effectively'.[29]

Despite the imperial mandate suspending discussion of the religious question, the estates met in Ansbach and addressed the articles. Casimir still wished to use the *Landtag* for political ends, but the clergy, and many secular officials, recognised that the leading agenda were the twenty-three articles.[30] The Ansbach *Landtag* represented the first official disputation of the religious problem in the margravate. The Catholic representatives were reluctant to attend; once there, they were reluctant to pass judgement; and as a whole they rejected the articles and took refuge in centuries of tradition and the possibility of a church council. The majority simply deferred the issue, as did the abbot of Heilsbronn: 'He does not know what to say about the matter. He has not studied such things and would let it remain as tradition and the councils have dictated (councils of not only clergy, but laity as well).'[31] The evangelical clergy, in contrast, offered a detailed tract in support of the articles. This came as no surprise, as they had already sent a supplication to the margrave before the *Landtag* asking for the basic Lutheran desires sketched in the articles along with 'whatever the Gospel inherently brings'. The evangelical articles, which were submitted to the margrave on 30 September 1524, offer a vivid picture of the strength of Lutheran belief among the clerical elite in the principality. From the true nature of the church, the proper interpretation of Scripture, the sacraments, confession, votive masses, German baptism, the intercession of the saints, free will, fasts and Holy Days, to the essential principle of Lutheran theology – justification by faith alone – the evangelical pastors of Ansbach presented a comprehensive digest of Luther's ideas. Published the following year, the articles left Casimir in little doubt about the depth of the clergy's convictions. At the same time, other members of the *Landtag* also supported the faith. Though they were less ardent, the nobility as a whole welcomed the preaching of the Word. And the cities – the twelve representatives of the cities – demanded the same.[32] In 1524 Casimir aired the religious issue in a public forum, and the evangelical party proved to be the most forceful contingent.

Casimir did not grant the desires of the reforming party; and yet, though he has

[29] M. J. H. Schülin, *Fränkische Reformations-Geschichte* (Nuremberg, 1731), p.17; Krodel, 'State and Church', pp. 158–161.

[30] Schornbaum, *Die Stellung des Markgrafen Kasimir*, pp. 38–40.

[31] Schornbaum, *Die Stellung des Markgrafen Kasimir*, p. 40. The Catholics drew up a proposal, which they submitted once they were absent from the council. It was a rejection of the articles. Their objections are reprinted in Schülin, *Fränkische Reformations-Geschichte*.

[32] Schülin, *Fränkische Reformations-Geschichte*, pp. 1–94; Johann Wilhelm von der Lith, *Erläuterung der Reformationshistorie vom 1524. bis zum 28. Jahr Christi incl. aus dem Hoch- Fürstlich-Brandenburg Onolzbachischen Archive an das Licht gebracht* (Schwabach, 1733), pp. 47–59; Sehling, p. 66. The cities included Ansbach, Schwabach, Crailsheim, Kitzingen, Neustadt, Gunzenhausen, Uffenheim, Wassertrüdingen, Kulmbach, Hof, Bayreuth, and Wunsiedel.

been maligned by generations of historians for his lack of religious conviction, margrave Casimir's reaction was not necessarily detrimental to the evangelical cause. On 1 October 1524 he published a resolution which effectively shelved any sort of final decision and simply asked:

> that throughout His Grace's domain and territories the holy gospel and divine Word be preached clearly and purely ... according to the right and true understanding, and that nothing [be preached] that is contrary [to the divine Word], so that the common Christian people are not scandalized and misled. [Resolved] that all pastors and preachers of the divine Word should in their sermons restrain themselves from speaking evil of anyone in particular, [or from preaching in such a way as] to cause quarrels, scandals or uproar; as it is stated above, they should preach only God's Word unadulteratedly and purely, so that only God's praise and honor, and the salvation of the common Christian people are ... promoted.[33]

The call to broadcast the Word 'clearly and purely' without unwanted human additions was a central mandate of the reform movement. There is little doubt that this resolution, while not endorsing positive action, at least granted the reformers the opportunity to preach the Gospel unmolested. But it did not sponsor reform, and as the leaders of the movement in the principality well knew, they could not implement religious change without explicit margravial sanction. The evangelical party continued to press Casimir for further reforms. If the margrave is to be believed, not a day passed without a request from one of his subjects asking for the suspension of old rites and observances and a church order founded on the pure Word of God. Soon after the margrave's refusal to concede to the demands of the reforming party in Schwabach (4 February 1525), Hans Herbst published an anonymous pamphlet in an effort to convert the margrave to the cause.[34] *A True, Christian, and Profitable Warning* ... was written to urge Casimir to take a firm (Lutheran) stand in religious affairs. It was not enough to allow for the spread of the Word, wrote Herbst. Rulers who did not implement reform measures, and thus did not realise the implications of the Gospel's message, were guilty in God's eyes – no less guilty than Herod or Pilate. Johann Rurer published a similar work the following year. Rurer's *A Christian Instruction from a Pastor to his Lord* ... was an even more explicit attempt to force Casimir to recognise God's will.[35] Unmoved, Casimir left the religious question in abeyance.

---

[33] I use the translation in Krodel, 'State and Church', p. 159, n.19. Original text in Sehling, pp. 80–1.

[34] Hans Herbst, *Getrewe Christenliche und nutzliche warnung/etlicher öbrigkait die das Evangelion zü Predigen zülassen un[d] befelhen/Und straffen doch desselben volziehung.* (1525). The authorship is established in Matthias Simon, 'Eine unbeachtete Flugschrift zur Reformationsgeschichte der Markgrafschaft Brandenburg-Ansbach', *ZbKG*, 22 (1953), 183–92; Krodel, 'State and Church', pp. 180–1.

[35] Johann Rurer, *Cristliche unterrichtung eins Pfarhern an seinen herrn/ein Fursten des heyligen Reychs/ auff viertzig Artickel und puncten gestelt/was eins rechten/waren/ Evangelischen Pfarhern oder Predigers/Predigen und lere sein soll/mit einfürung etlicher sprüch in heiliger geschrifft gegründt/das solch lere/das ware wort Gottes sey/Auch ableynung viler vermeinten einreden/ fast nützlich un[d] tröstlich zu lesen unnd zuhören.* (1526).

Even in the face of repeated entreaties from neighbouring princes, Casimir would not take a resolute stand in confessional politics. In the late 1520s the major Lutheran powers began to look for allies. Unlike outright supporters of Luther, such as the princes of Saxony and Hesse, margrave Casimir did not contemplate a union in defence of religious liberty. Certainly he never considered an anti-imperial alliance. Casimir continued to honour the traditional Hohenzollern policy of fostering close ties with the imperial house. He worked in the service of Charles V and fought for archduke Ferdinand in Hungary. This was not mere opportunism. As detailed above, Casimir did not take a resolute stand in religious matters; he granted the preaching of the Word 'clear and pure', allowed for religious disputation at the meetings of his estates, but Brandenburg-Ansbach-Kulmbach never officially adopted the Lutheran faith while he was in power. Casimir was therefore not pressed to join a defensive alliance. This is not to say that he avoided negotiation. He was very intrigued by the idea of a coalition against the bishops and the Swabian League, for instance, though this came to nothing. And he treated with both Johann of Saxony and Philipp of Hesse as they sought confessional allies, though he would not enter into a union with them. For this lack of (religious) commitment Casimir has been judged harshly by historians. But this is unfair. The Emperor had not yet dictated a certain course of action. There was every reason to believe that the much-promised general council would settle the issue. Casimir would gain nothing if the Empire was divided and unstable. Always the good Hohenzollern, Casimir's religious stand was subordinate to his quest for aggrandisement. His primary concern was the status of his house in the Empire. The most effective way for him to realise his imperial aims was to remain non-committal.[36]

The Peasants' War of 1525 forced Casimir to act. In Franconia, as in other south German imperial districts, peasant unrest was widespread. Casimir considered this uprising a manifestation of the religious unrest and confusion thought to have been boiling away in the parishes since the early 1520s. As it was perceived by contemporaries, as will be discussed below, this was the reality. The Reformation in the rural parishes of Ansbach and Kulmbach followed no distinct evolutionary pattern. Chaos, rather than ordered reform, reigned. To a certain extent, the peasant uprising in the principality was a corollary of Casimir's failure to legislate religious order in the face of widespread calls for change. The Peasants' War was symptomatic of a religious movement left to foment in a rural context with no formal guidance. Unlike the urban setting, where reform might be directed and controlled by interest groups, the Reformation in the countryside was given a broader

---

[36] Reinhard Seyboth, 'Die Reichspolitik Markgraf Kasimirs von Ansbach-Kulmbach 1498–1527', *Zeitschrift für bayerische Landesgeschichte*, 50 (1987), 63–108; Schornbaum, *Die Stellung des Markgrafen Kasimir*, pp. 74–86.

concourse and very little constraint. A state of unrest, rebellion, and uncertainty and confusion proved to be the harvest of Casimir's indecisive religious policy.

The rebellion of 1525 was not unexpected. Casimir had been far more prescient in this respect than most other Franconian potentates. Many of his efforts at the meetings of the estates had been directed towards forming a coalition to arm against growing sedition; he treated with the Swabian League and the Franconian bishops in order to erect a standing army as a security measure. But the bishops could not be won, nor would Casimir enter into a religious pact with Saxony and Hesse, and so the margrave took matters into his own hands.[37] In the Spring of 1525 Casimir began to assemble a troop to deal with the uprising. By this time, the reach of popular support had penetrated deep into the parishes. (If a confession from Wunsiedel is representative, sometimes up to half of the parishioners – presumably men – were involved in the uprisings.[38]) The threat, however, was short-lived. The peasants failed to present a uniform front. Despite widespread references to the Gospel as law, there was no trans-communal ideology binding the rebels together, and the weak and sequestered peasant armies proved no match for the forces mustered against them. After making concessions to the movement, including actions, such as the confiscation of the monasteries and the purloining of church wealth, perceived by the leaders of the peasant armies as signs of sympathy for their cause, Casimir gathered a force together on 13 May 1525 and put down the war in a series of brutal slaughters and show-piece trials.[39] He then used the pretence of the war to impose further secular control over the clergy and usurp the powers of diocesan jurisdiction: Clerical tax privileges were suspended, monasteries were catalogued and the wealth tallied, the clergy were taxed one-tenth, and they fell under the control of the secular courts.[40] The revolt itself proved an ephemeral threat; the real issue was the fragile atmosphere that gave rise to the unrest.

Reacting to events in a manner calculated to reduce the possibility of further agitation, Casimir looked to contain religious discourse, if not govern it, and thereby curtail the freedom of interpretation exercised by the 'unsuitable, godless preachers' who, in his eyes, were responsible for the outbreak of the Peasants' War. The margrave still shied away from offering a definite statement for or against the new faith. In the April 1525 resolution, Casimir failed to offer

---

[37] Schornbaum, *Die Stellung des Markgrafen Kasimir*, pp. 67–73.

[38] For a detailed account of the movement in Ansbach, see Carl Jäger, 'Markgraf Kasimir und der Bauernkrieg in den südlichen Grenzämtern des Fürstentums unterhalb des Gebirgs', *Mitteilungen des Vereins für Geschichte der Stadt Nürnberg*, 9 (1892), 17–164; StaB, C2 160, fasc. ii, fol. 88 'dann es sey woll der halbtheill der gemeind im spill...'.

[39] J. M. Grossen, *Burg und Marggräflichbrandenburgische Kriegshistorie der löblichen Fürstenthümer Kulmbach und Ansbach*, (Bayreuth, 1748), pp.134–49.

[40] Krodel, 'State and Church', p. 162.

anything beyond the former, definition of the faith as the holy Gospel preached clearly and purely. He granted some concessions to the evangelical party, paramount being the inclusion of the clergy in civic duties. And while this worked to stave off complete alienation from potential Lutheran allies, his policy did nothing but legislate confusion in the parishes. Greater precision was needed, but Casimir did not take the steps. No constructive measures were issued, only decrees and resolutions designed to maintain the balance or stifle discontent. The 1525 preaching mandate was the apogee of this policy.[41] This sermon, drafted perhaps by Rurer, supplied a foundation for the idea that the real freedom of the Christian man was obeisance to earthly authority. It was a Lutheran apology, used by the margrave to avoid religious faction, and we may safely assume that it was read to the parishioners on at least one occasion. The objective was twofold: to contain the spread of divisive ideas and to limit the growth of partisan disquiet.

The picture that emerges from the parishes during Casimir's reign is not one of isolated confessional groupings, but rather one of confusion and uncertainty. Lutheranism had not been uniformly established through popular support. Even at this early date, the evangelical clergyman Adam Weiß feared for the survival of the evangelical movement.[42] Weiß claimed that masses and Catholic rites were still dominant, and even in those places where the Gospel was preached the Word was being abused. Chancellor Georg Vogler was able to prompt margrave Albrecht to write to Casimir and register the common man's fear that the Catholic mass would once again be the only service available, the laity once again denied the chalice.[43] But this is the voice of an educated Lutheran minority. The Catholic mass had not yet been officially abolished, and it is unlikely that most parishes were home to a consistent evangelical service. At this early stage the faith of the parish was the faith of the incumbent – or perhaps two faiths if religious sympathy was divided. In Feuchtwangen, in 1526, the congregation first heard Georg Vogtherr preach against pilgrimages and then witnessed the local Catholic clergyman stand up and cry out against the sermon. This struggle must have continued throughout the year. While Vogtherr was attempting to usher in the new faith, Hans Dietrich was defending the Catholic mass, the sacramentals, the Pope, and

---

[41] Sehling, pp. 84–7. See the analysis of the contents by Krodel, 'State and Church', pp. 164–6. Krodel sees the sermon as a triumph of *Politik* over religion, as Casimir was now acting in the capacity of a bishop in telling the clergy what to preach. The sermon defined the freedom of the Christian man as obedience to the secular authorities. Krodel is certainly correct to point out that Casimir believed the unrest had been spread by the unqualified preaching of the Word. As the introduction to the sermon reads: 'nachdem die gewesen aufrurn nit wenig aus ungeschickten, gotlosen predigen entstanden sind...'. Sehling, p. 84.

[42] On Weiß, see Martin Brecht, 'Via Antiqua, Humanismus und Reformation – der Mainzer Theologieprofessor Adam Weiß', *Zeitschrift für Kirchengeschichte*, 102 (1991), 362–71.

[43] Johann Baptist Götz, *Die Glaubensspaltung im Gebiete der Markgrafschaft Ansbach-Kulmbach in den Jahren 1520–1535* (Freiburg, 1907), p. 81.

denying the parishioners the right to interpret Scripture.[44] Even if many of the clergy adopted a wait-and-see attitude, as did Hans Dietrich, the innovations suggested by the reform-minded clergy would give rise to faction and confusion. 'My children', was how Hans Dietrich soothed his parishioners in the quarrel cited above, 'because all is presently in such error I will start with nothing new ... I wish to remain a Thomist for the moment and do nothing until I see [how things turn out].' The parish clergy waited on a definite statement from Casimir.

When the margrave did finally react to events it was, from a Protestant viewpoint, in a negative way. He had already been named imperial commissioner for the Diets of Augsburg (1525) and Speyer (1526), and in 1526 he was also appointed the supreme commander of the imperial army in the war against the Turks. With his other attempts at forming a united front having failed, he began to concentrate on his relationship with the Habsburgs.[45] Following the Diet of Speyer (1526), whose vague solution to the religious problem did not really console either party (reform was allowed in so far as it could 'answer to God and his imperial Majesty'), Casimir made preparations for his service in Hungary. His last important act as margrave of Brandenburg-Ansbach-Kulmbach was the resolution of the October 1526 Ansbach *Landtag*. The resolution was clearly in part a response to the growing threat of the bishops (who had begun negotiations with the Swabian League), and its intent appears to have been to put an end to innovation in the parishes. Casimir acknowledged that it was not a final solution; he hoped to deal with the religious question upon his return.

The 1526 resolution was strongly Catholic: Latin mass, the tabernacle, auricular confession, maintenance of Holy Days and foundation masses, religious brother-hoods, and clerical celibacy. It was essentially a move toward the reestablishment of the Catholic form of worship. Concessions to the reformers included German for the Gospel readings and the mass Epistles, baptism in the vernacular, a reevaluation of fast days, and, most significantly, the Lord's Supper in both kinds where it was already practised as such (as had been conceded at the Diet of Speyer). Moreover, also in a Lutheran vein, it helped to strengthen Casimir's control over the church. His pastors were commanded to preach the Word 'clearly and purely ... and nothing else which is contrary [to the Gospel]' while the margravial officials monitored the parishes for religious unrest. Church

---

[44] Lith, *Erläuterung der Reformationshistorie*, pp. 188–90; StaN, *Ansbacher Religionsakten*, III, Tom. II, no. 37, fos. 162–4. Georg Vogtherr to Georg Vogler 'Montag nach dem Pfingstag 1526', in answer to some charges against his sermon:

> der halben ich von wegen des abgelauten Mißbrauchs der walfart, dar innen begriffen, got sey lob, hart vervolgt wirde, Also das ich von der selbigen predig her, nye uff die Cantzel komen, Sonder vom dechant und pfarher unverclagter sach gantz abgestossen bin, Ist auch der pfarher wider mich Am Sontag Exaudi uff gestanden und mit etzlichen puncten wider mich geschrien...

[45] Schornbaum, *Die Stellung des Markgrafen Kasimir*, pp. 92–106.

finances fell under the purview of the secular powers; secular law was extended to include the clergy.[46] The resolution was a compromise. Since the seventeenth century, scholars have been commenting on its hybrid nature – *mixtum quid ex Papismo et Evangelismo*. It worked on two levels: as a general concession to Catholic observance, it was meant to minimise religious discord, whether in the parishes or between the margrave and the bishops; as an initiative of the margrave, it was meant to consolidate his power over the territorial church. It failed on both counts.

The Catholic powers were unmoved by Casimir's gesture. The bishop of Bamberg continued to press for action against Casimir with the Swabian League. All of the bishops recognised, quite correctly, that the margrave's intervention in ecclesiastical affairs infringed upon their powers as keepers of the parishioners' souls. As the margravate was subdivided by three dioceses (Eichstätt, Würzburg, Bamberg) and touched upon by two others (Regensburg, Augsburg), it is little wonder that the prelates soon brought suits against the margrave before the imperial courts. As early as the 1524 Diet of Nuremberg, it became clear to Casimir that the bishops were a threat. He hoped to construct a united secular front of Franconian powers against them, and he summoned meetings in Kitzingen and Windsheim to this end. Despite his efforts, however, it was the bishops who first banded together and brought their grievances to the attention of the imperial authorities. The bishop of Bamberg was untiring in his efforts. He managed to have a penal mandate directed at the margrave in response to the forced taxation of the clergy, though ultimately it amounted to nothing. The political atmosphere in the Empire after the Diet of Speyer (1526) was so unstable the Swabian League could not act and nothing came of the bishop's efforts.[47]

In the evangelical camp, Georg Vogler, Johann Rurer, Philipp von Hesse, even Martin Luther himself – all reacted unfavourably toward the resolution.[48] The Ansbach clergyman Johann Rurer would not accept the mandate, claiming that it was against his conscience and would bring eternal damnation should he comply. Although Rurer asked the margrave to spare him a forced conversion, his arrest was ordered and he and his chaplain fled 'in search of the teaching of Christ from one city to another'. (Rurer had heard a number of threats directed against him should he refuse to accept the 1526 resolution, including the fulmination of Casimir's wife, who wanted to put him in a sack and drown him, and the bishop of Würzburg's warning, who wanted to summon Rurer before his court.[49]) Margrave Georg, who had sent letters of encouragement to Casimir to strengthen

---

[46] Analysis based upon Krodel, 'State and Church', pp. 203–4; Sehling, pp. 88–97. Gerhard Müller and Gottfried Seebaß (eds.), *Andreas Osiander D. Ä. Gesamtausgabe* (Gütersloh, 1979), vol. 3, p. 173, no. 6. set the date of issue at 11 October 1526 rather than 10 October 1526 as in Sehling.
[47] Schornbaum, *Die Stellung des Markgrafen Kasimir*, p.108.
[48] Götz, *Die Glaubensspaltung*, pp. 85–7.
[49] StaN, *Ansbacher Religionsakten*, III, Tom. II, fos. 273–4; Lith, *Erläuterung der Reformationshistorie*, p. 186.

his resolve, later disavowed the corrections made to the 1526 resolution, along with any approval for its publication, claiming that he had not given his full consent.[50] At the level of the local parish the resolution triggered latent disputes and gave rise to conflict. The state of the church in Brandenburg-Ansbach-Kulmbach in 1527 demonstrates that the Reformation, as a popular movement, was too disparate and contentious an issue to be implemented at the rural level without state intervention.

Many of the clergy could not agree. The pastor of Egersheim, fearing 'it is dangerous to do something against one's conscience', looked to neighbouring clergymen for advice.[51] Other pastors thought the people would soon abandon the new faith if the clergy honoured the 1526 resolution, for surely such a *volte face* would cast doubt on their former claims.[52] The resolution divided the local official Michael Prenner and the clergyman of Plofeld, for the latter believed that the Catholic mass was 'no use or good but rather heresy'. When Prenner opened the church to allow for a visiting Knight of the Teutonic Order to have a mass performed, the pastor took offence and accosted Prenner. The pastor would not allow for the chaplains to say the early mass without intervening. As a result of this dispute, the parishioners became even more bold and quarrelsome and the parish divided.[53] A similar situation existed in Geilsheim. The clergyman wanted someone to fetch salt from 'old Sibill' so that he could bless it. The sexton opposed sacramentals, as the clergyman knew, but he was advised that such ceremonies were to be maintained in accordance with the mandate and tradition. At this point the sexton countered: 'Yes, but those ceremonies which are dealt with in the Gospel!.' The clergyman then offered a defence of consecrated salt with reference to the Old Testament; but this did not convince the sexton, who insisted that the blood of Christ washes sin from this world. 'Over this the priest laughed and mocked',

---

50 Georg's letters were published as a pamphlet: *Etlich schrifften, so Marggraff Georg von Branden-burg, an seyner gnaden Brüder und desselben Rethe gethan hat, das wort Gottes und desselben verkünden zu handthaben.* (1526). As they were co-rulers, Casimir needed Georg's approval before he could publish the resolution. He met with Georg in Prague and Vienna. According to Schornbaum, Georg approved the draft only because he thought it would be valid for one year alone and the state of the principality required such a compromise. Schornbaum, *Die Stellung des Markgrafen Kasimir*, p. 106. If a subsequent letter from Georg can be trusted, the published resolution (1527) differed from the draft he and Casimir had discussed: 'Nun werden wir aber bericht, als dann solchs offenwar, datz solche schrifften in drukh komen, offenlich außgangen, und dartzue in etlichen worten geendert sind, darab haben wir nit wenig misfallen, auch solchs nit geschafft, noch bevolhen...'. StaN, *Ansbacher Religionsakten*, III, Tom. II, no. 51, fo. 248.

51 StaN, *Ansbacher Religionsakten*, III, Tom. II, no. 69, fos. 277–9.

52 StaN, *Ansbacher Religionsakten*, III, Tom. II, no. 63, fo. 272. Statement of Jorg Rostaller. 'Thue ichs, so ist zubesorgen die leut, so solch vorgemelt predig von mir gehoert, werd sprechen der hatt auff disse zeit gepredigt, und thut ytzo stragks darbider [dárwider], eß mueß freilich falsch gebest sein.' Rurer expressed a similar concern in his letter to the Ansbach council.

53 StaN, *Ansbacher Religionsakten*, III, Tom. II, no. 71, fos. 285–8, 287: 'ist zubesorgen das er Sampt seinen anhengern, mit der zeytt zwischen den pawern zu ploveld nichtzig guts machen und aufrue erwecken werde, nachdem etlichen sein wesen gefellig und den andern nitt...'

vouched the sexton, 'as is usual with these unlearned clerics'.[54] Johann Nagel of Leutershausen did not know what to do when some neighbouring parishioners approached him and asked for communion in both kinds. He feared the bishop of Eichstätt.[55] The whole chapter of Gunzenhausen expressed a similar concern: if they maintained the order, the bishop would prosecute them, if they did not, they fell under the wrath of the margrave.[56] Casimir himself realised the opposition that was being offered to his resolution. He ordered the regional official of Uffenheim to forbid the sale of works that might provoke antagonism in light of it.[57] But his efforts came to nothing – though to be fair he did not have much time to correct the situation. Margrave Casimir died while in the service of the Emperor on 27 September 1527.

MARGRAVE GEORG THE PIOUS AND THE IMPLEMENTATION OF THE REFORMATION

After Casimir's death, Georg the Pious returned from Silesia and assumed rule in both Ansbach and Kulmbach. This turn of events was not necessarily to his advantage. Georg's Silesian principality of Jägerndorf had proved a lucrative acquisition. The wealth he had accrued through marriage and his contractual annexation of both Oppeln and Ratibor (still pending in 1527) had made him a substantial power in Silesia. There is little reason to suppose that margrave Georg was cheered at the prospect of returning to Brandenburg-Ansbach-Kulmbach, a land in religious disarray, suspect in the Empire, and over 550,000 gulden in debt. Georg did return, however, and on 3 March 1528, following the first Ansbach *Landtag*, he issued a resolution which dealt directly with the religious question and the confessional status of the Franconian principality. (It was the duty of the prince, as he explained in a letter to the Emperor, to tend for the souls of his subjects, not just their temporal welfare.[58]) Acting as guardian for Casimir's son Albrecht – thus extending the range of his rule to include Kulmbach as well as his inherited lands of Ansbach

---

[54] LKAN, MKA, Spez. 343, fo. 21 (19 July 1528).

> da hat pfarhr zu mir [sexton] gesagt, Ir halt selbs nichts auf saltz weihen, und wist das in meins g.h. mandat stat man soll alle ceremonien halten wie vor alter herkomen, daruf ich gesagt, Ja die ceremonien aber die im evangelio begriffen sein, daruf er gesagt das saltz und wasser haben im alten testament die sund abgewaschen vil mer im newen testament, und ich wols segnen, wens mir laid were, daruf ich gesagt, das plut Cristi wesch unser sund als im newen testament... daruber pfarhr gelacht und gespot, wie dann der ungelerten pfaffen gewonhait ist...

[55] StaN, *Ansbacher Religionsakten*, III, Tom. II, no. 76, fo. 290.
[56] StaN, *Ansbacher Religionsakten*, III, Tom. II, fo. 267.
[57] LKAN, MDU, 3, fos. 8–9. 'und kain lateinisch oder teutsch buch faÿl haben lassen, das ain schmachbuch, oder wider dises unser ausschreiben sein mag, damit allerlej ergernus und nachtail, so sonst daraus volgen möcht fur khommen werde...'
[58] Reinhard Seyboth, 'Markgraf Georg von Ansbach-Kulmbach und die Reichspolitik', *Jahrbuch für fränkische Landesforschung*, 47 (1987), 45.

– Georg confirmed Casimir's 1525 and, less convincingly, 1526 acts as fiats in favour of the evangelical cause. In this way he was able to imply that failure to conform to the new faith was a form of rebellion and always had been. The proper religious service was still defined as the Word preached 'clearly and purely' and nothing contrary to Scripture. Regional officials were ordered to monitor the parish sermons. The resolution affirmed that no Christian is bound to any form of worship or rite contrary to the Word of God; the Church is built upon Scripture alone. At this point the margrave was most concerned with establishing control over the development of the church in his principality. In the *Mandate for the Implementation of the Reformation* Georg made it clear that the clergy under his immediate patronage would be dismissed if they did not honour his demands.[59]

Georg recognised that the church needed greater precision, not only in its outer maintenance but in its creed. He was able to address both of these questions by following events in Saxony and adopting the idea of a visitation. Adam Weiß, pastor of Crailsheim, had suggested this to the margrave soon after the margrave's return to Ansbach. Georg acted, wrote to Johann Schopper of Heilsbronn for advice, and on 18 May 1528 Weiß, Althamer, and Schopper were meeting in Ansbach to discuss the possibility of a visitation. In neighbouring Nuremberg, at the same time, Lazarus Spengler and Kasper Nützel were drawing up plans for a visitation in the parishes of the imperial city. Despite the traditional animosity between these two Franconian powers, and indeed the fact that a jurisdictional dispute between them was before the supreme imperial court during the late 1520s, Spengler and Vogler entered into a correspondence over the religious issue in the hope that the two powers might benefit from cooperation. Spengler recognised the advantages to a joint visitation: not only would it heal some of the ill-will between the two powers, but a united front would offer security against the encroaching bishops and the Swabian League. Spengler first suggested the idea of a joint visitation in May 1528; by June Volger and Spengler were once again in communication, urged on by the margrave. Chancellor Vogler suggested that representatives meet for formal discussion at a proposed site. The parties agreed to gather at Schwabach, 14 June 1528.[60]

Although the Ansbach and the Nuremberg clergy had been commissioned independently to draft theological testimonies for the Schwabach meeting, the resulting religious mandates and ordinances were the product of mutual deliberation and consent. Ansbach sent its leading Lutheran sympathisers: Georg Vogler, Johann Rurer (who returned to replace Johann Schopper), Adam Weiß, and the district official of Schwabach, Wolf Christoph von Weisenthau.

---

[59] Sehling, pp. 102–4, 105.
[60] The following analysis is based upon Müller and Seebaß (eds.), *Andreas Osiander D. Ä. Gesamtausgabe* (1979), vol. 3, pp. 123–42; 187–248.

Nuremberg delegated Lazarus Spengler, Martin Tucher, Dominikus Scheupner, and Andreas Osiander. The representatives arrived on 14 June; deliberations began the next day. The text first put before them was Osiander's list of twenty-three visitation articles, drawn up as a means of instruction for the clergy. These articles were soon accepted. Ansbach's similar evangelical agenda, the thirty articles, were thought superfluous by the Nuremberg theologians; nevertheless, they were approved as a statement of the faith. The proposal for a common church ordinance was a more difficult matter (later proven by the points of division, especially the problem of the clerical ban). It was not only points of theological subtlety which held a solution at bay, but the basic architecture of the church in question. The principality of Ansbach required a different reforming strategy than the imperial city of Nuremberg. Very little is know about the actual composition of the church ordinance. Rough drafts of related topics aside, it is unlikely either party arrived at Schwabach with a useful blueprint of a church order. Ansbach had sent 'memoriale' to Nuremberg in early June under the headings *Ordnung der Visitation* and *Memorial der Visitation*, both of which Osiander had seen before composing his twenty-three articles. But there is no evidence to suggest that these statements formed the basis of the 1528 church ordinance.[61] The final ordinance seems to have been a summary of the principal points of the faith as both parties addressed them at Schwabach.

The 1528 ordinance was not envisioned as a final testament of the evangelical faith in either Brandenburg-Ansbach-Kulmbach or Nuremberg. It was primarily a visitation ordinance, a temporary measure until such time as a definite statement was forthcoming from the Lutheran factions. (Of the leading participants, only Johann Rurer referred to it as a church ordinance.) The authors stated clearly that further additions would be made after the results of the visitation were known. Georg the Pious did not want to publish it, fearing the ire of the bishops – further notice of its provisional nature. The real purpose of the Schwabach gathering was to organise a visitation, not to draft a finished church ordinance. Consequently, the 1528 ordinance was lacking theological precision. Undoubtedly, it was a Lutheran manifesto: baptism was to be held in German, salt and oil omitted; it called for communion *sub utraque*, with the mass spoken in the vernacular; it considered the sermon the focus of the service. But it was not a comprehensive statement of the faith, as was necessary at this time when many village pastors (and certainly parishioners) were still confused. Rather than offer comprehensive justification or instruction, the ordinance simply admonished the pastors to refer difficulties to the visitors. Parishioners were to be instructed by the clergy as problems arose. The church ordinance did not really legislate religious change. The real significance of the 1528 church

---

[61] Müller and Seebaß (eds.), *Andreas Osiander D. Ä. Gesamtausgabe*, (1979), vol. 3, p. 190.

ordinance lies less in its role as a blueprint for the new church than the guidance it provided for the first church visitation in the principality. The margrave viewed the visitation as his window on the religious complexion of the principality and the most effective way to introduce religious reform. Thus it is little wonder that Georg the Pious was eager to get the visitation under way. On 4 August 1528 he ordered all region officials to compile a report on the clergy in their districts (along with their patrons and religious dispositions). On 15 August 1528 the Ansbach clergy were ordered to appear before the visitation committee in Ansbach.[62]

The introduction of the Reformation in the principality met with resistance. Following the accession of Georg and the visitation of 1528 the bishops stepped up their efforts. They continued to press the Swabian League for action against the margrave; the League in turn advised Georg to stay all innovation until a general council and 'not give cause for war and unrest'. (The Nuremberg councillor Lazarus Spengler, incensed by the bishop's intrusion, wrote a treatise for the League justifying the recent visitation.) And it was not the bishops alone who took offence at the visitation: Archduke Ferdinand wrote to the margrave in a state of frustration demanding an end to the innovations. The visitation also raised the ire of the dukes of Bavaria and the Palatinate counts. But the bishops were the most persistent. At the Diet of Augsburg (1530) Bamberg and Würzburg presented their grievances to the Emperor. The Swabian League then issued a statement to Georg ordering him to justify his actions at the forthcoming Diet at Nördlingen (6 July 1531), where the bishops of Bamberg, Augsburg, Eichstätt, and Würzburg would be in attendance. The bishop of Bamberg outlined the extent of Georg's offences:

[The margrave] continues to impair diocesan jurisdiction, invest churches, foundations, and monasteries and insists on enforcing the Lutheran teaching [in such places]; moreover he forces the clergy to accept the new teaching, and those who will not suffer it he chases [from their posts]; the interdictions issued by the Swabian League he simply abuses and mocks...[63]

Georg answered the charges brought against him with a point-by-point defence: the bishops had first usurped his ecclesiastical jurisdiction; they had neglected their offices; they had let false preaching spread; he had a Christian duty to protect the souls of his subjects. But the success of his defiance was rooted in rather more mundane soil. The Swabian League was too weak, and the political climate too uncertain, to allow for intervention. Although the bishops continued

---

[62] Karl Schornbaum, *Aktenstücke zur ersten Brandenburgischen Kirchenvisitation 1528*, (Munich, 1928), pp.1–14; Müller and Seebaß (eds.), *Andreas Osiander D. Ä. Gesamtausgabe* (1979), vol. 3, pp. 187–205; Sehling, pp. 135–9.

[63] Schülin, *Leben und Geschichte*, p. 137.

to press their case, with the peace of Nuremberg (1532) they were no longer an immediate danger.[64]

Margrave Georg's main concern remained the creation of a Lutheran church in the principality. Neither the 1528 visitation nor the ordinance was sufficient in itself as a means of moderating religious affairs. With theological precision still wanting and the status of the new faith uncertain in the Empire, many of the parishes in Ansbach and Kulmbach were home to a mixture of Catholic and Lutheran services. Religious confusion in the parishes did not abate. The clergyman Conrad Benger was unsure about the mass; as no definite service had been agreed upon, he pointed out in a letter to Ansbach, communion tended to vary in nature from parish to parish. 'And so one can truly say', he added, 'there are as many masses as there are priests.'[65] In all likelihood the only pure services available at this time were found in the monasteries and foundations, but as these were Catholic services, and as the neighbouring parishioners insisted on the margave's resolutions being honoured, the state of confusion was multiplied rather than reduced.[66] The margrave acknowledged that progress had been slow at the parish level. On 28 February 1531 he issued a statement aimed at correcting the situation, accusing his subjects, both in the cities and in the countryside, of showing no respect for the word of God or the reform efforts. Soon after the consecration of the Eucharist, it read, they filed out of the church and made their way to the inns or the market place.[67] The margrave's edicts, it seemed, had had little effect. As margrave Georg realised soon after the visitation in his principality, there could be little hope of planting the faith in the parish communities unless the clergy had a published statement of the faith. This insight was the genesis of the 1533 church ordinance.

Soon after the completion of the 1528 visitation, the Nuremberg council commissioned a group of theologians to draft a more comprehensive church ordinance. Andreas Osiander, Nuremberg's leading theologian, delayed work on the project. Burdened with other duties, and waiting on his meeting with Luther at Marburg, Osiander did not finish a draft until January 1530. Once Osiander had submitted it, Spengler criticised the draft; the councillor took umbrage that Osiander had written the work on his own, without consultation, and he believed

[64] Karl Schornbaum, *Zur Politik des Markgrafen Georg von Brandenburg vom Beginne seiner selbständigen Regierung bis zum Nürnberger Anstand 1528–1532* (Munich, 1906), pp. 91 ff.; Hans Westermayer, *Die Brandenburgisch- Nürnbergische Kirchenvisitation und Kirchenordnung 1528–1533* (Erlangen, 1894), pp. 42 ff.; Schülin, *Leben und Geschichte*, pp. 126–39; Theodor Dorfmüller, 'Aeltere kirchliche Geschichte von Culmbach', *Archiv für Geschichte und Alterthumskunde des Ober-Main-Kreises*, 1, (1831), 38–41; Gerhard Kolde, 'Zur Brandenburgisch-Nürnbergischen Kirchenvisitation 1528', *Beiträge zur bayerischen Kirchengeschichte*, 19 (1913), pp. 275–81.

[65] LKAN, MKA, spez. 720, fos. 14–15 (11 August 1529). 'Und so es zimlich wer zu sagen, als vil prister, als mancherleÿ meß'.

[66] StaN, *Ansbacher Religionsakten*, III, Tom. XI, fo. 44, St Sebastian's Day, 1529. Letter from Althamer and Rurer to the margrave.

[67] StaB, C3 49, fos. 13–24. (28 February 1531). This was later published as a pamphlet.

the draft was unclear on the principle points of the Lutheran faith. Spengler returned the draft to the commission (now in session without Osiander's help) and it was reworked, incorporating many of Spengler's proposals. But this draft too came to nothing. The matter was dropped with the sitting of the 1530 Diet of Augsburg, and the two drafts were sent on to the margrave. With Nuremberg drawing back from the project, Georg the Pious now provided the impetus for further progress. The margrave submitted both drafts to a council of his theologians in Kulmbach (a gathering of scholars that also included the Schwä-bisch Hall reformer Johannes Brenz). After suggesting a few changes, the theologians sent the revised copy on to Nuremberg (1 March 1531). Again the Nuremberg council hesitated. The imperial city hoped for a general church ordinance of the Protestant princes in the Schmalkaldic League. In fact it entertained this hope into the final months of 1531 (well after margrave Georg had abandoned the notion). It was not until late in the year that the council was willing to renew its efforts and exchange views with Ansbach over the composition of the ordinance. Various drafts were exchanged between the two powers while they delayed a final decision until after the imperial Diet (1532). Finally, in July 1532, a copy of the church ordinance was sent to Wittenberg.

Luther and the Wittenberg theologians suggested alterations. Exclusion from the Lord's Supper should occur without any civic consequences (*bürgerlichen Folgen*); all masses without communicants should be abolished; and lastly – inevitable in a work which had suffered so many revisions – the ordinance should respect greater uniformity. It was the work of too many hands; one man, perhaps Osiander, should be commissioned to finish it. After so much close cooperation, however, it was unlikely that one (Nuremberg) man would be entrusted with the task. Johannes Brenz, as the representative for Ansbach, made his way to the imperial city and worked at Osiander's side. This consultation marked the final stage in the development of the ordinance. Certain revisions were made: Brenz prepared a preface for the Ansbach version, while margrave Georg offered some changes (too late) in January 1533. But the ordinance, in its conclusive form, was complete. Printing began in December 1532, with 800 copies earmarked for Ansbach. Distribution commenced in February 1533.[68]

The 1533 Brandenburg-Nuremberg church ordinance represents one of the first detailed Lutheran church orders to be published in Germany. Although it followed the Nuremberg armistice of 1532, and thus appeared in a period of relative calm, the religious question was still a flash point in the Empire and there was large degree of risk associated with its appearance. Margrave Georg had been advised by his brother Albrecht to delay publication and wait for an ordinance from the presses of Saxony, but both Brandenburg-Ansbach-Kulmbach and Nuremberg went ahead without waiting for the general Protestant church order,

---

[68] Müller and Seebaβ, *Andreas Osiander D. Ä. Gesamtausgabe* (1979), vol. 3, pp. 468–606; (1981), vol. 4, pp. 219–56; 373–396; (1983), vol. 5, pp. 37–181.

or the union of Lutheran states, for which they had so long aspired. And indeed, as scholars have noted, the 1533 church ordinance was in many ways a model for this united Lutheran agenda. Once it was published, the ordinance was adopted by cities as far afield as Regensburg, Donauwörth, Weißenburg, and Windsheim. It was used, to offer select examples, in the duchies of Oettingen and Hohenlohe, the principalities of Henneburg, Mecklenburg, and Neuberg.[69] Inside the principality where it was issued, its significance was no less profound. With the publication of the 1533 church ordinance, Brandenburg-Ansbach-Kulmbach became officially Protestant. The parish clergy now had a detailed abstract of the Lutheran faith at their disposal. And while it did not deal with administrative or regulatory matters to any extent – such as the formal construction of the church – on matters of theology and church service it was a precise exegesis. It rounded off the efforts begun by margrave Georg in 1528 when he inherited a land in religious disarray and it set the tone for future evolution. Up to the year 1527, the process of reform in the parishes of Ansbach and Kulmbach had been frustrated by a lack of decision, from the year 1528, forestalled, however forgivably, through the lack of a theological standard. The 1533 Brandenburg-Nuremberg church ordinance put an end to both of these shortcomings.

RECEPTION OF THE EVANGELICAL MESSAGE IN THE PARISHES

Were the parishioners of Brandenburg-Ansbach-Kulmbach interested in the reform movement? Did they embrace Luther's teachings? Much of modern day Reformation historiography is based upon the premise that Luther – and if not Luther then Huldrych Zwingli, Thomas Müntzer, or any of the 'radical' reformers – preached a message to the urban and rural subjects of the German-speaking lands which soon found a vast resonance. Work on the Reformation in the cities has repeatedly borne out this notion: civic magistrates legislated religious change, the urban populace demonstrated their affection for the reform movement and worked to consolidate the evangelical faith within the town walls. Often the historian is helped by the wealth of sources in a city archive. It is frequently possible to recreate the spread of Luther's message in detail and register the impact of his ideas on the urban inhabitants. However, a study of the rural populace and the Reformation must do without equivalent sources, and in the absence of sufficient testimony the historian is left to reconstruct the religious convictions of the peasantry by inferring their wants from their collective actions. For many years attention has been focused on the events of 1525, the uprising known as the Peasants' War. Historians now have a number of peasant-war studies to choose from and a host of explanations for the uprising. Some of these explanations, it is maintained, are altogether unrelated to the reform movement

[69] Sehling, pp. 122–3.

and have little to do with religion. And yet none of these explanations explains away the large number of parishioners who rose up in defence of the 'clear and pure' preaching of the Word of God.[70] Thus the dilemma once confronting the historian of urban reform now challenges the historian of rural Germany: what was the appeal of the evangelical message and why did it muster so much support?

Although no theory, however broad, can hope to account for all of the motives behind a parishioner's decision to act in the name of religion, some approaches allow for a wider scope of interpretation than others. The traditional (Protestant) understanding of the Reformation movement saw its success in providential terms, the inevitable result of the Word revealed to a desperate age. Luther's criticisms of the Catholic church were supported by the Christian faithful because they were perceived as not only justified but divinely inspired, an expression of God's will. The subsequent theological breakthrough that took shape during the 1520s was then considered the standard of true religion. This sentiment permeated the work of Lutheran historians for centuries. It was enough for the eighteenth-century scholar Johann Wilhelm von der Lith to claim that the Reformation succeeded in Brandenburg-Ansbach-Kulmbach 'through the power of the divine Word' alone.[71] Even Catholic polemicists endorsed the notion that the evangelical movement owed its success to its theological appeal. Writing against the Brandenburg-Nuremberg church ordinance in 1533, Johann Eck reprimanded Luther for wishing to make Pauline theologians out of handworkers and farmers. The appeal of Luther's teaching for the common man, Eck continued, was the doctrine of Justification, which gave rise to laxity in worship and a disregard for penance among the masses. Sacred law was being abused, interpreted as a lawyer or a doctor might read Scripture, so that the common man believed a Christian could seek easy remedies for the illness of sin ('*so mag er darnach artzney un[d] besseru[n]g süche*'.[72] Eck's concern shared a similar premise to that of the Protestant historians: the appeal of the movement should be considered in strictly religious terms.

Social historians are doubtful in the face of conversion theory, though very few are willing to discount religious conviction outright when coming to terms with

[70] See the reviews and the literature cited in Tom Scott, 'The Peasants' War: A Historiographical Review', *The Historical Journal*, 22, 3 (1979), part 1: pp. 693–720; Part 2: pp. 953–74; H. C. Erik Midelfort, 'The Revolution of 1525? Recent Studies of the Peasants' War', *Central European History*, 11, 2 (1978), pp.189–206; Bob Scribner and Gerhard Benecke, *The German Peasant War of 1525 – New Viewpoints* (London, 1979), pp.19–23.

[71] Cited in Fritz Hartung, 'Die Literatur über die Reformationsgeschichte der Markgrafschaft Ansbach-Kulmbach', *Beiträge zur bayerischen Kirchengeschichte*, 14 (1908), p. 81. Compare A. G. Dickens and John M. Tonkin, *The Reformation in Historical Thought* (Oxford, 1985), pp. 7–57; Bernd Moeller, 'Problems of Reformation Research', in (trans.) H. C. Erik Midelfort and Mark U. Edwards, Jr (eds.), *Imperial Cities and the Reformation* (Durham, 1982), pp. 3–16.

[72] Johann Eck, *Christenliche underricht Mit/grund der gschrijft, wider die Angemaßten/setzer unnd angeber, vermainter Newer/Kirchen Ordnung, Jüngst in der obern Marg/graffschaft un[d] Nürmberger gebiet, Im tau/sent fünff hundert un[d] drey unnd dreyssi/gsten Jar, Außgangen...* (Ingolstadt, 1533).

the Reformation. Current Reformation historiography tends to view the process of religious change as an essentially 'social phenomenon' brought about by the weight of 'collective action'. Individual belief is no longer a sufficient determinant for an episode as profound as the Reformation. Religion is now placed in a more complex matrix. At present, within this paradigm, two schools of thought dominate in the search for an answer to the question 'Why was the evangelical faith found appealing by the subjects of rural Germany?'.

The first approach, exemplified in Reformation studies by the work of R. W. Scribner, works on the premise that popular belief was both appropriated and expressed in social collectivities. In order to understand why the people of sixteenth-century Germany adopted the evangelical faith, it is necessary to analyse their public actions, for a culture's shared values and convictions – conveyed overtly – condition a people's reception of ideas. The investigation of ritual and ceremony, the communal display of structures, signs, and associations, yields the following result: the evangelical message was either adopted or opposed in so far as it served a function within the complex of gestures, rites, and perceptions comprising the mental world of the peasantry.[73] Scribner's work focuses more on the means of appropriation than the reasons why certain ideas were adopted, but he has made it clear that the two are related, largely by means of the pragmatic attitude through which religious ideas were applied to people's social and material circumstances.

The second approach roots the filiation of evangelical ideas even more firmly in the social context of the day. The historian Peter Blickle, building upon a number of earlier studies of rural relations in southern Germany, has suggested with his notion of the 'communal Reformation' (*Gemeindereformation*) that the Reformation was centred, both theologically and socially, in the parish commune, the local units of peasant government.[74] According to Blickle, the peasants adopted Luther's call to reform as they saw in this movement the culmination of a long drive towards local autonomy. Blickle's theory addresses the problem of appeal directly: peasant communities adopted the evangelical faith because (as they saw it) it granted them the right to elect a pastor, monitor local ecclesiastical finances, control the parish church, and base religious relations on the principles of cooperation and the common good – all to be realised through the commune, through the efforts of the 'common man'. Franziska Conrad, one of Blickle's students, has proposed the notion that the communal Reformation might also be viewed as an attempt by the parishioners to alter ethical relations to accord with God's will and act as a means to salvation.[75]

[73] R. W. Scribner, *Popular Culture and Popular Movements in Reformation Germany* (London, 1987), pp. 1–47, 103–22. Compare E. P. Thompson, *Customs in Common* (London, 1993); N. Z. Davis, *Society and Culture in Early Modern France* (London, 1975).

[74] Peter Blickle, *Gemeindereformation, Die Menschen des 16. Jahrhunderts auf dem Weg zum Heil* (Munich, 1987).

[75] Franziska Conrad, *Reformation in der bäuerlichen Gesellschaft. Zur Rezeption reformatorischer Theologie im Elsass* (Stuttgart, 1984).

Reception of the evangelical message

A common element is present in all of the models discussed above: the evangelical message was appropriated and manipulated by the parishioners to serve their own ends. Only the motive differs. For Johann Eck, the faithful were most concerned with abstract theological truth, searching for a shortcut to salvation. For historians of the sociological bent like Blickle and Scribner, the commune integrates the message of the Gospel into the context of social relations or the system of religious practice. In an effort to come to terms with the spread of the evangelical movement in the countryside and its appeal for the rural inhabitants of Brandenburg-Ansbach-Kulmbach, the following analysis will examine the spread of the evangelical movement in light of these two considerations: the relative importance of religious conviction and the role of social context.

Before examining the reception of the evangelical message in the countryside, it is worth noting that the participants of this predominantly oral culture tended to discuss contentious matters among themselves, in familiar surroundings, after the initial message had been broadcast in a sermon or an open-air lecture.[76] The importance of the spoken word was well known to the authorities. In 1532 Nuremberg published a mandate forbidding the discussion of the Eucharist in the marketplace, the inns, the bath, or other public gatherings.[77] (The inns were an especially volatile atmosphere for parishioners and clergy alike, and it was not unusual for clients to quarrel with one another about religious issues.[78]) Local pastors and foreign clergymen, sympathetic to the new ideas, would lecture to an audience assembled from neighbouring parishes. The chronicler of Hof mentioned Nicolaus Storch, who preached at mid-day to a 'great concourse and gathering of people' in 1525. Others could be cited, preachers who spoke in the open air or took refuge in the forests. Even in Würzburg, the Catholic see, inhabitants were spiriting evangelical clergy through the city gates late at night so that they might preach 'the holy Gospel and the Word of God' to the common people.[79] Given that so few people could read, the spoken word was of central importance. This is not to deny the significance of printing. References to pamphlet literature (*buchlein, tractetlein*) and the reading of illicit materials are not uncommon.[80] But most parishioners would have heard the Word before they read it. During the Peasants' War and the early years of the Anabaptist movement,

---

[76] See Scribner, 'Oral Culture and the Diffusion of Reformation Ideas', in *Popular Culture and Popular Movements*, pp. 49–70.

[77] StaN, *Ansbacher Religionsakten, III*, Tom. XI, fo. 396.

[78] For examples of religious disputes in local inns, see Heinz Dannenbauer, 'Die Nürnberger Landgeistlichen bis zur zweiten Nürnberger Kirchenvisitation (1560/61), *ZbKG*, 11 (1927), 232; (1928), pp. 44, 221; 227; (1929), pp. 59, 115; (1933), p. 219. On occasion the local inn, such as at Bergen, would be protected by the nobility. StaB, C2 1827, fo. 42. 7 October 1589.

[79] LKAN, MKA 343, fo.10; Karl Schornbaum, *Quellen zur Geschichte der Wiedertäufer. (Quellen und Forschung zur Reformationsgeschichte)*, 16 (Leipzig, 1934), vol. 2, Markgraftum Brandenburg, pp. 4, 62; Lorenz Fries, *Die Geschichte des Bauern-Kriegs in Ostfranken* (Würzburg, 1883), vol. 1, p. 79.

[80] Schornbaum, *Quellen zur Geschichte der Wiedertäufer*, pp. 1, 24, 166.

men would travel from place to place, visiting peasant dwellings, and read aloud to an assembled audience in return for food and lodging. Ulle Nodler, suspected of Anabaptism in 1527, admitted:

He had once been invited to Hans Nodler's house for supper. After they had eaten, following the meal, Frau Meier from old Erlangen along with a small boy came in to Nodler's house. They had a book with them, though he [Ulle Nodler] does not actually know whether it was the Bible or an evangelical book. From this the boy began to read, and when he had read an entry, they told him to stop, and Frau Meier and Hans Nodler put their heads together, disputed, and interpreted the passage.[81]

Topics of a foreign nature were familiarised through confidential discourse. Religious topics were conveyed in traditional peasant rapport and were thus subject to manipulation. Cultures reliant upon the transmission of news by word of mouth, as might be expected, often distorted information once it was in the public domain, either through the whims of its oral circuit or the manipulating influence of a shared expectation or a general fear. Rumour and the run of 'public opinion' were especially significant during times of unrest, such as the Peasants' War of 1525, when subjects reacted *en masse* to the 'general cry'.[82] Even in times of peace, in an area no larger than a village, a 'public' statement might fall prey to manipulation or distortion in the hands of its audience. The remarks of the clergy were no exception. When the pastor Johann Wunniglich offered his parishioners a unique interpretation of the sixth commandment, news of the sermon spread through the parish as a fable or a proverb, from mouth to mouth as a means of illustrating a moral.[83] Caspar Baumacher recognised in 1566 that his feud with a local official had become the subject of discussion, but he would not accord such chatter the status of truth – it was street talk.[84] The transmission of evangelical ideas might be viewed in relation to the language of myth and legend. A local legend acquires its significance just because its moral rhetoric is made sensible with concrete or familiar referents.[85] In a similar manner, the abstract evangelical message acquired significance only after it was placed in a familiar context. In many instances the subject of discussion was so abstract it could only have

---

[81] Schornbaum, *Quellen zur Geschichte der Wiedertäufer*, pp. 17, 67, 116.

[82] Ernst Schubert, '"bauerngeschrey": Zum Problem der öffentlichen Meinung im spätmittelalterlichen Franken', *Jahrbuch für fränkische Landesforschung*, 34/35 (1975), 883–907.

[83] Wunniglich had declared that should a young man go to a spinning bee and get a girl pregnant, God would forgive him if he asked for mercy while on the way home. The congregation laughed when this was said. Later Lenhardt Straubinger reported: 'Seÿ auch nun mehr ein sprichtwort under den knechten im dorff Ir pfarrer sagt es sei nit unrecht, das wir fenstern und do ein knecht, einer diene schwengere, und Gott darüber bitt umb vergebung, so seÿ er wider frum und gerecht vor Got, so dan das war ist, wollen wir erst recht fenstern gehn.' The pastor excused his behaviour by claiming that the devil spoke through him. LKAN, MDG, 71, fos. 103–4, 1579/80. On *Fenstern*, see chapter 4.

[84] LKAN, MDL, 234 T.1. fo. 4 (23 January 1566).

[85] Jacqueline Simpson, 'The Local Legend: A Product of Popular Culture', *Rural History*, 2, 1 (1991), 25–30.

meaning once invested with traditional values. Parishioners of Geilsheim saw the demise of the contemporary German princes in a sermon on Herod. A villager of Rohr saw only himself in a biblical tale involving theft. The congregation of Neudrossenfeld was said to invert the significance of the pastor's sermons and invest them with personal meaning. Local figures often believed the sermon was about themselves. 'Such', said pastor Johann Conrad, speaking of his own parishioners in Leutershausen, 'is their logic' [*Dialectica*].[86]

The demand for the Word of God – an explicit reaction to the evangelical movement – should be viewed in light of the peasants' proclivity to manipulate a theological message or a religious slogan. Parish supplications throughout the 1520s demanded the preaching of the Word. The Wendelstein parishioners requested a pastor who would read the Gospel. In 1528 the people of Freudenbach wanted 'to be educated and instructed in the Word of God'. Supplications from the cities of Schwabach, Uffenheim, Kitzingen, Gunzenhausen, Ansbach, and Bayreuth called for the preaching of the Gospel. The parishioners of Feuchtwangen celebrated the discovery of the Word and the knowledge they had subsequently gained.[87] The regional reports of 1528, preceding the visitation, revealed that the villagers expected their clergymen to honour the 1528 Ansbach resolution and preach the Gospel in a comprehensible manner.[88] At times the parishioners' interest in Scripture drove the clergy to exasperation. It is unnecessary that the laity interpret the Word themselves, so concluded the pastor of Bürglein. They fail to understand the meaning, added the Puschendorf incumbent.[89] The sheer novelty of the Gospel, read aloud in the native tongue, held a fascination in itself. Nicolaus Storch amassed a following of laymen because of his familiarity with Scripture. Hans Hut, it was claimed, counted as his followers those who cannot read or understand Scripture [*der schrift*]. Georg Nespitzer confessed on 12 June 1530 that he had become an Anabaptist because 'he had, his whole life, never heard the Gospel preached'.[90] The examples are myriad, but what did this demand for the Word of God signify?

As mentioned above, Blickle's notion of a 'communal Reformation' has placed the reform initiative firmly in the hands of the peasant commune. The peasant mind interpreted the Reformation within the parameters of parish experience and hoped to realise its promises within the confines of parish reality. Franziska Conrad, building upon this, has suggested that the evangelical movement (as perceived by an Alsatian peasantry whose thoughts were saturated by the religious

[86] LKAN, MSK, 131, T.1. Letter of Johann Decker 1545; StaB, C3 1223, fo. 100 (13 October 1568); LKAN, MKA Spez. 343, fo. 11; LKAN, MKA Spez. 500 (8 December 1589).

[87] LKAN, MKA Spez. 992 Wendelstein 1480–1658 (6 January 1525); StaN, *Ansbacher Religionsakten III*, Tom. VIII, fasc. II, fo. 497; StaN, *Ansbacher Religionsakten III*, Tom. II, fos. 158–161. (1526).

[88] Schornbaum, *Aktenstücke*, pp. 77–8, 81–2, 89, 92.

[89] Schornbaum, *Aktenstücke*, pp. 78; 82: 'so heist er uns auf offener canzel narn, wir versteds nit, wein wyrs schon lesen, wyr haben pustaben auf dem leickkuchen gefressen.'

[90] Schornbaum, *Quellen zur Geschichte der Wiedertäufer*, pp. 9, 79, 186–7.

demands of the medieval Catholic church) exercised an appeal because it was thought the Gospel offered an alternative route to salvation. Subscription to the Gospel's norms was a means of avoiding the wrath of God, another apotropaic measure in the arsenal of popular piety. It was not just the Word itself, however, that interested the peasants, but the Bucerian notion of living in accordance with the directives of the Bible in a manner pleasing to God. The Gospel as the standard of a Christian life was how the peasants viewed the importance of the preaching of the Word and why it was necessary for salvation.[91] Scripture assumed a tropological significance. It was, as Conrad observes, Catholic works-righteousness in another guise. Did the peasants of Brandenburg-Ansbach-Kulmbach show similar motives?

When a causal relationship between the Gospel and salvation was made explicit, similar to the type suggested by Conrad, the author was usually theologically sophisticated. The Kitzingen common chest ordinance (1523) presented the notion that the Gospel should determine social relations: the Word of God should be integrated within the community, 'brotherly love' would reign, and salvation would result. This ordinance, influenced by the Nuremberg common chest ordinance, was first subject to change in Ansbach before it was approved.[92] Perhaps it was revised by the same men who drafted the 1524 Ansbach articles, wherein it was claimed 'The fruit of the Spirit is love, pleasure, peace, forbearance, friendliness, goodness, belief, gentleness, and chastity'.[93] The 1525 Bayreuth supplication called for the evangelical mass, 'so that we may recognise the fruits of the same and better ourselves' before God. This was a copy of a common draft, written by either Johann Rurer or Georg Vogler.[94] The Schwabach supplication read the same; and indeed in Schwabach the year before a pamphlet had appeared justifying the construction of a common chest with the observation that 'brotherly love' was Christ's own command – 'Oh, blessed is the man who observes the fruit of love and lives by it'.[95] Even the *Wendelstein Church Ordinance*, that manifesto of evangelical demands forwarded and published by the rural commune of Wendelstein in 1524, is not, upon closer examination, evidence of an understanding or an assimilation of the faith among the peasantry. The ordinance was in fact written by the reform-friendly Schwabach *Stadtrichter* Hans Herbst. When called to account by Casimir soon after its appearance, the parishioners

---

[91] Conrad, *Reformation in der bäuerlichen Gesellschaft*, pp. 93–105; Franziska Conrad, 'Die "bäuerliche" Reformation. Die Reformationstheologie auf dem Land am Beispiel des Unterelsaß', in P. Blickle, A. Lindt, and A. Schindler, (eds.) *Zwingli und Europa. Referate und Protokoll des Internationalen Kongresses aus Anlaß des 500. Geburtstags von Huldrych Zwingli* (Zürich, 1985), pp. 137–50.

[92] Sehling, p.76; Demandt and Rublack, *Stadt und Kirche*, pp. 51ff.

[93] Schülin, *Fränkische Reformations-Geschichte*, p. 77.

[94] StaB, C3 1554, fos. 1–4.

[95] *Ein Gesprech/Von dem gemeinen Schwabacher Kasten/als durch brüder Heinrich Knecht/Ruprecht Kemerin Spüler/und irem maister/des hantwerks der wullen Tüchmacher. Anno MCXXIIII*, in Oskar Schade, *Satiren und Pasquille aus der Reformationszeit* (Hanover, 1856/8), p. 201.

were quick to deny the implications of its contents, and disavowed the former claim that they had the right to appoint or dismiss the local clergyman.[96]

Village supplications do not offer any evidence to suggest that the relationship between the preaching of the Gospel and the realisation of its contents was at issue. The desire to hear the Word was widespread, but not for theological reasons. The parishioners considered the clear preaching of the Word their right as subjects of the margrave.[97] The demand for the implementation of the margrave's religious resolutions conflated with the demand for the Word of God and the teaching of the Gospel 'clear and pure'. The villagers expected the pastor to read the Gospel from the pulpit in a manner they could understand. The pastor of Wettelsheim had been cited before Ansbach for the reason that, aside from his Catholic proclivities, he read the Gospel incomprehensibly, refused to provide interpretations, and cut his sermons short.[98] The parishioners of Wiesenbach were grieved that their clergyman preached in an incomprehensible manner and thus nothing was learned. Similar complaints emerged from the parishes of Freudenbach, Burglein, and Mörlbach.[99] In 1527 the Geilsheim residents opposed Johann Siebentail for having said 'man has no need of books, of Scripture, of sermons...and has no understanding of the new faith (*new wesen*).'[100] In 1530 a chaplain fell prey to criticism for his failure to preach clearly and thereby enlighten 'the simple folk'.[101] Parishioners would generally take umbrage at the suggestion that 'the Gospel is not the Word of God' or the refusal on the part of the clergyman to read Scripture before the congregation, but it does not appear that the evangelical message was elevated to the status of a 'good work' whose message would help to secure salvation when applied to social relations. The pastor Johann Siebentail observed that, far from producing social coherence, the message was sponsoring a laxity in morals.[102]

The peasantry in Ansbach and Kulmbach expressed a desire for the Word of God, but some qualifications must be made before this is construed to represent a

---

[96] StaN, *Ansbacher Religionsakten III*, Tom. 1ᵇ Supplementorum, fo. 61: 'Aber nit der maynung das wir unns damit selbs gewalt geben wolten einen pfarer zubesetzen und zuentsetzen sonder wie In E.f.g. ambtman nach altem herkommen und Ius patronatus eingesetzt haben wir uns gutlich settigen lassen, und gar nicht willens gewesen und noch nit, mit eignem gewalt Ins lehen zegreÿffen wie das mag angezaigt werden.'

[97] I do not mean by this the *Göttliche Recht* that served as a legitimating principle for so many peasant revolts. The peasants in Ansbach and Kulmbach were demanding the preaching of the Word, but they were not justifying their demands with reference to Scripture. On the appeals to *Göttliche Recht*, see Peter Bierbrauer, 'Das Göttliche Recht und die naturrechtliche Tradition', in Peter Blickle (ed.), *Bauer Reich und Reformation* (Stuttgart, 1982), pp. 210–34.

[98] LKAN, MKA Spez. 1007, fo. 2. (29 June 1529).

[99] Schornbaum, *Aktenstücke*, pp. 61, 75, 78, 92: 'wiewol er die epistel und evangelion zu teutsch sage, so leg ers inen doch nit verstenglich aus.'

[100] LKAN, MKA Spez. 343, fos. 1–3, Point 4 (1527).

[101] Matthias Simon, 'Die kirchlichen Verhältnisse in Neustadt a. d. A im Jahre 1530', *ZbKG*, 36 (1967), 85.

[102] LKAN, MKA Spez. 343, fo. 11.

systematic trend in belief. Both Casimir and Georg had published resolutions (1524,1525,1528) declaring that the Gospel should be preached 'clearly and purely', for only then could the margrave's subjects be assured of salvation.[103] And in almost all instances, whenever the Gospel was demanded by the parishioners, it was followed by a reference to the margravial order. The peasants of Meinheim wanted a man who would preach 'God's sacred word, clear and pure, of the Old and New Testament, in accordance with the command of God and [margrave Casimir's] mandate.'[104] The village mayor and commune of Freudenbach requested a pastor who would preach the evangelical faith along the lines stipulated in the mandates.[105] The Wettelsheimers opposed their pastor because he would not honour the mandates in his sermons. The parishioners of Berolzheim prepared their list of grievances, including the lack of evangelical sermons, for the same reason.[106] On those few occasions when the parishioners expressed a concern for the Gospel, the words they used to impart their dissatisfaction matched the formula in the margravial resolutions. Repeatedly the parishioners appealed to the secular authorities to ensure that the word of God was preached in complete accordance with the stipulations of the margraves' mandates and resolutions – not the Word as commanded by God, as promised by Scripture, or as championed by Martin Luther, but the Word avouched in 'the Christian ordinances of our princely Grace [margrave Georg]'.[107] As subjects of the margrave, and thus one pole of the reciprocal relationship inherent in the nature of power relations (*Herrschaft*), the peasants felt that they had a right to hear the Word preached in the evangelical manner.[108] The resolutions of the 1520s had made it law.

What then was the reason for the interest in the Gospel? Two related explanations offer an answer. First, the peasants continually asserted that the Word had been promised to them by the margrave; it was a service outlined in the mandates and expected of the pastor. It was their right as subjects of the margrave. Second, the peasants considered the Gospel the voice of God, a divine gift, and they wished to hear it proclaimed. It was their right as subjects of God.

The discord between the Catholic priest Johann Siebentail and the parish (*Gemeinde*) of Geilsheim illustrates these points. When Siebentail arrived in 1525 the parish was already home to the evangelical faith, yet he tried to reimpose the old order. The parishioners took issue, and ultimately forty-three grievances were ranged against Siebentail.[109] Signed by 'the commune'

---

103 Sehling, pp. 80, 82, 102–3.
104 LKAN, MKA Spez. 572, fo. 28.
105 StaN, *Ansbacher Religionsakten III*, Tom. VIII, fasc II, fo. 497.
106 LKAN, MKA Spez. 1007, Bd. 1, fo. 1. 1529; StaN, *Ansbacher Religionsakten III*, Tom. VIII, fasc. II, fo. 569 (1529/30).
107 StaN, *Ansbacher Religionsakten III*, Tom. VIII, fasc. II, fos. 495, 506, 569.
108 On *Herrschaft*, see David Warren Sabean, *Power in the Blood* (Cambridge, 1984).
109 LKAN, MKA Spez. 343, *Johanns Sibenthalls pfarrers zu Geÿlsheim gpredigt Artickel. So Ein gemaÿnd daselbs bestendig die also Gepredigt haben und sunsten auch gehandelt*, fos. 1–3.

(*Ein Gemaÿnd*), the grievances suggest that some parishioners had a comprehension of certain points of the evangelical faith. Siebentail, it was alleged, cast doubt on the powers of the Gospel, placed weight on the fulfilment of the Laws, looked to the saints for aid, and consecrated salt and water.[110] And yet an equally dominant theme in the articles is the dim view the parishioners took of Siebentail's challenge of margravial powers and, as they saw it, their right to the Gospel. Siebentail made a series of claims which enraged the parishioners: the Pope was an 'earthly God', superior even to the Emperor; forty knights would soon appear and all of the evangelicals would be hanged from the trees; the world had been in decline since the bishops had been deprived of power; Jan Huss would remain in Hell until the new movement came to an end. In conclusion, Siebentail declared himself a subject of Eichstätt, not Ansbach. He thus questioned the validity of the margrave's actions, pledged his allegiance to a foreign power, and insinuated that the faith was contrary to natural and supernatural order.[111] Not only did he oppose the idea that the common man should have access to the Gospel preached 'clearly and purely', but he doubted the very efficacy of the movement, for it lacked the approbation of the Lord and was the religion of tricksters.[112] His great offence was not his theological inclination, but the fact that he called into question the church formed by order of the margrave and the spread of the Gospel as commanded by God.

Beyond the demand for the Word preached 'clearly and purely', a formula cribbed from the mandates, it is difficult to discern any interest or understanding on the part of the villagers for the evangelical faith from the year 1528 to the publication of the 1533 church ordinance. In the parish reports of 1528, the parishioners were encouraged to assess the local pastors.[113] Select Catholic clergymen were cited as having spoken of 'a Lutheran knave or three in the village' or badgered the 'Lutheran dogs' from the pulpit, but it does not appear that Lutheranism had many public followers.[114] Demands for the elimination of Catholic practices and the institutionalisation of Lutheran alternatives were rare. To offer an example, the 1526 resolution allowed for baptism in German, yet not a soul asked for a German baptism in Gnodstad. The pastor of Wertsheim confessed he would have done so, 'but no one had

---

[110] LKAN, MKA Spez. 343, fos. 1–3. Points 4, 7, 8, 12, 37–8. The sexton, an evangelical sympathiser, may have been responsible for the articles.

[111] This latter point was emphasised in his suggestions that hail would rain down on the believers and nuns would give birth to *hüren kinder*. He was, in short, a rebel in the face of both the margrave and God (*aufrurisch* is the term used by the parishioners).

[112] LKAN, MKA Spez. 343, fo. 1, Point 26: 'Es seÿ gleych ein ding mitt dem newen predigern in diesem Land wie ainem gokler der ein katz auβ seinem sack gokle und sey doch nichts da'. Karl Schornbaum, 'Geilsheim in der Reformationszeit', *ZbKG*, 22 (1953), 173–82. Schornbaum points out that Geilsheim was very active in the Peasants' War.

[113] Schornbaum, *Aktenstücke*, pp. 80, 84.

[114] Schornbaum, *Aktenstücke*, pp. 93–4.

asked him to baptise the children in German'.[115] If a grievance was forwarded with reference to a clergyman, it usually referred to a moral failing (bad behaviour, sexual misconduct) or the *fact* of his resistance to honour the 1528 mandate. No real knowledge of the evangelical faith is betrayed.

In 1530 a feud raged in the parish of Roβtal between the incumbent and the Catholic mass priest of Buttendorf which encapsulates this lack of understanding. In theological terms, the division was clear. The Buttendorf clergyman had lectured against the 1528 ordinance, the preaching of the Word, and had once sarcastically observed how 'God has made the fools into wisemen, in that they don't want to honour the mother of God'. The Roβtal clergyman, on the other hand, was a Lutheran and read a German mass.[116] An investigation into the quarrel revealed that the parishioners had no idea of the reasons for the theological division between the two clergymen. Peter Voller of Buttendorf admitted the two were in disagreement, but the authorities soon realised that 'he also knows nothing on it ... understands nothing about it'. This testimony was followed by others marked 'also knows nothing'. Aside from the observation of Hans Dürer that the mass in Roβtal was different from the Latin mass in Langenzenn, the parishioners had no comprehension of the fundamental differences in confessions, and they did not rise up to defend either [*wiβ auch nit welcher recht unrecht hab*]. The revealed attitude was one of resignation and indifference. 'When someone comes to Roβtal', observed Hans Keyner, 'then he must believe the clergyman there. When someone comes to Buttendorf, then he must also believe the clergyman at that place. It is as if a man must have two faiths.'[117]

Between the years 1525 and 1528, the parishioners had enough leeway to pursue the evangelical faith without real threat of persecution. With the arrival of margrave Georg the Pious in 1528 all threat of persecution was removed. With this in mind, the most striking aspect of the 1528 regional reports is the sheer lack of opinion as to what comprised a preacher of the true faith and what rites were commensurate with a church 'born out of God's word'. At least nineteen parishes were home to a clergyman in 1528 who read the Gospels and epistles in German but performed an otherwise traditional service.[118] A definitive statement of the faith was still lacking, but if the Gospel had elicited support among the rural populace it seems unlikely that the parishioners would have been so silent and so restrained when given the chance to express their religious views. Three years after the mass uprising of the Peasants' War in defence of the Gospel, the fact that

---

[115] Schornbaum, *Aktenstücke*, pp. 72–4.
[116] StaN, *Ansbacher Religionsakten III*, Tom. XI, 1530, fos. 425–6. Buttendorf was incorporated with Roβtal.
[117] StaN, *Ansbacher Religionsakten III*, Tom. XI, 1530, fo. 425: 'so einer khum gein Rostall, so muβ er dem pfarrer doselbst glauben, khum dan einer gein Puttendorff, muβ er dem frümesser daselbst auch glauben. Als das nott wer das einer zween glauben hette.'
[118] Schornbaum, *Aktenstücke*, pp. 52–4, 58–9, 61, 64, 71, 72, 74, 79, 80, 83, 93, 94. In some cases two services – evangelical and Catholic – were performed in the same church.

so many uncommitted pastors and imprecise services could persist – in a land, moreover, where communion *sub utraque* was conceded – is a significant measure of the mild intensity of evangelical commitment among the parishioners.

Any suggestion of a 'mild commitment', even if it is in reference to post-1525 events, must contend with the mass uprising of the peasantry that took place in the years 1524 and 1525 – partly in defence of the Gospel – from which the lands in Ansbach were not immune. As early as 13 March 1524 Casimir issued a mandate instructing the district officials to keep an eye open for disturbances in the parishes. Influenced by events in Rothenburg, Windsheim, Würzburg, and Nuremberg, the peasantry in Ansbach began to assemble in the spring of 1525. On 19 March 1525 the margrave's officials discovered a gathering in Wassertrü-dingen. On 31 March Ansbach officials were commissioned to investigate unrest in Crailsheim, and from there they went to Feuchtwangen. Subjects of Nuremberg threatened that their numbers would include the inhabitants of Forchheim and Herzogenaurach, both home to peasants of the margrave. Around the same time Kitzingen was visited by disturbances, then Uffenheim, the region around Schwabach and Roth, and the south-east districts of Stauf and Landeck, with the monastery of Anhausen falling subject to plundering. Peasants also gathered in Bayreuth, but wide-spread agitation did not result.[119]

Casimir estimated that the peasant bands were thousands strong.[120] To counter the threat he began negotiations with the estates of Franconia. Meetings were held in Neustadt, attended by the bishops of Bamberg, Würzburg, and Eichstätt, in addition to representatives of Hesse, Bavaria, Saxony, and the Palatinate. At the second meeting Casimir suggested a unification of troops under his command; but the bishops were wary, and instead looked to the Swabian League. Casimir also treated with the peasant bands themselves. He was in communication with Stephan von Menzingen and the peasant army of Dinkelsbühl, and he had been invited to the peasant parliament in Schweinfurt. Nothing came of his efforts. On 2 June the peasants were defeated at Königshofen by the Swabian League. Following this it was simply a matter of consolidating victory within the margravate.[121]

Central to the peasant demands was the free preaching of the Gospel and the Word of God, but this demand was bound up with so many other issues it is

---

[119] Jäger, 'Markgraf Kasimir und der Bauernkrieg', pp. 29–37; Götz, *Die Glaubensspaltung*, pp. 58–66; Schornbaum, *Die Stellung des Margrafen Kasimir*, pp. 64–76; Heinrich Wilhelm Bensen, *Geschichte des Bauernkriegs in Ostfranken*. (Erlangen, 1840), pp. 387 ff; Klaus Arnold, 'Die Stadt Kitzingen im Bauernkrieg', *Mainfränkisches Jahrbuch*, 27 (1975), 11–50; Rudolf Endres, 'Probleme des Bauernkriegs im Hochstift Bamberg', *Jahrbuch für fränkische Landesforschung*, 31 (1971), 91–138; Hans-Christoph Rublack, 'Die Stadt Würzburg im Bauernkrieg', *ARG*, 67 (1976), 76–100; Roy L. Vice, 'The Leadership and Structure of the Tauber Band during the Peasants' War in Franconia', *Central European History*, 21, 2 (1988), 175–95.

[120] Otto Merx (ed.), *Akten zur Geschichte des Bauernkriegs in Mitteldeutschland*. (Darmstadt, 1964), vol. 1, p. 3.

[121] Götz, *Die Glaubensspaltung*, pp. 59–66.

difficult to determine where religious verve begins and traditional discontent ends. Peter Blickle has viewed the emergence of the evangelical movement – the appropriation of God's Word in particular – as the catalyst for a state of unrest native to pre-Reformation rural society. The 'common man' attempted to over-come the crisis of feudalism through a reshaping of social and seigniorial relations on the basis of Scripture.[122] Ansbach fits this model. Feudalism did not play such an oppressive role in Franconia as it did in Blickle's Upper Swabia, but it is clear that the burden of rents and taxes was a source of resentment and despair for the parishioners and that the call for the Gospel prefaced and guided subsequent demands. 'Concrete economic and social problems among large sections of the rural and urban population', writes Rudolf Endres, 'together with various socio-psychological factors, provided grounds for the uprising in Franconia. What sparked it off was the preaching of the Gospel.'[123] Quoting the Gospel in defence of their rights, the peasant armies in Franconia – Ansbach and Kulmbach included – submitted articles of grievance designed to eliminate or level the estate prerogatives in the principality. Peasant manifestos aimed to purge the land of the burdens considered unfair, without base in tradition, or without reference in Scripture. Numbered among these burdens were as follows: restrictions on the use of water and wood, the extension of hunting rights, restrictions on the running of sheep, the small tithe, arbitrary disciplinary measures, freedom of the clergy from the secular courts, unfair tax burdens, and the number of lords to whom the peasantry had to render up their dues.[124] As this abridged list suggests, it is difficult to disentangle the many interlocking reasons for the peasant uprising.

Although the appeal to the Gospel was a constant theme throughout the rebellion – present in the vast majority of supplications – it would be mistaken to assume that Scripture itself, ingested and understood by the peasantry, worked as a handbook for revolt. 'It is true that the religious question had often sparked off uprisings', Endres observes, 'but rebellious movements soon took another turn and pushed social, economic and political issues much more into the foreground, which rebels themselves regarded as well in tune with holy writ.'[125] Later interrogations illustrate how the impulses that led to revolt were so parochial and pragmatic they preclude any type of broader social, economic, or ideological

[122] Peter Blickle, *Die Revolution von 1525* (Munich, 1983).
[123] Rudolf Endres, 'The Peasant War in Franconia', in Benecke and Scribner (eds.), *The German Peasant War of 1525 – New Viewpoints*, p. 70; Rudolf Endres, 'Franken', in Horst Buszello, Peter Blickle, Rudolf Endres (eds.) *Der deutsche Bauernkrieg.* (Stuttgart, 1984), pp. 134–53.
[124] Lorenz Fries, *Die Geschichte des Bauern-Kriegs in Ostfranken* (Würzburg, 1883), vol. 1, pp. 7, 14–17, 43–4, 196ff, 294–5; vol. 2, pp. 28, 47, 56–7, 179–80, 199, 234; Günther Franz, *Der Deutsche Bauernkrieg. Aktenband* (Darmstadt, 1977), nos. 164, 168, 170, 171, 174; Merx (ed.), *Akten zur Geschichte*, p. 11; 148, 68–70. Jäger, 'Markgraf Kasimir und der Bauernkrieg', pp. 39ff; Bensen, *Geschichte des Bauernkriegs*, pp. 395–6; Lorenz Fries, *Geschichte, Namen, Geschlecht, Leben, Thaten und Absterben der Bischöfe von Würzburg und Herzoge zu Franken* (Würzburg, 1849), vol. 2, p. 67; StaB, C2 161 fo. 119; StaB, C2 160 facs. II fos. 61, 89, 153.
[125] Endres, 'The Peasant War in Franconia', p. 72.

interpretation. Alliances were made, between 'rich and poor', as secret pacts; discontent was directed toward the authorities, indiscriminately on occasion, or with greater definition at other times.[126] Anti-noble sentiment was rife, but there was nothing especially new about this. It was the momentum of the rebellion that prompted many of the rebels in Ansbach and Bayreuth to join up in 1525. Hans Franck of Bayreuth, for instance, heard of the anti-noble uprising in Creußen and advised the regional official that the Bayreuthers should do the same. The latter advised against it (*Liber frank ich widerrats*), but this did not dissuade Hans from goading those present to cross a line and join him. After all, he added, Bayreuth was no different than Creußen.[127] The sheer number of men assembled in groups aroused the curiosity of peasants like Eberlein Stedelman, who went to Gesees 'to see why so many peasants were gathered'.[128] Later confessions, suspect perhaps for their innocence, reveal participants who claimed that they had no idea as to why the unrest started. They simply heard, as in the case of Thomas Groß, that someone wanted to cause trouble, but they did not know why.[129]

Caution should be taken before a scholar assigns blanket motives to a movement as variegated and disparate as the Peasants' War of 1525. This is not to suggest that the discontents outlined in the articles were not shared, the burdens were not real, or the structure of society was not at threat. The point is this. The complex of factors underlying the unrest is not easily separated; the demands placed before the authorities are not a transparent account of the participants' concerns. The call for the Gospel in 1525 is not evidence of a general allegiance to the principles of the evangelical faith. As the investigation of parish religion in 1520s reveals, the Lutheran faith had made little impression. In the years immediately following the revolution, the religious grievances of 1525 no longer surface, nor were they defended with any vigour. The tithes withheld in 1528 (the few cases cited in the district reports) were refused because the clergyman neglected to perform one of his expected, and traditional, functions, not because Scripture failed to offer sanction.[130] Parish tithes, as later disputes reveal, were not reduced by the conflict. Nor did the laity have greater control of the clergy. In 1531 margrave Georg released the pastors from the secular burdens imposed by Casimir.[131] If the idea of a 'communal reformation' had ever taken hold in the principality – that is, with Scripture serving as the guiding authority – the silence in the sources suggests that it had all but disappeared after 1525. The parish, the commune (*Gemeinde*), perceived as a collective body, persisted, but the Gospel did not work to harmonise and justify relations. The Peasants' War does not provide evidence for

---

[126] StaB, C2 161, fos. 119, 284; StaB, C2 160, fo. 136; StaB, C2 160, fo. 164.
[127] StaB C2 160, fos. 89–90; 95. 'so sein die von Creüsen nür ein dorff gegen uns...'; Lang, *Neuere Geschichte*, vol. 1, p. 207.
[128] Stab C2 160, fos. 163, 161.
[129] StaB C2 160, fos. 164 ff; fos. 136, 138, StaB C2 161, fo. 277.
[130] Schornbaum, *Aktenstücke*, pp. 57, 78, 81, 90–1, 92.
[131] StaB, C3, 49, fo. 22. (28 February 1531).

a widespread assimilation of the evangelical message in Brandenburg-Ansbach-Kulmbach.

An investigation of the reception of the evangelical message in the parishes of Ansbach and Kulmbach thus yields two general observations. First, it is clear that the villagers expressed a sincere desire for the Word of God, to be preached aloud without distortion. Parishioners in Ansbach and Kulmbach demanded the spread of the Gospel. But as the investigation of parish religion in the 1520s illustrates, there is little evidence to suggest that the evangelical message was integrated or understood by the parishioners to a degree which would warrant the notion of mass conversion; nor is there much evidence to support the notion that the precepts of the faith were applied to social relations. The communal Reformation did not occur in this principality. Secondly, it is clear that the villagers viewed the Reformation as an 'act of state', ordained by the margrave, and they expected their pastor to preach the Word 'clearly and purely' in line with the mandates. Religion was bound up with the idea of authority; parish demands were couched in a language more 'political' than religious. Behind the demand for the Word of God was a secular agenda: a desire to maintain the relationship between the parish and the margrave, to uphold the rights of the parish (*Gerechtigkeit*), and to sustain traditional filiations of rule.

To return to the discussion taken up at the outset of this section, the appeal of the new faith cannot be explained solely with reference to either religious conviction or the inducements of the social context. An investigation of the reception of the evangelical message in the parishes of Ansbach and Kulmbach in the 1520s suggests a mixture of the two: the demand was for the Word of God, but it was provoked by secular concerns. Parishioners demanded the Word of God because the margrave had commanded as much; it was their right as subjects. This is a rather patent conclusion, but its implications are considerable. The question to ask now is less why the Reformation exercised an appeal on the rural populace than how the parishioners articulated their interest. This issue will arise again later in this work.[132]

[132] See chapter 4.

2

The Lutheran church in Brandenburg-Ansbach-Kulmbach

THE EVOLUTION OF THE CHURCH

The reform leaders in Brandenburg-Ansbach-Kulmbach followed Luther's line of reasoning when they justified the margrave's usurpation of ecclesiastical power. In the Franconian Confession, Luther's idea of the Two Kingdoms provided the context for a discussion of the church. The real church, the community of true believers, is invisible, ruled through Christ alone (*Gewalt Christi*). However, as it is necessary for the external form to maintain order, the rule of the church (*Gewalt der Kirche*) prescribes the service and the organisation of the assembly. The former deals with salvation, the latter with peace and unity among believers. In order to maintain peace and order on earth, the margrave laid full claim to powers of supervision over the rule of the church. (This was a bid for power rather more emphatic than Luther's early notion of 'emergency bishops' who were acting in a temporary and exceptional capacity.) A threefold support is offered for the margrave's claim: First, he inherits the task by default, as the bishops would not comply with the principles of reform; secondly, as protector of the public peace and possessor of high jurisdiction (*Hochgerichtsbarkeit*) – an office granted by God – he has an obligation to maintain accord; lastly, as a member of the Christian estate and one soul among many in the priesthood of all believers (though *praecipuum membrum ecclesiae*), he was obliged out of Christian love and duty to watch over his fellow man. Johann Rurer, the Ansbach clergyman, was emphatic in his support of the margrave's intervention: the sovereign powers had a divine obligation to tend for their subjects' souls.[1] According to such a notion, the laws governing the secular realm and the ecclesiastical realm merge; the church on earth may take form according to the laws of natural order, so long as these laws comply with Scripture and do not threaten salvation. The margrave acts as the divine sanction integrating all of his subjects into a single moral compact.

[1] Bernhard Schneider, *Gutachten evangelischer Theologen des Fürstentums Brandenburg-Ansbach/Kulmbach zur Vorbereitung des Augsburger Reichstags von 1530* (Neustadt a. d. Aisch, 1987), p. 31: 'Die Obrigkeit hat nämlich ihr Amt von Gott und deshalb hat sie ihre Gewalt für Gott einzusetzen zum Nutzen, Heil und Seligkeit der Untertanen'; Schülin, *Fränkische Reformations-Geschichte*, pp. 2–10.

The Ansbach reformers were quick to invest the secular powers with the right to oversee reform, but they were somewhat slower providing practical guidance. The true church, 'the community of believers', was invisible; the earthly nature of this institution, however, its constitution and its makeup, was not specified.[2] In the absence of an alternative church structure, the authorities plotted the course of reform using the means at hand: In Ansbach and Kulmbach religious directives were executed and enforced by the secular authorities. In the resolution of 1524, Casimir ordered that religious disputation be kept to a minimum, and he charged all of his leading secular officials (...*gnedigen herren hauptleut, amptleut, kastner, vögt, schulthaißen, richter, bürgermeister und räte...*) with the task of monitoring the parishes within their jurisdiction. A similar order was issued in 1526 and directed at the regional officials, councillors, and mayors. The secular authorities thus usurped the functions once exercised by the diocesan officials. The regional officials were empowered to judge the quality of the sermons, assess the clergy, and act as the mediating authority in the appointment and dismissal of the pastors.[3] This reliance on secular officials for the implementation and regulation of ecclesiastical policy was in part a self-conscious step in the growth of the territorial church. And yet in the 1520s, there was not really an alternative course of action. No detailed blueprint for church governance had yet been provided by the reformers as a model or a guide.

Secular officials thus assumed the mantle of reform in the 1520s, but this *ad hoc* solution proved inadequate. After the completion of the 1528 visitation, it became apparent that a separate commission of church officials was necessary in order to maintain constant vigilance. The Ansbach clergyman Andreas Althamer offered a solution in a letter to Georg the Pious. Althamer advised the margrave to establish the office of superintendent (*Speculatoren* or *Superattendentes*) – an office invested with powers granted by the margrave – so that the work of the visitation would not be in vain.[4]

Althamer's model was provided by Saxony. The biblical office of super-intendent – as interpreted by the Lutheran reformers – was first given shape by Philipp Melanchthon in 1527.[5] Melanchthon thought it necessary that some clergymen in the larger cities should be selected to watch over the pastors and the state of worship in the parishes under their jurisdiction. The office soon incorporated other responsibilities. In addition to examining the qualifications of

2   For the emergence of the Lutheran church in general, see Irmgard Höss, 'The Lutheran Church of the Reformation: Problems of Its Formation and Organization in the Middle and North German Territories,' Buck and Zophy (eds.) *The Social History of the Reformation*, pp. 317–39.

3   Sehling, pp. 80, 89, 102.

4   StaN, *Ansbacher Religionsakten III*, Tom. VIII, fasc. II, fo. 467. Althamer stressed that the superintendents should 'fürstlichen gewalt und bevelch haben ... das man etwas umb sie geb: Wir sorgen es werde sunst alles mit einander verloren sein.'

5   Heinrich Nobbe, 'Das Superintendentenamt, seine Stellung und Aufgabe nach den evangelischen Kirchenordnungen des 16. Jahrhunderts', *Zeitschrift für Kirchengeschichte*, 14 (1894), 414.

the clergy and the school personnel, the superintendent had to supervise parish finance and exercise provisional control over marriage law in cooperation with the regional officials.[6] The limits of each superintendent's region corresponded to the secular divisions, while the judicial aspect of the office was roughly equivalent to that of the former archdeacons. True to Luther's ideas, the reformers did not assign the superintendent any greater sacerdotal status than the common parish clergyman; he simply had more involved duties. And even without this theoretical limitation, the powers of the regional superintendents were few. It was clear from the outset that the superintendents would have to answer to the Elector's regional officials. Their scope of independent action was severely circumscribed.[7]

The 1528 church ordinance established the office of superintendent in Ansbach. Like his Saxon counterpart, the Ansbach superintendent was commissioned to watch over the faith and correct abuses in the parishes. Where matters could not be settled locally, the superintendent referred them to the margrave.[8] These men were given no independent powers and had to work in close cooperation with the secular authorities. The region, or operational basis, of each superintendency was divided to match the secular divisions in the principality rather than the chapters, since the ecclesiastical partitions encompassed parishes that did not belong to the margrave, but rather to Eichstätt, Bamberg, Würzburg, other territorial princes, or imperial cities such as Rothenburg. Althamer first suggested the election of one or two superintendents for each division in the wake of the 1528 visitation, and this had been carried out exclusively in accordance with the secular divisions by secular officials. The basic idea was simply to add a clergyman to support the often inefficient work of the regional officials.

In many ways the appointment of superintendents was an eleventh-hour attempt to solve the immediate problems of church governance. In Brandenburg-Ansbach-Kulmbach, the office proved ineffective. The regional districts were of unequal size and demand. Uffenheim, for instance, had twenty parishes while Mainbernheim had – at various times – only two or three, yet both were assigned a single superintendent. Moreover, the superintendents did not have an adequate system of church government to support or monitor their efforts. Final recourse for all disputes was the distant margrave's court in Ansbach.[9]

The 'visible' church in Brandenburg-Ansbach-Kulmbach was slow to evolve.

[6] Georg Müller, 'Verfassungs- und Verwaltungsgeschichte der sächsischen Landeskirche', *Beiträge zur Sächsischen Kirchengeschichte*, 9 (1894), 96–109.

[7] Nobbe, 'Das Superintendentenamt', p. 564; Westermayer, *Die Brandenburgisch-Nürnbergische Kirchenvisitation und Kirchenordnung*, p. 43.

[8] Sehling, p. 139. 'Superatendenten sollen den bevelch haben, das, wie sie aus dieser visitation und anderen wissentlichen bevelhen der obrigkeit ir gemut versteen, das, wo etwas wider Gottes wort oder solche ir gute ordnung geschehe, konten sie das fur sich selbs wenden und pessern gewißlich, das sie es teten, wo nit, das sie es an die obrigkeit ließen langen alles mit vorbehaltner unser bederseits enderung und besserung'.

[9] Gustav Bossert, 'Die ersten Schritte zur Neuordnung der Kapitel in der Markgrafschaft Brandenburg-Ansbach 1528ff', *Blätter für bayerische Kirchengeschichte*, 3 (1887), 33–9.

Despite its theological sophistication, the 1533 church ordinance said very little about the structure of the church. The church ordinance dealt with the service and its teachings; it did not provide the Lutheran authorities with a concrete reform strategy. As a consequence, the inchoate 1528 system of superintendencies remained in place until further steps were taken in the middle of the century.[10] Althamer outlined the failings and inadequacies of this type of church government in a letter to the margrave. The 1533 ordinance was opposed in many parishes, he wrote, the catechism was neglected, schools were empty and dancehalls were full. Often the superintendents were hindered in their duties, if not publicly opposed, by the regional officials. Friedrich Myconius described a similar problem in Saxony: the Gospel was not 'everyman's thing' and the Lutheran superintendents frequently encountered resistance from the secular officials.[11] Althamer suggested that a yearly synod or gathering of the clergy should be held, and he advised the superintendents to watch over the parishioners and report abuses to the margrave or his council. Finally, in the margin of this letter, Althamer made the note: 'Inquire into places in which there are no superintendents'.[12] But Althamer's advice was not heeded.

In general, the years following the publication of the 1533 ordinance to the further construction of the church in 1556 was a time of stagnation and even decline for the Lutheran church in Brandenburg-Ansbach-Kulmbach. Catholic services continued unabated in some Ansbach parishes. A Kulmbach clergyman complained that there was no unity in worship; each pastor wished to be his own bishop.[13] The chancellor Georg Vogler tried to repair the situation by introducing a second visitation. While in exile in Windsheim, Vogler extended the efforts he had begun at the Ansbach court. Writing to such men as the Crailsheim clergyman Adam Weiß, the Ansbach academic Zeigler, and finally the margrave himself, Vogler was able to strengthen his case by detailing the set-backs facing the evangelical religion in the parishes. Pastors were calling the margrave a heretic; noblemen were reinstituting the Catholic mass; moreover, the superintendents, according to Vogler, refused to make reports. Vogler's efforts were rewarded. The visitation was carried out in 1536 – but its impact was ephemeral.[14]

The church was also set back by unfavourable political events at mid-century. In 1541 Casimir's son Albrecht Alcibiades, scourge of the Lutheran moralists, came of age and inherited the lands of Kulmbach. In 1543 Georg the Pious died

---

[10] Friedrich Vogtherr, 'Die Verfassung der evangelisch-lutherischen Kirche in den ehemaligen Fürstentümern Ansbach und Bayreuth', *Beiträge zur bayerischen Kirchengeschichte*, 2 (1896), 212.

[11] Paul Drews, 'Der Bericht des Mykonius über die Visitation des Amtes Tenneberg im März 1526', *ARG*, 9 (1905), 15.

[12] Theodor Kolde, *Andreas Althamer, der Humanist und Reformator in Brandenburg-Ansbach* (Erlangen, 1895), pp. 126–7.

[13] Dorfmüller, 'Aeltere kirchliche Geschichte von Culmbach', p. 25.

[14] Karl Schornbaum, 'Zur zweiten brandenburgischen Kirchenvisitation 1536', *Jahresbericht des historischen Vereins für Mittelfranken*, 53 (1906), 1–22.

and a regency ruled for his son. A further threat emerged in 1548, when both principalities were faced with the imposition of the Interim. In Ansbach, the regency hoped to append the service with a few alterations intended to please the Emperor (elevation of the host, increased Latin for the mass); the clergy, however, rejected the suggestion. The issue was readdressed at Heilsbronn, with the Kulmbach clergymen in attendance (28 August 1548), but once again the theologians rejected the attempts of the council. Disconcerted, the Ansbach regency submitted a list of proposed alterations to two leading clergymen, who drew up what was in effect an appendix to the church ordinance and presented it to a meeting of the clergy on 31 October 1548. This appendix was approved and accepted; entitled the *Auctuarium*, it included an increase in the amount of Latin used in the service and the elevation of the host.[15] It was designed to serve as a bridge between the Interim and the church ordinance, and its ambivalence won few admirers. Albrecht Alcibiades, a self-professed Catholic, wanted to introduce the Interim in its entirety in his Kulmbach lands, but the clergy continually opposed his efforts. Despite a series of meetings overseen by the margrave and the introduction of a revised church ordinance, the changes were not enforced in Kulmbach.[16] Only in Ansbach did the compromise *Auctuarium* find its way into the parishes, where it simply introduced confusion and resentment. The clergyman Georg Karg observed (as did the widow of Georg the Pious) that services varied from parish to parish.[17] It was not until 1556, following the Peace of Augsburg, that a more definitive Lutheran church structure emerged.

The final form the Lutheran church assumed was the work of Georg Karg and margrave Georg Friedrich. Georg Karg entered the principality as the city pastor of Schwabach in 1547; five years later he was transferred to Ansbach. Once in Ansbach, he submitted reports detailing the poor condition of the church: not only the city church, but the church in general. Karg's struggle to purge the parishes of the *Auctuarium* had opened his eyes to the need for a centralised authority in the church. In 1556 Karg pointed out the deficiencies and abuses of the church, both in Ansbach and the outer principality, in a series of letters to the margrave.[18] He then detailed the reforms and innovations he thought were necessary in order for the Lutheran church to prosper. First, to counter the autonomy and license enjoyed by the rural clergy, Karg proposed that each pastor should be made subject to a superintendent (or deacon – the titles were

---

[15] Simon, *Evangelische Kirchengeschichte Bayerns*, p. 254; Karl Schornbaum, 'Das Interim im Markgraftum Brandenburg-Ansbach', *Beiträge zur bayerischen Kirchengeschichte*, 14 (1908), 1–27, 49–79, 101–26.

[16] Lang, *Neuere Geschichte*, pp. 206–12; Wilhelm Kneule, *Kirchengeschichte der Stadt Bayreuth* (Neustadt a.d. Aisch, 1971), Part 1, pp. 29–31; Löhe, *Erinnerungen*, pp. 145–65.

[17] Christian Meyer, 'Aktenstücke zur Geschichte des Interims im Fürstenthum Brandenburg-Ansbach', *Jahresbericht des historischen Vereins für Mittelfranken*, 40 (1880), 48–51.

[18] The original letters are in LKAN, *Allgemeine Kirchenangelegenheiten*, Gen. 18, nos. 11 & 12. A transcribed copy is printed in Karl Schornbaum, 'Die Ansbacher Synode 1556', *Beiträge zur bayerischen Kirchengeschichte*, 27 (1921), 106–9.

interchangeable) in a pre-determined chapter. Where no chapter existed, one should be founded, and a superintendent and a coadjutor should be appointed from among the clergy encompassing those administrative districts making up a reasonable ecclesiastical chapter. Secondly, each superintendent should hold a yearly synod where the clergy could gather and discuss the faith, thus enabling the superintendent to emphasise the principles of the religion and oversee unity of belief. Thirdly, once the new clergyman had been accepted and confirmed by the margrave, each superintendent along with a regional official should invest the pastor into his new parish. Fourthly, and of paramount importance, each superintendent and his assistant should maintain close supervision of the clergy under their charge. Finally, Karg ended his report with the suggestion that the clergy meet once a year in Ansbach. These directives, Karg believed, would enforce orthodoxy in religious observance and offer some protection for the parish clergy who, he added, were often treated worse than the Jews.[19]

With the threat of Karg's self-exile to support it, this proposal soon found a response at court. Two of the margrave's councillors contacted Karg and agreed to rectify the situation in the Ansbach church of St Johannis at the earliest opportunity. The council was also ready to address the wider problems of church governance. In October 1556 a synod was held in Ansbach and Georg Friedrich submitted a motion of his immediate intentions. The margrave presented three topics for discussion and counsel: the matter of the superintendents, an appropriate catechism, and a marriage court.[20] As each of the issues was dealt with in turn, most of Karg's reform suggestions were accepted.

The clergy drew up a proposal for church government which essentially agreed with the earlier efforts of Karg. The territorial church was divided into chapters or superintendencies, exact divisions which formed the administrative district for each superintendent. Along with the five original chapters of Crailsheim, Cadolzburg, Gunzenhausen, Wassertrüdingen, and Feuchtwangen were added Uffenheim, Kitzingen, Schwabach, Wülzburg, and Leutershausen. A superintendent headed each chapter, empowered to invest the clergy, keep a watch over vacancies and election, and maintain unity in worship and morals (the latter task being ameliorated through yearly synods). The regional officials now had to refer all church disciplinary matters to the superintendents.[21] Each new pastor had to be examined in Ansbach – the general chapter – before assuming duties in the parish. The proposal also offered solutions for the problems confronting the discipline of marriage, the pastors' personal powers of excommunication and discipline, the state of education, and the maintenance of

[19] Schornbaum, 'Die Ansbacher Synode 1556', pp. 108–9; Hans-Martin Weiss, *Vom notwendigen Verstand der Lehre* (Neustadt a/d Aisch, 1991), pp. 104–34; Georg Wilke, *Georg Karg (Parsimonius), sein Katechismus und sein doppelter Lehrstreit* (Scheinfeld, 1904), pp. 15–40.
[20] Schornbaum, 'Die Ansbacher Synode 1556', pp. 10–11.
[21] Weiss, *Vom notwendigen Verstand*, p. 65.

parish buildings.[22] In 1565 the foundation ordinance consolidated the work begun at the synod. Two new chapters were added to the principality of Ansbach: Neustadt and Baiersdorf. As had been established at the Ansbach synod, a superintendent chaired each district, but now he was joined by two *Seniores*, elected by the clergy, who were to act as his aides. The *Camerarium* was also created to deal with financial matters. Each superintendent was to hold a yearly synod; each clergyman was expected to appear, 'with no exceptions', and his learning was to be assessed against the observed theological texts.[23]

The church order established by Georg Karg and margrave Georg Friedrich extended the reach of its innovations and reforms into the parishes. The rural clergy were now much more accountable to the margrave. The power to appoint and invest the Lutheran pastor was, as before, reserved for the margrave. The clergyman had to appear before the higher clergy for evaluation before he could be placed into office. Once the pastor was approved, he was invested by the superintendent alongside a secular official.[24] (On 22 May 1572 this mandate was extended to include the lands of Kulmbach.)[25] From the moment of application to the day when the pastor was introduced to his future congregation, the margrave and his higher officials were in control of the clergyman's fate. Once in office, the pastor was under the constant surveillance of his fellow clergymen. The synods kept the clergy in check through a policy of mutual incrimination: if a pastor knew anything at all about the life or the teaching of another who was suspect, he was to report it to the superintendent.[26] All of these measures strengthened the margrave's hold over the church; but perhaps most significant of all, at least with reference to the impact the mandate made in the parishes, was the super-intendents' obligation to undertake an annual visitation, the so-called special visitation.[27] As will be discussed below, the visitation proved to be the most effective way to monitor the religious life in the villages.

[22] Schornbaum, 'Die Ansbacher Synode 1556', pp. 33–7, 151–8.
[23] *Corpus Constitutionum Brandenburgico-Culmbacensium* (Bayreuth, 1746), Part 1, pp. 350ff. Vogtherr, 'Die Verfassung', pp. 215–16. Sehling, pp. 346–59. Löhe, *Erinnerungen*, pp. 177–85. Lorenz Krauβold, *Geschichte der evangelischen Kirche im ehemaligen Fürstenthum Bayreuth* (Erlangen, 1860), pp. 134–63.
[24] *Corpus Constitutionum Brandenburgico-Culmbacensium*, (1746), p. 358.
[25] Sehling, pp. 362–3; *Corpus Constitutionum Brandenburgico-Culmbacensium*, (1746), p. 347. The principality of Kulmbach-Bayreuth led what Sehling had termed a 'Sonderleben' in religious matters until the last few decades of the century. Most of the religious decisions were supervised by the *Hauptmann und Räten auf dem Gebirg*. Events in the parishes were not as well monitored as in Ansbach. Generally the pastors of the four administrative centres – Hof, Wunsiedel, Kulmbach, and Bayreuth – acted in the capacity of superintendents from 1528–29 until the reception of the synodal mandate in 1572, which then confirmed their status. Krauβold, *Geschichte der evangelischen Kirche*, pp.136–44.
[26] *Corpus Constitutionum Brandenburgico-Culmbacensium* (1746), p. 353. The clergymen should 'sagen und zeugen, was inen kund und wissend ist, wo er sich in seinem Amte, in seiner Haushaltung, oder sonst in seinem Leben ungebührlich gehalten hätte ... oder unfleissig in seinem Amte und Dienste gewesen, Weib und Kind übel gehalten, oder sonst ärgerlich gelebt hätte'.
[27] *Corpus Constitutionum Brandenburgico-Culmbacensium* (1746), p. 351.

By the 1560s the foundations of the Lutheran church in Brandenburg-Ansbach-Kulmbach had been established, though the church was slow to work as an integrated unit. For instance, the Ansbach council of 1556 had called for yearly chapter synods, and while it might not be representative to isolate a single chapter, it is however clear that these did not take place every year in Uffenheim. In 1560 the councillors of Ansbach observed that 'since the death of Johann Schilling, former pastor of Uffenheim [1556], no synod or gathering [*Capitell oder versamblung*] of the dependent clergy of the same has been held'.[28] The superintendent Johann Dannreuther was instructed to resurrect the yearly synod. Yet four years later the clergy of Uffenheim still complained that the synods in Uffenheim had been left in abeyance (*ein zeitlang unterlaßen*), and even Dannreuther himself submitted a list of parish abuses to the margrave.[29]

The reform of the visible church did not provide an immediate solution to the problems faced by the Lutheran authorities. Ill-behaviour in the parishes – as viewed through a Protestant glass – continued unabated in other chapters besides Uffenheim. It would be unrealistic to attribute all perceived failings to a loose system of ecclesiastical discipline,[30] and yet the glacial development of church government, and the frail lines of command, go a long way in explaining the freedoms exercised by the parishioners. Recognising the lack of order, Georg Friedrich held another general synod in Ansbach in 1578, in the presence of the theologian Jakob Andreae, and the 1565 ordinance was reworked.[31] The problem, however, lay not in the theoretical groundwork: rather, the network of chapters waited upon an administrative hub, an epicentre other than the prince's court, which could deal with church concerns as an autonomous unit and issue directives in the margrave's name. Consequently, in many ways, the proficiency of Georg Karg's structure of church government ran parallel with the emergence of the consistory.

THE CONSISTORY

Since it was lacking in scriptural justification, the sacramental nature of marriage was rejected by Luther and greater emphasis was placed on the earthly state of matrimony. In one fell swoop, centuries of ecclesiastical law amounted to nothing. Luther's reinterpretation of marriage thus suspended the jurisdiction of the ecclesiastical courts, but no similar institution emerged in the Lutheran lands as a replacement. The regulation of marriage became a concern for the secular

---

28 LKAN, MDU, 3, fos. 44–5 (5 March 1560).
29 LKAN, MDU, 3, fos. 60–2, 1564. A section of Dannreuther's letter is printed in Sehling, p. 296; Rudolf Herold, *Ein Stück Kirchengeschichte. Geschichte des Dekanates Uffenheim* (Gütersloh, 1891), p. 50.
30 Though this was certainly stressed by Karg in 1571. LKAN, *Allgemeine Kirchenangelegenheiten*, Generalia 18, no. 20, 1571.
31 Vogtherr, 'Die Verfassung', p. 216.

authorities; and, like many other aspects of the moral order projected by Lutheran theology, the regulation of marriage became a matter of public discipline, a contest between individual choice and the maintenance of secular order.[32] At the outset of the evangelical movement the local officials, together with the superintendent or the visitation commissioners, would judge over the less controversial cases, while the more difficult cases were referred to court. But this system soon feel into disuse. A more stable, centralised forum was needed.

The Lutheran consistory in Germany emerged to fill the vacuum left through the atrophy of the visitation commission and the suspension of the marriage courts. In 1539 a Lutheran consistory was established in Ernestine Saxony. It functioned almost exclusively as a marriage court. Although it was revised in 1542, extending its field of competence to include legal supervision of the clergy and church property, it remained a court of appeal (*Gerichtshof, Kirchengericht*) rather than an administrative apparatus.[33] A few years later in Albertine Saxony steps were taken to construct a consistory that seemed to presage later developments – examination and ordination of the clergy, broadening the spectrum of supervision – but in Albertine Saxony, as in northern Germany as a whole, the consistory remained a dependent church court.[34]

The development of the Lutheran church, and in particular the evolution of the consistory, was greatly encouraged by the reform measures introduced in Württemberg. By the year 1553, a college of advisers was in session in the Württemberg territorial church invested with administrative functions and actively directing ecclesiastical affairs. The college (*Kirchenrat*), which found full expression in the 1559 church ordinance, was responsible for the supervision of church governance. Unlike the Saxon model, full management of the church was in the hands of the secular and ecclesiastical officials comprising the college.[35] This was the second of the two consistorial models; while the Saxon consistory acted as a judicature, the Württemberg institution was more of an administrative centre for the maturing territorial church. The consistory that evolved in Ansbach was a composite of both the Württemberg and the Saxon institutions.

In the early 1520s, even before the Ansbach reformers began to advise the secular authorities on what should be done in the absence of diocesan regulation, many evangelical pastors and reform-minded princes simply processed marriage disputes independently, without paying heed to the bishops' remonstrations. In the chapter of Kulmbach, for instance, the clergy assumed the burden at the expense of Catholic jurisdiction. 'I have been informed by reliable people,' or so

---

32 Thomas Max Safley, *Let No Man Put Asunder: The Control of Marriage in the German Southwest: A Comparative Study, 1550–1600* (Kirksville, 1984), pp. 1–32.

33 Karl Müller, 'Die Anfänge der Konsistorialverfassung im lutherischen Deutschland', *Historische Zeitschrift*, 3 (1909), 5–8.; Nobbe, 'Das Superintendentenamt', pp. 557–9; Höss, 'The Lutheran Church of the Reformation', p. 327.

34 Müller, 'Die Anfänge der Konsistorialverfassung', p. 11.

35 Müller, 'Die Anfänge der Konsistorialverfassung', p. 16.

The Lutheran church

claimed the bishop of Bamberg in 1523, that a number of men in Bayreuth – secular and spiritual officials – had ventured to process a marriage dispute between themselves without consulting the bishop's court. Casimir denied the charge, or at least reinterpreted it, for he did not wish to part company with the bishops yet. But it does seem that pastor Johann Prückner took the initiative and processed a marital case in private, claiming that he did it out of 'brotherly love'.[36] The facts are clear: the evangelical clergymen of Bayreuth decided this case without recourse to the Bamberg ecclesiastical court. Nor does this appear to have been an isolated instance; it may stand as a solitary example of a general trend.[37] Pastor Prückner's actions represent the difficulties and the resultant confusion that arose following Luther's reinterpretation of the sacramental status of marriage and his rejection of the ecclesiastical courts.

The Ansbach resolution of 1526 attempted to limit some abuses,[38] but the problems confronting the regulation of marriage were not really taken into hand until Georg the Pious returned in 1528. Georg wanted to confer the vacant archdeaconry of St Gumbertus on the evangelical clergyman Johann Rurer. Rurer would sit on a committee which, 'with the advice of the pastor here in Ansbach and other learned men', would settle contested marriage cases. The provost of St Gumbertus at the time was Georg's brother margrave Friedrich, and he would not agree to the plan. Georg then sought the advice of Johannes Brenz, who sent the margrave a draft of suggestions in 1529; but Brenz's suggestions were never developed, his draft was not incorporated into the 1533 church ordinance, and the imposition of a uniform marriage law hung fire.[39] Not until 1535, with the publication of the *Mandat wider die heimlichen Verlöbnisse*, was the supervision of marriage embodied in print, and then in a limited way.[40] During this period marriage disputes were settled by the local officials in consultation with the pastor. If the authorities felt the case was beyond their capabilities, the matter was referred to Ansbach.

---

[36] StaB, C2, 1814, fos. 3–4, 8–11. Letter from the bishop of Bamberg (1523). The clergy involved included Johann Prückner, Nikolaus Schamel, and 'andern Briester zu Bayreuth'. The bishop also complained that the mandates and summons issued from his court were not being obeyed and that his beadles were beaten and thrown in the water by the peasants (at the request of the clergy). The bishop concluded that the margrave was threatening his jurisdiction and depriving him of power.

[37] StaB, C2, 1814, fo. 27. Point 8 of the *Verzeychnus der Beschwerde, so dem geystlichen Bambergischen decanat gericht begegnen* suggests that many of the parishioners responded to the initiative taken by the clergy: 'Zum achten, so werden auch zuzeiten etlich person welche laut geschribens rechtens kein Ehe beschliessen mogen, Auch wider derhalben am geystlichen gericht ergangen urtheil eingeleyt, mit verachtung aller Censür, dagegen als billich fürgenommen, an etlichen orten enthalten und beschutt.'

[38] Sehling, p. 95. *Von der weltlichen uneelichen beisitz.*

[39] Heinrich Gürsching, 'Die Entstehung des Ansbacher Konsistoriums', *ZbKG*, 4 (1929), 17–18; W. Köhler, 'Brentiana und andere Reformatoria IV', *ARG*, 11 (1914), 241–89. In 1531 Brenz, along with the Ansbach theologians, suggested the establishment of a consistory after the fashion of a court of morals and marriage, but the plan was rejected by Nuremberg. Vogtherr, 'Die Verfassung', p. 216.

[40] *Corpus Constitutionum Brandenburgico-Culmbacensium*, (1746), pp. 289–90.

The consistory

The laws and practices regulating marriage in Brandenburg-Ansbach-Kulmbach were not fundamentally modified until Georg Karg's reforming efforts in 1556. Heinrich Gürsching has written a detailed article on the emergence of the consistory in Ansbach and it is telling how he passes by the years 1528 to 1556 in relative silence.[41] The council of theologians and officials in Ansbach – strictly speaking the three principal clergymen of the city – oversaw the difficult cases; these men formed something of a college, and later, from among the general assembly of officials in charge of church affairs (*verordnete examinatores*), there emerged a group of men who seem to have specialised in marriage cases and represented the nucleus of the marriage court (*verordnete in ehesachen*).[42] It appears that the examiners were referring to themselves as a consistory before 1556, since Karg complained in his letter of the same year that, aside from his duties examining the clergy, he had to attend the meetings of the consistory of marriage matters as well.[43] But Karg may have been using such terminology indiscriminately, for at this date the margrave had not yet founded an independent institution to oversee marriage disputes.[44]

With the publication of the synod ordinance in 1556 a marriage court was finally established in its own right. In Ansbach, the officials in charge of marriage disputes now met on Wednesdays to settle contested cases. Marriage articles, issued in 1565 and reissued in 1573, provided pastors and higher officials alike with a list of objective standards for the entire principality.[45] The marriage court (or consistory), as the 1567 Kulmbach institution illustrates, now had a definite form and role:

The consistory should be chaired by a doctor or otherwise a councillor from our government learned in the ways of the law (*rechtsverstendiger*), the superintendent, and the pastor and chaplain(s) of Kulmbach. The superintendent should be the judge. They should have their own court secretary (to which purpose a chancery scribe might be used) and they should meet each week on a certain day, whether Wednesday or Thursday, at a convenient location in the city of Kulmbach [and there] process matters and hold court. They should also have their own seal.[46]

---

41 Gürsching, 'Die Entstehung', pp. 19–21.
42 Gürsching, 'Die Entstehung', p. 21; Weiss, *Vom notwendigen Verstand*, p. 116.
43 Vogtherr, 'Die Verfassung', p. 218. Original letter in LKAN, MKA, *Allgemeinen Kirchenangele-genheiten*, no. 11, fo. 3.
44 In Kulmbach the situation appears to have been even more chaotic. In 1538 Johann Schnabel went to Wittenberg for advice on the grades of consanguinity: 'von wegen der verpoten grad der blutfreundschafft und schwagerschafft etc. und ander den gleichen'. The same year the clergy had confessed to Melanchthon that the margrave had not yet appointed officials who could deal with contested marriages: 'biβher nit sonderlichen personen solche Eesach zu handeln beuolhen haben und den selben vollen gewalt geben in Ehesachen zehandeln sondern zu zeytten von sich geschoben'. StaN, *Ansbacher Religionsakten*, III, Tom. XI, fos. 459–61.
45 Sehling, pp. 367–76; *Corpus Constitutionum Brandenburgico-Culmbacensium*, (1746), pp. 291–5, 296–304.
46 Sehling, p. 371.

Gradually the assembly began to take on wider functions, and out of this evolved a type of church court, annexed to the marriage court, which met on Thursdays and served as a forum for the clergy.[47] The court was strictly a legal assembly, now separated from the margrave's chancellery, which dealt with disputes and altercations involving the clergy. It was still a church court (*Kirchengericht*) similar to the Saxon model; it did not deal in any great depth with ecclesiastical administration.[48]

At this stage, in the early 1560s, the young margrave Georg Friedrich was under the tutelage of his father-in-law Hans von Brandenburg-Küstrin and his chancellor Wolf von Kötteriz. Both men recognised the need for a central administrative agency for the church, if only to channel the many legal disputes in a single direction and away from the Ansbach chancellery. To this purpose they planned to use the monastery at Heilsbronn and the foundations in Ansbach and Feuchtwangen, but the beneficiaries of these institutions, some of whom were councillors, did not wish to see them dissolved, and the construction of a consistory fell prey to court politics.[49] The main concern during this period remained the need to remove the many ecclesiastical proceedings away from the court. In general, the majority of formal church pronouncements at this time were still more likely to be extended *ex consilio* rather than *ex consistorio*. On other occasions, for example in a 1575 tithe dispute, judgement was rendered *des Consistory in Ehesachen zu Onolzbach [Ansbach]*, although the lawsuit had nothing whatever to do with marriage.[50]

The guidance for further evolution came from outside the principality. In 1580, at a time when most Protestant states welcomed cooperation from their confessional counterparts, Jakob Andreœ began to offer his considerable talents to Ansbach. A consistory ordinance was drafted in 1580, based upon the equivalent in Ernestine Saxony, which outlined an institution capable of dealing comprehensively and independently with the supervision of church affairs.[51] Alterations to the ordinance were made in 1580, 1588, until the final version was published in 1594. By the last decade of the century, both Ansbach and Kulmbach were home

[47] Gürsching, 'Die Entstehung', p. 36. Up to that point the Ansbach council had dealt with such matters. See *Konsistorium für Kirchensachen*. Sehling, p. 366.

[48] Sehling, pp. 298, 366. Gürsching, 'Die Entstehung', p. 37. Ernst Hirschmann, 'Das Konsistorialrecht der evangelisch-lutherischen Kirche im ehemaligen Fürstenthum Bayreuth' (Jur. Diss., Erlangen, 1949), p. 26.

[49] Gürsching, 'Die Entstehung', pp. 24–38.

[50] LKAN, MKA, Spez. 394, Bd. 1 1525–1581, fos. 251–2 (24 March 1575). The reference may have been to the building rather than the college of officials involved, but it illustrates nonetheless that an independent forum for these disputes did not yet exist.

[51] Gürsching, 'Die Entstehung', pp. 38–42. Sehling, pp. 298–9. Simon, *Evangelische Kirchengeschichte Bayerns*, p. 290. 'Unter dem Einfluß Andreäs, der von Württemberg her ein Konsistorium nicht nur als Gericht, sonder als Verwaltungsgröße kannte, wurden 1580 diese Gerichte in Ansbach zu einem Konsistorium im Sinne eines Kirchenregiments vereinigt und ausgebaut.'

to consistories with the power and the competence to regulate church affairs free from constant reliance on, or the constant supervision of, the margrave's secular councils. When the pastor of Weimersheim wrote to the chancellery in 1594 to announce the death of a pastor (which was the proper procedure) a hand had scribbled on the back of the letter: 'Should be given to the consistory' – *Ex Consilio.*[52]

The 1594 ordinance classified the consistory and its membership retrospectively; it systematised procedures that had been in operation 'for many years'. Three theologians along with three members of the margrave's council staffed the main offices, with one of the secular officials serving as the president. The consistory had the power to issue decrees in the name of the margrave. In general the margrave or his council was contacted whenever it was a question of jurisdiction or expenditure – for instance the approval of the clergy, the punishment of recalcitrant parishioners, or the construction or repair of ecclesiastical buildings – otherwise the consistory's functions were clearly delineated and we can assume that it dealt with the following with some regularity: supervision of unity of teaching, worship, and ceremony in the parishes; the learning of the pastors, their behaviour, and the defence of their rights if they should seek legal aid; supervision, selection, and examination of all the church servants (which included the sextons and the schoolmasters); yearly registers and investigations of the financial state of the parish churches; and the annual inventory of the visitation returns.[53]

The ultimate goal of the consistory was not only to regulate religious affairs and preserve the faith, but to exercise the margrave's power in such a way that the Lutheran faith became synonymous with the will of the margrave. The consistory was a means to discipline the subject population, affecting clergyman and parishioner alike. The consistory was called to life 'for the maintenance of constant unity, discipline, order, and honour among the clergy and their audience, and to punish and make an example of evil in our land and principality in the name of God'.[54] Although it had accrued extensive prerogatives by century's end, the margrave was always the ultimate arbiter of the consistory's functions and the final reach of its powers in the principality. There is no doubt that the 1594 ordinance illustrates the dominance of the prince in ecclesiastical affairs and his unabashed claim to dictate the course of religious reform. Like the other councils at Georg Friedrich's disposal, the consistory worked as an arm of the emerging territorial state. His control of the church was complete.

[52] LKAN, MKA, Spez. 861 (12 March 1594).
[53] Sehling, pp. 379–96. *Corpus Constitutionum Brandenburgico-Culmbacensium* (1746), pp. 253–84. Vogtherr, 'Die Verfassung', pp. 270–5.
[54] Sehling, p. 380. '...zu erhaltung guter bestendiger ainigkeit, disciplin, zucht und erbarkeit under den lehrern und zuhorern, auch zue anscheu und strafe des uebels in unserm land und fürstenthumb in Gottes namen...'

The Lutheran church

Georg the Pious, it has been claimed, read Melanchthon's *Instructions for the Visitors of Parish Pastors in Electoral Saxony* while in Kulmbach in 1528.[55] Whether the stimulus for the visitation was so elementary might be suspect, but there is no doubt that the visitation in Ernestine Saxony served as a model for coterminous events in Ansbach. Not long after Melanchthon had drafted his *Instructions for the Visitors...*, the first visitation in the principality of Brandenburg-Ansbach-Kulmbach took place. Thinking that a parish-to-parish visitation was too dangerous in 1528 (given the religious climate in the Empire and the sabre-rattling of the bishops)[56] the margrave ordered the clergy to appear in Ansbach, with a suitable member of the congregation in tow, where they would be interrogated by the clergymen Johann Rurer and Andreas Althamer at the house of the former mayor Jörg Hamer.[57] At this stage, without a published church ordinance, it was easier to realise reform by subjecting the clergy to the margrave's demands directly, rather than diffusing his orders through the still ineffective system of superintendencies. In early 1529 the margrave attempted to extend the visitation to the lands of Kulmbach. Althamer suggested that the margrave invest him with a special commission, so that the visitation could be taken in hand.[58]

A second visitation did not occur in Ansbach until the year 1536. Whereas the 1528 visitation functioned as a type of interrogatory tribunal – its main concern was whether the parish clergyman honoured the 1528 resolution – the 1536 visitation broadened its field of investigation to include the physical, social, and economic aspects of parish religion.[59] The sheer scale of interest presaged later developments. Yet however detailed the visitation ordinance became, the visitations themselves were slow to develop. After the death of Georg the Pious in 1543, a regency assumed power for the minor Georg Friedrich. Due to the uncertainty of the confessional situation in the Empire, especially after the defeat of the Schmalkaldic League in 1547, there was no talk of further visitations until 1555, the year of the Peace of Augsburg. In 1556, at the Ansbach synod, the idea of yearly visitations was once again mooted and tentative steps were taken. And in

---

[55] Schornbaum, *Aktenstücke*, p. 1.

[56] Nor was this reserve overcautious, as the pastor of Obernzenn Philp Getreu made clear after his efforts to visit the neighbouring parish in the same year. Getreu encountered insults and abuse from the parishioners and indeed feared for his welfare. StaN, *Ansbacher Religionsakten III*, Tom. VIII, fasc. II, fo. 561. 'Aber der durch ich in grosse gevard kome von dem mererin thail under den ich visitiren sollte und visitirt habe ... mit grossen iniuren und schmach worthn angedast das ich nit frolich oder sicher in dorff noch auβ dem dorff geen darff...'.

[57] Götz, *Die Glaubensspaltung*, pp. 128–9; Westermayer, *Die Brandenburgisch-Nürnbergische Kirchenvisitation und Kirchenordnung*, p. 3.

[58] Götz, *Die Glaubensspaltung*, p. 137. Original in StaN, *Ansbacher Religionsakten III*, Tom. XI, fasc. II, fo. 402.

[59] Sehling, pp. 317–24.

fact general visitations did occur between the years 1557 and 1564 (which called the pastor and a parish representative to meet the examiners as a predetermined spot), but the records from this period are sparse; not until the year 1565 is it possible to determine whether the parishes were inspected by the superintendents in person or whether the clergy were examined at a stipulated location. Speculation ends with the 1565 chapter ordinance: Each year the superintendent had to visit the parishes within his chapter. From 1565 to 1600 special visitations occurred with some regularity.[60]

The visitation was designed to accommodate the rural parishioners. It took place in the autumn, in September, October, or November, when the field work would not be adversely interrupted.[61] The superintendent, accompanied by one of his senior officials (and a secular authority if it was considered necessary), travelled from village to village in a wagon, with each parish providing the driver from one location to the next.[62] Once in the village, the visitors usually stayed at the parsonage, while the pastor's wife cooked up a meal at the expense of the local church. This notion of parish-sponsored meals could be met with resistance. Some parishioners, like the official of Auernhofen, would not allow the visitors food until they paid; others, less well-placed, simply railed against the injustice of it all.[63] In general such complaints were rare. The parishioners did not necessarily consider the visitation progress a financial burden; indeed, on occasion the visitors would figure as part of the tally the small coins they had passed out among the promising catechumens. And in any event, the visitation itself was fleeting: the examination lasted no longer than mid-day, when the visitors would remount the wagon and head off for the next village. The prescribed schedule for the 1576 visitation progress in the district of Creglingen required the visitors to make a daily trip ranging from 2.5 to 12.5 kilometres, hold examinations before lunch the following day, and reach the next parish before nightfall.[64]

When the visitation came to an end the superintendent drew together the

---

[60] Gerhard Hausmann, 'Das Bemühen des Ansbacher Konsistoriums um kirchliche Ordnung und reine Lehre im Zeitalter der Orthodoxie', *ZbKG*, 59 (1990), 81, n. 39; Weiss, *Vom notwendigen Verstand*, pp. 78–9. In some years the visitations were not undertaken in certain chapters. Scattered examples include: Kitzingen 1590; Wiltzburg 1575 (the superintendent wished to be excused due to his wife's illness. He was told that similar requests had emerged – and had been approved – from Schwabach and Neustadt). Georg Friedrich allowed for the visitation in Schwabach to be suspended in 1575. The visitation in Neustadt was cancelled in 1585 due to the plague (which also took the superintendent's wife).

[61] Most visitations at the end of the century took into account the rhythms of rural life. For instance the 1554 Mansfeld *Visitationsordnance* chose a specific time so that the peasants would not be inconvenienced: 'sonst sind die Dorfleute mit ihrer Haushaltung beschwert, dass sie solchem christlichen, nötigen und guten Werke nicht können ohne Schaden auswarten.' Nobbe, 'Das Superintendentenamt', p. 49.

[62] Sehling, pp. 350–1.

[63] LKAN, MDU, 8, Near Holtzhausen (23 September 1572); LKAN, MDL, 51, Unternbibert 1588: The miller claimed: 'Item, wir [Visitors] hetten keiner befhel zu visitiren, geschehe nur umb freßen und sauffen willen.'

[64] Distance in kilometres is approximate. LKAN, MDU, 8, no. 44ᵃ. 1576.

reports and sent a statement to the authorities in Ansbach. In Ansbach, the officials would look through the reports and then dispatch orders to the appropriate officials. A superintendent's failure to submit the results could elicit a harsh reminder, as happened to the Wülzburg superintendent Stephan Schnitzlein, who was cited to appear in Ansbach along with the overdue returns.[65] As the century progressed, the routine became more familiar; the consistory officials would take each chapter as a separate unit and then sift out the abuses and forward suggestions to the superintendent. There was no set pattern, however, to the interests of the sixteenth-century visitations in Ansbach and Kulmbach. Certain features, certain concerns were stressed at different times, but the spectrum of interests had not yet succumbed to the grey mechanics of the 1717 protocols, wherein a series of numbered points are followed by *ja, nein,* or the emotive *ja gar wohl.* The returns tend to relate the observations of a concerned participant rather than hollow compliance to a formula dulled by routine.[66]

The area of the visitation fell within the bounds of the margrave's jurisdiction. The local nobility were asked to present their clergy for examination, and they were assured that it would not infringe upon their jurisdictional prerogatives. The visitation, as the margraves repeatedly stressed, was not to extend into the properties of a foreign lordship without leave.[67] Despite these caveats, some noble families remained wary of the visitation. In 1528 the subject clergy of the Seckendorff, Castell, and Pappenheim families were forbidden to attend the visitation.[68] The lords of Blassenberg allowed the visitation in their parish, as did Jobst von Kinsberg, but Adam von Kinsberg would not allow it, nor would he give his pastor leave to attend a hearing in the parish of Lindennardt.[69] The lords of Guttenberg drafted a letter for the superintendent stating that they would welcome the visitation in Melkendorf only if their rights of presentation were preserved.[70]

[65] LKAN, MDWz, 86 (6 October 1578).
[66] To my knowledge the visitation returns used in this work represent the entire collection as it is known to exist for Brandenburg-Ansbach-Kulmbach. The scarcity of remaining visitation returns was observed as early as 1804. A writer remarked: 'Ich habe schad- und mangelhaffte Concepte der Visitationis protocolle ... [gelesen]' only to find 'daß schon 1565–1568 und weiters viele...nacheinander dergl[eichen] visitationen gehalten worden'. Assuming that these were the Wülzburg returns, it appears that they no longer exist. LKAN, MDWz, 87 Visitationen 1566/90 1571/1804. fo. 50 (27 February 1804).
[67] Gustav Bossert, 'Der Stand der Reformation in der Markgraffschaft Brandenburg-Ansbach nach den Berichten der Aemter im Jahre 1528 vor abgehaltener Visitation', *Jahresbericht des historischen Vereins für Mittelfranken,* 40 (1880), 63; F. H. Medicus, 'Die brandenburg-nürnbergische Kirchenvisitation vom Jahre 1528', *Blätter für bayerische Kirchengeschichte,* 4 (1888), p. 53; *Corpus Constitutionum Brandenburgico-Culmbacensium,* (1746), p. 357.
[68] Sehling, p. 115.
[69] LKAN, MSK, 157, fo. 6. 1572; LKAN, MKA, Spez. 897 (23 January 1578). fos. 122–3.
[70] LKAN, MSK,157, Melckendorf (14 November 1558). 'doch uns an unsern lehenschaften, und habenden gerechtigkeiten one nachtheil und schaden...'.

Many of the parishioners, and the clergy as well, heeded the confrontational words of their lords. In 1567 pastor Johannes Zoberer of the Nuremberg parish of Bruck advised all of his parishioners to 'stay at home' when the visitors arrived.[71] Although the margrave exercised high jurisdiction and the right of patronage in Wallmersbach, the visitor observed in 1565 that 'the people subject to Conrad of Enheim will neither appear before us or the public examination', while the local mayor had belittled the visitation in a public gathering.[72] Not that the parishioners had to be foreign subjects to oppose the visitation. When the visitors arrived in an Ansbach village in 1567, the local inn was afire with activity 'as if it were the middle of Hell', and a man emerged from its infernal depths only to curse the visitors as he stood before them: '*Pfu dich teuffel, friß pfaffen, und scheiß munch.*'[73] Similar greetings were extended by the parishioners of Meinheim and Altheim.[74] Even the margrave's secular officials, such as those in Kitzingen, offered resistance to the visitation process.[75] The reason for this resistance is not hard to fathom: the Protestant visitation represented the most intense investigation of parish life that had ever been undertaken before.

From the state of the church, the quality of local marriages, the dealings of merchants, to the frequency of catechism classes and worship – the visitors inquired into every aspect of village affairs. Nothing remained immune. Each official, whether secular or spiritual, was expected to answer every questionnaire with honesty, in full allegiance to the prince. In 1536 parishioners were admonished to relate

whether they themselves had, or knew of, any faults concerning the life and teaching of their clergy ... [such as] if a pastor or other clergyman teaches contrary to the word of God, speaks dishonestly or contemptuously of the Mass, [whether they] are lazy and neglectful of their office, lead evil, unpleasant lives and dispositions ... or refuse to honour the church ordinance of our gracious lord ...[76]

Again in 1565, it was the parishioners' duty 'to speak the truth and not remain in silence concerning whatever failings and deficiencies they have in the church personnel or otherwise dishonest or unpleasant [things] which they know of them'.[77] And it was a two-way process. Even before the clergy themselves fell under scrutiny, they had divulged the sins of their congregation to the superintendent:

---

71   StaN, 16a B-Laden Akten, Lade 177, no. 9, (6 September 1567).
72   LKAN, MDU, 8, no. 148, fo. 26. Wallmerspach 1565. Enheim was not integrated into Uffenheim until 1599.
73   LKAN, MDG, 71, fo. 6.
74   LKAN, MDG, 71, fo. 68. 1578.
75   Weiss, *Vom notwendigen Verstand*, p. 136.
76   Sehling, p. 321.
77   Sehling, p. 352.

Whether the parishioners [*das Vollck*] are keen to hear sermons and sing the Psalms
Whether the parents send their children and dependants [*gesindt*] to catechism class, and
attend themselves...
If and when they receive the Sacrament [of the Mass]
Whether they dance, play, or drink and pursue other laxities [*leichtfertigkeit*] during the
service [*zur stundt des kirchgangs*]
Whether idols are being worshipped.

The list ended by reminding the visitors to root out blasphemers, sorcerers, wisewomen, adulterers, feuds, lax sexual morality, usury, and gluttony.[78] The 1565 chapter ordinance reduced the range of interests to the following catalogue: 'The parish and church service, schools, church personnel, maintenance, buildings, parishioners (taken as a whole or in particular), public vice such as blasphemy, magic, contempt and neglect of God's word and the Holy Sacrament, dissolved marriages, gluttony, and usury'.[79] As more and more visitations were carried out, the list of parish abuses became increasingly detailed and local activities categorised with a developing exactitude.[80]

It would seem that the hegemonic rise of 'elite' or 'learned' culture at the expense of local or 'popular' traditions of belief – the so-called 'triumph of Lent' – was in no small part aided by and informed through the visitation process.[81] Contemporaries, Luther among them, looked to the visitation as a panacea to cure the ills of immoral behaviour and wayward belief. When it was clear that the event itself was not enough to secure reform, or indeed respect, the authorities began to view it more as a juridical corrective or disciplinary measure than its original 'supervisory' function would suggest:

'We have therefore considered necessary that punishment be taken in hand', concluded the visitors of Bayreuth in 1592, 'because the contempt and neglect of this Christian work [visitation] is very great, so that through these means a fear may be raised in the people. Hopefully they will, without any doubt, appear somewhat more eagerly in future visitations.'[82]

The work of historians would suggest that the visitation, in its capacity as an extension of the early modern regime's push for absolute surveillance, was a success. German scholars have noted that the contradiction that emerged in 1527

---

[78] LKAN, MDU 8, no. 1, fos. 2–3. 1558.
[79] Sehling, pp. 351–2.
[80] For instance the 1578 additions to the 1565 draft include a much more detailed list of forbidden parish activities and beliefs, in addition to an understanding of what aspects of clerical life intersected with village politics and thus what questions were the most effective to reveal the local situation. This point will be developed in chapter 4. Other sources for the above paragraph include: LKAN, MDL, 143 Errichtung & Ordnung des Kapitels Lehrberg / Leutershausen – Visitation 1556–1834, 1563, fos. 3 ff.; LKAN, MDWz, 86 Visitationsakten.
[81] Peter Burke, *Popular Culture in Early Modern Europe* (London, 1978), pp. 207 ff.
[82] StaB C2 1823, *Bericht Von Visitation der zür Superintendents Beyrrheüt gehörigen Kirchen Anno 1592*, fo. 3. The visitors suggested making a list of all absentees who would be cited in Bayreuth and threatened with a monetary fine or enjailment.

Saxony (that is, how the visitation, as a curative for an ailing church, must necessarily involve princely intervention) became more marked as the territorial church took hold, until such time that the visitation simply served to strengthen the position of the secular authority.[83] The Lutheran superintendent, Wolfgang Reinhard has suggested, became no less an agent of the state than the later *Intendants*, the props of French Absolutism.[84] Even Gerald Strauss, who has questioned the impact of the visitation process, admits that 'the visitation was a true expression of the early modern bureaucratic state'.[85] The visitation in Brandenburg-Ansbach-Kulmbach is easily seen as a political tool wielded by the margrave to augment his power over the subject population.[86] But an investigation of the visitation process must pay heed to the crucial distinction between expression and deed. The claims of the early modern state over its subjects were comprehensive in their scope, but the actual implementation of these claims and their fulfilment at the local level was another matter. These observations can be developed by examining the points of contact between the Reformation movement and the rural parish.

[83] Ernst Walter Zeeden and Peter Thaddäus Lang (eds.), *Kirche und Visitation: Beiträge zur Erforschung des frühneuzeitlichen Visitationswesens in Europa* (Stuttgart, 1984), p. 11; Martin Honecker, 'Visitation', *Zeitschrift für evangelisches Kirchenrecht*, 17 (1972), 341–3.

[84] Wolfgang Reinhard, 'Zwang zur Konfessionalisierung? Prolegomena zu einer Theorie des konfessionellen Zeitalters', *Zeitschrift für historische Forschung*, 10 (1983), 275.

[85] Strauss, *Luther's House of Learning*, p. 259.

[86] Bernard Vogler, 'Le role des visites dans les eglises protestantes et leur utilisation comme source d'histoire religieuse et sociale', in *Sensibilité religieuse et discipline ecclésiastique*. (Strasbourg, 1973), p. 94.

3

The clergyman in context: the extension of the Reformation to the parish

THE CLERGY

In *Praise of Folly* Erasmus took aim at the Scholastics. He ridiculed the maxims, paradoxes, 'tortuous obscurities', and ingenious subtleties spun in the schools of theology, and he scoffed at the Scholastics for seeing themselves as a new Atlas, bearing the weight of the Church 'on the props of their syllogisms'.[1] Yet for all her wit and satire, Erasmus's Folly said very little about the parish clergy of her age. The early Reformers did not miss the chance, however, and a bitter polemical war was waged in the first few decades of the evangelical movement directed at the laxities and failings of the Catholic clergy.[2] Nor was it sheer invention. Medieval Christendom witnessed its share of clerical abuses: absenteeism, pluralism, ignorance, exploitation of excommunication or the sacraments, and moral failings such as drinking, fighting, blasphemy, and sexual licence.[3] No doubt the parishioners of Ansbach and Kulmbach witnessed the same misemployments. A 1480 visitation in the neighbouring diocese of Eichstätt revealed that the clergy were heavy drinkers of wine, frequented the inns, gambled, fought, danced, and

---

Sections of this chapter have appeared in a different format as 'Rural Resistance, the Lutheran pastor, and the territorial church in Brandenburg-Ansbach-Kulmbach, 1528–1603', in Andrew Pettegree (ed.), *The Reformation of the Parishes* (Manchester, 1993), pp. 85–112. I would like to thank Manchester University Press for allowing me to reprint this material.

[1] Erasmus, *Praise of Folly*, trans. Betty Radice (London, 1988), pp. 154–62.

[2] A campaign which drew upon a medieval tradition of satire such as Sebastian Brant's *Ship of Fools* (1494). Brant said this of the average parish clergyman:

> If he be foolishe or of his wit unstable,
> Misshapen of his face, his handes or his feete,
> And for no busynes worldly profitable,
> For the holy Church then thinke they him most meete...

Translation by Alexander Barclay Priest, *The Ship of Fooles, wherin is shewed the folly of all States, with divers other workes adioyned unto the same, very profitable and fruitfull for all men* (1570), pp. 143–5.

[3] Gerald Strauss (ed.), *Manifestations of Discontent in Germany on the Eve of the Reformation* (Bloomington, 1962). For the English church, see Peter Heath, *The English Parish Clergy on the Eve of the Reformation* (London, 1969). For France, see Paul Adam, *La vie paroissiale en France au XIVe siècle* (Paris, 1964), pp. 148–89; Jacques Toussaert, *Le Sentiment religieux en Flandre à la fin du moyen-âge* (Paris, 1963).

paid little heed to their vow of chastity.[4] With all this evidence in her favour, why did Folly not ridicule the parish priest? Erasmus recognised, perhaps, that the Catholic clergyman had little scope for true folly; the range of his duties was tightly circumscribed by the dictates of the medieval church.

The range of tasks facing a late-medieval clergyman was limited to a prescribed ritual. Once invested, he was saddled with *cura animarum et custodia reliquiarum*: he had to perform the requisite sacerdotal services – *inter alia*, the mass, baptism, extreme unction, confession – and satisfy the demands of his immediate religious community, which might mean honouring local saints or venerating the parish relics. Stephan May, vicar of Hilpoltstein in the diocese of Eichstätt (thirty kilometres from Nuremberg), divided most of his time in the year 1511 between the demands of his office (masses, sermons, provision of the sacraments) and the attendant religious duties expected of the Hilpoltstein priest (veneration of local relics, numerous processions, and the observance of foundation or confraternity holidays).[5] The Catholic church expected the clergyman to have some knowledge of Scripture, a grasp of the Ten Commandments, the Apostles' Creed, and the Psalter, and the ability to recite the formulae for mass, confession, and baptism. The level of clerical learning might be low, but so too were the intellectual demands placed upon the clergyman. Sermons were generally limited to analyses of the more notable events in the Bible, the life of Christ and the saints, the pleasures of Heaven or the torments of Hell, all of which could be gleaned from ready-made biblical concordances, *exempla*, and model sermons.[6] Late-medieval parish Catholicism was a religion of ritual and example; it was enough for the priest to perform the salvific duties expected of him and live a life free of grotesque moral failings.

Reformation theology placed stronger emphasis on the clergyman's role as teacher and interpreter of Scripture. Central to the evangelical faith was the preaching of the Gospel, which was at once tradition and innovation levelled at the supposed failings of the Catholic church. For although Paul had invested the bishops with the obligation to preach and educate (argued the evangelicals), the prelates had long neglected their offices, leaving the lower clergy to inherit these duties. And yet, aside from an audience with the occasional itinerant preacher, it is unlikely that the average villager of pre-Reformation Europe had regular exposure to sermons on Holy Writ. Only with the advent of the evangelical movement was the idea even mooted that the laity should have regular access to God's word in

---

4   Peter Thaddäus Lang, 'Würfel, Wein und Wettersegen – Klerus und Gläubige im Bistum Eichstätt am Vorabend der Reformation', in Volker Press and Dieter Stievermann (eds.), *Martin Luther: Probleme seiner Zeit* (Stuttgart, 1986), pp. 219–43.

5   Johann B. Götz, *Das Pfarrbuch des Stephan May in Hilpoltstein vom Jahre 1511* (Münster, 1926), pp. 27–39.

6   Friedrich Wilhelm Oediger, *Über die Bildung der Geistlichen im späten Mittelalter* (1953), pp. 46–57, 98–121; Adam, *La vie paroissiale*, pp. 89–97; D. Catherine Brown, *Pastor and Laity in the Theology of Jean Gerson* (Cambridge, 1987), pp. 11–17.

the vernacular; and it followed from this that knowledge of Scripture, and the ability to relate that knowledge to the parishioners, became the pastors' principal obligation.

As the 1533 church ordinance advised the clergy, teaching the unlearned was not an inconsequential onus, but the greatest and highest wisdom of man.[7] The pastor was expected to use his knowledge of Scripture to strengthen the resolve of the weak or uncertain, admonish the intractable to change their ways and convince them of their errors, and teach the members of the congregation, old and young, the nature of, and justification for, the evangelical faith along with its central tenets and rites, from baptism to free will.[8] And of course in addition to his pedagogical role, the Lutheran pastor had the other duties of office: officiating the sacraments, visitation of the sick, exercising the small ban, safeguarding local morality, and maintaining the parsonage. It was crucial that the church in the principality was staffed with a clerical estate competent enough to carry out the duties expected of it, just as it was crucial that a process of selection and examination watched over their appointment.

In the absence of a centralised bishopric, the margrave exercised control over the appointment of clergy. This usurpation of the bishops' prerogative was not only an inevitable consequence of the margrave's appropriation of ecclesiastical power, but the logical corollary of his practising philosophy: the prince had a God-given right to exercise control over the visible church. The 1526 resolution stipulated that no pastor or chaplain should be invested into a parish without first consulting the margrave or one of his district officials. Georg the Pious repeated this injunction in 1528.[9] In the 1520s, the margraves feared that the bishops would fill vacant posts with Catholic clergymen. To guard against this, the secular authorities kept watch over unoccupied parishes and waited for the council to dispatch instructions. In 1528 the district official of Gunzenhausen confiscated the keys to the church and the sacristy in Aha following the death of Georg Sorg. The foundation of Rebdorf, as patrons, claimed that they had the right of presentation and had already decided on a candidate. This posed a problem for the official, who was not certain whether he should hand over the keys or wait on the margrave's orders.[10] In 1532 the property of a deceased clergyman in Alfershausen was confiscated by the local official so that it would not fall into the hands of the bishop of Eichstätt. The benefice was held in suspension until the Ansbach council issued further orders.[11] In 1541 the margrave's officials safeguarded the parish of Rohr and advised the Ansbach council: 'so that the clergy of Eichstätt [*die Eystetischen*] do not appoint a pastor according to their pleasure, we have

[7] Sehling, p. 141.
[8] Sehling, p. 143.
[9] Sehling, p. 90, 105.
[10] LKAN, MKA, Spez. 11, fos. 1–5.
[11] LKAN, MKA, Spez. 14, fos. 19, 18–26.

locked the church and ordered that no one without authorisation [*on bevelch*] be allowed access.'[12] The battle over patronage was enmeshed within the wider struggle for religious supremacy, and its affects seeped down to the level of the parish. The secular authorities and parishioners near Meinheim, for example, came to the support of Johann Fröschlein in 1525 when his evangelical sympathies got him into trouble with the bishop of Eichstätt. Fröschlein refused to appear in Eichstätt: 'For I feared the use of force, and worried that I would not be allowed a hearing but rather immediately placed under arrest.'[13] A correspondence between Eichstätt and Ansbach worked out a compromise. The absent clergyman Leonhard Bart would let Fröschlein retain office for three years; when the contract came to an end, however, a Catholic man was empowered to exercise the office (4 February 1528). The Catholic clergyman ultimately made his way to Meinheim, where he was greeted by the parishioners (Fröschlein's relatives prominent among them): '*Pfaff*, take yourself and your letter out of this village or we'll chop off your hands and feet. The Eichstätt clerics are no longer the patrons of our church; we know of other patrons.' Fröschlein remained in Meinheim until 1558.[14]

Some disputes lasted the century. When the evangelical clergyman of Binzwangen died in 1540, he was not immediately replaced. Both Ansbach and Eichstätt issued instructions forbidding a replacement outside of their respective confessional folds. During this interim, the Binzwangers were forced to bear their children to neighbouring parishes for baptism.[15] When a Catholic substitute finally did arrive (appointed by the foundation of Spalt as active patrons), the Colmberg official wrote to the margrave seeking advice. The official feared unrest.[16] The Ansbach council, assuring the official that the authority of Binzwangen (*die fraischlich Obrigkeit*) belonged to 'none other than our gracious Lord margrave Georg,' ordered him to replace the man with a suitable evangelical pastor. The secular official carried out this order in the same year (1543) and the evangelical clergyman Leonhard Baudenbacher remained in office until 1547. The

---

[12] LKAN, MKA, Spez. 720, fo. 19.
[13] LKAN, MKA, Spez. 572, fo. 6. 'Ist nit zu verwundern, noch (als ich hoff) mir zuverweysen dann ich gewalt forchtet, und besorgt man würd mich nit zu verhor lassen kumen, sonder als bald in kessel gefangen liegen...'.
[14] LKAN, MKA, Spez. 572, fo. 23. Although religious sympathy was the central concern, other issues were involved in this dispute, such as the bad will and misdealings that arose between Bart and Meinheim over the extension of Fröschlein's contract. See Karl Schornbaum, 'Der Beginn der Reformation in Altmühltale', *Beiträge zur bayerischen Kirchengeschichte*, 16 (1910), 1–27.
[15] The *Landesherrschaft* over Binzwangen was disputed between Ansbach and Eichstätt. LKAN, MKA, Spez. 109, fos. 5ff:

> dan mein genediger herr auch derselben Ambtleut auβ bevelch Irer fürstlichen gnaden kein Bebstler zu Binzwang haben leiden wollen, dagegen Eistet auch kein Ewangellischen verordnet, derhalb die armen leut nun im das dreithalb jar das wort gottes Beraubt, und Ire kindlein in andere pfarr Windelsbach Sterberg und Fulzbach zu tauffen tragen.

[16] LKAN, MKA, Spez. 109, 1543: 'werd mit der zeit aufrur und nichts guts darauβ entsteen'.

Eichstätt bishopric did not surrender its claims, however, and from 1547 to 1601 the parish of Binswangen was once again home to a Catholic service.[17] The margrave was less guarded in his dealings with noble patrons and parish communes than he was with the bishops. Noble families were expected to forward their candidates to the margrave's ecclesiastical officials for examination; they could not appoint or dismiss the pastor independently. When Peter Hochmuther, pastor of Döhlau, protested in 1590 that the Rabenstein nobles had taken the church key from his daughter in a effort to bar him from the church (ultimately dismissing him altogether by 1596), the Kulmbach council made it clear in the subsequent investigation that the power to dismiss or to appoint a clergyman was not within the purview of the nobility.[18] As the regional official of Birkenfels advised the nobility in his district, the margrave had exclusive right to present and invest the clergy, in keeping with his right to exercise high jurisdiction over his subjects. By virtue of the Treaty of Passau and the 1555 Peace of Augsburg, the margrave was acting *summus episcopus*: patrons could forward candidates, but they could not appoint or dismiss.[19] Similar restrictions were placed on parish communes (*Gemeinde*) with powers of patronage. Increased regulation and maintenance of local religious affairs through the commune may have figured large in peasant demands during the 1525 uprising,[20] but the commune's power of appointment found limited application in practice. The documentation consulted for this study provided eight occasions when the villagers forwarded or suggested a candidate. Five of these proposed candidates were rejected by the examiners. The three remaining candidates were approved due to special circumstances, as the examiners' testimonies explained.[21] The margrave and his councillors exercised exclusive control over the installation of the clergymen.

Pastors were examined, approved, and appointed by the margrave's officials in Ansbach and Kulmbach. Superintendents and district officials notified the Ansbach authorities once a parish became vacant. On occasion the superintendent or the district officials extended a suggestion for a replacement themselves, otherwise the consistory would supply a clergyman, chosen from the many transfer applications and direct requests that had emerged once news of the

---

[17] LKAN, MKA, Spez. 109, fos. 8–16.
[18] LKAN, MDH, XX, 3, fos. 7, 1–7 (7 May 1596).
[19] LKAN, MKA, Spez. 655, Birkenfels (28 March 1560); G. Braun, 'Eine Pfarrbesetzung aus dem Jahre 1611', *Beiträge zur bayerischen Kirchengeschichte*, 6 (1900), 31.
[20] Blickle, *Gemeindereformation*, pp. 50ff.
[21] LKAN, MKA, Spez. 1010, fos. 40–2. Weiboldshausen 1574; LKAN, MKA, Spez. 443, fos. 23–5. Holtzhausen 1559; LKAN, MKA, Spez. 724, fos. 82, 86–7. Roßtal 1546; LKAN, MDLz, 703, fo. 22. Cadolzburg 1581 & LKAN, MKA, Spez. 169, fos. 90–101; LKAN, MKA, Spez. 813 (10 August 1556). The examiners approved the choice of the *Gemeinde* Johann Reuter ('des lateins ungeübt') for the chaplaincy of Geilsheim since he was a 'dorffkind' and his functions would be limited – 'Aber wo es ein pfar were wolten wir nit bewilligen'. LKAN, MKA, Spez 346, fo. 23. (1551). Konrad Langer was approved in 1537 by Johann Rurer for the parish of Buch am Wald (despite his youth) because of the paucity of available clergymen ('sonderlich in solchem mangel der kirchendiener, so zu diesen zeitten wirt gespurt'). LKAN, MKA, Spez 135, fo. 12.

vacancy was broadcast. The applicant could write directly to the margrave himself, as did pastor Elias Körber in 1577, or in the stead of another, as did Michael Stiber in his efforts to secure an incumbency for his son in 1587. At times the vacancy of a substantial parish could generate a fugue of solicitations, as happened when David Glantz of Sickerhausen died on 4 January 1579.[22] Once proposed, the candidate appeared before the examining board (*verordnete examinatores*) to undergo the process of confirmation. The Kulmbach council outlined the routine in 1596: the patron should present the council or consistory with a pious man, bearing a letter of recommendation, who would then undergo examination. If the man was found suitable, he was ordained for office at Kulmbach, where he also took the clerical oath. Once confirmed, and with letter of presentation in hand, he was referred to the appropriate superintendent.[23]

All candidates were subject to a trial sermon, followed by an examination of their knowledge of Latin and German, basic Scripture, and the body of texts comprising the faith: Luther's catechisms, the Augsburg Confession, Melanchthon's doctrinal works, the Schmalkaldic Articles, and the 1533 church ordinance. Ordination had become a crypto-sacrament; the ritual was abolished in Ansbach, but in Kulmbach the clergyman Johann Schnabel was writing to Wittenberg in 1538 looking for something to fill the void, and it appears that by 1546 a ritual of sorts was practised.[24] After approval and confirmation the clergyman, accompanied by a commissioned secular official (*eines weltlichen bevelchhabers*) and two neighbouring clergymen, was invested into the parish by the superintendent. The superintendent introduced the parishioners to the man, admonished them to obey and honour him, and then a common prayer from the church ordinance was said, in which the words of Matthew were evident: 'Then saith he unto his disciples, The harvest truly is plenteous, but the labourers are few; Pray ye therefore the Lord of the harvest, that he will send forth labourers into his harvest.'[25]

What was the quality of the clerical estate in the principality of Brandenburg-Ansbach-Kulmbach in the sixteenth century? Evaluations of parish clergymen are often coloured by confessional bias. Either the clergy were beacons of the new faith and competent in office, or they were, at best, the same as their Catholic predecessors: lazy in office, lax in morals, a burden on the parish. In each instance the clergy are measured against the standards of the faith. But how did the clergy fare against the standards of their parishioners? In general the clergy in Ansbach and Kulmbach were suitable ministers of the faith; given the scope of their duties, they were able to perform what was demanded of them. Anticlericalism, when and

---

22 LKAN, MKA, Spez. 500, fo. 179, 1577; LKAN, MKA, Spez. 655 fo. 85 (22 July 1587); LKAN, MKA, Spez. 813, post-1578 *passim*.
23 LKAN, MDH, XX 3, fos. 41–5 (20 July 1596). The parish of Döhlau (in question) was in the superintendency of Hof.
24 Simon, *Evangelische Kirchengeschichte Bayerns*, pp. 304–5.
25 Sehling, pp. 354–5, 388–9.

where it surfaced, was more a reflection of a disruption in village norms than the failings of an individual. Let us examine these points in detail.

Bernard Vogler's study, *Le clergé protestant Rhénan au siècle de la Réforme (1555–1619)*, makes a number of observations about the Rhineland clergy which hold true for most of Protestant Germany. In his study of social origins, Vogler noticed that the majority of the first and second generation Protestant clergy were themselves the sons of clergymen, and he concluded from this that the entrustment of sacred office from a father to a son was encouraged by the authorities.[26] In addition to this 'clerical caste,' a large proportion of the Protestant clergy stemmed from modest bourgeois households, a class of people covering a spectrum of stations, from merchants to artisans. On the other hand, Vogler adds with reference to the heavy middling-class bias to his findings, both the nobility and the peasantry were poorly represented. Similar studies support these observations.[27] In the face of such evidence, and mindful of the role played by family custom in early-modern society, it is not too far-fetched to speak of a type of guild which emerged with the second generation of Protestant pastors. While in many ways his Catholic predecessor was simply custodian of a repository of supernatural rites and remedies, effective *ex opere operato*, the Protestant pastor had additional responsibilities – preaching in particular – requiring a fair degree of ongoing application. The office of Protestant pastor gave rise to the 'pride of craft' familiar to guilds; pastors fashioned their sons to follow in their footsteps; handworkers and artisans, attracted by the security and honour of a legitimate station, valued employment in the church.

Vogler's second point follows the first to its logical conclusion: the majority of these clergymen had been educated at a university. In the Electoral Palatinate, by 1605, up to 90 per cent of the clergy had spent some time at a university.[28] This was a comparatively high number of matriculated clergy compared with some areas of Germany, but a university education was common to most Protestant pastors in the latter decades of the century. In Württemberg, of 2,700 clergymen in the sixteenth century, 1,779 (65 per cent) had attended a university.[29] Such statistics must be weighed against the historical situation. It is unlikely that the standard of the clergy at the beginning of the century, when there was a dearth of candidates, was as high as the standard fifty years later. In Ernestine Saxony, only 20 to 31 per cent of the first-generation clergy in the

---

[26] Bernard Vogler, *Le clergé protestant Rhénan au siècle de la Réforme (1555–1619)* (Paris, 1976), pp. 21, 18–21.

[27] Martin Brecht, 'Herkunft und Ausbildung der protestantischen Geistlichen des Herzogtums Württemberg im 16. Jahrhundert', *Zeitschrift für Kirchengeschichte*, 80 (1969), 172–3; Bruce Tolley, 'Pastors and Parishioners in Württemberg during the Late Reformation (1581–1621)', PhD thesis, Stanford University, 1984, pp. 42–55.

[28] Vogler, *Le clergé protestant Rhénan*, p. 57.

[29] Brecht, 'Herkunft und Ausbildung', p. 170; Heinrich Richard Schmidt, *Konfessionalisierung im 16. Jahrhundert* (Munich, 1992), pp. 60–1.

Altenburg district had attended a university.[30] As late as 1548 a pastor in Kulmbach was reported to have said: 'At the present time tailors, cobblers, and the like come forward and preach as priests and preachers, without understanding the Word of God.'[31] But generally by the end of the century, as the number of students attending university increased, the majority of Protestant clergy were university-educated.[32]

Hermann Jordan's investigation of the clergy in Ansbach and Kulmbach yields the following figures. In 1540, 28 per cent of the clergy had attended a university; in 1560, the number rose to 32 per cent.[33] On the whole, using Matthias Simon's compilation of Ansbach clergymen (*Ansbachisches Pfarrerbuch*) as the source, the trend in Ansbach would seem to reflect the picture described above. Over the course of the century, as the new faith became more secure, the educational quality of the clergy improved. A survey, categorised according to twenty-year periods, bears this out. There was a 25 to 30 per cent increment in the proportion of university-educated clergy from the decades 1520/40 to 1580/1600.[34] The number of parish clergymen that had matriculated at a university may have been as high as 80 per cent. The visitation returns from 1580 to 1591 in the Neustadt superintendency reveal that at least 80 per cent of the parishes in this region had a university-educated pastor.[35] If the educational background is a fair standard by which to judge the quality of the Protestant pastors, the clergy of sixteenth-century Ansbach and Kulmbach had the educational qualifications to perform the tasks expected of them.[36]

In order to measure the quality of the clergy once they were in office the researcher is left with the judgement of two sections of the populace: the higher clergy and the villagers. The higher clergy were unlikely to mention a local pastor unless he had fallen foul of the faith or the synodal ordinances. In the 1520s and

[30] Susan C. Karant-Nunn, *Luther's Pastors: The Reformation in the Ernestine Countryside* (Philadelphia, 1979), p. 19.

[31] Cited in Hermann Jordan, *Reformation und gelehrte Bildung in der Markgrafschaft Ansbach-Bayreuth* (Leipzig, 1917), vol. 1, p. 299.

[32] Cameron, *The European Reformation*, pp. 390ff.

[33] Cited in Bernard Klaus, 'Soziale Herkunft und theologische Bildung lutherischer Pfarrer der reformatorischen Frühzeit', *Zeitschrift für Kirchengeschichte*, 80 (1969), 45.

[34] Calculated from a survey of 330 clergy, based upon the date when they took the clerical oath or entered office in the principality. Simon's collection, though by his own acknowledgment far from comprehensive, would seem to increase Jordan's figures by some 20 per cent. Matthias Simon, *Ansbachisches Pfarrerbuch. Die evangelisch-Lutherische Geistlichkeit des Fürstentums Brandenburg-Ansbach 1528–1806* (Nuremberg, 1955/57).

[35] D. H. Clauß, 'Kirchenvisitation des 16. Jahrhunderts im Dekanat Neustadt a. A.', *ZbKG*, 9 (1934), 155–8.

[36] A university education was not necessarily superior to that offered by a good Latin school. In Ansbach, as in other places, institutions were emerging specifically designed to supply the church with competent pastors. In 1536 Luther commended the margrave's efforts to convert the monastery of Heilsbronn into a school for potential young clergymen. Other institutions were created for the same purpose; and existing schools were improved to deal with the growing need. Klauß, 'Soziale Herkunft', p. 46.

1530s, many of the clergy were still Catholics, and if not Catholic, then half-hearted Protestants, so the results are bound to be skewed. Out of a total of fifty-two candidates, the 1528 visitation counted twenty-one as good, thirteen as mediocre, thirteen as bad, and five as very bad.[37] No doubt many of the clergy who received a bad review were Catholic sympathisers; and we should measure the words of these early visitations with caution, when expectations were so high and realities so uncompromising. General appraisals of the clergy do not surface again until the visitations were established from 1565 onward, and as such it is not possible to trace the development of the clergy to mid-century; but it is clear that by the end of the century complaints from the higher clergy about the local pastors were rare. Although there were always a few exceptions, the lack of complaints and unfavourable citations in the visitation reports would suggest that the majority of the clergy had an adequate knowledge of the faith and were considered suitable incumbents. Justus Bloch, the Bayreuth superintendent, concluded in his 1572 report:

For although they did not respond in the manner which the office and strict necessity demands, all of them, however, (God be praised), have been found to be of good mind and understanding in the principal articles of our Christian religion and our faith as defined by Holy Writ and the Augsburg Confession.[38]

Twenty years later the review was the same. The superintendents were generally satisfied with the level of learning and the theological make-up of the parish clergy.

One reason for this satisfactory state of affairs was the lack of theological diversity among the parish clergy. Ansbach remained true to the teachings of Martin Luther. In the first decade of the reform movement, when margrave Georg issued a statement ordering the clergy to draw up theological reports for the impending Imperial diet at Augsburg (1530), the tone of religious harmony had been set: Luther and Melanchthon were the touchstone theologians. On occasion Johannes Brenz or Urbanus Rhegius might be mentioned, but no crucial theological issue was at stake.[39] This was due, in part, to the fact that neither Ansbach nor Kulmbach was home to a leading Reformer. Andreas Althamer and Johann Rurer were certainly competent men, but they did not challenge Luther or test the limits of Reformation theology. Georg Karg alone among the higher clergy introduced dissension from within with his theories on the Real Presence and *Satisfaktionslehre*, yet this type of discord was rare. When theological dissonance surfaced, it did not emerge from within the parishes, but rather from an external source, such as the imposition of the Interim or the efforts of a foreign religious sect, like the Anabaptists or the (suspected) agents of Matthias-Flacius

---

[37] Sehling, p. 115.
[38] LKAN, MDK 157, *Bericht der Spetial Visitation, In der Süperintendentz Beÿrreuth Ao 1572*, fo. 3.
[39] Schneider, *Gutachten evangelischer Theologen*, pp. 140–71.

Illyricus, to infiltrate the principality.[40] On the whole the land was free of wide-spread religious disharmony.[41]

Pastors were also assessed by the parishioners under their charge. The visitations encouraged the officials of the village, or any number of parishioners (depending on the visitation process), to evaluate the life and learning of their pastor and forward any grievances they might have to the visitors. In the larger towns, towns such as Bayreuth, this was done in the presence of a secular official. With the clergy absent from the room, the official would take each person in hand and collate the results.[42] On the whole, complaints about the pastor's performance of his religious duties were infrequent. The entire visitation progress of the 1576 Neustadt superintendency unearthed a single grievance – and this concerning the pastor's personal nature (*seltzamen und strittigen Kopffs halben*), nothing about him in his office. By far the most regular comment in all visitations was 'no complaint at all about the pastor'. The twenty-three parishes visited in the superintendency of Neustadt in 1579 registered complaints about only two clergymen. The visitation protocol from Gunzenhausen tells the same story: 'It is very seldom that the representatives of the parish forward a complaint about their pastor ...' In Kulmbach the vast majority of parishes were 'well satisfied with the life and teaching of the pastor'.[43] The results of a Bayreuth visitation (1592) might be taken as paradigmatic: eighteen of the clergymen received 'a good appraisal', 'a really good appraisal', or 'a very good appraisal', two 'a reasonable appraisal', while the pastor of Pegnitz alone was considered to be inadequate.[44] The rural parishioners of Brandenburg-Ansbach-Kulmbach were generally satisfied with the professional qualities of their clergymen.

But a discrepancy existed between the standards of the church and those of the parishioners. Although the Bayreuth superintendent considered Georg Pöschel of Pegnitz to be the worst clergyman under his charge, the parishioners found nothing wrong with his teaching and sermons. In 1579 the parishioners of Lenkersheim approved the teaching (*Lehr*) of their pastor, and yet a report proved he neglected communion, baptism, and burial sermons, failed to preach

---

[40] In 1578 the official of Uffenheim was instructed 'ein vleiβiges aufsehen [zu] haben' for the agents of Illyricus. LKAN, MKA, 3, fos. 78–81.

[41] StaB, C2 1833 (18 September 1567):

Wir müsen es aber gleichwol in warheit für ein grose gaben unsers lieben Gottes erkennen und preisen, das in eur f. g. landen ... kein strictt oder hanckh, auch kein gefehrliche und unnotige disputationes der lehre oder der heiligen sacrament halben, sich zugetragen, Sondern das wort an im selbst einfeltig wird schlecht, still und in ruhe geleret, und dem volck zu keinen frembden Opinionen oder furwitzigen nachdencken ursach geben.

[42] StaB, C2 1823, fo. 31.

[43] StaN, *Ansbacher Neues Generalrepertorium*, no. 49, rep. nr. 103e. fo. 14; 1576–94 *passim*; L. Clauβ, 'Aus Gunzenhäuser Visitationsakten des 16. Jahrhunderts', *Beiträge zur bayerischen Kirchengeschichte*, 3 (1925), 102; LKAN, MSK, 157, *passim*.

[44] StaB, C2 1823 1592 Bayreuth Visitation, *passim*.

on Fridays, and sloughed off catechism classes.[45] The villagers did not share the same set of values as the higher clergy. The examiners, and later the visitors, assessed the pastor in relation to the church ordinance. The degree to which the pastor could accommodate his expressed beliefs and practices within the bounds of theological accuracy defined his suitability.[46] 'It was perhaps this splitting of subjective experience from objective life', David Sabean concludes, 'which lay at the heart of Luther's teaching and continued to inform the perspective of the churchmen-administrators later on in the century'.[47] The villagers, in contrast, were more concerned with concrete transgressions of village norms. If a pastor drank, fornicated with the local women, brawled, swore, refused traditional services, or was in dispute with his villagers, he was cited before the officials. His actions, set against custom and normality, defined his status; the theological acumen he displayed once in office was often incidental. Anticlericalism, perceived as a range of action directed against a pastor's theological or sacerdotal competence, was rare to non-existent in the rural parishes of Ansbach and Kulmbach in the sixteenth century. The following study of village grievances bears this out.

ANTICLERICALISM

On 24 May 1570 the parish of Langenzenn (*Burgermeister rathe und gantze Gemain*) submitted a letter of complaint against their pastor Daniel Langer. The town authorities, as they later confessed, drafted the letter without first consulting the commune, but the contents of the draft would suggest that the pastor's conduct affected the entire parish.[48] According to the letter, Langer had alienated everyone in the village through his abusive conduct ('almost no one wants to go to his sermons') and he was accused of abusing the adjunct clergymen and the village schoolmaster. Parishioners would often go to the church services in neighbouring parishes to escape his wrath. To aggravate matters even further, Langer imposed a fee on the parishioners (a measure of wine) for the proclamation of marriage and the rites of burial and baptism. This demand for accidental fees, to cite the authors, was a novelty (*Neuerung*) in the parish and could not be tolerated. In short, sighed the town authorities, nothing could be done with Langer (*nichts früchten*). They concluded the letter by asking for Langer's dismissal and the

---

45 StaN, *Ansbacher Neues Generalrepertorium*, no. 49, rep. nr. 103ᶜ. fo. 34.
46 Of course the church also policed the conduct of the clergy once they were in the parish. A detailed corpus of strictures and norms emerged defining proper behaviour, from the type of clothing to suitable company. Were the clergy to transgress these norms, however, it was the villagers who would have to bring this to the attention of the authorities. *Corpus Constitutionum Brandenburgico-Culmbacensium* (1746), pp. 361–6.
47 Sabean, *Power in the Blood*, p. 43.
48 LKAN, MKA, Spez. 527, fo. 87, 91. '...wiewol ein gantze gemain in der clagschrifft unterschrieben, das doch der weniger theil solchs wissenstrag...'. Langenzenn was a substantial parish of perhaps 1,200 communicants, fos. 23–4.

appointment of a more learned clergyman in his place. Daniel Langer, it would seem, was an inadequate, or at least an inappropriate, pastor.[49]

The Langenzenn authorities painted a markedly negative picture of their pastor, the image of an opportunist groping for more wealth while he neglected his congregation, but there is little evidence to bear out their claims. Langer had been educated at the universities of Jena and Wittenberg and his behaviour in office, up to this point, had not elicited the attention of the authorities. In an effort to buttress his meagre income, he had asked for an addition the year before from the neighbouring monastery; but by all appearances, he was not an unreasonable, greedy, or incompetent man. This dispute in Langenzenn was less the product of Langer's failings than Langer's intrusion into parish affairs. As the secular official of Cadolzburg advised Ansbach, the quarrel was fuelled 'more out of premeditated hate and envy than pressing reasons':

It looks as though the petitioners have very little regard for the obedience before the secular and spiritual authorities demanded of them by God, especially before the holy ministry. For if such sentiment were found amongst them, without a doubt they would have more thanks for the efforts of their church servants, and fewer letters and complaints.[50]

The initial investigation, which cleared Langer of blame, was followed by a brief interim, a break in the proceedings while the settlement was pending. Langer was considered for a parish in Kulmbach. But before he could be relocated, and before the Ansbach authorities forwarded their final decision to the parish, the Langenzenn magistracy submitted another letter of complaint. Now, it was suggested, the pastor barred people from communion without good cause. If the accusations are true, Langer may have been reacting to the offensive behaviour of the plaintiffs, who were denying him the use of the common wood for the grazing of his pigs. Langer claimed the run of the common wood was a right his predecessor enjoyed; the village officials denied it. In their eyes it was 'a novelty, and no old, customary, traditional right *(gerechtigkeit)*'.[51] This violation of village norms is what the dispute revolved around. Langer demanded forms of payment, or an increase in payment and an access for his pigs, which the leading characters in this dispute viewed as a novelty, a violation of custom and right. Langer's demands displaced certain parish norms and thus sparked off accusations smacking of clerical laxity.[52]

The dispute in Langenzenn illustrates the nature of anticlericalism in Brandenburg-Ansbach-Kulmbach. The pastor was evaluated according to the norms or the standards of village custom and expectation. Once the pastor violated a norm, tradition, or standard, he became the object of derision and

---

[49] LKAN, MKA, Spez. 527, fos. 107–110.
[50] LKAN, MKA, Spez. 527, fo. 91; fos. 92–3 (26 July 1570).
[51] LKAN, MKA, Spez. 527, fos. 107–10 (8 September 1571).
[52] LKAN, MKA, Spez. 527, fo. 115 (17 September 1571).

antagonism. A quarrel between pastor and parish then assumed the dimensions of an 'anticlerical' suit: the competence of the clergyman was questioned by the parishioners, his abilities in office were challenged, his religious convictions were placed in doubt. These 'anticlerical' sentiments were secondary to the dispute, if not outright fabrications. Fundamental to the conflicts between the clergy and the parishioners in Brandenburg-Ansbach-Kulmbach was the degree to which the pastor could integrate into village life without disturbing traditional parish relations.[53]

In the same year of Langer's troubles in Langenzenn, the parish of Wendelstein, so impressive in 1524 when the commune demanded the pastor to bend to its needs, advised the authorities that they could command little respect from pastor Christoph Popp. Nuremberg informed Ansbach that Popp 'gives an unpleasant, wicked example' and was often in quarrel with the parishioners.[54] The judge of Wendelstein cited Popp as lax in his duties, especially baptism, and in too many disputes with the locals. The mayor Michael Maurer concurred: Popp was in conflict with the townspeople and drank far too much – '*In summa* the pastor is no use'.[55] The local witnesses, those not in regular communication with margravial authorities, did not deny that Popp drank 'like a pig' and failed to baptise the children, but it is interesting how they were even more eager to point out that Popp was a thief. Veit Vogel, the church warden, answered immediately that 'almost everyone in the parish knows that the pastor is suspected of thievery and takes whatever he finds.' Hans Schmidt suspected Popp of having taken twenty-four gulden lost by the judge – as did the rest of the parish. Vogel made it clear that Popp's worth as a pastor (using this infraction as the central example) was not judged according to the abstract moral imperatives of the Lutheran church, but rather the customary trial of honour. Michael Otter had publicly termed him a thief: 'And if the pastor had been right in this matter, he would not have borne it in such silence'.[56] In this case, as the example above, the pastor was judged according to traditional moral standards. Popp was an enemy of the parish first, only then was he weighed against a backdrop of Lutheran standards and his clerical laxities came to the fore.

A pastor did not have to be on bad terms with an entire parish to fall prey to anticlerical abuse. Johann Decker was dismissed from the parish of Rohr in 1546 through the efforts of a single man, the secular official of Rohr, Wolf Schmidt. Decker, it was claimed, abused Schmidt's wife (calling her a *frantzhosische Müter*),

---

[53] See the similar conclusions in Gerald Strauss, 'Local Anticlericalism in Reformation Germany', in Peter A. Dykema and Heiko A. Oberman (eds.), *Anticlericalism in Late Medieval and Early Modern Europe* (Leiden, 1993), pp. 625–37.

[54] LKAN, MKA, Spez. 992. fo. 83.

[55] LKAN, MKA, Spez. 992, fo. 85: 'las sich gegen den armen burgern in Rechtfertigung ein wider alle billicheit. Setze sich in die wirtsheuser und bezech sich von ainer mitternacht zur andern.'

[56] LKAN, MKA, Spez. 992, fo. 86: 'Und mocht der Pfarrer seinersachen so recht gehabt haben, er wurds nit allso stillschweigend vertragen haben lassen.' Most of the other witnesses, as a result, did not explain it away, but 'auf Im ligen lassen'.

while Schmidt's son called Decker's wife 'a whore and a priest's whore'. Schmidt once approached Decker and greeted him in much the same way (*dü böswichtse faff* [sic] *und diebstefaff...*). Decker responded by calling Schmidt a thief. The pastor also once penned his desire 'that they should lie in the deepest sea with stones around their necks'. While the feud is not recorded in any great detail, it appears as if the problem in this instance was one of property rights. Decker cursed Schmidt's wife because she had removed some of his fencing.[57] To aggravate matters, Schmidt's son had stolen some goods from his glebe lands. A quarrel over boundaries and rights was enmeshed in a defence of honour and status in the parish.[58] In this instance the pastor was eventually dismissed.

Matters of jurisdiction, use of property, or the scale of clerical maintenance would often given rise to quarrels between the pastor and the parish. Quite regularly, a strictly legal or contractual concern developed into a parish-wide battle, with the clergyman suffering discredit as a result. To return to Peter Hochmuther in the parish of Döhlau: as mentioned earlier, the Rabenstein nobleman, as patron of the church, had taken the keys from Hochmuther and refused him entry. Hochmuther claimed this was due to Rabenstein's wish to deny him the harvest of a property that had traditionally supplied more than half of the clergyman's income. Since he could not discredit Hochmuther's capacity in office, Rabenstein tried to starve him out of the parish.[59] Although the margrave's authorities investigated the matter, the quarrel was not resolved and Hochmuther wrote another letter of complaint in 1591 accusing Rabenstein of portioning the pastor's income himself (*er wil betzaler sein*) while refusing to pay him tithes.[60] The disputed property became ever more important.

In 1596 both parties were cited to appear before the Kulmbach chancellery. Testimony made it evident that the property dispute had been commuted into a struggle of personal honour – parish-wide – which then incorporated Hochmuther's qualities as a parish pastor. The later interrogation was almost exclusively focused on his alleged abuses as a Protestant clergyman: his knowledge of prayers and hymns, his execution of the mass, confession, absolution, and his comportment in the parish.[61] Ultimately the entire parish

---

57 LKAN, MDS, 131 T.1. (No pagination) Letter of Decker to Ansbach 1545.
58 LKAN, MDS, 131 T.1. *Antwort des Pfarrers zu Rohr uf Schmid Wolfs clag Samstags den 3 Septembris 1545*. The pastor continued: 'Daß wolff Schmid sein ampt und pflicht mermals ubersehen und verraten, das er selbs unainigkeit und hader anricht, auch wider mein leib ehr und guth...'.
59 LKAN, MDH, XX 3, fo. 2. (30 January 1590): 'so wil er mich enterlauben und dieweil er mir an lehr und leben halben nicht kan peÿ kommen, Gott lob, so wolt er mich gerne weg hungern, den Ich das heürige zinß geraid weder mit guten und hartten wortten nit khan von ime bekommen und andere kirchenspeis...'.
60 LKAN, MDH, XX 3, no. 5. (18 October 1591).
61 LKAN, MDH, XX 3, nos. 13–14. *Interrogatoria darauf Hans Frederichen Rabensteiners zu döla, wieder Peter Hochmuttern Pfarherrn furgestelte Zeugen exofficio beffracht undt examinirt worden*. One of the charges suggested that Hochmuter was prone to forget his place during sermons and once said: 'eÿ lieber, wo sein wir? helf mir einer wieder darein' (my punctuation).

(*alle eingepfarrten*) was cited before the officials of Hof. Whether everyone appeared cannot be known, but of the fifteen people who did testify, each of them confirmed some or all of the accusations brought against Hochmuther by Rabenstein.[62] And yet they had not complained before; nothing emerges from the 1589 visitation returns.[63] Once again it was the pastor's status in relation to desired parish norms which gave rise to complaints. His alleged abuses were a corollary (true or false).

Dissatisfaction with the clergy could also be the product of general apprehension or fear. On occasion the parishioners would cite a pastor before the Ansbach authorities because he threatened the communal peace. In Uttenhofen, Pankraz Spitznagel was said to curse and rail at his congregation from the pulpit. He had received a warning from the secular authorities, but he had not honoured it, and instead cursed everything within his range of vision ('us, our women, children, livestock, even the precious crop in the field' was how the victims described it).[64] Accusations levelled against his clerical competence followed. He once refused to bury an old man in the graveyard; then, when the latter's wife grew ill, he would not extend the sacrament to her. Spitznagel may have been correct to exclude the old man from the burial ground; such punishment was meted out to unrepentant sinners. (The woman was involved in a quarrel and may have been unprepared for the sacrament.) But the theological justification for his actions was never in question, just the actions themselves. Understandably, Spitznagel's proclivity to threaten the congregation, as he did Christmas Day when he wished for 'a fresh pestilence ... and in conclusion, amen, amen, that such became true and should happen', was the matter at issue.[65]

It did not necessarily take a prophet of doom such as Spitznagel to waken the ire of the villagers. Johann Stieber of Weimersheim was cited before the authorities by members of his congregation in 1573 for far less. According to the parish report, Stieber favoured a Catholic notion of divine forgiveness, wished ill upon his enemies, held public rather than private confession, argued with the schoolmaster in the church, swore, drank, and his wife was little better.[66] So too did he cast doubt (it seemed) on the villagers' status before God: 'The pastor preaches publicly, that amongst one hundred, scarcely one is blessed [*selig*]'. Yet Stieber may have been the victim of his own competence. Testimonials in a

---

[62] LKAN, MDH, XX 3, nos. 29–36. (4 June 1596) Witnesses testified that he refused confession to a pregnant woman, began communion only to discover that he had no wine (so he sent his daughter to get some), was lax in catechism classes, and let the host fall to earth on occasion.

[63] StaB, C2 1827 *Relation der im herbst deß 1589 Jars gehaltener Visitation Inn der höfer Superintendentz, passim.* On the other hand, already in 1572 complaints were brought forward in the visitation about the Rabenstein nobility and their neglect of worship. LKAN, MDH, V 1a, fo. 66.

[64] LKAN, MDU, 330 (14 January 1586).

[65] LKAN, MDU, 330 (14 January 1586), Point 7.

[66] LKAN, MDG 71, fo. 50.

subsequent inquisition gave him a good witness.[67] It seems that Stieber had run foul of certain high-placed parishioners and they grew determined to discredit him. Ludwig Harder, an official in Weimersheim, had grown to dislike the pastor, and it may have been due to Stieber's sheer application in office.[68] His very diligence, in that he honoured to the letter the expectations of the Lutheran church, irrespective of the parishioners who might be affected, ushered in his downfall. Certainly the public confession was the outcome of Stieber's concern for the welfare of his flock. During the Easter service (1572) Stieber stormed out of the church in frustration as the schoolmaster and a member of the parish were causing a ruckus. When he came back, eight people remained. He said to them: 'Dear friends, you see how it goes with me; and against my will I have kept you waiting for too long. And as it has grown so late, so that I can't hear each of you in private, as I rightly should do...' Stieber gave a public confession, the first and last, if his word is to be trusted.[69] In this instance the alleged faults of a pastor came to light because he had alienated certain members of the parish in the execution of his clerical duties. He was, in a sense, too strictly true to his calling.

In all of the above-cited examples a common element is present. The parish (or a member of the parish) was at odds with the pastor *in situ*, not with the broader concept of what a proper Lutheran clergyman should be. If a grouping of charges against the pastor's competence in office preceded or followed an investigation, it was the derivative of a more pedestrian village quarrel or a legal disagreement. In each instance the original complaint evaluated the clergyman according to traditional or 'functional' norms. Gerald Strauss has recently made the similar observation that local anticlericalism was very rarely 'principled opposition to a sacerdotal presence in the community'.[70] This is not to deny that a more general form of anticlericalism was voiced during the 1520s which transcended local situations;[71] but a close study of discord between pastor and parish reveals a hidden agenda, and this agenda, more

---

[67] LKAN, MDG 71, fos. 51–3. The testimonies of Michael Hüfftlein (*Vierer*), Caspar Minderlein (*margraflich vierer*), Johann Stor (*Vierer*), Georg Stoë (?) (*weisenburgisch vierer*) in particular. The inquisitors also implied that Stieber was a competent pastor: 'das examen so wir in der kirchen gehalten, gibt dem pastorn seines vleiβ ein guttes gezeugniβ, dan die jügendt auff das, so sie gefragt worden, zimlich antwortt geben haben'.

[68] In his defence Stieber reproached the parishioners for their lack of Christian humility and strength of worship. But in specific he mentioned Harder, with whom he was in dispute about marriage matters (Harder forbade the parishioners to seek assistance from the pastor). Harder was also threatening the pastor's family. *Inquisition die Weimmarschheimschen special visitation betreffende.* LKAN, MDG 71, fo. 48.

[69] LKAN, MKG 71, fos. 50–1.

[70] Strauss, 'Local Anticlericalism', p. 627.

[71] Henry J. Cohn, 'Anticlericalism in the German Peasants' War', *Past & Present*, 83 (1979), 3–31; Hans-Jürgen Goertz, 'Aufstand gegen den Priester. Antiklerikalismus und reformatorische Bewegungen', in Peter Blickle (ed.), *Bauer, Reich und Reformation* (Stuttgart, 1982), pp. 182–209; Hans-Jürgen Goertz, *Pfaffenhaβ und groβ Geschrei. Die reformatorischen Bewegungen in Deutschland 1517–1529* (Munich, 1987); Scribner, *Popular Culture and Popular Movements*, pp. 243–56.

often than not, was a composite of routine village concerns. The Protestant clergyman was measured against the norms of the community, not the standards of religious dogma.

Isolated acts of injustice and moral shortcomings figured large amongst the complaints brought before the visitors. Clergy who drank too much on their own, or 'ran from one tavern to the other', were obvious targets of reproach. Pugnacious incumbents – those in frequent quarrel with other clergy, or with villagers – were also high on the list. Sexual licence was looked down upon by the community.[72] Even less tangible misdeeds, such as insults, dishonouring the community, suggestions of novelties or unwarranted demands, were a source of friction. Complaints against the clergy thus increased in line with the degree of intrusion into parish affairs. In Saxony, in progress with the first century of reform, the nature of anticlericalism changed as the scope of the church's reach into parish life developed – from problems of maintenance in the first instance, to conflicts over parish custom and tradition as the parishioners' deportment became subject to greater scrutiny.[73]

In general, the pastor was expected to toe the collective line as any other member of the community. If he fell suspect he could be discredited by the whole parish. Johannes Bermouth made it clear in 1597: if his sexton continued to be rude to him,

makes us suspect with the parishioners, has pleasure at our misfortune, gives a clear impression that he pays us no heed, abuses us, or fails to return our greetings, then all sorts of suspicion will be aroused amongst the common run [*gemeinen pöbel*], who are quick to believe, especially whatever is being said about the clergy.[74]

The pastor was no less, and no more, than what the villagers would tolerate; until, that is, he violated their patience or their trust, and then he was viewed against the backdrop of the church. 'It is a common feature of many such conflicts in rural parishes', observes one historian, 'that a trivial disagreement or a minor complaint often let loose a deeper reservoir of resentment and set off a chain reaction of dissension and bitterness that seemed to subvert the very basis of the cure of souls.'[75]

Nowhere is the concern with the parish status quo more apparent than in the villagers' habit of citing clergymen before the visitation commission to answer for the machinations of their wives. Judging by the frequency of this concern, it

---

[72] LKAN, MDL 165. *Beschwerungs Puncten wider Johan Cunrad Pfarrer zu Leutershaussen*; LKAN, MDG 71, fo. 88; LKAN, MDG 71, fos. 115–17; StaN, *Ansbacher Neues Generalrepertorium*, no. 49, rep. nr. 103ᵉ. fo. 235; LKAN, MKA 998, fo. 44.
[73] Susan C. Karant-Nunn, 'Neoclericalism and Anticlericalism in Saxony, 1555–1675', *The Journal of Interdisciplinary History*, 24 (1994), 615–37.
[74] LKAN, MDLz 665 (10 January 1597).
[75] R. W. Scribner, 'Pastoral Care and the Reformation in Germany', in James Kirk (ed.), *Humanism and Reform: The Church in Europe, England and Scotland, 1400–1643* (Oxford, 1991), p. 97.

would seem that the pastor's wife was difficult to integrate into the parish.[76] This may have been due to new social expectations, in a bilateral sense. The peasantry probably continued to view these women on much the same terms as their predecessors, the concubines. The pastors' wives, in contrast, now given divine warrant to abide in the parsonage, may have tried to use their status to advantage. The source materials do not relate such subtle conceits; but it is clear that the pastor would suffer 'anticlerical' abuse if his wife was not kept in check. Clerical wives were repeatedly described as termagant scolds in quarrel with the entire village. The pastor's wife in Colmberg was a drunkard, she abused her employees and claimed that 'there is not one devout [*fromb*] wife in the whole village, just pure whores'.[77] The pastor of Aschbach, it was claimed, had a troublesome wife who fought with the villagers at the inn, drank herself full of wine, blasphemed terribly, and would not bear punishment.[78] (Secular authorities were often faced with this difficulty: the pastors' wives would not obey the rulings of the village officials.) The wife of Johann Schatz, the old Catholic priest in Berolzheim, went so far as to oppose the visitors and tear up their notices.[79]

The tension and unease created by a quarrelsome pastor's wife provides a useful model with which to explain the causes and course of parish conflicts. The Reformation ushered in a sequence of novelties (not the least of which was clerical marriage) which placed a greater demand on the parish to provide maintenance for the pastor and, while doing so, pay heed to his bidding. Less manifest, though no less real, were the innovations introduced by the change in status and power of a rural pastor (and his wife) commensurate with the emerging territorial church. As has been noted above, dissatisfaction with a clergyman was the outgrowth of a personal quarrel or a perceived violation of traditional village relations. Anticlericalism was merely the symptom of an underlying condition of social tension between pastor and parish. The pastor could assimilate himself in the parish only in so far as his presence was not a burden or a disturbance; and he could be successful as a Lutheran clergyman only in so far as he could penetrate the web of social relations and make his presence felt. The extent of his assimilation is a question of maintenance; the measure of his status is a rather more comprehensive issue, forcing the historian to examine the impact of the Reformation movement as a whole.

---

[76] StaN, *Ansbacher Neues Generalrepertorium*, no. 49, rep. nr. 103ᶜ. fo. 91; LKAN, MSK, 157, Monchberg 1578; LKAN, MDH, V 1a, fo. 48; LKAN, MDG 71, fo. 34; LKAN, MDG 71, fo. 63.

[77] LKAN, MDL 131, *Acta, in sachen einer Inquisition, den pfarern zü ... Colbergk 27. Aprilis. Anno 1586.*

[78] LKAN, MDG 71, fo. 25.

[79] LKAN, MDG 71, fo. 28; Clauß, 'Aus Gunzenhäuser Visitationsakten', pp. 102–3

CLERICAL MAINTENANCE

For the visitor of Kulmbach in 1572, the equation was straightforward: 'When there is not enough parish wealth to support the pastors, then preachers cannot be maintained; when there are no sermons, there is also no Word of God; where there is no Word of God, there is no chance of salvation.'[80] The preaching of the Word required a trained clergy, and a trained clergyman required an income and a home. The introduction of the evangelical faith did not solve the problems associated with clerical maintenance; in fact it compounded the difficulties. Sources of income were eliminated outright or gradually atrophied with time; masses for the dead, foundations, monasteries, and church offices disappeared with the Catholic church. At the same time, clerical marriage meant that the number of people in a clergyman's household increased. (Johannes Kellner of Seibelsdorf, for example, fathered over twenty children.) Clerical maintenance became one of the chief complications facing the nascent territorial church. For it was imperative to the growth of the Lutheran church that the clergy, in addition to being suitable for office, be suitably maintained once they were in office. As the higher clergy advised, the pastor should be able to stay clear of 'base' economic concerns without suffering too dearly as a result.

Attempts have been made to chart the rise and fall of clerical incomes in the sixteenth century.[81] Where the source materials yield enough information, the evidence suggests that the first two or three generations of Lutheran pastors suffered financial hardship; the average pastor was not really in a secure financial position until the end of the century. Susan Karant-Nunn has surveyed the fortunes of the clergy in the Ernestine countryside and it seems that, by degrees, their lot did in fact improve.[82] But tallying a cross-section of salaries, as she notes, ignores the wider context. Incomes varied greatly – from cash to kind to labour service. The average cash salary in Ansbach and Kulmbach (taken from a composite of sixty-eight mid-century incomes) equalled roughly fifty gulden, with figures ranging from twenty-three gulden to 225.[83] No doubt the higher salary denotes a more lucrative post, but a cash income was only one part of the yearly intake. Using Karant-Nunn's categorisation, we can divide a pastor's income along the following lines: ground rent (*erbzins*) on land situated on the property of the local church; the quarterly offering (*opferpfennig*) given by each communicant on feast days; *accidentia* – services rendered for tasks

---

80 LKAN, MSK 157, fo. 12 (my pagination).
81 Vogler, *Le clergé protestant Rhénan*, pp.149–89; Karant-Nunn, *Luther's Pastors*, pp. 39–53; Susan K. Boles, 'The Economic Position of Lutheran Pastors in Ernestine Thuringia 1521–1555,' *ARG*, 63 (1972), 94–125.
82 Karant-Nunn, *Luther's Pastors*, pp. 43–52.
83 StaB, C3 1229, *passim*.

such as baptism, marriage, or burial;[84] the tithe, usually in sacks of threshed grain; less regular dues (chickens, lambs, bread, beeswax) which varied according to local custom; and labour service (*frondienst*), expected of the parishioners at specific times of the year.[85] Given the range of possibilities, it is small wonder some clergymen in Ansbach received very little in cash. Grain, traditional gifts, and labour services formed the better part of their income.[86]

Even if the historian were granted data reliable enough to estimate an average yearly income, there is no guarantee this would represent the pastor's salary in real terms. Salaries varied from year to year, as an inspector in the super-intendency of Gunzenhausen (1573/4) found to his dismay: 'It is impossible for me to know exactly the pastors' yearly income, and how much each has brought in from year to year.' The clergy rarely helped the inspector with the tally, since they thought an investigation worked to their disadvantage; and time was always against the likelihood of a general investigation: it was not possible to calculate the income until the crops had been gathered, sold, and stored away, and this was considered to be a matter for God to decide (*do man des segen Gottes erwarten müß*).[87] Of course the parishioners were unlikely to be very helpful, either with the drafting of the annual tally or in the distribution of the tithes. In Gunzen-hausen, for example, the residents harvested the crops, including the pastor's share, and meted out the ration according to their pleasure at a time of their own choosing. The clergyman was forced to negotiate for his income, an event that inevitably ended to his disadvantage.[88]

Aside from the word of the parish residents, whose collective memory might have a precarious hold on the truth, the authorities had to rely on the parish registers for an accurate rendering of the parish income. But the registers were often missing or destroyed. Sometimes the old Catholic clergyman took the

---

84 The payment of *accidentia* continued after the introduction of the Reformation, but there was little standardisation in the amounts that could be demanded or the services for which it could be charged. In Halsdorf a pastor (1583) could expect seven pfennig for a baptism (which held true for many parishes) and up to twenty-one for a burial. LKAN, MSK 133, *Jährliches einkommen der pfarr harsdorff, wie hernachfolgt*, 1583. In other places, such as Wernsbach, the pastor charged as he or the parishioners felt fit (or according to the ability to pay). For baptism and marriage, some clergy received wine, others money, but for the visitation of the sick they did not charge. LKAN, MDL, 234 T.1 (5 June 1619). The chapter ordinance conceded that a pastor might expect a considerable fee for baptism or marriage if it was custom in the parish. Sometimes the amount was fixed, as at Oberferrieden where in 1491 it had been stipulated that for such services the pastor received seven pfennig. LKAN, MDS, 122 T.1 (3 March 1575).
85 Karant-Nunn, *Luther's Pastors*, pp. 39–42; Boles, 'The Economic Position of Lutheran Pastors', pp. 96–101.
86 Karl Schornbaum, 'Pfarrbesoldungen im 16. Jahrhundert', *Beiträge zur bayerischen Kirchen-geschichte*, 14 (1908), pp. 42–5; Werner Sprung, 'Zehnten und Zehntrecht um Nürnberg', *Mitteilungen des Vereins für Geschichte der Stadt Nürnberg*, 55 (1968), pp. 2–6.
87 LKAN, MDG 71, fos. 54–6. The clergy believed 'das Inen solche nachforschung mehr zum nachthail, dan zw Iren nutz geschehe'.
88 LKAN, MDG 71, fo. 20.

register with him when he left, on other occasions fires or wars were to blame. A missing register also meant that the pastor had to turn to the parishioners for help when he needed information on a plot of land or the annual dues, and it surprised no one when the visitor in Kulmbach (1572) reported how

> up to now there has been a failing in all the visitations, in that there is hardly a single pastor who has a certain and continual register of his annual income and parish worth. The fees and dues therefore must be gathered according to the peasant accounts. Every now and again, as a consequence, many rights belonging to the parish [church] are being lost.[89]

A comparative study of the incomes of parish clergymen in the sixteenth century would be fraught with incomplete registers and figures with hidden values.

How did the Lutheran church in Brandenburg-Ansbach-Kulmbach deal with the problem of clerical maintenance? In the absence of a reliable guide to the value of clerical incomes, the following investigation will examine the type of problems confronting the Lutheran pastor, rather than the relative degree. How well maintained was the pastor in the parish? What were the remedies suggested by the Ansbach authorities? To what extent were the Ansbach proposals implemented? How were the problems addressed at the level of the parish? To what degree was the Lutheran prince willing to intervene?

Soon after margrave Georg's return from Silesia in 1528, the pastor of Crailsheim, Adam Weiß, wrote to the Ansbach chancellery describing the ill-effects religious change was having on his income. Since the introduction of the Lutheran faith, claimed Weiß, the income of the Crailsheim incumbent had declined by up to 130 gulden. Previous sources of wealth, such as mass offerings and foundation endowments, were no longer available to the Crailsheim incumbent. In another letter Weiß presented his income, his debts, and the loss of potential wealth, and he added in conclusion that he found himself preaching the Gospel to the people at his own expense.[90] Clerical poverty was not new, as the 1480 Eichstätt visitation revealed, but Weiß was certainly correct to point out that many of the foundation masses, *accidentia*, and feast days – all previously valuable sources of income – had disappeared. This situation was not quick to improve. The Ansbach folklorist Karl-Sigismund Kramer's conclusion holds true for the entire sixteenth century: 'The poor pastor was the rule.' Reliant as he was upon the cooperation of the parishioners, the village clergyman was never in a position of financial security. 'The realisation that they [parishioners] could keep the pastor tied to their apron strings because they were responsible for his upkeep lasted many decades.'[91]

---

[89] LKAN, MSK 157, *Bericht der Spetial Visitation, In der Süperintendentz Beÿrreuth A[nn]o 1572*, fo. 12 (my pagination).

[90] StaN, *Ansbacher Religionsakten III*, Tom. XI, fos. 39–41, 297–8. Weiß had to maintain two chaplains.

[91] Karl-Sigismund Kramer, *Volksleben im Fürstentum Ansbach und seinen Nachbargebieten 1500–1800* (Würzburg, 1961), p. 166.

The visitation returns of the latter-half of the sixteenth century support Weiβ's claims. Throughout the parishes of Ansbach and Kulmbach pastors lived in dire poverty. The Seibelsdorf incumbent was hard hit by the removal of the *opfergeld*; the parishioners saw it as a continuation of Catholicism (*Babstisch grifflein*) and refused to pay. The clergyman of Kurzenaltheim could not maintain his wife and four children on his salary without an increase. The income of the pastor of Joditz (1572) was so sparse he was forced to catch fish and birds to supplement his diet. Other pastors were compelled to go door to door and beg. Gerson Reis of Meinheim looked to the Jews for a loan in his need.[92] In Gunzenhausen, the clergyman could not improve his income because the citizens insisted on dividing up the tithe themselves. Mainstockheim's Erhard Döberlein suggested in a sermon that while costs continued to rise, the desire among the parishioners to pay had declined:

The preachers these days must have more income than before, since everything is nearly three times more expensive now than it was ten years (or less) ago; and, moreover, the people are no longer as charitable as those people were when the Gospel was first broadcast. For almost nothing, or very little, is being given to the preachers these days.[93]

Döberlein's lament on the expensive times was a common one. Many supplications began with 'in these dear years' or 'during these gaunt, expensive times'. It was not just rhetoric. During the course of the sixteenth century the population in Franconia rose, food demand increased, prices doubled and trebled, while the salaries of the middling professions, especially one so precarious as that of a clergyman, remained fixed.[94] The dire situation in Franconia mirrored a general trend in the German-speaking lands, where the onset of inflation influenced the price of basic foodstuffs, such as rye and grain, to the detriment of many rural inhabitants.[95] A tight budget, or 'bad economy', could impair the pastor once he was in office. 'The economy hinders him [the pastor of Mistelgau] and other pastors in the countryside in their studies', was the conclusion of a Kulmbach visitor.[96]

The problem was augmented for those clergymen forced to service a parish which was just too big to handle. Lukas Korneffer of Merkendorf preached the

[92] LKAN, MSK, 133, *Antwort uff des Herren Decani schreiben. Pfarhers zu Seÿwolβdorff den 11. Decemb* (1583), fo. 8 (my pagination.); LKAN, MDG 71, fo. 8; LKAN, MDH, V 1a, fo. 64; LKAN, MSK 157, Joditz (22 October 1573); LKAN, MSK, 157, Lehenthal 1573; LKAN, MDG 71, fo. 81; LKAN, MDG 71, fo. 17 (Meinheim).

[93] LKAN, MKA, Spez. 564, fo. 96.

[94] Rudolf Endres, 'Zur wirtschaftlichen und sozialen Lage in Franken vor dem Dreiβigjährigen Krieg', *Jahrbuch für fränkische Landesforschung*, 28 (1968), 5–52; Herms Bahl, Wilhelm Otto Keller, and Karl-Ludwig Löffler, 'Ansbachs wirtschaftliche Situation in der zweiten Hälfte des 16. Jahrhunderts und die Almosenordnung von 1581', in *Ansbach – 750 Jahre Stadt* (Ansbach, 1971), pp. 65–83.

[95] Wilhelm Abel, *Agrarkrisen und Agrarkonjunktur* (Hamburg, 1966), pp. 113ff; Thomas Robisheaux, *Rural Society and the Search for Order in Early Modern Germany* (Cambridge, 1989), pp. 148–9.

[96] LKAN, MSK, 157, Mistelgau 1578/9.

Lutheran faith in a parish surrounded on all sides by Catholics. His duties were compounded by isolation and the sheer scale of his parish. 'The incumbency is difficult, sprawling, arduous, and big ... but the benefice is small, and meagre', is how he assessed the situation.[97] Some clergymen suffered because the patron would not grant them the parish funds, perhaps due to an aversion to Lutheranism, perhaps due to a belief that the elimination of the bishoprics necessitated their intervention. Faced with such problems, most of the clergy would approach the superintendent, a secular official, or the margrave himself in their search for aid.

The Lutheran pastor inherited the parish residency of the Catholic priest. In most instances a village parsonage was an old dwelling built of wood, small, draughty, and structurally unsound. 'The residence ... is an old, poorly built wooden house ... a poor wooden building' are two reviews conveying the general idea. The visitation returns are littered with complaints of crumbling dwellings in an imminent state of collapse. In Kulmbach (1573) approximately 80 per cent of parish returns mentioned an unsuitable residence. There are too many examples to cite; representative examples must suffice. A filial parish of Baudenbach saw its pastor's residence blown to earth by the wind. Other residences in the same superintendency, lacking a roof, a floor, a cellar, a door, or an annexed stable, were considered so run-down they were not worth repair. The Ergersheim pastor related to the visitors in 1589 how his household lived in constant fear of their 'life and limbs' in his house. In Pilgramsreuth, 'one piece after another falls in, and he [the pastor] and with his wife and child are for no moment, day or night, safe of life and limb'. In Lehenthal (1573) the pastor could not escape the elements, winter or summer. In Weidenbach the clergyman was victim to the rain, even when he was in bed; nor did the rain do the contents of a house any good (*verderbe ains hie, das ander dort*). Similar circumstances forced the pastor of Busbach to leave the parsonage altogether and live elsewhere.[98] But to avoid the house did not eliminate the fact that it was falling down. Moreover, as Ambrosius Büttner, pastor of Rockingen, observed, a dilapidated residence was not just an eyesore, but a potential source of misfortune in a parish: it welcomed thievery, remained a fire hazard, and a cold house required heating, in an age when wood was scarce.[99]

The number of references to decrepit churches is less. The church was *the* object of communal concern in Ansbach, a point made more explicit by the lack of

---

[97] LKAN, MDG 71, fos. 31–2. A similar situation existed in Oberndachstetten. LKAN, MKA, Spez. 655, no. 44.

[98] Sources for the paragraph: LKAN, MDH, V, 1a, fos. 44; 65 (1572); LKAN, MSK, 157 *Verzeichnus der Baufelligen Pfarr und Pfründt Heusern in der Superattendentz Culmbach* (c.1572/3–a stray folio.); StaN, *Ansbacher Neues Generalrepertorium*, no. 49, rep. nr. 103e. fos. 167; 228 (17 October 1591); LKAN, MSK, 157, Untersteinach 1558; LKAN, MSK, 157, Trumsdorf (17 September 1572); LKAN, MDU, 8, no. 155; StaB, C2 1827, fo. 87 (29/30 October 1589); LKAN, MSK, 157, Lehenthal 1573; LKAN, MDG 71, fo. 22; LKAN, MDG, 71, fo. 70. Gunzenhausen 1578; LKAN, MSK, 157, Busbach 1578.

[99] LKAN, MKA, Spez. 709 (4 July 1565).

other public buildings in the villages of middle Franconia.[100] All the same, some churches were in a fragile state, suffering from buckling roofs, yawing bell towers, broken windows, leaks, gaps, holes, and rotting wood. Pastors complained of water dripping onto the lectern, rotten floorboards surrounding the pulpit, and sparrows nesting in the nave and disrupting the sermon. Often the visitors recommended immediate repair, lest a ceiling or tower collapse and 'destroy everything'.[101] Churches fell to the destruction of war, others to neglect, the mismanagement of funds, legal disputes, questions of patronage, and sheer poverty. The church was in many ways a mirror on the fortunes of a parish.

In the visitation of 1528 the margrave instructed the regional officials to inspect the parishes within their jurisdiction. In the following visitation of 1536, the directives were more explicit: the financial state of the parish and the condition of the church became objects of inquiry.[102] Two years later a large-scale investigation took place in Kulmbach. Georg the Pious wrote to the mayors and councillors of Hof, Bayreuth, Kulmbach, and Wunsiedel instructing them to aid the efforts of Heinrich Blechschmidt, who had been ordered 'to establish a register [*Salbuch*] and make a record of the foundations [*die Spitall*] and churches which have special rents and assets, and also of their old conventions and privileges'.[103] This seems to have followed a general effort in 1538 to inventory the wealth of church property in both principalities.[104] With the advent of special visitations in 1565 it was possible to inspect the financial condition of the parishes (*underhaltung, gepeu*) on a yearly basis. Administrators of local monasteries were instructed to visit dependent parishes and examine the church buildings. The 1560s (the Hof chronicler suggested 1567) was the period in which a serious programme of inspection began. A letter to the administrator of Feuchtwangen indicates that a widespread effort was being made to keep track of the condition of the residences.[105] Overspending was a central concern of the Ansbach authorities, and often the local officials themselves were the prime suspects.[106] By the year 1611 margrave Joachim Ernst was dispatching printed mandates regulating the amount

---

[100] Kramer, *Volksleben im Fürstentum Ansbach*, pp. 29–35.
[101] LKAN, MDG 71, fo. 63. Beroltzheim 1576; LKAN, MSK, 157, Schauenstein (1 October 1572); StaN, *Ansbacher Neues Generalrepertorium*, no. 49, rep. nr. 103e. fo. 55.
[102] Sehling, p. 318.
[103] StaB, C3 1223, fo. 20 ('Mittwoch nach Michaelis 1538').
[104] StaB, C3 1223, fo. 18.
[105] LKAN, MDF, 1, no. 15, (10 January 1569):

> Obwohl von dem dürchleuchtigen hochgebornen fursten unserm gnedigen herrn, Marggraf Geörg Friderichen ... zuerbauung und besserung der pfarr und pfrundtheuser die verschinen Jhar uber, grosser uncost ufgewendet, und auch darauf von Iren f. g. allenthalben in die Embter bevelch gethun worden, das solche pfarr und pfrundtheuser Jhärlich besichtigt werden, und solch einsehen geschehen soll, damit dieselben von den kirchendienern in Beulichen wesen erhallten werden das wir doch täglich erfharen, wann gleich an etlichen ortten die pfarrheuser oder andere gebew, aintweder von Neuem gebauet, oder sunsten nach aller notturfft widerumb zugerichtet worden sein...

[106] LKAN, MDLz, 676a (31 March 1591).

that could be spent on reconstruction and restricting the liberties taken by the secular officials.[107]

In order to supplement an income or buttress a crumbling residence the margrave had recourse to two basic sources of wealth: the parish itself – the church fund, the tithes, the defunct votive masses – or an external source, such as a neighbouring monastery or foundation. According to the 1594 consistorial ordinance,

> Where we [the margrave] have the right of patronage [in a parish] not incorporated into one of our foundations or monasteries, the cost of construction will be taken in part from the church funds [*von den Gottesheusern*], where such is possible, and part from the parish commune [*Gemein*] in gratis contributions and taxes. And in the case where these combined assessments will still not suffice, the rest will be reimbursed from us out of the church property.[108]

The parishioners were reluctant to render gratis dues to the pastor, whether for his maintenance or the construction of a residence. And it was rare for the village to suggest a possible alternative source of wealth in a supplication, though a grouping of villagers in a large parish might propose that the inhabitants of a incorporated hamlet assume a greater share.

The confiscation of local masses and endowments was treated with some circumspection at first. The 1526 Ansbach provincial *Landtag* ruled that real Christian endowments were those dedicated to the service of God or the welfare of a neighbour. If a clergyman could not fulfil the functions expected of him while in the possession of such an office without endangering his conscience, he should step down.[109] If the donors were still living, as Melanchthon advised, the money could be returned to them (not, however, to their heirs). Since the church ordinances do not go into detail about the fate of endowments, it seems safe to assume that each was incorporated according to local conditions or needs. 'In time they were probably incorporated into the *Grosse Almosen* or elsewhere into the common chest ... Otherwise, the state treasury incorporated them when there was no longer an interested party.'[110] By 1536 the towns were expected to have a common chest and most endowments simply merged with this central fund. Both this fund and the church buildings were managed at the local level by laymen – the church wardens – as had been the case before the Reformation. These men went under the title of *Heiligenpfleger* or *Gotteshausmeister* and were called to answer before the visitation commission. In general, the Reformation did not uproot the existing system of endowments, but rather integrated the funds and benefices into the new ecclesiastical system.

---

[107] LKAN, MDL, 1 (12 December 1611).
[108] Sehling, p. 394; *Corpus Constitutionum Brandenburgico-Culmbacensium* (1746), p. 279.
[109] Hans Liermann, 'Protestant Endowment Law in the Franconian Church Ordinances', in Zophy and Buck (eds.), *The Social History of the Reformation*, p. 343.
[110] Liermann, 'Protestant Endowment Law', pp. 345–6.

On a grander scale the Reformation brought with it the secularisation of the monasteries and the confiscation of their wealth. The Benedictine monastery of Wülzburg, already in a state of moral and administrative disarray, was taken over by Casimir in 1523. He set about reforming the administration, including apportioning of income, eventually deciding to turn it into a secular foundation. Casimir appointed a secular official to watch over administration; in 1525/6 an inventory was taken.[111] Using the Peasants' War as justification for his intervention, Casimir ordered a similar inventory of all of the monasteries in Ansbach. He promised that the wealth would be returned after the war, as it was just a precautionary measure.[112]

It is unlikely that Casimir ever contemplated returning the wealth he had purloined to rout the peasants, but it is clear that the fate of the monasteries did present something of a problem for him, as it did for his successor, margrave Georg.[113] Georg wrote to Luther for suggestions. Luther advised that the monasteries be left in relative peace until the last of the Catholic clergy died out or were willing to accept a pension (reception of novices was correspondingly forbidden).[114] Luther agreed that the wealth might be used for religious ends (scholarships, schools), but the foundations should not be rent to the ground. Through this strategy the monasteries were gradually emptied and the wealth put to use. Evangelical preachers lectured to the remaining members and the 1533 church ordinance was introduced.[115]

In order to grant the confiscation of the monasteries a modicum of legality Georg the Pious began a series of negotiations with the Pope, but his efforts led to a stalemate.[116] Undaunted, the margrave used the wealth of the monasteries to support preachers and educators and to fund pensions and salaries for the higher officials and clergymen, while a substantial sum went to pay off the margrave's debt. The monasteries' material wealth, above all the treasures and valuables of the more ancient houses, went either as gifts or was melted down and minted in Schwabach. Of course these liberties were not enjoyed without opposition, nor

---

[111] Karl Schornbaum, 'Die Säkularisation des Klosters Wülzburg,' *Sammelblatt des Historischen Vereins Eichstätt*, 24 (1909), 1–18; Schornbaum, *Die Stellung des Markgrafen Kasimir*, pp. 8–10.

[112] Many of the clergy left the monasteries during the Peasants' War, only to return afterward by order of Casimir. The nun Veronica Gross later claimed that as she left Frauenaurach during the war for the safety of the stronghold in Cadolzburg she took with her four silver cups worth about 28–30 gulden. Once in the castle, however, a servant and a local official opened her trunk and took her goods, 'with the words, I should be silent, for they had orders from the margrave'. StaB, C3 1555, II, fos. 25–6.

[113] Karl Schornbaum, 'Zur Klostersäkularisation des Markgrafen Kasimir', *Beiträge zur bayerischen Kirchengeschichte*, 10 (1904), 129–140.

[114] For example, the nuns of Sultz. StaN, *Ansbacher Religionsakten III*, Tom. XI, fo. 199.

[115] Götz, *Die Glaubensspaltung*, pp. 185–202; E. F. H Medicus, *Geschichte der evangelischen Kirche im Königreiche Bayern* (Erlangen, 1863), pp. 35–6; Georg Muck, *Beiträge zur Geschichte von Kloster Heilsbronn* (Ansbach, 1859), pp. 131–9; R. G. Stillfried, *Kloster Heilsbronn* (Berlin, 1877), pp. 25–30.

[116] Götz, *Die Glaubensspaltung*, pp. 210–13.

was this usurpation without its vocal critics; but the bishops were too remote, the local Catholic clergy too insubstantial, and the local nobility too reliant upon princely favour to present effective opposition. In 1529 margrave Georg ordered a principality-wide inventory and gradually all of the monasteries fell under the control of the margrave.[117] Administration was managed by a margravial official, though an abbot or prior might stay on if he worked in the same capacity. These men were consulted when it was necessary to repair a neighbouring residence or supplement a pastor's income.

A survey of the post-Reformation church in Brandenburg-Ansbach-Kulmbach would suggest that the margraves did have ecclesiastical funds at their disposal. Some of it was the inheritance of the medieval system of dues and endowments, some of it was appropriated after the introduction of the evangelical faith. All of it, however, was reliant upon the participation of the parishioners if it were to be raised or implemented effectively at the local level. It remains to be seen whether the reform of clerical maintenance was helped or hindered by the rural inhabitants, and whether these problems, if they existed, could be overcome.

TITHES, LABOUR, AND THE REFUSAL TO PAY FEES

On 15 September 1568 a group of neighbouring parishes drafted a note of complaint against their pastor. Emphasising their poverty, the parishioners claimed that some clergymen had incomes to equal those of the nobility. One pastor in particular, whose parish, they insisted, would maintain three or four incumbents, wanted to build a house to match his wealth: 'for he proposes to have a castle and not a pastor's house.' To add to this, the parishioners continued, he used their wood for his alchemy, insulted them from the pulpit, denied them the sacrament, and wished an infamous illness upon them (*frantzossen kranckheÿdt*). At the conclusion of the draft, they asked for a new pastor.[118]

The superintendent of Kulmbach ordered a resident official (*Forstmeister*) to investigate the dispute, and an inquiry soon followed. The investigation revealed that the complaint stemmed from the parish of Neudrossenfeld; it was directed against the clergyman Kaspar Günther. The official, however, waived most of the accusations aside. When he heard that Günther was at odds with his parishioners, the official's initial reaction was one of suspicion. He put it down to the machinations of 'a number of fiendish people, of whom one is not certain what belief they are'.[119] The *Kastner* of Wunsiedel, Desiderius Hedler, commissioned to aid the *Forstmeister* in the investigation, also cleared Günther of all

[117] Götz, *Die Glaubensspaltung*, pp. 144–5.
[118] StaB, C3 1223, *Sűpplication Etlicher gemainden im Ambt Culmbach und Bayreuth von wegen allerley beschwerűng wider Ihren (doch unbenanten) pfarrern*, fos. 90–3.
[119] StaB, C3 1223, fos. 94–7 (19 October 1568).

blame. Hedler pointed out that the parish was far from lucrative, as Günther was expected to support a chaplain on a salary that did not extend beyond 130 gulden, and his house was modest. Hedler suggested a more extensive investigation, to bring the 'authors of this conspiracy' to justice as an example for the rest. A local nobleman also expressed his concern over the 'poisoned' letter and gave Günther a very good reference.[120] The superintendent absolved Günther of all blame.

If he was a suitable pastor, or at least innocent of the faults placed before the authorities, what was the motivation behind the accusations directed at Günther? In an earlier deposition (23 July 1568) Günther pointed his finger at a small clique of outlying villagers who refused to help in the construction of the parsonage. This defiance continued, despite the margrave's orders to the contrary, and the term of imprisonment they had suffered for their earlier refusal. In the words of a parish participant, they stood fast as sworn brothers (*geschworne Brüder*) against the pastor.[121] This union of inhabitants believed that the construction of the house – more specifically the aid they were to supply – was detrimental to, or at least in contravention of, their traditional rights. An earlier copy of the complaint (9 December 1567) illustrates the problem:

Each village community complains strongly that such a condition should be introduced by this pastor, which, to the best of their knowledge, has never been done by any pastor before; and (more especially) nor have the parishioners in the past ever been burdened or troubled with the construction of the pastor's residence.[122]

The 'league of conspirators' insisted that previous clergymen had set aside a small store of money for construction, a type of fabric fund. Kaspar Günther was the first pastor to ask for help from the parishioners with the construction of his residence. The parishioners feared Günther's novel demands would take permanent root, thus entering the cycle of annual dues and labour services already extended to the church. Resistance built up to Günther's plan, until some parishioners were meeting in the local inn discussing alternative possibilities (a pseudo-parliament (*Reichstag*) of like-minded beer-swillers, according to the pastor). The Ansbach officials confirmed the picture painted by Günther.[123] Two or three neighbouring communities had set themselves against the pastor; the other parishioners could do nothing. Once the conspirators had committed themselves to resisting Günther's demands, they then won over other members of the parish, and not without resorting to

---

120 StaB, C3 1223, fos. 94–9 (25 October 1568); 100–1 (13 October 1568).
121 StaB, C3 1223, fos. 107–8.
122 StaB, C3 1223, fos. 123–6. *Copia wie sich die Bauern Beschweren als wolle Ihnen der pfarher zu drosenfeldtt Neuerliche Beschwerdt aufdringen.*
123 StaB, C3 1223, fos. 143–54. *Aussage Etlicher Personen in genumener Inquisition den Pfarrherr zu Drosenfeldt und seine Pfarrkhinder betreffent.*

threats.[124] The authorities responded by promising to punish the ringleaders and reimposing the former demands. Associated documentation ends in the year 1568.

A number of related issues emerge from this dispute. There is no doubt that a few parishioners of Neudrossenfeld opposed the impositions simply because they did not want to pay. But two observations of more general application can be adduced from this quarrel.

First, the Lutheran authorities were often forced to impose material change on a community of inhabitants still in thrall to the immutability of nature. Raw materials were available in limited quantity; the regeneration of wood and farm land occurred at a slow, uncertain rate in accord with seasonal rhythms. Labour, at the same time, its yields and its demands, was fixed. The dynamics of distribution and the degree of yearly fluctuation experienced in a regular lifetime was largely absolute; 'a faithful execution of traditional ways in this sphere helped to create a moral atmosphere within the more practical dimensions of tradition which could maintain their force.'[125] That Günther should have made unprecedented demands was not only an inconvenience, and a violation of custom and right,[126] but an infraction against the moral order. His status as a Lutheran pastor did not grant him the right to demand more from the parish without offering something in return. The parishioners thought as Desiderius Hedler suspected: 'I believe however that the godless peasants focused their attack to this end: that this or any other pastor should be paid according to the sermon, like the artisans according to the piece or the daily wage, and no more.'[127]

Secondly, while a demand for income or labour may have precipitated a quarrel, underlying tensions and unresolved disputes often flamed into being as a result. Günther claimed that the very same people who first rallied against him were those who had been punished five years earlier because of their recourse to a wise woman. Günther had refused them confession and an extended quarrel followed.[128] Like some of the clergy who suffered attacks of anticlericalism due to their devotion to

---

[124] As Heinz of Waldau testified, he did not want to speak against the pastor, but he was threatened with exclusion and violence should he not comply: 'Er thue nicht gern wieder den Pfarrer, habe sich aber nicht durffen von der gemeinde sondern, dan sie sich gegen ettlichen vernomen laßen, so sich von Ihnen in diesen bösen handel absondern wollen, Ihnen die gemeinde zuverbietten, und Ihre heuser zu vermachen, oder zuverschlagen'. StaB, C3 1223, fo. 148. One interesting testimony compared the dispute with the snowballing resistance common to the Peasants' War: 'wan er [witness] von diesem handel zü Reden pflegte, vergleichett er den selben mitt dem anfang des Bauernkriegs und sage er haltte von dieser wiederspenstigkheitt eben so viel alß von dem Ergangenem Bauernkhrieg, In welchem das Spiell uber den Bauern auß gangen were, diese ungehorsamen sollten sich auch fursehen'. Stab, C3 1223, fo. 148.

[125] Michael R. Mauss, 'Folklore as an Ethnographic Source: A "Mise au Point"', in Jacques Beauroy, Marc Bertrand, Edward T. Gargan (eds.), *The Wolf and the Lamb: Popular Culture in France* (Saratoga, 1977), p. 118.

[126] This was clearly a concern. For example the fear that 'es möchte ihnen iherlich zw einer gerechtigkeit aufferben.' StaB, C3 1223, fo. 117.

[127] StaB, C3 1223, fo. 98.

[128] StaB, C3 1223, fos. 120; 129–142.

office, Günther may have experienced a similar fate. (One witness testified that he was too diligent in office.) The attempt to rebuild Günther's house, and the unprecedented demands it evinced, gave rise to a dispute which was soon subsumed under the interests of long-term local discontent. The Lutheran authorities may have mounted large-scale efforts to reform clerical maintenance, but each parish, with its distinct concerns, was the context in which they would take hold.

In order for the authorities to effect reconstruction of a pastor's residence or add to a pastor's salary it was often necessary – as the example of Neudrossenfeld illustrates – to overcome deeply embedded animosities and an innate aversion to change, all shaped by local traditions of regulation and concession. What was the nature of this resistance? Was the opposition directed at the church or the state? How were the practical problems of construction and income additions overcome? Is it possible to assess the effort to reform clerical maintenance in general terms?

Although the elimination of the small tithe was one of the main demands of the peasant manifestos in the war of 1525 (on the basis that tithes could not be justified by Scripture and were thus human invention) a rejection of the tithe on religious grounds did not play a role in the disputes later in the century. In 1524 opposition to tithes in Nuremberg's territorial lands had become a source of concern for the council, who were ultimately forced to abolish the collection of tithes during the revolt (1525), but this was a period of violence brought about, in no small part, by clerical preaching against tithes.[129] The lands of Ansbach and Kulmbach were affected in the same manner, but again this should come as no surprise, given the overtly anti-tithe stance of the pamphlet literature and peasant manifestos like the Twelve Articles.[130] Yet this anti-tithe sentiment appears to have ended with the war itself. The visitation of 1528 revealed tithe disputes, but on each occasion the peasants withheld the tithe only when the pastor failed to resume or acknowledge traditional services.[131] There is no evidence to suggest that the evangelical faith, with its emphasis on Holy Writ, engendered a new attitude toward the payment of the tithe, or its non-payment, among the peasantry in Brandenburg-Ansbach-Kulmbach.

An analysis of extant tithe disputes bears this out. In pre-Reformation Oberferrieden (1491) the parishioners were unwilling to pay a tithe on lambs, since it was 'not a convention from the past' (*von alter nit als herkommen sei...*). In 1575, when a quarrel over clerical income resurfaced, the dispute was settled by reference to the 1491 contract. All forms of payment remained constant ('aside from the Papal superstitions and mass' which the Reformation had eliminated);

---

[129] Lawrence P. Buck, 'Opposition to Tithes in the Peasants' Revolt: A Case Study of Nuremberg in 1524', *Sixteenth Century Journal*, 4 (1973), 11–22.

[130] 'Everywhere in Franconia rebels' grievances are directed against small tithes with no biblical justification'. Endres, 'The Peasant War in Franconia,' p. 68; Merx, *Akten zur Geschichte*, vol. 1, p. 11; Tom Scott and Bob Scribner, *The Peasants' War: A History in Documents* (London, 1991), p. 181; Fries, *Die Geschichte des Bauern-Kriegs*, vol. 1, p. 7.

[131] Schornbaum, *Aktenstücke*, pp. 57, 78, 81, 92.

there was no attempt to diminish the tithe payments with reference to a law outside of the original agreement.[132] Repeatedly, tithe disagreements were contested and settled with reference to an original, pre-Reformation contract. The parishioners would justify their refusal, as at Frommetsfelden in 1571, on the basis of a written agreement, an 'old sealed letter established one hundred years before'.[133] Parishioners of Hechlingen went so far as to refuse certain tithes when their original (1448) sealed contract was at hand; whenever it was thought to be lost, however, they would render up dues without resistance.[134] When the tithe in Ansbach and Kulmbach was refused or contested – and these occasions were few – it was not placed within the framework of a theological or specifically evangelical discourse. Both the parishioners and the clergymen made reference to local custom, tradition, and the powerful endorsement granted by a margravial contract. For all parties involved, a tithe dispute was a local concern; it had specific legal and temporal reference, and nothing to do with God's Word.[135]

The rarity of open resistance to the tithe, and the lack of theoretical alternatives to tithe payment, point to an attitude which was very much a medieval inheritance. Resistance to the tithe was provoked by the conditions of individual parishes; a supraregional uprising against tithe payment, such as the Peasants' War of 1525, was rare.[136] This is not to say that such dues were suffered gladly. The visitors of Kulmbach labelled a schoolmaster's lament over the parishioners' reluctance to pay his salary 'a common complaint in all places'. Sebastian Faßnacht wondered whether Christ himself could get the tithes with any greater ease, were he the pastor of Schalkhausen.[137] But there was nothing fundamentally rebellious about this behaviour. It was rather indicative of the peasant mentality, a *Bauernschläue* overinterpreted by Luther to mean a crafty ingenuity, when in truth it was a native pragmatism, employed by the peasantry in all of their dealings – from trade to faith to magic – to secure the utmost advantage from a limited reservoir of possibilities.[138]

James C. Scott, in his work on peasant resistance, has identified a stratagem behind this reluctance to pay fees. Scott entitles it 'resistance without protest' or 'everyday acts of peasant resistance' which he views, over the long term, as more

---

[132] LKAN, MDS, 122 T.1 (Sunday before Saint Veit's Day 1491); (8 August 1575).
[133] LKAN, MKA, Spez. 135 (8 May 1571).
[134] LKAN, MKA, Spez. 394, fo. 218.
[135] Source materials for the above paragraph: LKAN, MDL, 51 Geslau 1588; LKAN, MDG 71, fos. 20; 44; 63; 138; LKAN, MKA, Spez. 394, fos. 1–282. Hechlingen tithe dispute 1525–76; LKAN, MKA, 135, (3 May 1574–26 May 1574); StaB, C2 1858, (28 October 1581–29 April 1583); StaB, C2 986, 1592; LKAN, MKH, XX 3, fo. 5.
[136] Giles Constable, 'Resistance to Tithes in the Middle Ages', *The Journal of Ecclesiastical History*, 13 (1962), 172–85.
[137] LKAN, MSK, 157. Steinbach (2 October 1572); LKAN, MKA, Spez. 756, 'Anno Nativitatis Christi 1552' (seventeenth-century copy of original).
[138] Not unlike the notion of limited resources common to many tribal societies. See G. M. Foster, 'Peasant Society and the Image of Limited Good', *American Anthropologist*, 67 (1965), 293–315.

deleterious to the appropriating authorities than explosions of discontent like rebellions or mass movements. The most damaging type of tithe resistance occurred in forms of flight, evasion, misreporting, false declaration, fraud, concealment, and noncompliance. Often this violation of a tax, rent, or property became a custom or tradition, acquiring an authority of its own.[139] The gradual transmutation of resistance into custom hardened the parish mind to reform or correction and resulted in discord between the pastor and the parish. Such a mentality, in addition to the problems associated with the increase in population, the denuded woodlands and clearings, the general economic malaise, and the complex of underlying social tensions in the parishes, made the effort to improve clerical maintenance difficult.[140] How did the authorities overcome these problems?

The margrave could approach the reform of clerical maintenance from two angles. He could effect improvement from within, keeping a check on the management of funds in the parish, or he could impose order from above, at the expense of local traditions of rule.

In order to secure an addition, the clergyman could either submit an application to a higher official, secular or spiritual, or he could send his request directly to Ansbach. Upon reception of the application, a regional official made an inquiry so as to determine whether the increase could be shouldered through parish funds alone or whether it had to be raised from an external source. If support from an external source was necessary, the wealth from a local foundation was used and integrated into the church fund. Small foundations, most commonly in the form of a chapel, were generally used *ad pias causas* in accordance with the Peace of Augsburg (1555). They were not ravaged and destroyed for secular ends; but with the original purpose lost, they fell prey to the erosion of time and neglect, either disappearing altogether or assimilated into the church.[141] In other instances, if the request for an increase was approved, a neighbouring monastery might be expected to raise the money. (It was not unusual at the end of the century for the monastery administrators to plead poverty to the demands stemming from the chancellery.)[142] Once the necessary steps had been taken, the addition was joined with the parish funds and this wealth was managed by the wardens of the church.

The visitation returns are littered with complaints about the mismanagement of parish funds. The fund itself might be very meagre, composed of what was collected

---

[139] James C. Scott, 'Resistance without Protest and without Organization: Peasant Opposition to the Islamic *Zakat* and the Christian Tithe', *Comparative Studies in Society and History*, 29 (1987), 417–52; James C. Scott, *Weapons of the Weak. Everyday Forms of Peasant Resistance* (London, 1985); James C. Scott, *Domination and the Arts of Resistance: Hidden Transcripts* (London, 1990).

[140] On the scarcity of natural resources and the difficulties this caused, see Karl Hasel, 'Die Entwicklung von Waldeigentum und Waldnutzung im späten Mittelalter als Ursache für die Entstehung des Bauernkriegs', *Allgemeine Forst- und Jagdzeitung*, 138 (1967), 141–50.

[141] Johann Sigmund Strebel, *Franconia Illustrata*. (Schwabach, 1761), p. 17; Stieber, *Historische und Topographische Nachricht*, p. 288; Simon, *Evangelische Kirchengeschichte Bayerns*, pp. 293–5.

[142] LKAN, MKA, Spez. 537, fo. 7; Muck, *Beiträge zur Geschichte von Kloster Heilsbronn*, p. 191.

The clergyman in context

during services.[143] The church fund might be in debt; indeed, parishioners themselves might owe the church large sums of money.[144] Patrons interfered with the parish audit, thinking that the wealth was under their care. In the chapter of Gunzenhausen, parish funds fell to the management of men ranging from the officials of Gunzenhausen, the superintendent, the officials in Eichstätt, the regional official of Hohentrüdingen, the administrators of Heidenheim and Ansbach, or, in the case of Windsfeld (a *freidorff*), the parishioners alone.[145] It was quite common for the pastor to be excluded from the yearly audit altogether, in spite of the margrave's continued effort to eliminate this offence.[146] The caretakers of the church fund often used the money for private ends. A report from Langenzenn in 1584 made it clear to the margrave '[that] we must assume from this that they [the wardens] would fain want to have, as has happened up to now, a free hand with provisions and other things … which, however, is in no way to be permitted to them.'[147]

To counter such license the margrave introduced yearly audits. Although the 1536 visitation ordered inspection of the common chests, it was not until the visitations of 1565 that an annual inspection threatened the church wardens to any real degree.[148] In 1578 the chapter ordinance commissioned the superintendents to investigate whether the church wardens handled the church funds with honesty and whether they made the requisite repairs to ailing parish buildings (which would include the church, the pastor's residence, and the school). By 1594 the margrave expected the elected representatives in charge of the parish fund to keep an orderly register of all income and expenses, which they would then present before the superintendent in the annual visitation.[149] Abuses continued despite this crusade; but it is one measure of the effort made to reform the management of parish funds that the complaints brought forward in the visitations rarely repeat themselves from year to year. Examples of such abuse in the visitation returns were, in the majority of cases, investigated and corrected. In the realm of church finance, parish liberties were severely curtailed.

It was not always feasible to regulate matters from within the parish. In the case of a reconstruction or a sizeable increase in a clerical salary, the margrave and his

---

143 LKAN, MSK, 157 (22 October 1572). 'Das Gottshauβ ist arm, und hat nichts mehr, den was die Sontag ins Secklein gefellet…'
144 StaN, *Ansbacher Neues Generalrepertorium*, no. 49, rep. nr. 103ᵉ, fo. 161; LKAN, MKA, Spez. 625, fos. 25–7. The indebted parishioners of Oberferrieden asked the margrave to bear their borrowing with patience. Some parishioners were up to twenty-three gulden in debt.
145 LKAN, MDG, 71, fo. 72 (1578).
146 StaN, *Ansbacher Neues Generalrepertorium*, no. 49, rep. nr. 103ᵉ, fo. 13; LKAN, MKl, 51, *Acta Specialis Visitationis Capituli Leütershusain 1584*; StaB, C2 1831, fo. 1, *Visitation Acta der Superinte[n]dents Wunsiedel Anno 92*; LKAN, MSK, 157, Stammbach (6 November 1589). This was a problem in the pre-Reformation church as well. See the comments in Götz, *Das Pfarrbuch des Stephan May*, p. 82.
147 LKAN, MDLz, 676 T.1 (22 June 1584).
148 Sehling, p. 320, 352–3.
149 *Corpus Constitutionum Brandenburgico-Culmbacensium* (1746), pp. 365, 280–2.

98

officials were forced to intervene directly, without waiting on local initiative. Reform was interposed on the parish, not coerced from the parish officials. Three cases from the year 1562 illustrate the nature and extent of this intervention.

In July of 1562, upon the conclusion of the visitation, the secular officials of Uffenheim were commissioned to inspect the condition of the residences in Langensteinach and Adelhofen. The officials inspected the church funds (*heÿligen*) of both villages and found that neither could support the proposed reconstruction. Ansbach acknowledged this state of affairs and suggested that the monastery of Heilsbronn, which exercised patronage, should supply the needed support for Langensteinach. The abbot was ordered to render up the appropriate building materials and whatever wealth was needed from the monastery's stores. The building fund would then be given to the church wardens of the parish. In reaction to the Ansbach directives, the administrator of Heilsbronn pleaded poverty. Lacking in cash, he suggested that the monastery's woodlands be used to supply the materials, as they could be had for minimal expense.[150] Ansbach followed this advice, and the council delegated a member of the parish to oversee the construction and to keep a list of all expenses.[151] In Adelhofen, in a similar manner, the wealth was gathered from local foundations. The official was to keep a record of all transactions; he was to inspect the buildings on a yearly basis, and indeed all parish buildings within the compass of his district.

One year later the pastor of Münchenaurach, Andreas Trebel, wrote to Ansbach requesting repairs to his 'very small and meagre' quarters. A monastery official in the company of a group of men versed in the construction trade inspected the building and recommended repairs running to at least forty gulden.[152] Negotiations continued for the next few years over the construction of a cellar, and it was not until 1587 that the possibility of reconstruction was once again reconsidered. As before, the monastery official assessed the house as in need of repair; it should be built from scratch, he added, and the expense must be supplied from margravial coffers, since the parish in question had no independent income.[153] Blueprints and estimates were drawn up by the monastery administrator. According to the official report, the residence had been visited in the past by the regional official of Cadolzburg, an authority from Ansbach, and the chief engineer (*Bawmeister*) himself.[154] Ansbach gave the orders to rebuild in June 1588. The construction was expected to take place in line with the proposals drafted at court and the parishioners were to help with shipment and repairs.[155] As the parish was home to subjects of Eichstätt and the nobleman Ernst von

---

[150] LKAN, MKA, Spez. 537, fos. 2–9. (23 July 1562); (30 July 1562); (26 August 1562).
[151] LKAN, MKA, Spez. 537 (9 September 1562), fo. 11: 'und furter yemandt auß der Gemeinde des orts uber solchen Baw verordndne und gebürliche Rechnung von Inen nemen.'
[152] LKAN, MDB, 324 (6 May 1564).
[153] LKAN, MDB, 324 (16 May 1587).
[154] LKAN, MDB, 324 (13 April 1588).
[155] LKAN, MDB, 324 (21 June 1588 & 21 August 1588).

Crailsheim, some of the outlying hamlets (*eingepfarte*) resisted, pleading poverty. Even the margrave's subjects in Münchenaurach protested that such service was not possible: it would force them into beggary. Indeed, the regional official of Cadolzburg supported their objections, suggesting that neighbouring subjects of the monastery be inducted for the task.[156] But Ansbach was unmoved; the parishioners were forced to assist. In 1589 the house was largely completed, and the following year a detailed inventory was taken, exposing to the authorities the use, and misuse, of funds in Münchenaurach.[157]

In the year 1562, as the pastor Johannes Schmidt of Offenbau waited for an increase in his salary, measures were taken to rebuild his house. Instructions from the chancellery outlined the process of reconstruction: all of the parishioners were to help with transport and construction; forty-five gulden was to be provided from an ecclesiastical source; the villagers themselves had to undertake the reconstruction.[158] The sources fall silent about the rebuilding. In 1576, however, the parishioners of Offenbau wrote another letter of complaint about Schmidt.[159] Schmidt was accused of letting the residence fall into disrepair. It seems that this accusation was in part the dénouement of a latent power struggle within the parish.[160] The parishioners had refused to help the pastor from at least 1574 onwards. By 1585 another supplication from the pastor spoke of a crumbling residence; two years later he claimed a new stable had been necessary for fourteen years.[161] Ansbach mounted an investigation. All of the neighbouring subjects in and around the parish were listed (answering, in total, to five different lords). The church fund was assessed. In 1592 the directives went out to rebuild. In order to overcome the poverty of the church fund, and to ensure that the village quarrel would not preclude reconstruction, a local tax was introduced (*paw steur*) and the responsibility of repair was placed directly upon the parish.

In each of the cases cited above, the margrave was able to facilitate reform of clerical maintenance by shifting the locus of control away from the parish to the chancellery or to one of its district appendages. The very process of investigation and correction defused the impediments hampering reform. If a pastor needed an addition to his income an official was sent to the parish, tithes were catalogued, church funds were assessed, village rights, prerogatives, customs, and claims were reviewed, and all of this was done by a margravial official, who then inherited the annual job of scrutinising the parish audit. If a church building had to be repaired

---

[156] LKAN, MDB, 324 (24 September 1588): 'andern benachtbartten Ämptischen und Clösterischen Unterthonen...'.

[157] LKAN, MDB, 324 (28 August 1590).

[158] LKAN, MKA, Spez. 640 (16 September 1562). The official was to ensure 'das von den eingepfardten zu solchem Baw mit fueren und auch anderer handt raichung zur notturfft hulff gethon'.

[159] LKAN, MKA, Spez. 640 (30 June 1576).

[160] LKAN, MKA, Spez. 640. Letter from Schmidt, 1576.

[161] LKAN, MKA, Spez. 640 (2 March 1587).

or rebuilt, the church was inspected, supplies were sought, first from within the parish, and then from a neighbouring foundation; once the construction began, building was supervised by a monastery official, a district authority, or a parish resident commissioned by the margrave. The margrave supervised every stage of the process. The parishioners were given specific duties; if they resisted, their legal status was investigated; if a village quarrel hindered progress, an investigation was mounted or a solution was proposed (like the above building tax) which could, by its very nature, circumvent local disputes. This type of investigation, as the authorities observed in 1570, was not a legacy of the past, but a recent innovation.[162] The process of rebuilding and remuneration was slow, often punctuated with years of inactivity or resistance, but a start had been made and a policy was in motion. The Reformation in Ansbach and Kulmbach brought with it a greater degree of supervision and control over the parish church and the maintenance of its servants.

The introduction of the Lutheran pastor affected the lives of the rural inhabitants. The territorial church in Brandenburg-Ansbach-Kulmbach did have a clerical estate suitable enough to preach the faith; the authorities did take concrete steps to improve income and housing; the margravial officials did intervene into local affairs and defuse resistance to fees and dues. The territorial church, in its efforts to maintain a Lutheran pastorate, made its presence felt. But this was only one aspect of the Reformation, and the regulation of parish wealth was only one step in the process of religious change. In many ways, an analysis of the reform of clerical maintenance obscures as much as it reveals. The Lutheran authorities were able to staff the rural parishes with a working clerical estate, but their efforts often unleashed considerable resistance at the parish level. As will be shown, the Lutheran reformers did not encounter a rural populace quite as pliant as the weathered churches they endeavoured to repair.

---

[162] LKAN, MDLz, 666, no. 213 (16 March 1570). A correspondence dealing with the supervision of the construction and maintenance of the church buildings near Langenzenn by the court. It contains the observation: 'solches beÿ der herschaft mit alters nit herkommen gewest'.

4

The Reformation and parish morality

VILLAGE CULTURE AND RELIGIOUS CHANGE

A woodcut of 1540, attributed to Lucas Cranach the Younger, depicts the charred remains of four criminals, each bound to a stake, with the slightly altered text of Romans 13:4 providing a moral for the reader: 'The sovereign powers are not to be feared by those who do good, but rather by those who do ill. For they do not wield the sword in vain. They are God's servants – against those who do evil, an avenger.'[1] The juridical complex of sixteenth-century Germany was a brutal system of punishment and discipline, exercised in the public realm. Punishment was theatrical, a 'theatre of horror,' and it sent out its message to the subject population: the sovereign powers would exact revenge with violence in equal proportion to the crime; they would not tolerate disorder; they alone had the divine right and exclusive authority to dispense justice.[2] The Reformation did not directly challenge or displace this notion. Indeed, in their need to secure the foundations for their respective faiths, the reformers invested the secular authorities with even greater power. Martin Luther, by limiting the powers of Christ's kingdom to purely spiritual concerns and granting the sword to the temporal realm alone, 'sanctioned an unparalleled extension of the range of their [secular authorities'] powers'.[3] Although the secular rulers had been extending the range of their powers before Luther offered his theological justification to this trend, the Reformation did grant an unprecedented strength of rule to the early modern state. It is perhaps significant that the four criminals mentioned above met their fate in Wittenberg.

The relationship between the early modern state and the church in this confessional age has become a subject of interest for historians of sixteenth- and seventeenth-century Germany. Scholars have begun to investigate the implications of this close association of church and state and its effect on the subject

---

A condensed version of this chapter appears as 'The Reformation and Parish Morality in Brandenburg-Ansbach-Kulmbach,' *Archiv für Reformationsgeschichte* (1996).

[1] Max Geisberg, *The German Single-Leaf Woodcut: 1500–1550* (New York, 1974), vol. 2, p. 639.

[2] Richard van Dülmen, *Theatre of Horror. Crime and Punishment in Early Modern Germany*, trans. Elisabeth Neu (Oxford, 1990); Michel Foucault, *Discipline and Punish. The Birth of the Prison* (New York, 1977), pp. 3–69.

[3] Quentin Skinner, *The Foundations of Modern Political Thought* (Cambridge, 1978), vol. 2, p. 15.

Village culture and religious change

population. Gerhard Oestreich, for example, originated the notion of 'social disciplining' to describe the complementary developments taking place in political, philosophical, and religious thought, all of which worked to a similar end: the creation of obedient subjects. Oestreich's observation that confessional change might be seen as just one kindred element in a broader context of social change throws a different light on sixteenth-century developments. Scholars such as Ernst Walter Zeeden have since suggested that the Reformation and Counter-Reformation were simply variations on a structural theme. Both movements, Catholic and Protestant, were in essence similar programmes of reform. Heinz Schilling and Wolfgang Reinhard have gone one step further by developing the concept of confessionalisation. Confessionalisation assumes that religion and the more secular aspects of society were inexorably linked; the church was of central importance to sixteenth-century life and any attempt to reform religion would necessarily include the wider dimensions of German society.[4]

Confessionalisation thus brings much into view, including the categories of social history, the paradigm of state building, the investigation of power relations and the apparatus of rule, the related philosophies on the role of the state, and the intellectual impact of the reform movements on the popular mind, the study of *mentalités*. The growth of the modern state and the fixing of confessional boundaries was part of the same process. As John Calvin saw it, the result was 'a public manifestation of religion ... among Christians', guided and maintained by the civil government.[5]

Confessionalisation, as an explanatory model, runs the risk of concealing as much as it reveals. It would be all too easy for the historian to overlook the particulars of the process in order to save the appearance of the whole. As Heinz Schilling has warned, 'We must strictly maintain the epistemological and methodological distinction between analytical concepts of this kind and historical reality in order to prevent them from assuming an existence independent

---

[4] Gerhard Oestreich, *Neostoicism and the Early Modern State* (Cambridge, 1982); Ernst Walter Zeeden, *Die Entstehung der Konfessionen. Grundlagen und Formen der Konfessionsbildung im Zeitalter der Glaubenskämpfe* (Munich, 1965); Ernst Walter Zeeden, *Konfessionsbildung: Studien zur Reformation, Gegenreformation und katholischen Reform* (Stuttgart, 1985). On Confessionalisation, see Wolfgang Reinhard, 'Zwang zur Konfessionalisierung? Prolegomena zu einer Theorie des konfessionellen Zeitalters', *Zeitschrift für historische Forschung*, 10 (1983), 257–77; Wolfgang Reinhard, 'Konfession und Konfessionalisierung in Europa', in *Bekenntnis und Geschichte* (Augsburg, 1981), pp. 165–89; Heinz Schilling, *Religion, Political Culture and the Emergence of Early Modern Society*, trans. Stephen G. Burnett (Leiden, 1992); Heinz Schilling, 'Sündenzucht und frühneuzeitliche Sozialdisziplinierung. Die calvinistische, presbyteriale Kirchenzucht in Emden vom 16. bis 19. Jahrhundert', in Georg Schmidt, (ed.), *Stände und Gesellschaft im Alten Reich* (Stuttgart, 1989), pp. 265–302; Heinz Schilling, 'Reformierte Kirchenzucht als Sozialdisziplinierung? Die Tätigkeit des Emder Presbyteriums in den Jahren 1557–1562', in Wilfried Ehrbrecht and Heinz Schilling, (eds.), *Niederlande und Nordwestdeutschland* (Cologne, 1983), pp. 261–327. For a bibliographical essay, see R. Po-Chai Hsia, *Social Discipline in the Reformation. Central Europe 1550–1750* (London, 1989), pp. 188–212.
[5] Cited in William J. Bouwsma, *John Calvin. A Sixteenth Century Portrait* (Oxford, 1988), p. 213.

of the historical record'.[6] This chapter will examine the 'historical reality' of one aspect of the broader notion of confessionalisation: the extent to which the Lutheran authorities were able to discipline the parish population.

The ability to discipline and control the parishioners was a central priority of the church, whether Lutheran, Calvinist, or Catholic. This is not to suggest that the desire to reform parish morality was the only dimension to the process of religious change, for neither the Reformation nor the Counter-Reformation was exclusively concerned with morality; but of the many concerns and issues addressed by the theological writings of men such as Luther, Calvin, Peter Canisius, and Martin Bucer, morality was given a high profile. Without a doubt, the realms of church and state discipline retained certain boundaries throughout the sixteenth and seventeenth centuries; and yet, as the notion of confessionalisation has suggested, there was an unprecedented fusion of interests in this period. The discipline of the parishioner was one area where church and state in the Lutheran principalities joined together to realise a common goal. What were the stages of development in this campaign to reform parish morality? And did it actually affect the individual in the parish?

The Reformation was introduced into the lands of the Holy Roman Empire over the space of many decades; different territories advanced in different stages.[7] Nevertheless, it is useful to highlight certain stages in the Protestant lands when social disciplining and the growth of local confessional power, still true to the passions that saw their intensification, were at their height. Heinz Schilling has set this dynamic of religious and state reform in four stages: The first stage, the 1540s to the 1560s, was a period of preparation; this was the era of quarrels, debates, and meetings while the reformers ironed out the theological complexities. The second stage, running through the 1570s, was a decade of confessional confrontation: distinct churches evolved and the battle lines were drawn. The third stage (1580–1620) saw the high point of confessionalisation as the religious groupings made efforts to consolidate the faith within their secular borders.[8] Schilling suggests that this development penetrated into the towns, the villages, and ultimately into the household. Finally, the condition of war and the Peace of Westphalia (1648) saw the weakening of the process. Schilling's analysis views events in broad terms and enfolds a wealth of factors under its approximate headings, but it does offer a plausible division for the process of reform as it occurred in Brandenburg-Ansbach-Kulmbach.

The German parishioner in the Lutheran territories was subject to increasing

---

[6] Schilling, *Religion, Political Culture*, 196.
[7] Walter Ziegler, 'Territorium and Reformation. Überlegungen und Fragen', *Historisches Jahrbuch*, 110, (1990), 52–75.
[8] Schilling, *Religion, Political Culture*, pp. 205–45.

scrutiny as the mandates and ordinances issued to dictate his behaviour grew more complex and substantial.[9] This was not a radical break with the past: the medieval ruler had been just as concerned with the moral comportment of his subjects. Nor was secular intervention into the realm of ecclesiastical affairs new, as some secular rulers had exercised considerable control over the pre-Reformation church in their territories.[10] But this period did see an unprecedented union of disciplinary realms: there was little or no distinction between secular and spiritual surveillance by the close of the century. For the historian, it might be germane to delineate between two processes, between the 'history of crime' and the 'history of sin', as long as we do not lose sight of the obvious: the object of disciplinary control was always the individual, whether for his 'deliberate and malicious intent against another person's rights' or his disruption of the 'sacral-transcendental unity of the eucharistic community'. Both the church and the state wished to impose uniform moral control, and the Reformation allowed for many principalities – Ansbach and Kulmbach among them – to accelerate that trend.[11] The parishioner, as a consequence, was subject to greater scrutiny.

In the early decades of the evangelical movement, religious change in the parishes of Ansbach and Kulmbach was implemented and contained by the secular authorities, in particular the leading officials of each administrative district. Casimir's 1524 resolution, anticipating the widespread unrest of the following year, ordered the secular officials to pay close attention to the nature of religious disputation. Parishioners who abused the Word of God or incited agitation, whatever their standing, were to be punished. Georg the Pious also relied upon his local officials to oversee parish religion. The 1528 Ansbach resolution invested the district authorities with the task of monitoring sermons and reporting suspect clergy to the margrave; the same officials had to hold vacant benefices in suspension until the margrave approved the appointment of a pastor and, when necessary, the officials might remove recalcitrant Catholic priests from office.[12]

In 1528, Georg the Pious, following the advice of the Ansbach clergyman Andreas Althamer (who was inspired by the Reformation in Saxony), established the ecclesiastical office of superintendent. As we have seen, superintendents were, in effect, coadjutors for the district officials: the region, or operational basis, of each superintendency matched the secular divisions in the principality. From the

9   Compare Paul Münch, *Zucht und Ordnung. Reformierte Kirchenverfassungen im 16. und 17. Jahrhundert* (Stuttgart, 1978).
10 Manfred Schulze, *Fürsten und Reformation. Geistliche Reformpolitik weltlicher Fürsten vor der Reformation* (Tübingen, 1991); Helmut Rankl, *Das vorreformatorische landesherrliche Kirchenregiment in Bayern (1378–1526)* (Munich, 1971).
11 This paragraph refers to the observations made by G. R. Elton in his introduction to J. S. Cockburn (ed.) *Crime in England 1500–1800* (London, 1977), pp. 1–14 and Heinz Schilling, ' "History of Crime" or "History of Sin"? Some Reflections on the Social History of Early Modern Church Discipline', in E. Kouri and T. Scott. (eds.), *Politics and Society in Reformation Europe* (London, 1987), pp. 289–310.
12 Sehling, 80–1, 103, 105–6.

late 1520s until well into mid-century, the highest ecclesiastical officials (super-intendents) and the margrave's district officials performed similar roles in the same jurisdictional districts.[13] It was a system of governance, as Althamer pointed out in 1534, which was easily abused;[14] but it was not improved upon until 1556, when margrave Georg Friedrich and the pastor Georg Karg devised a lasting constitution for church government. As has been detailed above, the principality was divided into chapters (superintendencies) with a superintendent (or deacon) at the head of each chapter and two consistories, one in Ansbach and the other in Kulmbach, to centralise the flow of command. Thus by the end of the century the church and its officials had some degree of self-governance, though the super-intendents were never entirely independent of the district officials, and the district officials were still called upon to assist the superintendents in their ecclesiastical duties. The yearly visitations, for instance, took place in the presence of a superintendent and a district official.[15]

The Reformation was legislated from above by the margrave. Throughout the sixteenth century secular mandates, church ordinances, and visitation orders were issued from Ansbach setting the course of reform. As the Lutheran church became more secure in the principality, and as the machinery of government became more efficient, the number of mandates increased and the contents became more detailed. Moreover, as the century unfolded, the publications began to probe deeper and deeper into parish affairs; the conduct and belief of the parishioners became central concerns. At century's end visitation ordinances empowered the visitors to amass a detailed inventory of village life. The development is clear to see. The second visitation of 1536 concerned itself with traditional 'church' affairs: the schools, the piety of the parishioners, the conduct of the pastors, parish funds, the nature of the local service. In 1565, the visitors began to investigate the frequency of blasphemy, magic, gluttony, usury, and the rate of attendance at formal worship. When the visitation orders were expanded in 1578, suspect parish customs and activities were listed explicitly (i.e. ...*rock-enstuben, scheidweg oder letzrocken*...), rather than falling under the general heading of 'unsuitable pastimes'. The 1594 consistory ordinance considered 'blasphemy, profanation of the Sabbath, contempt for the Word of God, sin and vice, adultery, whoring, sexual offence, irreconcilable hate, injury to life and limb, drunkenness, forbidden games, theft, usury, unjust contracts, [and] lies' as matters in need of correction.[16]

In addition to the church edicts and visitation orders the margrave had the traditional secular mandates at his disposal. Secular mandates, such as the police

---

13 The 1556 synod ordinance, for example, expected the district official (and the other higher officials in his district) to assist the superintendent in almost all aspects of church affairs – including the appointment, discipline, and punishment of clergy. Sehling, 338–43.

14 Kolde, *Andreas Althamer*, pp. 126–7.

15 Sehling, 350, 360, 335–43, 346–64, 379–96.

16 Sehling, 317–24, 346–59, 352, 386.

ordinances and the criminal court ordinances, generally dealt with infractions of the peace – murder or robbery – or crimes against the property of the margrave and his subjects. But there was no strict boundary between secular and spiritual offences: German princes often punished crimes traditionally reserved for the ecclesiastical powers.[17] In Brandenburg-Ansbach-Kulmbach, there was also a considerable degree of overlap between the concerns embodied in the visitation ordinances and the secular mandates of the sixteenth century. The 1516 Brandenburg Criminal Court Ordinance (based upon the 1506 *Bambergensis*) invested the secular authorities with the power to process the crimes of blasphemy, gluttony, heresy, magic, and adultery.[18] Police ordinances, following suit, focused on village customs and gatherings intimately bound up with popular religious observance and village custom: baptismal feasts, marriage celebrations, and spinning bees. Ansbach issued police ordinances in 1549 and 1566, which were then superseded in 1572 when the Franconian estates drafted a police ordinance for the entire circle.[19] These secular mandates, like the ecclesiastical ordinances listed above, brought parish activities under the scrutiny of the margrave's higher authorities.

In Brandenburg-Ansbach-Kulmbach, there was thus a network of higher officials in place to enforce the conditions of the Lutheran church; there was also a thorough corpus of official publications detailing the conditions and expectations of the church as defined by the margrave and his theological advisors. To an extent unmatched by the pre-Reformation diocesan system, church governance became a concern of secular and spiritual authorities alike. In particular the desire to regulate the conduct of the parishioners and the drive to enforce the disciplinary regulations of the Lutheran church grew into a shared responsibility. The church and the state, in their pursuit to control and reform the behaviour of the parishioner, worked to similar ends. 'The secular process of social disciplining was attended and assisted by the religious disciplining of the new confessional churches.'[20] Once this union of purpose is conceded, the question naturally arises as to whether the reforming effort of the Lutheran church in Brandenburg-Ansbach-Kulmbach was successful. Did the Lutheran authorities realise the

---

[17] Roland Axtmann, ' "Police" and the Formation of the Modern State', *German History*, 10 (1992), 39–61.

[18] The relationship between the ordinances has been examined in Heinrich Zoepfl, *Die Peinliche Gerichtsordnung Kaiser Karls V. nebst der Bamberger und der Brandenburger Halsgerichtsordnung* (Heidelberg, 1842).

[19] *Polliceyord/nung etlicher pu[n]ct/unnd Artickel, in welchen/vermög des heiligen Römischen Reichs...Anno/MDLXVI.* Copy in LKAN, MDF, No. 1. For the emergence of the 1572 Franconian ordinance, see Rudolf Endres, 'Zur wirtschaftlichen und sozialen Lage in Franken vor dem Dreißigjährigen Krieg', *Jahrbuch für fränkische Landesforschung*, 28 (1968), 38–43. *Des löblichen Frenkischen/Reichskraiß, verainte und verglichne Policey/ordnung etlicher Puncten und Artickeln...Abgehandelt zu Nürmberg, den/12 Maij, Anno 72.* Copy in LKAN, MDF, 1, no. 26.

[20] Thomas Winkelbauer, 'Sozialdisziplinierung und Konfessionalisierung durch Grundherren in den österreichischen und böhmischen Ländern im 16. und 17. Jahrhundert', *Zeitschrift für historische Forschung*, 19 (1992), 320.

disciplinary aims of the territorial church at the level of the parish? The fate of some parish activities prohibited by the church provides insight.

The police ordinance, although a secular mandate, nevertheless dealt with behaviour within the purview of religious morality, behaviour policed by both secular and spiritual officials. Neither the nature nor the imputed consequence of immorality was considered in strictly religious or profane terms. According to the margrave, the ill-conduct outlined in the police ordinances enraged God; if it were not done away with, 'the wrath of the Lord' would visit the principality. As in the imperial mandates, fear for the parishioners' salvation was the opening overture. And yet this did not eclipse another real concern in the ordinances – 'superfluous and unnecessary expense'. Parishioners continued to hold large and expensive celebrations. According to a letter dispatched to the superintendency of Feucht-wangen, the limitations placed upon public celebrations in the 1549 ordinance were held in small regard. The traditional dichotomy, thought to be at the root of most social problems, was cited as the culprit: the common weal (*gemeiner nutz*) was suffering at the hands of a few individuals who pursued their own ends (*aignem nutz*) irrespective of the needs of the community.[21] The police ordinances prescribed the proper bounds: Marriage celebrations lasting more than two days were forbidden; numbers should be limited to forty-two people who could partake in no more than four meals.[22] In 1572 the numbers fell yet further to thirty people and two meals. Baptismal feasts could include no more than twelve close friends and relatives, and the meal should be done away with altogether, replaced by a simple bread and cheese repast. Other gatherings were forbidden. Drinking at the taverns had to end at nine o'clock in the summer, eight in winter. The stakes at gambling could not exceed half a gulden. The streets must be empty when the inns closed, and even in time of celebration night dances were disallowed. These restrictions were directed at the inhabitants of the towns and villages, sometimes less indulgently at those in the countryside. The nobility remained exempt.

That the ordinances should have focused almost exclusively on 'religious' events such as baptism and marriage comes as no surprise. The customs surrounding baptism and marriage were enmeshed within what has been termed the 'life cycle' of the European peasantry and figured large in daily life. Local rites and practices served the function of marking the passage of time and honouring the extended family, two important moments for a society in thrall to the earth and structured according to clan. The identity of the village and its members was bound up in the celebration, and the festivities and expense often took on gargantuan proportions to match local pride. Quite aside from the function these celebrations assumed as liminal periods in a rite of passage, it must be said that

---

[21] LKAN, MDF, 1 (12 october 1566).
[22] Urban authorities frequently issued independent mandates to limit the abuses at marriage feasts. Walter Bartl, 'Bayreuther Polizei- und Handwerkssatzungen in der ersten Hälfte des 16. Jahrhunderts', *Archiv für Geschichte von Oberfranken*, 72 (1992), 184–5.

they were also witness to great bouts of drinking, eating, and general excess. Jacob Wimpheling wrote of the Alsatian peasantry:

The peasantry in our region and many other parts of Germany have become lavish and arrogant on account of their wealth. I know peasants who spend so much at the wedding of their sons and daughters that, for the same sum, they could buy a house and a plot of soil, and still have enough for a small vineyard.[23]

The police ordinances attempted to eradicate the excess associated with baptismal and marital feasts, and the shift in religious authority ushered in by the evangelical movement helped sharpen the focus. The Reformation did not introduce the concern with village feasts;[24] but the state had never before had the moral justification, nor the reach of officials, as it did once it became the self-professed handmaiden of God. But how much control did the Lutheran authorities exercise?

The villagers paid little heed to the directives of the police ordinances. In the superintendency of Kulmbach, the traditional baptismal revelry lasted well into the latter decades of the century. As the Kulmbach visitor lamented in 1586, the 'unchristian and contemptuous life and nature' of the customs surrounding childbirth endured. On reception of an invitation, the godparents and neighbours would congregate at the nearest inn and drink a gulden or a thaler-worth of beer. When it was time to attend the baptism, the godfather was too drunk to go; he could neither stand nor speak. On occasion, the child's father was altogether too intoxicated to attend, and another man would go in his place.[25] Once they had left the church, the parishioners would return to the tavern and spend more money on beer.[26] (Women were singled out by one clergyman as being especially prone to spend time at the tavern following this rite. When reprimanded, they claimed that they did it for the infants' health.)[27] The visitation reports mention the waste, the expense, and the sheer duration of these forbidden practices. Baptismal celebrations continued throughout the century, despite the margrave's continual efforts to eradicate them. The practice of *Kretzentragen*, for instance, wherein the godparents would send the mother eggs, cheese, and other edibles expecting gifts in return, was expressly forbidden in 1580, but continued none the less.[28]

The campaign to curb the surfeit of 'immoderacy, coarseness, and excess' at

---

23 Cited in Alfred Hagelstange, *Süddeutsches Bauernleben im Mittelalter* (Leipzig, 1898), pp. 239–40.
24 See the 1488 Zurich mandate in Leo Zehnder, *Volkskundliches in der älteren schweizerischen Chronistik* (1976), p. 122.
25 LKAN, MSK, 157, *Acta Visitationis in der Culmbacher Superintendentz im 1586*, fo. 4. (my pagination); LKAN, MSK, 133, Untersteinach 1584.
26 Sometimes up to three gulden. This abuse persisted long enough to be a subject of concern in the 1594 consistory ordinance. *Corpus Constitutionum Brandenburgico-Culmbacensium* (1746), p. 275.
27 LKAN, MSK, 157, *Verzeichnus der furnembsten puncten in der visitation eingeben, den 5 Novemb: im 1589 Jar*, fo. 1 (my pagination): 'die weiber fur geben, sie thün es des kindes halben, sonderlich winterzeit, das sie es warmen, und wider recht einwindeln...'.
28 Lang, *Neuere Geschichte* vol. 3, p. 324.

marriage feasts registered the same modest results. Marriage festivities, with pipers and drummers, persisted into the twilight years of the century. Guests would arrive in tow with the bridegroom, 'especially in the villages [where], before the ceremony, loaded with excessive food and drink, quite besotted, they then come into the church'. After the church ceremony the merry-making moved to the streets, where it could last many days: 'The guests in the towns and villages, whether rich or poor, are invited for at least three days (though they are often together four or five days, indeed whole weeks ...). For this period they do nothing but live it up.'[29] What was worse, the problem waxed with its own energy. Families looked to outdo each other in cost and resplendence. When the authorities forbade one option, the peasantry simply looked for another alternative, moving the dances to the streets or other public places.[30]

Neither the clergy nor the district officials could impose the regulations of the police ordinances to the degree they wished. In part, the very logistics behind the enforcement of a uniform ordinance worked against them. Any attempt to impose unity of order and discipline on an area such as Franconia – home to so many lordships, free cities, polarized confessional boundaries, and disputed jurisdictions – was bound to encounter resistance. A uniform ordinance had to cut across the boundaries of custom, jurisdiction, and belief, and this proved a near impossibility. A sixteenth-century commentator has noted on the *Landeskirchliches Archiv* copy of the ordinance that the strictures against swearing, debasing the majesty of God, or belittling the holy sacrament could apply equally well to Zwinglians or Catholics as foulmouthed parishioners. There was no singularity of belief in Franconia, so the laws fell prey to this kind of interpretation. Moreover, the diversity of jurisdiction prevented full acceptance of the ordinance. Nuremberg and Ansbach, for instance, often had subjects in the same parish honouring different ordinances. Although the margrave wrote to the Nuremberg council asking the imperial city to obey the 1572 ordinance, so that unity of punishment and order could be maintained, Nuremberg policed swearing, baptismal parties, marriage gatherings and the like according to its own book of standards (*eines E Rhats Agendbuchlin*). The Nuremberg council was reluctant to cede to the margrave's wishes for fear that he would have too much power over its own subjects.[31]

In 1573 Nuremberg completed a report on how the other powers in the

---

29 LKAN, MSK, 157, Kirchleus (1 December 1558); *General* Kulmbach (4 June 1573), fos. 3–4 (my pagination); citation from *Verzeichnus der furnembsten puncten in der visitation eingeben, den 5 Novemb: im 1589 Jar*, fo. 1.

30 StaB, C2 1831, *Visitation Acta der Superinte[n]dents Wunsiedel Anno 92* fo. 12: 'Des gleichen werde auch das Mandat mit vier tischen zur hochzeit nit gehalten sondern weil bis weilten etlichen mehr tisch erlaubet, so wollens die andern auch haben und lade ein yder wie viel er will. Also geht es auch zu mitt der nach hochzeit, weil deß andern tags das tanzen uffm Rathhauß verpotten, so halten sie tentze uff den gassen und ofnen pletzen...'

31 StaN, 16a B–Laden Akten, Lade 212, no. 25, 1572.

Franconian circle were dealing with the imposition of a unified police ordinance. A clergyman close to the parishes of Eichstätt knew nothing about the publication of the ordinance; he could only assume, since marriage and baptismal feasts happened 'as before', that it was not in effect. The pastor of Lauf, north-east of Nuremberg, claimed that the subjects of Rothenburg held marriage celebrations as they had in the past. In the Palatinate, matters were worse: 'in the Palatinate nothing at all is being honoured'. The subjects of Bamberg, at least those in the district of Betzenstein, did not obey the 1572 ordinance, nor did those in Burkheim or Hilpoltstein.[32] Other, smaller lordships showed a similar type of disregard. Upon learning of this, Nuremberg decided to stick with many of its traditional directives and orders. Georg Friedrich was annoyed, and wrote to the city asking for standardisation;[33] but Nuremberg did not give way. We may assume that a degree of diversity, both in standards and punishments, was common throughout Franconia in the sixteenth century.

Even in the lands of Ansbach and Kulmbach the police ordinances were slow to take root. In some parishes, such as Schwarzenbach an der Saale, the ordinance was not honoured by the parishioners; as it was an isolated estate (*Rittergut*), the pastor was without the necessary support from the local lord.[34] Once such an enclave of relative indulgence was given room to develop, it was difficult for the local authorities to clamp down on the margrave's subjects without inciting their displeasure. The Hof visitors noted that in Pilgramsreuth 'the Rabenstein nobles want to be exempt from the police ordinance. This causes annoyance among the subjects of the margrave that they must obey it [the police ordinance].'[35] As the officials of Münchberg told the visitors, 'they would be pleased to enforce the ordinance; but it is a great problem that the same does not hold for the district of Stockenroth and those in Sperneck'.[36] Due to this type of disregard, endemic in many parishes, little heed was paid to the 1572 police ordinance in the immediate years after its publication.

'We have however found in the visitation', observed the Kulmbach visitors in 1573, 'that the police ordinance of the Franconian circle is being observed in very few places. Rather, with church fairs, marriage and baptismal customs, dances, etc., the former disorder and gross disobedience continues unabated.'[37]

---

[32] See the reports in StaN, 16a B–Laden Akten, Lade 212, no. 25. From 21 April to 6 May 1573.
[33] StaN, 16a B–Laden Akten, Lade 212, no. 25 (19 June 1573).
[34] LKAN, MDH, V, 1a, fo. 42 (7 October 1572). On the *Herrschaft* of the parish, see J. K. Bundschuh, *Geographisches statistisch-topographisches Lexicon von Franken* (Ulm, 1802), vol. 5 (1802), pp. 243–4.
[35] StaB, C2 1826, *Relation des Visitation Höfer Superi[n]tedents Anno 1576*, fo. 9.
[36] LKAN, MDH, V, 1a, fo. 52 (13 October 1572).
[37] LKAN, MSK, 157, *Mitt was Ordnung die Visitation des 1573 iares vorrichtet, und wie die raisen eingestellt worden...* fo. 3 (my pagination). This complaint continued until at least 1578 in Hof. See LKAN, MSK, 157, *Beschwerung und Ergernus* from Hof (1578/9), Point 13. The pastor of Sparneck did not even have a police ordinance. StaB, 1827, fo. 116: 'Die policeyordnung hab er nicht, vil weniger gelesen.'

Well into the final decades of the century, the pastors maintained that the refusal to obey the police ordinance was common to every parish. This was hyperbole, to be sure, but there was truth in it.

Illicit gatherings and night dances were another source of concern for the Lutheran authorities. For both the secular and the spiritual powers alike, late-night assemblies of parish youth were anathema. Nocturnal gatherings in general (the witches' sabbath being the most feared and infamous example) exemplified antisocial behaviour: arcane and sequestered, honouring rules unknown to God or man, any late-night assembly could be a source of unease. The Reformation did not originate the effort to police and eradicate these village fêtes; as early as the fourteenth century Nuremberg was dispatching mandates aimed at curbing 'dances in the night' and the excess thought to take place there. But the Reformers were quick to pick up on the immoral implications of late-night dances, and many Lutheran principalities singled them out as especially dangerous in the eyes of God.[38]

Brandenburg-Ansbach-Kulmbach had its fair share of dances and late-night gatherings. Georg the Pious observed in 1530 'that many of our subjects, as well as others, are attending public dances held in the villages ... and in great numbers, with piping and drumming'.[39] The nature and occasion of the dances could vary from village to village, even if certain customs did predominate. It is one measure of the sheer variety of custom in Germany that Johann Fischart took the liberty of inserting verbs for dancing into his sixteenth-century German translation and adaptation of *Gargantua and Pantagruel,* as if Rabelais did not realise that people 'danced, kicked, galloped, pranced, leapt, sung, limped, danced in chorus, clamored, swung, [and] danced in a ring' when they gathered.[40] The dances could be lewd, overtly sexual, an opportunity for the youth to behave in a manner usually reserved for carnival. The pastor of Zirndorf feared they were an invitation to 'whoring and sodomy,' symptoms of man's demise.[41]

The margrave called for the abolition of such customs. In 1566, Ansbach issued orders to eliminate the nocturnal celebrations on Holy Days, and in 1578 the visitors were instructed to keep an eye open for 'indecent night dances' within their superintendencies.[42] The authorities wanted to regulate the festive life of their subjects, for they viewed it as reckless and extravagant. And indeed, reckless and extravagant it may have been; but some gatherings had a definite social function and a regular place in the calendar of events – the assemblies of village youth (*Rockenstube* and *Spinnstube*) and the church fair (*Kirchweih*).

[38] Franz M. Böhme, *Geschichte des Tanzes in Deutschland* (Hildesheim, 1967), vol. 1, pp. 112–119.
[39] Karl S. Kramer, 'Ältere Spuren burschenschaftlichen Brauchtums in Mittelfranken', *Jahrbuch für fränkische Landesforschung,* 20 (1960), 383.
[40] Florence M. Weinberg, *Gargantua in a Convex Mirror: Fischart's View of Rabelais* (New York, 1986), p. 55; Böhme, *Geschichte des Tanzes,* pp. 49–63.
[41] LKAN, MDLz, 665 (4 May 1611): 'und also durch solche weis in meiner pfarr zu hürerej und sodomitischen leben thur und thor auffgethan wirdt...'.
[42] Sehling, p. 352.

Village culture and religious change

In Ansbach and Kulmbach the young gathered together in spinning bees (*Spinnstube* or *Rockenstube*), most commonly at night, whose central function appears to have been twofold: on the one hand the spinning bees were a convenient place for the women to meet in a single room, heated and well-illuminated, where they could knit, stitch, and sew; on the other hand they provided a forum in which the young people could vent their pent-up frustrations and observe customs of courtship.[43] The secular powers feared the moral license of such gatherings, however, and steps were taken to limit and ultimately eradicate these twilight assemblies. Georg Friedrich's police ordinance of 1566 limited attendance at spinning bees to the females of a single village:

And therefore in a village where there is a spinning bee no youth or man should enter or visit. Also, those who are having the spinning bee should not allow a youth or a man to enter, or indeed a foreign girl from other villages and hamlets.[44]

As might be expected, the suspect moral character of the spinning bee was also a concern for the church. The 1578 chapter ordinance advised the visitors to investigate the frequency of spinning bees and encourage the secular officials to punish wrongdoers.[45] Not surprisingly, given the threat a spinning bee represented to the moral order, parents and parish elders were also recruited to keep a watch over the young people. A Schwabach clergyman asked in a sermon that 'all elders, father and mothers' – peasants in particular (*Bawern und Bawrin*) – make sure that the young people under their care stayed clear of spinning bees. He ended his sermon with the threat: 'Whoever does not heed this advice may suffer the wrath of God and the authorities.'[46]

Spinning bees, notwithstanding the measures taken to purge the margravate of them, persisted throughout the sixteenth century. Superintendents at the latter end of the century lamented the continuance of this custom and the immoralities occurring as a result. The Bayreuth visitor observed that spinning bees survived in his superintendency regardless of the restrictions placed upon them; the young continued to gather and exercise their appetites 'in infinite ways'.[47] As even a cursory reading of the visitation returns attests, this aspect of parish life was largely untouched by the disciplinary powers set in place by the Reformation.

---

[43] Hans Medick, 'Village Spinning Bees: Sexual Culture and Free Time Among Rural Youth in Early Modern Germany', in David Sabean and Hans Medick (eds.), *Interest and Emotion: Essays on the Study of Family and Kinship* (Cambridge, 1984), pp. 323, 317–39. A 1524 print by Barthel Beham illustrates the assumed goings-on at an evening spinning bee. As one or two women labour in the corner of the room, the rest of the villagers frolic about in various stages of undress. Max Geisberg, *The German Single-Leaf Woodcut: 1500–1550* (New York, 1974), p. 133.

[44] *Polliceyord/nung etlicher pu[n]ct/unnd Artickel, in welchen/vermög des heiligen Römischen Reichs ...Anno/MDLXVI.*

[45] Sehling, 352.

[46] LKAN, MDS, 28. A stray leaf, undated and unsigned – *Copia Ehmahnung von Rockenstuben und anderer uppigkeit.*

[47] STAN, *Ansbacher Neues Generalrepertorium*, no. 49, rep. no. 103ᵉ, fo. 167; LKAN, MSK, 157, Bayreuth 1573; LKAN, MKA, Spez. 1023, no. 11 (6 March 1578).

Spinning bees remained a concern for the Lutheran church in Brandenburg-Ansbach-Kulmbach; the proscriptions were not enough to ensure their removal.[48] In part, this was due to the reluctance of the local authorities to act against them. To judge by the indulgence of the village elders, it would seem that the spinning bees were gladly tolerated, if not altogether encouraged. The village officials realised that a move to abolish spinning bees and similar gatherings would only work to inflame and anger the young people; at least a spinning bee was localised and terminal. Consequently, as the visitor of Kulmbach observed (1586): '[the local authorities] will not suffer talk or sermons against it. They say the young must have their diversions and merriment.'[49] Superintendents, it seems, could do little to prevent spinning bees once their visitation retinues had passed through the villages. And district officials, at least with reference to this pastime, held little sway with local officials. Spinning bees, as a result, remained a concern for the margrave's officials well into the latter years of the seventeenth century.

In addition to *Rockenstuben* and *Spinnstuben*, the Lutheran authorities tried to eliminate the numerous church fairs (*Kirchweihen*) dotting the annual festival calendars. For the rural inhabitants of Franconia, the church fair, held on the anniversary of a church's consecration, was the single most important local celebration of the year.[50] More than any other festival or gathering the church fair was a trans-communal event. The annual celebration at Mögeldorf, for instance, a village four miles east of Nuremberg of less than ninety inhabitants, might attract thousands of neighbouring parishioners.[51] The original purpose of the event was to honour the day of a church's consecration and the patron saint to whom it was dedicated; and indeed, bearing witness to their medieval origins, most church fairs began with a morning service and communal worship. By the sixteenth century, however, the main appeal of the church fair had become its secular entertainments: dancing, drinking, wrestling, pole-climbing, gambling, the host of market booths, the hucksters and charlatans, and the travelling performers, such as fire-eaters and acrobats. Urbanus Rhegius remarked on the dangers of this misplaced emphasis in his *Sermon on the Church Fair*: no longer pleasing to God, these celebrations had become haunts of the Devil.

Indeed, such blindness is among us. For we believe that the church fair is well and magnificently observed when we bedeck the mother church with flowers and twigs [*nesten*], when we hang banners from the belfry, a letter of indulgence on the church door, sing, pipe, and drink ... The devil rejoices more in one church fair than in a thousand Good Fridays...

[48] LKAN, MSK, 157, Melkendorf 1580: 'das Rockenstüben fur und fur gehalten werden' was a complaint common to most parishes.
[49] LKAN, MSK, 157, *Acta Visitationis in der Cülmbacher Süperintendentz 1586*, fo. 5.
[50] Kramer, *Volksleben im Fürstentum Ansbach*, p. 116.
[51] Alison Stewart, 'Paper Festivals and Popular Entertainment. The Kermis Woodcuts of Sebald Behaim in Reformation Nuremberg', *Sixteenth Century Journal*, 24 (1993), pp. 308–12.

Urbanus wondered in conclusion: 'Who is to say what excess and fury might result from this?'[52]

Excess and fury were what the Lutheran authorities feared, and the elimination of the church fair was one of their disciplinary priorities. 'Above all', wrote Martin Luther, 'we ought to abolish church anniversary celebrations outright, since they have become nothing but taverns, fairs and gambling places and only increase the dishonouring of God and foster the soul's damnation.'[53] The Lutheran authorities in Ansbach heeded these precautions; the local church fair became an object of investigation in the yearly visitations. Pastors were forbidden to attend these 'heathen' gatherings and instructed to report local excesses to the authorities. Secular mandates, such as the police ordinances, limited the number of guests that might gather, the quantity of wine and foods, and the hours when the rural inhabitants could remain out of doors. Finally, with the publication of the 1572 Franconian police ordinance, the authorities endeavoured to eliminate the large church fairs outright.[54]

But the church fair, like the spinning bee, remained a popular local custom in the sixteenth century. The Lutheran authorities in Brandenburg-Ansbach-Kulmbach were unable to uproot or markedly alter this tradition. As late as 1596 an official in the district of Uffenheim related how the people of Wallmersbach held their St Leonard's church fair, replete with a dance ('which the young men from the surrounding villages take care to attend') just as they had many years before.[55] Parishioners would plead overwork or poverty when justifying their lackadaisical church attendance, but, as the pastors would attest to the superintendents, the villagers always had the wealth and the time to attend the church fairs.[56] The visitation records contain numerous references to these celebrations; neither the super-intendents nor the district officials could impose the strict aims of the visitation ordinances or the police mandates. And again, the local authorities were largely to blame. 'It is an old custom', was the explanation given to the Kulmbach visitor in 1586 by a parish authority; 'people have held church fairs for one hundred years. There must always be one time in the

[52] Urbanus Rhegius, *Ain Sermon/von der Kyrchweyche*. (1522), Biii. I would like to thank Professor Keith Moxey for sending me a copy of this pamphlet.
[53] Cited in Keith P. F. Moxey, 'Sebald Beham's church anniversary holidays: festive peasants as instruments of repressive humor', *Simiolus*, 12 (1981), p. 126.
[54] Sehling, pp. 322, 357. Copies of 1566 and 1572 police ordinances in LKAN, MDF, 1.
[55] LKAN, MKA, Spez. 941, fos. 107–8 (24 May 1596). The superintendent of Bayreuth, Justus Bloch, concluded in 1572: 'und wiewoln hievorn fürstliche Mandata der dorfkirchweien halben publiciret, ists doch den maÿsten theil umb sonst, und vergebens geweßen.' LKAN, MSK, 157, *Bericht der Spetial Visitation, in der Süperintendentz Beÿrreuth Ao 1572*, fo. 6.
[56] STAN, *Ansbacher Neues Generalrepertorium*, no. 49, rep. nr. 103ᵉ, fo. 12: 'das sie weder zum sacrament noch zur lehr des Catechismi kommen, viel weniger das Junge gesind darzu halten, da Inen doch kein kirchweih oder tantz zu weit entlegen ist...'; LKAN, MDG 71, fo. 3: 'niemandt gehe zw dem Catechismo, lauffen zum dentzen, und kirchweihen, wan man zu kirchen leuth will man nit hörn, aber wan man zum dantz pfeiffet, laufft es mitt heuffe zw'.

year when one good friend may seek out another, when one might seek friendship from another.'[57] Local authorities, recognising the important social function of the church fair, were reluctant to press too hard for its removal. The church fair in Brandenburg-Ansbach-Kulmbach, like the church fair in the neighbouring parishes of Nuremberg, was a local celebration enjoyed without intermission in the early modern period.[58]

The offence of blasphemy or profanity was a transgression policed by both the secular and the ecclesiastical authorities. Blasphemy, swearing, and insult were considered powerful wrongs by the authorities, though for different reasons in different contexts. Ridicule and inversion might be seen as a threat to the social order; taking any name in vain that serves a legitimating function for the relations of power 'discloses the potentiality of an entirely different world, of another order, another way of life'.[59] Seen in this light, blasphemy and sacrilege are acts of resistance or revolution. More immediate for the sixteenth-century mind, however, was the fear that blasphemy would call down the wrath of God. The 1530 imperial police ordinance warned against insults directed at the majesty of God, the sacraments, Mary, or the 'body, members, wounds, death, [or] suffering' of Christ, as this would evoke the displeasure of God and threaten the moral order.[60] The margraves of Brandenburg-Ansbach-Kulmbach expressed a similar concern. When Georg Friedrich issued mandates against swearing and blasphemy in 1559 and 1562, he was alarmed at the damage done to the majesty of God and the damnation his subjects might suffer in return.[61] The margrave ordered the clergy to preach against such abuses and punish those who did not reform themselves. It was a policy with a considerable history. As early as 1525 Casimir had published a mandate against blasphemy, chastising the regional officials for letting the practice get the upper hand. He advised his subjects to report all transgressors, along with 'what

---

[57] LKAN, MSK, 157, *Acta Visitationis in der Culmbacher Superintendentz 1586*, fo. 3.
[58] This conclusion is based upon a study of the visitation reports. References to the church fairs are scattered throughout the reports. I have consulted the collections in the Landeskirchliches Archiv, Nürnberg, the Staatsarchiv, Nürnberg, and the Staatsarchiv, Bamberg. To my knowledge, the holdings in these archives represent the entire collection of extant returns. Stewart, 'Paper Festivals and Popular Entertainment', p. 327.
[59] Mikhail Bakhtin, *Rabelais and His World* (Bloomington, 1984), pp. 48, 1–58.
[60] 'Von Gottszlesterung und Gotts Schwören', in *Romischer Keyser/licher Maiestat Orde/nüng un[d] Reformation/güter Pollicei im Heylligen Romischen Reich/Anno M.D.rrr./zu Augsburg uff/gericht*. Copy in STAN, 16a B-Laden Akten, Laden 204, no. 17. Blasphemy (which might implicate Anabaptists and other marginal sects) was viewed as *the* fundamental reason why the Empire was visited with misfortune and was a primary concern when the imperial ordinances were drawn up. Karl Härter, 'Entwicklung und Funktion der Policeygesetzgebung des Heiligen Römischen Reiches Deutscher Nation im 16. Jahrhundert', *Ius Commune*, 20 (1993),93.
[61] Lang, *Neuere Geschichte*, vol. 3, p. 323; Kraußold, *Geschichte der evangelischen Kirche*, p. 155. Georg Friedrich also issued orders against blasphemy in his reformed criminal court ordinance of 1582.

words, and the cause ... and the number of witnesses', to the proper authorities.[62] This surveillance continued throughout the sixteenth century. The margraves continued to publish mandates against blasphemy, but the parishioners were never sufficiently reformed, the mandates were never adequately enforced, and the use of blasphemous language persisted. Andreas Osiander made the point in his 1533 catechism:

Not only do men and boys do it, women and girls do it as well. Even small children curse, and in the most horrible manner! They curse not only when they are angry, but also when something good happens to them. Today people curse for no particular reason at all, as if cursing were a virtue and to curse some kind of blessing.[63]

The most common complaint of the 1564 Bayreuth visitation was the frequency of blasphemy.[64] Most visitors, at one time or another, commented on 'the dreadful blasphemy, which is so common among the peasantry'.[65] In 1584 the visitor of Kulmbach observed that 'blasphemy in the name of God and verbal abuse of the Holy Sacrament is very common, especially at the inns, among high and low estate, young and old, male and female.'[66] In Neustadt, blasphemy was singled out as a 'common complaint' above such ills as magic, usury, theft, and gluttony. One clergyman declared that blasphemy was an ill endemic 'in all ends in the whole wide world'.[67] 'There are people', observed a pastor in 1603, still harping on the frequency of blasphemy and how it pleased the enemies of God, 'who would rather worship the devil than our Lord God.'[68] Like the church fair and the late-night gatherings of youth, the offence of blasphemy haunted sixteenth-century dreams of reform.

The offence of usury also persisted in the margravate, notwithstanding the attention given to this offence by the authorities. Both the secular and the ecclesiastical ordinances published by Georg Friedrich advised the authorities to police the parishes for usury. Nevertheless, the margrave's subjects continued to charge interest on goods and loans as part of their daily commerce. The Gunzenhausen clergy estimated in 1578 that 'all merchants in our chapter throughout are userers' as well as the innkeepers. Since no steps had been taken to guard against the evil other citizens began to follow suit. 'As the saying goes', observed the visitor, 'when the abbot lays down the dice, the monks will play.'[69]

---

[62] *Verbot der/Gots lesterung/Gots schwuere/und flueche* (Ansbach, 1525).

[63] Cited in Steven Ozment, *Protestants: The Birth of a Revolution* (London, 1993), pp. 106–7.

[64] Kraußold, *Geschichte der evangelischen Kirche*, p. 155; LKAN, MSK, 157, *Generalia* 1592: 'Es ist fast an allen orten nicht allein von den pastoribus sonder auch zum teil von den auditoribus uber das greuliche fluchen und Gotslestern und mißbrauch des H. namen gottes bej jung und alt....'

[65] STAN, *Ansbacher Neues Generalrepertorium*, no. 49, rep. nr. 103ᵉ, fo. 12.

[66] LKAN, MSK, 133 (10 February 1584).

[67] LKAN, MDN, 8, fo. 37; LKAN, MDG, 71, fo. 70: 'Gotslesterung, ist ein gemaines laister an allen enden in der gantzen witen welt'.

[68] Lang, *Neuere Geschichte*, vol. 3, 323.

[69] LKAN, MDG, 71, fo. 70.

The charging of interest on goods – from cash to grain to hay – was so common it was no longer considered a sin.[70] In fact, added pastor Pancratius Feindtel of Kirchleus, people considered usury to be a necessary skill for the maintenance of a household. As a consequence 'not only lots of rich, but also poor widows' were wont to charge interest during an exchange. When they were brought to justice and punished, they answered without reservation: 'they learn such things from the citizens [*bürgern*] in the cities.'[71]

MARRIAGE, THE MASS, AND THE FORTUNES OF DISCIPLINE

Another moral offence common to both the rural hinterlands and the urban centres was the infamy of illicit or invalid marriage. Like usury, blasphemy, the spinning bees, and the church fairs, the customs associated with marriage rites were inherited from the medieval period; unlike these offences, however, marriage became subject to secular jurisdiction only after the introduction of the Reformation. Prior to the Reformation, the bishops and their chapter courts had acted as final authorities in all matters relating to marriage. In the eyes of the Catholic church, marriage was a sacrament and thus subject to ecclesiastical law.[72] In the eyes of the laity, in contrast, marriage was an important social rite and had very little to do with religion.[73] Tensions between the laity and the clergy in marital matters were thus very common in the medieval period. The secular populace considered the church's intervention an unwarranted violation of their rights. 'I cannot goodly determine what I most abhor, detest, loathe, and abominate', concluded Rabelais' Gargantua in the face of this situation,

– whether the tyrannical presumption of those dreaded sacerdotal mole-catchers, who not being willing to contain and coop up themselves within the gates and trellises of their own mysterious temples, do deal in, meddle with, obtrude upon, and thrust their sickles into harvests of secular businesses, quite contrary and diametrically opposite to the quality, state, and condition of their callings, professions, and vocations; or the superstitious stupidity and senseless scrupulousness of married folks, who have yielded obedience, and submitted their bodies, fortunes, and estates to the discretion and authority of such odious, perverse, barbarous, and unreasonable laws.[74]

70 StaB C2 1827, fo. 22. 'Der Wucher ist kein Sunde mehr. Denn die vom adel, sowohl die Burger und Bawren, mit gelt, getreÿdig, hew und andern ungescheucht uber messig wucher treiben, und wird das hundert nicht allein uff 6 R weggelden, sonder uff zehen und ein höhers gebracht.'

71 LKAN, MSK, 352 (28 January 1584).

72 Gabriel Le Bras, 'La doctrine du mariage chez les théologiens et les canonistes depuis l'an mille', in *Dictionnaire de théologie catholique* (Paris, 1927), cols. 2123–317.

73 Richard van Dülmen, 'Fest der Liebe. Heirat und Ehe in der frühen Neuzeit', in Richard van Dülmen (ed.), *Armut, Liebe, Ehre* (Frankfurt, 1988), pp. 67–106; Robisheaux, *Rural Society and the Search for Order*, pp. 116–20.

74 François Rabelais, *Gargantua and Pantagruel*, Book III, Ch. 48. On Rabelais and clandestine marriages, see Jean Plattard, 'L'Invective de Gargantua contre les mariages contractés "sans le sceu et adveu" des parents', *Revue du Seizième Siècle*, 1 4 (1927), 381–8.

In response to these 'unreasonable laws' (and with Gargantuan mettle) the laity in the Middle Ages tended to ignore the dictates of the Catholic church and form alliances convenient to their interests. The medieval parishioner exercised a great degree of freedom over the regulation of marriage, going so far as to consider a marriage legitimate even when it was invalid in the eyes of the church.[75] Little notice was paid to the moral restrictions placed on unions by the Catholic church (such as mutual consensus or degrees of consanguinity) and the marriage courts were generally avoided, as proceedings often proved lengthy and expensive.

The Lutheran authorities capitalised on this native resentment. Casimir's officials were quick to deprive the Bamberg bishopric of its capacity to try marriage cases, claiming that the common people could not come away from the ecclesiastical courts without incurring debts and disadvantages (*on grossen schaden*).[76] Casimir thus freed his subjects from the jurisdiction of the ecclesiastical marriage courts; the difficulties associated with the regulation of marriage were from this point forward inherited by the secular powers. But it was Lutheran theology which provided a set of standards.

Marriage was a central concern of the Lutheran reformers. Martin Luther exalted the state of matrimony; while it was no longer a sacrament, marriage was sanctioned by God as one of his creations. Although still in a state of sin, through marriage man could realise the gifts of God and recognise the need for trust in the divine plan.[77] Marriage thereby lost the status it enjoyed in Catholic theology: it was no longer a sacrament. The secular arm assumed the right to legislate and regulate the laws relating to marriage. But the moral significance of a proper union remained as important as ever. For Luther, marriage figured large in the divine plan: 'The Lord God has wanted three things made right again before the Last Day: the ministry of the Word, government, and marriage'.[78] By 'made right' Luther was referring to the vow of celibacy instituted (as he saw it) by the Catholic church. In his tract *On Monastic Vows* (1521) Luther judged this vow as lacking in scriptural authority and contrary to the basic tenets of the Gospel, faith, Christian freedom, love,

[75] Jack Goody, *The Development of the Family and Marriage in Europe* (Cambridge, 1983), pp. 128–53; John Bossy, *Christianity in the West 1400–1700* (Oxford, 1987), pp. 19–26; R. H. Helmholz, *Marriage Litigation in Medieval England* (Cambridge, 1974), p. 31.

[76] StaB, C2 1814, 1523, *passim*.

[77] *D. Martin Luthers Werke: Kritische Gesamtausgabe* (Weimar, 1907), 10, 3, 'Vom ehelichen Leben 1522', p. 304

> das fleysch und blutt, durch Adam verderbt, ynn sunden empfangen und geporn wirt, lautts des 50. psalm, Unnd das keyn ehepflicht on sund geschicht, aber gott verschonet yhr aus gnaden darumb, das der ehliche orden seyn werck ist, und behellt auch mitten unnd durch die sund alle das gutt, das er dareyn gepflantzt und gesegenet hatt.

Hartwig Dieterich, *Das protestantische Eherecht in Deutschland bis zur Mitte des 17. Jahrhunderts* (Munich, 1970), pp. 33–5.

[78] Cited in Steven Ozment, *The Age of Reform 1250–1550* (New Haven, 1980), p. 381.

and common sense. Luther's followers flocked to his side and demonstrated their allegiance in a spate of marriages in the early 1520s. The Ansbach clergyman Andreas Althamer, for instance, defended his union in an address to the people of Schwäbisch Gmünd.[79]

But the Lutheran theologians did not limit their interest in marriage to how it related to the clerical estate. The Reformers soon realised that the laity needed instruction and guidance if their unions were to be pleasing before God. Moreover, now that the secular arm had the power to try marriage cases, the state required a corpus of law consistent with the Lutheran conception of legal and godly wedlock. Margrave Georg the Pious wrote to Johannes Brenz for advice in this matter, and Brenz agreed with the notion that the theologians should provide guidance for the margrave and his subjects. 'As the estate of marriage has been instituted by our Lord God himself', wrote Brenz, 'and confirmed through Jesus Christ, it is thus meet to comport oneself daily in marriage matters in fear of God and in compliance with his Word in accord with divine ordinance.'[80] The clergy soon set to work. The Ansbach theologians paraphrased Luther on clerical marriage: Marriage is in accord with God's will and the nature of man ('It is not good that man should be alone; that is, without a wife'). The twenty-three Nuremberg articles of 1528 repeated this injunction to the clergy, and the 1533 church ordinance also praised the holy state of matrimony.[81] A digest of marriage laws was in the making.

The regulations governing marriage grew apace with the growth of ecclesiastical institutions. Casimir's 1526 resolution simply admonished the authorities to police the parishes for couples cohabiting in a state of sin.[82] In 1528, the year of the joint visitation, margrave Georg the Pious advised Georg Hüter, the administrator of St Gumbertus, Ansbach, to settle disputes 'according to the Word of God' rather than canon law.[83] In 1535 margrave Georg issued his *Mandat wider die heimliche Verlöbnisse*, a mandate directed at young people who were exchanging vows without the consent of their parents or their elders.[84] From this point forward the margravial authorities and the higher clergy seem to have taken a greater interest in the statutes ruling marriage. (In 1538 the Kulmbach clergyman Johann Schnabel made a trip to Wittenberg in an effort to settle with Melanchthon over the forbidden grades of consanguinity and

[79] *Ain Sermo[n]/von dem ehelichem Stand, das/er auch den priestern frey/sey, gethon zu Schwe/bischen Gemünd/durch Andream/Althamer/im Jar/1525.*
[80] Johannes Brenz, *Wie inn Eesach/en unnd den sellern* [sic] *so/sich derhalben zutra/gen* (1531). Brenz forwarded his report 'On Marriage Issues' to the margrave 27 July 1529. Th. Pressel, *Anecdota Brentiana* (Tübingen, 1868), pp. 43ff.
[81] Schülin, *Fränkische Reformations-Geschichte*, pp. 68–71; Sehling, pp. 132; 200–1.
[82] Sehling, p. 95. *Von der weltlichen uneelichen beisitz.*
[83] Müller and Seebaß, *Andreas Osiander D. Ä. Gesamtausgabe* (1981), vol. 4, p. 438.
[84] *Corpus Constitutionum Brandenburgico-Culmbacensium* (1746), pp. 289–90.

affinity).[85] By mid-century pastors were instructed to keep a register of all marriages within the church.[86] Finally in 1556, the year in which a marriage court was established in Ansbach, it was recognised that the proration of independent judgement was causing confusion. Regional officials were instructed to send a written report of the proceedings recorded during marriage suits of complexity – and these included secret betrothals, pre-marital pregnancies, dissolved marriages, bigamy, and similar offences – so that some unity of purpose might result.[87] The result of this effort was the 1565 marriage articles, which were reissued in 1573.

The articles listed the offences common to illicit, invalid, and immoral marriages: First, no person should be married to more than one partner at once; second, no one should marry another person within the third degree of affinity; third, the young should not marry without the foreknowledge and the leave of their parents or their elders; fourth, following on this, no vows should be exchanged in secret; fifth, the couple should not 'mix flesh' or live together before the wedding; sixth, the wedding should take place within a reasonable time after the promise of marriage; and seventh, the union should last in a state of harmony.[88] Nothing in this list would have been out of place in the marriage courts of Catholic Germany, save perhaps the final stipulation, which was concerned with the moral quality of the union. Each of the wrongs had a corresponding solution and an appropriate punishment, which were later drawn up for the officials in the expectation that they would be enforced.[89]

The institutions responsible for the enforcement of the marriage articles developed at a similar gradual rate. Georg the Pious approached the Nuremberg council for guidance in 1531 and was advised that: 'It is regarded as useful, good, and necessary, that matrimonial matters should be processed (*gehandelt*) before learned, sensible people [who are] familiar with the law.'[90] But no immediate steps were taken to establish an independent marriage court. During the first few decades of reform, the local clergymen had to adjudicate between parties and seek the counsel of Ansbach when the case seemed without solution. At the latter part of the century, as has been detailed in an earlier chapter, both Ansbach and Kulmbach were home to consistories chaired by secular and ecclesiastical officials empowered to judge over cases of marriage disputes. Nevertheless, even after the publication of a comprehensive list of marriage articles in 1565, the pastor and the secular authorities would approach the consistory only if the matter was beyond

[85] StaN, *Ansbacher Religionsakten III*, Tom. XI, fo. 461. Schnabel reported in 1539 that he had gone to Wittenberg: '…Nemlich von wegen der Ordinirung etlicher personen zum priester ampt (der wir jtzet sieben zw wenig haben) und von wegen der verpoten grad der blutfreundschafft und schwagerschafft etc. und ander de gleichen'.
[86] Sehling, pp. 344–5.
[87] Sehling, p. 364. *Ausschreiben, irrung in eesachen betreffend.*
[88] Sehling, p. 367–8.
[89] Sehling, pp. 371–6. *Ehegerichtsordnung und Errichtung des Konsistoriums zu Kulmbach vom 18. Okt. 1567.*
[90] W. Köhler, 'Brentiana und andere Reformatia IV', *ARG*, 11 (1914), 247.

their capacities. The clergy remained the arbiter of moral standards at the level of the parish.

The pastors were unable to regulate the marital customs or the sexual behaviour of the parishioners. The marriage court in Ansbach had been established to reduce the frequency of 'adultery and whoring', but it had little direct impact. Mandates and articles had been issued to regulate behaviour, but they found little application. The superintendency of Gunzenhausen had a plague of children born out of wedlock; it was difficult for the pastors to know who the father was for the work of baptism.[91] In his list of parish misdeeds pastor Elias Körber of Weihenzell included 'the mischief of the betrothed couples who, against the issued and publicly announced marriage articles of the prince, cohabit together before taking their vows (*vor irem ehelichem kirchgang*) which, no doubt, results in mixing of the flesh'.[92] The parish of Neustadt alone was home to five men who lived in separation from their wives in 1576, one of whom lived in this condition for at least twenty years.[93] The margrave recognised this poor state of affairs. The marriage articles of 1565 made public his alarm over the problems rife in the estate of marriage and how they were damaging the conscience of his subjects.[94] Yet the articles had little effect. In Heidenheim (1572) it was observed that 'little of the marriage articles was being obeyed'.[95] As late as 1591 the pastor of Unternesselbach complained in a similar vein that the parishioners refused to obey the marriage articles.[96] In 1618 the clergy lamented that the offences against the state of marriage were a plague 'for all times ... in the smallest hamlets'.[97]

The parishioners would honour the marriage laws or appear before the marriage court only when an appeal to the law worked to their advantage.[98] For instance, the father of a Schwabach girl demanded that his child be absolved of the necessity to recognise a secret pledge of marriage (*Winckel eeh*) and asked the authorities to place her 'once again in his paternal charge'.[99] Else Stigler was also forced to return a thaler to her suitor because her parents disapproved of the match.[100] Paul Eberhardt, who longed to be dissolved of his marriage to his absent wife, simply wanted justice before the court (*füeg und*

91 LKAN, MDG, 71, fo. 71.
92 LKAN, MKA, Spez. 1023, no. 11 (6 March 1578).
93 StaN, *Ansbacher Neues Generalrepertorium*, no. 49, rep. nr. 103ᵉ, fo. 11; (1584) 118.
94 Sehling, p. 367.
95 LKAN, MDG, 71, fo. 46.
96 StaN, *Ansbacher Neues Generalrepertorium*, no. 49, rep. nr. 103ᵉ, fo. 232.
97 LKAN, MDU, 330, T.1., no. 12.
98 Compare Thomas Robisheaux, 'Peasants and Pastors: Rural Youth Control and the Reformation in Hohenlohe, 1540–1680', *Social History*, 6 (1981), p. 290; Robisheaux, *Rural Society and the Search for Order*, pp. 106–46; Lyndal Roper, '"Going to Church and Street": Weddings in Reformation Augsburg', *Past and Present*, 106 (1985), 62–101.
99 LKAN, MDS, 80 T.1 (Mittwoch nach Anthoni 1564). '...ime widerumb in seinen vätterlichen gewalt zustellen...'.
100 StaN, *Ansbacher Neues Generalrepertorium*, no. 49, rep. nr. 103ᵉ, fo. 101.

Recht).[101] For the same reasons parishioners would bring recalcitrant partners before the authorities to ensure a private pledge was honoured. Contz Ernst of Oberlaimbach was reprimanded by Helena Schülin because he demanded the return of his promissory gift two years after the initial pledge.[102] Margaretha Ziegler tried to hold Jorge Mümler to account for his flippant, though lucrative, promise of marriage one night in 1572.[103] Little heed, however, was paid to the moral standards set in place by the Reformation. Parishioners did not cite one another before the pastor or the marriage courts to answer for illicit 'mixings of the flesh', adultery, pre-marital intimacy, or suspect degrees of affinity. The concern with morality, so central to the Lutheran understanding of a godly marriage, was not shared by the laity. The contempt the villager had once shown for the marriage courts of medieval Germany was now spent on the Lutheran equivalent.

Indeed pre-nuptial intimacy and pre-marital sex, in the form of *Fenstern*, were a venerable tradition in Franconia. The custom of *Fenstern*, which went by many different names throughout Europe (*Fenstern, Gasselgangs, Kiltgangs*), involved the young males of the village visiting the unmarried maidens, climbing through their windows, and lying with them by night (though not necessarily engaging in sex). Often this happened with the tolerance if not the complicity of the parents. The French folklorist Arnold van Gennep described it as follows:

This custom which was openly approved by all the youths of the village and by the interested families allows the girl on certain nights, especially Saturday, to open the window or door of her bedchamber or the common bedchamber of all the nubile girls of the house successively to different gallants. The man chosen for the night rests completely clothed or partially clothed so that the principle act of love could not be accomplished. The night is spent in talking about the events which have taken place in the village or sleeping in each other's arms until early morning. Then the boy returns to his home or work. It is the girl who decides which gallant she will receive in her bed. These gallants are not necessarily amongst those from whom she will choose a fiancé. The *Kiltgang* [*Fenstern*] is neither a trial coupling nor a way to give preference in marriage. More important it is only exercised between boys and girls from the same village; rarely from the whole parish.[104]

---

101 LKAN, MDF, 99, 1582.
102 StaN, *Ansbacher Neues Generalrepertorium*, no. 49, rep. nr. 103ᵉ, fo. 152. (1588) A two-year delay after the initial promise would seem to be cause enough to bring Contz before the authorities. But it was not until he demanded the return of his *Leickauff* – accompanied with the promise 'der teufel soll in holen wenn er sie behalte' – that the pastor was consulted. He was forced to give her his hand, and promise once again, but Helena was doubtful ('...gleichwol nicht bald glauben...'). The visitation of the next year revealed that they still had not yet married.
103 LKAN, MDS, 80 T.1. *Verhorte kundschaft in der Strittigen ehesachen zwischen Jorgen Mumler zue Nembsdorf, und Margretha Zieglerin den 21 Julÿ Anno 72....*
104 Cited and translated in Sheldon J. Watts, *A Social History of Western Europe 1450–1720* (London, 1984), p. 73. See K. Rob V. Wikman, *Die Einleitung der Ehe. Eine vergleichend ethno-soziologische Untersuchung über die Vorstufe der Ehe in den Sitten des Schwedischen Volkstums* (Åbo, 1937), pp. 216–26, 356–62.

Certain of van Gennep's assumptions are idealised: the restraint of the pairings could of course vary; the suitors were often less 'chosen' by the girl than encountered; the youths involved did not always honour a traditional conduct or 'custom'. But other points are clear – above all, that the parents acted with complicity, and that the youths came from within the village boundaries. The margraves legislated against the practice throughout the sixteenth century; on 8 January 1584 it was considered so rife in Streitberg, Thüsbronn, and Muggendorf that the consistory was called upon to intervene. But it was too deeply imbedded in village culture to eradicate in the sixteenth century.[105] *Fenstern* remained a concern for the authorities in Ansbach and Kulmbach until at least 1698. The custom continued for centuries after the Reformation.[106]

Even a requirement as basic to the faith as regular attendance at the Lord's Supper could not be imposed by the Lutheran authorities. Parishioners were expected to attend communion at least two or three times a year; if they did not, they were subject to the disciplinary powers of the pastor. The pastor could exercise the small ban and exclude them from communion, godparenthood, and a Christian burial. The visitation instructions of 1558 advised the pastors to ban recalcitrant parishioners from communion, as well as baptism and burial, until they had taken steps to correct themselves.[107] The pastor would first admonish the parishioners in private (*gradus admonition privatæ*) and if this did not suffice he would refer them to the visitors (*gradus secundus*). Only when these two steps failed would the parishioner be referred to the consistory.[108]

Despite what would seem to be a fairly lax requirement, the parishioners failed to honour the demands of the church. Absenteeism remained a problem. Margrave Georg the Pious sought the advice of Luther and Melanchthon in 1531 over the matter of the parishioners' refusal to visit the church and whether he should reestablish votive masses (*winckel messen*) to encourage attendance.[109] The same year he published a mandate expressing his regret that the people were not giving proper respect to the mass:

[105] Lang, *Neuere Geschichte* (1811), vol. 3, p. 324.
[106] For Brandenburg-Ansbach-Kulmbach see Kramer, 'Ältere Spuren burschenschaftlichen Brauchtums in Mittelfranken', pp. 385ff.; Kramer, *Volksleben im Fürstentum Ansbach*, pp. 221ff.; Johann Andreas Schmeller, *Bayerisches Wörterbuch* (Munich, 1985), vol. 1, pp. 733–4.
[107] Sehling, p. 344. Correction meant proper preparation for mass:

> Auf das es nun ordenlich und recht zugee und alle mißbreuch sovil müglich verhütet werden, sollen sie dem volk ansagen, wer das heilig sacrament wöl empfahen, das er sich des abents zuvor oder, wo es ferne wegs oder ander zufell halben nicht sein könt, des morgens vor meßzeit dem pfarrer oder einem andern kirchendiener persönlich anzeigen: dann on soliche vorgeende anzaigung sollen sie fürohin niemand das heilig sacrament raichen.

Sehling, p. 185.
[108] Robert Dollinger, 'Evangelische Kirchendisziplin in den fränkischen Kirchen', *ZbKG*, 14 (1939), 48–52.
[109] StaN, *Ansbacher Religionsakten III*, Tom. XI, fo. 256.

our subjects seldom (or indeed never) attend the church, the sermon and the divine office of the true evangelical mass, along with the litany and other Christian services. Fewer still receive the most worthy and holy Sacrament of the Altar ... [and even when they do go to church] as soon as the Gospel has been read or spoken, or as soon as the blood and body of Christ has been consecrated in the mass, even before communion, they run out of the church.[110]

Deliberate absence from communion was not a rarity. A tally taken in the parish of Kirchleus at the end of the century counted 228 people in the village of Kirchleus itself, of whom 156 attended the prescribed two or three communions a year. This represents a 32 per cent rate of absence. The numbers at Gosserdörf [Gottersdorf?], with 178 parishioners and 113 regular communicants, also break down to around this percentage (37 per cent). And indeed the smaller hamlets and mill settlements register similar equations: nine out of fifteen in Rützjaβ, four for six in Weltzenmüll. Altogether, to take 906 names recorded in the survey, 590 were considered communicants (*zum sacrament*) – which leaves 316 parishioners who stayed away, or 35 per cent.[111] Thomas Rühr of Berneck noted in 1580 that of the 892 residents of the parish (*eingepfarten*), 590 were equivalent to what he termed communicants – again roughly 35 per cent of the populace did not go to mass even once a year.[112]

This type of inquiry was in fact a rarity; for the most part the historian is left with the names of the more deliberate and obstinate villagers only. There does not seem to be any regular pattern ruling correction or punishment (as evidenced by the list of those seen as contemptuous of the sacraments – *Contemptores Sacramenti* – in the superintendency of Neustadt between the years 1580 and 1594).[113] In the visitation mandate of 1558 the clergy were instructed to look into the plague of those who were 'contemptuous of the Word and the mass,' and this order was generally repeated with every visitation rescript thereafter. But the people could not be forced to attend the service. The clergy looked upon this offence as yet another instance in the calendar of the evils

[110] StaB, C3 49, fo. 15 (28 February 1531).

[111] LKAN, MSK, 352, *Nuhn volgen hernach die dorffer so in die pfar Kurleuβ gehörig auch wievil personen in ein jdem dorff siendt, und wie viel derselbigen zum Sacrament gehen oder nicht* (no date). The document mentions that the patron at the time was 'Hans Rüdingen von Güttenberg' (Hans Rüdiger III. von Guttenberg) who inherited the parish in 1580 and held it until 1609. See Johannes Bischoff, *Genealogie der Ministerialen von Blassenberg und Freiherren von (und zu) Guttenberg 1148–1970* (Würzburg, 1971), p. 43.

[112] LKAN, MSK, 133, *Ein Kurtze und Einseltige Verzeignis...* (1580). By Rühr's count, of the 416 children only 130 took communion (31 per cent), which would testify to the young age of the majority of children during this period of high infant mortality. It is significant that servants, or what Rühr termed *Dienstboten*, were regular fixtures at the mass. Of the 138 he included, 122 took regular communion (88 per cent). They were often forced to attend by their employers.

[113] StaN, *Ansbacher Neues Generalrepertorium*, no. 49, rep. nr. 103ᵉ, 1580–1594, *passim*. This label – *Contemptores Sacramenti* – does not refer to a religious sect, such as the Sacramentarians or the crypto-Calvinists, but rather to those parishioners who refused to attend communion, despite the pastor's blandishments.

'of this unthankful and unrepentant crude world' to which, alas, it was their lot to attend.[114]

In general, traditional village pastimes and customs survived the reforming efforts of the Lutheran church unscathed, despite the strength of purpose infused into the territorial church on the heels of the Reformation. The campaign to regulate the moral quality of marriages and enforce regular attendance at communion also fell short of the expressed goals. All of this is hardly surprising. No one has doubted that village culture lived beyond the sixteenth century. The mass of collections and compendiums of folk culture was prepared in the eighteenth and nineteenth centuries. All of the traditions and practices described above would be familiar to historians of modern Germany.[115] The examples cited above are not intended to prove a point by weight of evidence. Rather, reference to the Lutheran church's desire to reform or eradicate specific village activities, and its subsequent failure to do so, serves a narrative function in the general theme of this investigation. It is not the results the investigation yields, but the process it describes, which is of the most value. The Lutheran authorities set out to reform certain aspects of parish life; the church had a network of higher authorities in place to enforce the mandates and ordinances issued in defence of the faith. And yet, as the look at feasts, dances, spinning bees, church fairs, blasphemy, usury, marriage, and communion suggests, they clearly fell short of their goals. As a campaign to enforce discipline and morality, the Reformation failed. How can we account for this failure? The task ahead is to study the process of reform in detail and examine its workings.

What were the reasons for this failure? To the clergy the answer was obvious: the Devil had never been so prominent among the people as in the sixteenth century. 'It would be no wonder', concluded the pastor of Hechlingen, 'if fire fell from the heavens and consumed them all.' The visitor of Hof offered the same prediction, with the analogy of Sodom and Gomorrah to strengthen his case: 'There is seldom a month when one does not hear of evil dealings'. 'Few are those,' was the common complaint of the pastors in 1569, 'who follow the narrow road through life; many are those who march to Hell with the common herd. Lord have mercy.' The visitor of Kulmbach repeated this cry of desperation in 1572:

---

[114] LKAN, MDWz (15 September 1591).

[115] Rainer Marbach, *Säkularisierung und sozialer Wandel im 19. Jahrhundert* (Göttingen, 1978), pp. 131–54; Utz Jeggle, *Kiebingen – eine Heimatgeschichte. Zum Prozeß der Zivilisation in einem schwäbischen Dorf* (Tübingen, 1977), pp. 171–80; Andreas Gestrich, *Traditionelle Jugendkultur und Industrialisierung* (Göttingen, 1986), pp. 92–103; Andreas Gestrich, 'Protestant Religion, the State and the Suppression of Traditional Youth Culture in Southwest Germany', *History of European Ideas*, 11 (1989), 629–35; Hugh McLeod, *Religion and the People of Western Europe 1789–1970* (Oxford, 1981), pp. 54–74; Richard J. Evans, 'Religion and Society in Modern Germany', *European Studies Review*, 12 (1982), 249–88.

Marriage, the mass and the fortunes of discipline

But dear God in heaven, what should one do? It is sad to attend, that evil has now taken such an upper hand it is an ancient ill, which will not be righted through this reminder alone, as the experience of the past two visitations, now brought to light, unfortunately proves.[116]

The Gunzenhausen visitation offered a statement encapsulating this mood of cheerless resignation: 'The world is, and remains, the world. It has never been good, and for this reason there is little improvement by high or low.'[117] This was the voice of a clerical minority who, like the Ansbach clergyman Andreas Althamer, expected these recursive patterns of immorality and blindness from Man after the Fall: 'For I see that matters stand exactly as Christ and the Apostles have foretold.'[118] The pastor and part-time astrologer of Burgbernheim, Georg Caesius, warned the people of Ansbach that they were sure to feel God's wrath 'since sermons, warnings, and godly admonishments do not help, God must visit us for our many sins with plagues, unnatural weather, hail, and violent storms'. There was no truth, no love, no fear of God in the land.[119]

But the clergy of Ansbach and Kulmbach did not blame Fallen Man alone for the offences against the faith: many clergy blamed the local authorities. The problem lay not with the higher officials, the superintendents and the district officials, but with the subaltern officials under their charge and active at the level of the parish. The visitors of Wunsiedel (1592) identified the problem: 'The greatest deficiency is with the lesser officials [an der untern Obrigkeit], in that they do not honour the mandates, but rather let things run their course...'[120] Complaints about the local secular officials' reluctance to enforce the mandates and decrees began with the introduction of the Reformation movement and continued throughout the century.[121] On occasion the local elite would not cooperate because of their aversion to the faith. Andreas Althamer maintained (c. 1530) that in Kulmbach the majority of the officials were Catholic (mer papistisch

---

[116] Sources for citations as follows: LKAN, MDU, 3, fo. 62: '...der Teüffell seÿ in den leutten erger nie gewesen...' (1564); LKAN, MDG, 71, fo. 6; StaB C2 1827, Relation der im herbst deß 1589 Jars gehaltener Visitation Inn der höfer Superintendentz, 19; LKAN, MDG, 71, fo. 29; LKAN, MSK, 157, Bericht der Spetial Visitation, In der Süperintendentz Beÿrreuth A[nn]o 1572, fo. 7 (my pagination).

[117] LKAN, MDG, 71, fo. 29.

[118] Anzey/gu[n]g warumb/Got die Wellt so lang/hab lassen irrhen/Durch Andream/Althamer (Nuremberg, 1526).

[119] Georg Caesius, Prognosticon Astrologicum...1575 (1574); Georg Caesius, Prognosticon Astrologicum...M.D.LXXXVIII (1587), B.

[120] STAB, C2 1830, fo. 109; STAN, Ansbacher Religionsakten III, Tom. XI, fo. 402; LKAN, MSK, 157, Bericht der Spetial Visitation, in der Süperintendentz Beÿrreüth A[nn]o 1572, 6 (my pagination); LKAN, MSK, 157, Weisenstadt 1573; LKAN, MDG 71, fo. 29 (1569); STAB, C2 1823, fo. 26 (1592).

[121] Even after the Franconian Circle issued a general police ordinance in 1572, little attempt was made by the local nobility to enforce it in their regions. See the reports in STAN 16a B–Laden Akten, Lade 212, for the years 1572–73; LKAN, MDH, V, 1a, fo. 42 (7 October 1572); STAB, C2 1826, Relation des Visitation Höfer Superi[n]tedents Anno 1576, fo. 9; LKAN, MDH, V, 1a, fo. 52 (13 October 1572); LKAN, MSK, 157, Mitt was Ordnung die Visitation des 1573 iares vorrichtet...', fo. 3 (my pagination); LKAN, MSK, 157, Beschwerung und Ergernus from Hof (1578/9), point 13.

den Christen).[122] On a more mundane level, many local noblemen refused to punish their subjects because they saw this as a violation of their local freedoms and privileges.[123] Other officials would not force the parishioners to go to church, explaining that 'to bring the people to church is not their office; no one should be forced to go to church'.[124] In the villages, the officials would 'turn a blind eye' and refuse to enforce discipline.[125] Night dances, *Rockenstuben*, and special feasts were tolerated in many places; they were seen as a right or a custom.[126] This licence was a common characteristic of parish-level rule, and it allowed both the parishioners and the authorities a degree of liberty which undermined the threat of punishment. It was just this type of liberty, observed the visitor of Kulmbach, which weakened the potency of the disciplinary process and gave rise to greater boldness from the parishioners.[127]

As with many aspects of rule in early modern European society, a gap existed between injunction and practice, between the desired norms and real-life experience.[128] The reason for the failure of the Lutheran authorities to impose their disciplinary aims on the subject population in Brandenburg-Ansbach-Kulmbach can be located at the level of the parish, where discipline had to take root. The course of reform realised in the village was not always the same as the course of reform dictated by the margrave's mandates. Parish events were shaped by a more complex dynamic.

PARISH POLITICS

An enormous amount of work has been done on the growth of the village commune and its relation to the early modern state.[129] While scholars disagree over particular aspects of the parish or village commune (*Gemeinde*) in the German-speaking lands, most are in agreement that it was an autochthonous

---

[122] STAN, *Ansbacher Religionsakten III*, Tom. XI, fo. 402 (Althamer's letter).

[123] LKAN, MSK, 157, *Bericht der Spetial Visitation, in der Süperintendentz Beÿrreuth A[nn]o 1572*, fo. 6 (my pagination):

> Zum theil, wie wir hören, von wegen der amptspersonen, so uber solchen nicht gehalten, und dan derer vom adel halben, welcher etliche, solche Mandata, neben Iren unterthanen, nicht annemen wöllen, sondern halten viel mehr uber solchen ergerlichen sachen, als ob Iren freÿ-heitten und privilegien.

[124] LKAN, MSK, 157, Weisenstadt 1573.

[125] LKAN, MDG, 71, fo. 29 (1569).

[126] Though some officials looked the other way for rather more material reasons, such as the mayor of Casendorf who claimed that dances were good for local business, or the official of Wersberg, who was easy prey to the bribe of a goose. LKAN, MSK, 157, Casendorf 1592: 'drauff sagten vogt und Burgermeister wen man die Tentz nicht gestattet, So lieffen sie gen Pesten und Turnaw und käme zu Mittag Niemand in die Marck und die Kirchen'; LKAN, MSK, 157, Wersberg 1592.

[127] StaB, C2 1823, fo. 26 (1592).

[128] Roger Chartier, *The Cultural Uses of Print in Early Modern France* (Princeton, 1987), pp. 9–10.

[129] See the overview and the literature in Heide Wunder, *Die bäuerliche Gemeinde in Deutschland* (Göttingen, 1986).

growth from below, rather than shaped from above, and that there was some variation in development as the commune emerged in different regions of Germany. Village communes differ in kind in line with the economic, political, social, geographical, and religious conditions of the regions in which they are studied, but some generalizations can be made. Village communes emerged out of the Middle Ages when the strong feudal ties were loosened and demesne farming waned. Rural settlements began to emerge as effective economic units (often centred around an extended family) with a fair degree of independent action in the planning, reaping, and disposal of their own agricultural affairs. Peasants began to direct their goods toward a market, rather than forfeiting their income as feudal dues, and as standardised fees replaced feudal dues, the peasant found it easier to harvest a yearly quota without suffering the interference of the local lord. As the hold of the lords over the peasantry loosened, and as peasant mobility increased, settlements expanded. It became necessary for the peasants to work together in rural collectives so that they could manage the resources more effectively. The village commune, as a political or administrative unit, emerged in response to this need.[130] By the sixteenth century, the village commune was a prominent feature of the political landscape of Germany. In Franconia, for instance, a region of mostly pure tenant farming (*Grundherrschaft*) and favourable land-holding rights, where freedom from serfdom in the sixteenth century could be purchased relatively cheaply, the peasantry was faced with favourable conditions very early on, gathering together in political collectives with a fair degree of autonomy over local affairs.[131]

At the time of the Reformation, the Franconian village, like the Württemberg villages studied by David Warren Sabean, might be described as 'one of self-administration with strong external controls.'[132] In Brandenburg-Ansbach-Kulmbach, the strong external control was exercised for the most part by the margrave. In each of the administrative districts in the margravate a district official (*Amtmann*) represented the interests of the margrave at his Ansbach court. The district officials dealt with all aspects of sixteenth-century governance, including taxation, legal affairs, criminal jurisdiction, and ecclesiastical matters.

---

[130] Jerome Blum, 'The Internal Structure and Polity of the European Village Community from the Fifteenth to the Nineteenth Century', *Journal of Modern History*, 43 (1971), 542–76; Wunder, *Die bäuerliche Gemeinde*, pp. 33–67; Blickle, *Gemeindereformation*, pp. 165–200; Karl Siegfried Bader, *Dorfgenossenschaft und Dorfgemeinde* (Weimar, 1962), pp. 30–114.

[131] Hanns Hubert Hofmann, 'Bauer und Herrschaft in Franken', in Günther Franz (ed.), *Deutsches Bauerntum im Mittelalter* (Stuttgart, 1976), pp. 424–64; Karl-Sigismund Kramer, *Die Nachbarschaft als bäuerliche Gemeinschaft* (Munich, 1954); Ingomar Bog, *Dorfgemeinde Freiheit und Unfreiheit in Franken* (Stuttgart, 1956), pp. 59–65; Rudolf Endres, 'The Peasants' War in Franconia', Scribner and Benecke (eds.), *The German Peasant War of 1525*, pp. 63–83. It has been suggested that the very fact the Franconian lords began to formalise their rights in relation to the villages (contained in the late-medieval *Weistümer*) reflects the emergence of a strong communal political unit. Klaus Arnold, 'Dorfweistümer in Franken', *Zeitschrift für bayerische Landesgeschichte*, 38 (1975), 855, 819–76.

[132] Sabean, *Power in the Blood*, p. 14.

The district official, however, did not act alone: he was helped in his office by a host of subaltern officials who carried out specific duties in the name of the margrave. The peasantry rarely dealt directly with the district official, but rather with these attendant officials: chief administrative officers (*Vogt*), custodians of margravial property (*Verwalter*), judges or members of a court (*Richter*), and officers of finance (*Kastner*). In the village itself, the chief administrative official or mayor (*Schultheiß*) represented the rights of the margrave. (The mayor might be the representative of another lord within the principality if the lord had been invested with the power to execute low jurisdiction.) In his tasks the mayor was aided by the officials constituting the court (*Gericht*) and the council (*Rat*). All of these men in the court and council, including the mayor, might be chosen or elected from among the inhabitants of the village, and in some instances the commune itself might be in control of election. On the whole, however, the function of these officials was very much defined by the powers of the overlord.[133]

The other external authority exercising control over the villagers was the superintendent. With the introduction of the Lutheran faith there came a reshuffling of ecclesiastical authority; the power of the bishops was removed altogether, and in their place the margrave constructed a network of chapters, each headed by a superintendent, who in turn answered to the consistories in Ansbach or Kulmbach. The superintendent's officer in the village was of course the pastor, but it is remarkable how often the superintendent personally intervened in parish affairs.

The self-administrative character of the village commune is rather more difficult to define. Unlike the higher officials in the service of the margrave, village officials did not leave much evidence as to the day-to-day workings of parish rule. Often the village leaders were given voice only when they were in contest with the pastor over a disputed property or appealing to the margrave to preserve a traditional parish right.[134] Parish documentation from this period, therefore, could be misleading if it were used as a means of recreating the concerns of village governance. Village ordinances – the laws, rules, and customs regulating local government and administration – are perhaps more representative of the true record, offering an idea of the scope and functions of village

---

[133] Bog, *Dorfgemeinde*, pp. 1, 66; Wunder, *Die bäuerliche Gemeinde*, pp. 45, 64–76; Kramer, *Volksleben im Fürstentum Ansbach*, pp. 126–36; Sabean, *Power in the Blood*, pp. 12–20.

[134] The autonomy of the village commune in Franconia was gradually eroded as the state began to extend its competence. For the Franconian *Gemeinde* under threat, see Rudolf Endres, 'Absolutistische Entwicklungen in fränkischen Territorien im Spiegel der Dorfordnungen', *Jahrbuch für Regionalgeschichte*, 16 (1989), pp. 81–93; Rudolf Endres, 'Stadt- und Landgemeinde in Franken', in Blickle (ed.), *Landgemeinde und Stadtgemeinde*, pp. 101–17. While Endres's overall theme is the decline of communal autonomy, he points out that the process was slow. Not until the eighteenth century did the margrave interfere in the life of the villages to any great extent. Endres also makes it clear that communal life in Bayreuth was almost non-existent, a point which Kramer has made as well.

magistracy.[135] The main organ of government was the communal assembly (*Gemeindeversammlung*), which included all the single male property owners or residents granted the right to live in the village. In theory, the voice of the majority was necessary for a proposal to be implemented. This was also the assembly at which the village rulers (*die Dorfmeister*) were elected. In most villages of Ansbach four men (*Vierer*) exercised the office of village leaders, though one or two men might bear the official title of village mayor (*Bürgermeister, Dorfmeister,* or *Bauernmeister*). These village elite were then responsible for the installation of the lesser officials, such as the common herdsman (*Dorfhirte*), men to watch over the shared lands (*Dorfflurer*) and the forests (*Holzwart*), night watchmen, fire inspectors, and a markstone supervisor (*Steiner*).[136]

The complexity and reach of village government might be considerable. In some lands in the Empire village communes became enfranchised members of the territorial government, promulgating laws binding for the whole community (a legal resource usually reserved for the local lords).[137] In Ansbach and Kulmbach, however, the powers wielded by the village commune were more modest. For the most part, the village authorities regulated local economic affairs, such as the use of woods, water, and land – in short, the common weal – to avoid the type of 'division and disunity' feared in an Ansbach village ordinance of 1586.[138] The eighteenth-century legal historian Johann Christian Siebenkees outlined the duties expected of the village officials: the formal appointment and oath-taking of new officials; the enforcement of local police measures (those that could be tried at the level of the village); the inspection of mills, wells, roads, bridges, and streams; the maintenance of fair weights and measurements; the calling of the common assembly and the annual reading of the parish accounts; and the preservation, allotment, and remittance of the common lands.[139] On occasion a commune might demonstrate powers and ambitions that would seem to draw it into conflict with the margrave, but nowhere in Brandenburg-Ansbach-Kulmbach did the village corporation ever challenge the right of the margrave to rule or endorse itself as an alternative form of government. The political aspirations of the village commune remained rooted in the parish, and there was very little, at that level, which

---

[135] What follows is taken from Heinrich Rauschert, 'Dorfordnungen in der Markgrafschaft Ansbach', Diss., Erlangen, 1952; Bader, *Dorfgenossenschaft und Dorfgemeinde*, pp. 266–383. For other ordinances in Franconia, see M. Hofmann, 'Die Dorfverfassung im Obermaingebiet', *Jahrbuch für fränkische Landesforschung*, 6/7 (1941), 140–96; Walter Scherzer, 'Die Dorfverfassung der Gemeinden im Bereich des ehemaligen Hochstifts Würzburg', *Jahrbuch für fränkische Landesgeschichte*, 36 (1976), 37–64; and the literature cited in Wunder, *Die bäuerliche Gemeinde*, p. 163.

[136] Rauschert, *Dorfordnungen*, pp. 40–93.

[137] Peter Blickle, *Deutsche Untertanen. Ein Widerspruch?* (Munich, 1981), pp. 29–36; Blickle, *Gemeindereformation*; Bog, *Dorfgemeinde*, p. 66.

[138] Rauschert, *Dorfordnungen*, Anhang II.

[139] Cited in Endres, 'Absolutistische Entwicklungen in fränkischen Territorien', p. 82. From the original *Beyträge zum teutschen Recht* (Nürnberg, 1786), pp. 211–13. Also cited in Rauschert, *Dorfordnungen*, pp. 13–14.

escaped its notice. It can safely be said that 'the community interfered in the daily existence of everyone and in the greatest events of the collective life'.[140]

Into this pattern of power relations stepped the pastor. On a day to day level, the pastor was more likely to deal with the members of the village commune than the margrave's officials. But there was not always a strict separation between the interests of the village elite and the interests of a resident margravial official. In many cases, the official might be the local nobleman; the rights of the parish were thus bound up with the prerogatives of a neighbouring lord. Whatever the situation facing a particular pastor, the need to secure the cooperation of the secular officials was paramount if the pastor wished to control the behaviour of his parishioners. The pastor needed to have enough support at the local level for his presence to be felt, whether it meant having a working relationship with the leaders of the village commune or the compliance of the margrave's officials. The disciplinary aims of the Lutheran church would be realised only if the resident pastors were able to penetrate the network of village or parish government and have their rulings enforced. How successful were the Lutheran pastors at commanding the cooperation of the local secular officials? To what degree were the pastors able to consolidate their powers of discipline in the parish? An analysis of the relationship between the pastor and the parish in Brandenburg-Ansbach-Kulmbach, as illustrated by the parishes of Weidelbach, Leutershausen, and Hechlingen, brings the problems confronting reform to life.

In January 1580 the single women of Weidelbach, an Ansbach parish, submitted a letter of grievance against their pastor, Georg Jung, to the district official of Feuchtwangen. According to the draft, Jung had sullied the honour of the women in a public address. Above all they cited his statement of 27 December 1579, that when the women visit the dances in neighbouring parishes the people see them approaching and say: 'Here come the Weidelbach whores.'[141] No honourable woman, Jung claimed, would be seen near them. A list of similar accusations, all depreciating their collective reputation, followed. The women ended the supplication with a request for Jung's removal and the appointment of another pastor.

Georg Jung was given the chance to answer the charges brought against him, and on 3 March 1580 he drafted a lengthy defence.[142] According to Jung, the offending statement had emerged from a sermon on celibacy and good conduct. Jung had admonished the women of his congregation to live honourably in the three key stages of a woman's life: virginity, marriage, and widowhood. The pastor was convinced that many of his female parishioners refused to heed the

---

[140] Léopold Genicot, *Rural Communities in the Medieval West* (London, 1990), p. 60.

[141] LKAN, MKA, Spez. 1015, *Underthenige Bitliche Supplication Aller Jungfrauen und dienstmegten sampt und sonders zu Weidlbach* (January 1580). 'Item wann wir andererorten ausser dem fleckhen zum dentz giengen so fraget und sagt man do kommen die hurn zu weidelbach stunde auch kein erliche Jüngfraw zu uns, sonder tretten von uns ab.'

[142] LKAN, MKA, Spez. 1015, *Antwort Georgen Jüngen auff die Clag der vier Maigd zu Weÿdelbach, welche Clag mir nach meinem urlaub zukomen* (3 March 1580).

Word of God or yield to the moral dictates of the visitation ordinances. Jung cited the continuance of *Rockenstuben* within the village and the rash of late-night dances as proof. And he was able to make specific accusations: he singled out three women who had openly violated one or more of the marriage articles. One woman in particular had once kept very late company with a man, drinking, dancing, and singing so heartily it frightened the children. The din was so overwhelming it seemed, Jung opined, 'as if a number of devils had escaped from Hell and sought shelter there.' In his letter of defence the pastor referred to his repeated efforts to bring this behaviour to the attention of the local official, all of which failed to help. Jung was not able to govern the behaviour of his parishioners.

When Jung contacted the Ansbach authorities, they suggested to him that, since many of his parishioners were the subjects of the Teutonic Order in Dinkelsbühl, he should approach the Order's local official in Weidelbach, Michael Schmidt.[143] Jung followed this advice and, in doing so, multiplied his difficulties. Franconia was a region of multiple lordships and it was not unusual for a pastor to have to deal with more than one lord. The Teutonic Order of Dinkelsbühl had been enfeoffed with the parish of Weidelbach and the Order had traditionally exercised patronage over the appointment of clergymen. In 1566, however, the Teutonic Knights acquiesced to the installation of an evangelical pastor. Although the Order offered some initial resistance, the margrave was able to integrate the parish into the superintendency of Feuchtwangen. In 1571 visitations were extended to the parish.[144] The Reformation, in a legal sense, had been implemented; but the traditional relations of rule, as Michael Schmidt soon demonstrated, were still in place.

When Georg Jung was appointed in early January 1577, the parish had been home to an evangelical service for over a decade. Jung soon found, however, that many of his duties and rights as a pastor were being challenged by Michael Schmidt. In a letter to the margrave (3 September 1578) Jung reproached Schmidt for his refusal to pay his share of the pastor's maintenance, his efforts to deprive Jung of his rights (*pferliche gerechtigkeÿt*), and his habit of letting his animals run roughshod over the glebe lands. To make matters worse, Schmidt and his wife were trying to incite general enmity against the pastor, going from house to house in an effort to persuade the parishioners to withhold tithes. Jung had brought Schmidt's behaviour to the attention of a higher official in Dinkelsbühl, but the official had answered Jung in return: 'He can not help me; they [the family Schmidt] no longer set any store by him.'[145] Jung then turned to the margrave's officials in Feuchtwangen for help, and with some success, as Schmidt was imprisoned for thirteen days in 1578. But this only kindled greater

---

143 LKAN, MKA, spez. 1015 (8 April 1580). An official of the Teutonic Order in Dinkelsbühl referred to Schmidt as 'unsers ordens vogt zu Weÿdelbach'.
144 LKAN, MKA, Spez. 1015, fos. 108–10.
145 LKAN, MKA, Spez. 1015 (3 September 1578).

bitterness, as Jung observed: 'as soon as they [Schmidt and his wife] came out of jail they were only all the more infuriated.'[146] Georg Jung could accomplish very little in the parish in the face of Schmidt's opposition. In 1580 the translation the pastor had first requested on 2 March was granted: Georg Jung was transferred to the parish of Colmberg.

Nine years later in the parish of Leutershausen the pastor was facing similar problems as those which beset Georg Jung, including, ironically, an attempt to remove him from office and replace him with the pastor of Colmberg.[147] Leutershausen provides a long-term view of developments between the pastor and the parish. Leutershausen was a wealthy parish, with a surfeit of foundations, when the Reformation was introduced in the 1520s.[148] Johann Nagel became the first evangelical pastor; he participated in the 1528 visitation and was nominated for the superintendency. Nagel was dismissed, however, in 1530 (due perhaps to his Anabaptist sympathies) and was replaced by the aged Lutheran clergyman and pamphleteer Johann Eberlin von Günzburg.[149] Eberlin soon found himself in conflict with members of his parish. The local official (*Kastner*), in particular, was very abusive to Eberlin. He accosted Eberlin at the inn, where he said to him: 'you are a rogue, and if you were pious, you would not have come here'. On another occasion the *Kastner* held his fist before the pastor's nose and vowed: 'See, you rogue, your life is not safe before my hand!' Soon other members of the parish began to follow this bad example, until it got to the point where children would sing songs about the pastor and his family in the open streets. On one occasion, as Eberlin and his wife left the church, 'there was such shouting and singing about us from Jorg Losen's house that all the neighbours ran to their windows'.[150] Eberlin was not able to overcome this antagonism.

A subsequent pastor of Leutershausen, Johann Conrad, was no more successful than Eberlin at taming the wilfulness of his parishioners. Conrad had been cited before the consistory in 1589 by the local officials of Leutershausen as lazy, in dispute with many of his parishioners, and wont to vent his frustrations from the pulpit. 'It would be no wonder', he is once supposed to have said, 'if God should strike this city to earth with thunder and hail.'[151] Conrad defended himself in a series of letters to the consistory. The pastor made it clear that the parishioners

---

[146] LKAN, MKA, Spez. 1015 (3 March 1580).
[147] LKAN, MKA, Spez. 500 (8 December 1589), point 3.
[148] Leutershausen was a market town of between 600–700 people in the sixteenth century. E. Keyser and H. Stoob, *Bayerisches Städtebuch* (Stuttgart, 1971), 1, Leutershausen.
[149] Karl Schornbaum, 'Leutershausen bei Beginn der Reformationszeit und das Ende Eberlins von Günzburg', *Beiträge zur bayerischen Kirchengeschichte*, 11 (1905), 5–34, 78–92; Christian Peters, ' "Der Teufel sieht mich hier nicht gern" Die Zwölf Briefe Johann Eberlins von Günzburg aus seiner Zeit als Pfarrverweser in Leutershausen (1530–1533)', *ZbKG*, 59 (1990), 23–68; LKAN, MDL, 165 (20 August 1529). For the list of complaints from Heßberg, see Peters, 45–49.
[150] Schornbaum, 'Leutershausen bei Beginn der Reformationszeit', pp. 22–3; LKAN, MKA, Spez. 500, fos. 48–50.
[151] LKAN, MKA, Spez. 500 (30 October 1589) (10 November 1589).

were reluctant to pay their tithes, and even more reluctant to hear the Word preached in its purity. He often cited passages from the Bible and parables from sacred history, he explained, that were misinterpreted by his parishioners and then used against him. 'You godless knave', he once asked an accuser, 'how can you know what I meant? Are you God? Are you in my mind or my heart?'[152]

Johann Conrad, like Johann Eberlin von Günzburg before him, was at odds with the parishioners of Leutershausen, to the point where he could no longer command their respect. And in both instances the two pastors of Leutershausen were opposed, rather than supported, by the local secular officials. Eberlin was abused by the local official Veit Gattenhofer as soon as he arrived in the parish. Gattenhofer would not cooperate with Eberlin or heed the pastor's censure, and he exercised a freedom of rule characterised by the pastor as 'tyrannical'. He took liberties with the marriage laws; he did not attend communion; he abused the parishioners; and he once accused Eberlin of paying to much heed to the chancellery mandates.[153] Resistance did not end there. The district official Wolf von Heßberg also resented Eberlin's presence in the parish, going so far as to submit a list of grievances against the pastor.[154] Neither of these men helped Eberlin realise his will in the parish.

Over fifty years later, Johann Conrad suffered the same problems. Conrad's alleged failings had been brought to the attention of the Ansbach authorities by the mayor and councillors of Leutershausen and an official (*Vogt*) by the name of Hans Schreier. Schreier was particularly threatening to the pastor: 'God help you, my dear little priest [*Pfaffe*]. Now you must hurry away, and when you have a mountain before you, no excuses will help you then.'[155] Schreier was perhaps alluding to an attempt the authorities had made to secure Conrad's dismissal. In his November letter of defence, Conrad referred to the *Amtmann*'s efforts to have him removed from office; he was too old, no use, the accusations ran, and he should go to Schwabach or seek his rest at the monastery of Heilsbronn. Needless to say, Conrad could not elicit the help of these secular officials. The result, as Conrad noted with his penchant for aphorisms, was a stand-off: 'When the ecclesiastical and the secular rules are not united (as experience teaches), it is ill-fortune.'[156] Johann Conrad was transferred to another parish; in his stead, the parishioners welcomed their choice, Abdias Wickner from Colmberg.

A final example of this type of deadlock between pastor and parish is offered by the case of Hechlingen. In July 1574 the parish of Hechlingen, the 'whole commons, complete and unanimous', sent a letter of grievance to the margrave against their pastor, Christoph Planck.[157] The pastor was in dispute with his

152 LKAN, MKA, Spez. 500 (18 November 1589) (8 December 1589).
153 Peters, 'Der Teufel sieht mich hier nicht gern', pp. 54–6.
154 LKAN, MKA, Spez. 500, fos. 57–9.
155 LKAN, MKA, Spez. 500 (8 December 1589). 'Haec sunt verba Johan Schreier.'
156 LKAN, MKA, Spez. 500 (8 December 1589).
157 LKAN, MKA, Spez. 394, fos. 163–6.

parishioners over a plot of land in Hechlingen. The central issue in question was whether the plot should remain free of tithes. The parishioners, during the course of this feud, made a number of claims about Planck's deportment in the parish and capacity in office which would suggest that the relationship between the pastor and the congregation was strained. According to the letter of grievance, Planck was taking the tithe by force; he frequented taverns and inns, drank from one midnight to the next, and was often seen in bad company. When asked for absolution by sick men and women, he refused them the sacrament. Indeed, the parishioners later testified, Planck went so far as to deny them communion: 'He does not have the time today to extend the Lord's Supper', were his alleged (and unlikely) words on one such occasion, 'he has to go to the Meinheim church fair.'[158] The parishioners insisted they could no longer tolerate Planck. 'With this pastor there can be no hope of improvement', they wrote in 1575 and asked for a new clergyman.[159]

Planck made it clear to the Ansbach authorities that he felt himself under siege in the parish and helpless in the face of their aggression. The accusations against him were fabricated; the parishioners, whose only concern was keeping the contested plot of land immune from tithes, acted out of a 'bitter envy'. Planck compared his plight in Hechlingen to that of Christ surrounded by the Jews: 'They would soon crucify me or kill me, only that they do not have the power.' Hechlingen, Planck vowed, is well known as a den of rogues. The administrator of the Heidenheim monastery had said as much: if you want to send a pastor among devils, send him to Hechlingen.[160] Even after Christoph Planck was dismissed from the parish he could get no rest. The parishioners continued to abuse Planck as he waited for another office, refusing his animals the run of the common lands and threatening him and his wife in their beds. In 1576, following a search for a new parish that took him as far afield as Austria, Planck returned to Ansbach, to the 'pure motherly milk of God's Word', and became the new pastor of Schauernheim.[161]

To an even greater degree than Georg Jung, Johann Eberlin von Günzburg, or Johann Conrad, Christoph Planck was at odds with the local secular officials in his parish. Two of the village officials (*Vierer*), Hans Büssel and Caspar Lengle, were singled out by Planck as the leaders of the village movement to remove him from office.[162] Büssel and Lengle worked behind the pastor's back, sending draft after draft of grievances to the regional

---

[158] LKAN, MKA, Spez. 394, fo. 209.
[159] LKAN, MKA, Spez. 394, fos. 248–50, 241.
[160] LKAN, MKA, Spez. 394, fos. 233–40, 234, 238, 239: 'der Verwalter zu Haÿdenhaim gewarnet und gesagt, ja, wen er pfarer unter die Teuffell woll ziehen, so solle er zu denen von Hechlingen ziehen.' On a similar note, when the visitors arrived in Hechlingen in 1567 to the blasts of drunken revelry it sounded as if they were 'in the middle of Hell'. LKAN, MDG, 71, fo. 6.
[161] LKAN, MKA, Spez. 394, fos. 270–3, 280–2.
[162] LKAN, MKA, Spez. 394, fo. 176.

authorities of Hohentrüdingen (the administrative district) in an effort to discredit Planck and effect his translation to another parish. Even as the outcome of the tithe feud was pending in Hohentrüdingen, Büssel and Lengle, along with a few of their 'consorts', sent a letter directly to the margrave himself 'in order to ask for another pastor'.[163] Given the animosity directed at him, it is unlikely that Planck could elicit any cooperation at all from these men. The installation of the sexton, for instance, a formality which involved the participation of the pastor in the Ansbach parishes, (if not always his full supervision), occurred without Planck's approval and against Planck's will.[164] The situation in Hechlingen was thus similar to the situation in Weidelbach and Leutershausen: the pastor was unable to overcome local resistance. Unlike the other parishes, however, the pastor in Hechlingen was not opposed by the higher officials of the margrave residing in the parish, but by members of the village rule themselves. As Planck observed: 'what the provocateurs and ringleaders of this matter enjoy as rule and dynasty [*erbes Leben*] amongst themselves and their sons and daughters is known to both the authorities and many in Hechlingen.'[165] Christoph Planck was transferred to another parish in 1576.

There are common threads running throughout the studies presented above. In each case, a state of discord rather than concord describes the relationship between pastor and parish, and in each case, the secular authorities heightened, rather than limited, the pastor's isolation and impotency. Lutheran pastors in Brandenburg-Ansbach-Kulmbach often fell foul of their parishioners the moment they attempted to introduce stricter disciplinary measures. In the eyes of the local authorities, this drive to reform the parish in line with the moral directives of the Lutheran church seemed a threat to local rule. The character of this local rule, however, was very different from the type of government associated with communal rule. The vast majority of parishioners played no role in the disputes. The pastors were opposed by a ruling elite – whether the higher officials in the service of the margrave or a cabal of village leaders – who sought to preserve their local autonomy against the pastor's intervention. And what is perhaps of greatest interest, the secular authorities looked to justify their dissent with reference to the standards of the very institution responsible for the pastor's actions in the parish: the Lutheran church. Let us now examine these points in greater detail.

If there was a conflation of moralising instincts with the onset of the Reformation (as the reforming ambitions of the church combined with those of

---

[163] LKAN, MKA, Spez. 394, fo. 241.
[164] LKAN, MKA, Spez. 394, fo. 234.
[165] LKAN, MKA, Spez. 394, fo. 239. The lack of higher officials in this dispute may be due to the fact that Hechlingen enjoyed a fair degree of autonomy, as it was a fairly large village with its own court. Hanns Hubert Hofmann, *Gunzenhausen–Weissenburg* (Munich, 1960), pp. 62, 127–8.

the state) it is not surprising that the Lutheran pastor was viewed with resentment as he worked to impose these norms in the parish. Clergymen driven to correct or reform the behaviour of their parishioners often encountered hostile reactions. When Georg Jung tried to impose greater order on the parish of Weidelbach his parishioners protested: 'There is now an effort to maintain a regulation of discipline ... before this time no one paid such close attention.' The wife of Michael Schmidt, Jung's rival in Weidelbach, made the most poignant reference to this intrusion (as recorded by Jung): 'Since this Lutheranism has arrived there has been no prosperity nor benefit, for the unrepentant life is being punished.'[166] Pastors were often begrudged for their reforming zeal. The troubles Johann Eberlin von Günzburg experienced with the secular officials in Leutershausen were due in no small measure to the officials' aversion to Eberlin's disciplinary measures. 'They do it purely out of the fear that they will have to accept good order', was Eberlin's conclusion.[167] Johann Conrad, later pastor of Leutershausen, was deeply resented by the parishioners and officials alike because of his unyielding commitment to the Lutheran ordinances. 'The Devil be our pastor! It is a pity we should have such a learned man', was the lament of his congregation. In response, Conrad cited the counsel of Martin Luther: pastors who let sins go unpunished will go to the Devil. But for Johann Conrad, and many others like him, the attempt to introduce stricter disciplinary measures only incited the parishioners to greater antagonism. The result in many cases was a stand-off between the pastor and his congregation.[168]

That the pastors should have encountered resistance is not surprising. The extent to which the local secular officials deliberately impeded the reforming efforts of the pastors, however, does offer a unique view of the Reformation as it was implemented in the parishes. The local secular officials considered the Lutheran pastors a threat to their independence of rule. In some cases, all manner of parish affairs were in the hands of a few individuals. Johann Conrad observed in 1589 that the local officials wanted 'to reform [*verneuern*] not only the secular offices, but also the ecclesiastical [institutions], the church and the schools'.[169] The pastor of Repperndorf, Jacob Sumpffelder, made the same observation (albeit in a drunken stupor) about the higher authorities in his parish: the *Schultheiß* wanted to be master of all; but he was the *Schultheiß*,

---

[166] LKAN, MKA, Spez. 1015 (3 September 1578). A similar sentiment was expressed by a woman in the Nürnberg parish of Tennenlohe (1561): 'Sie sagt auch weil Lutherus [...] die lehr auffbracht hat, seÿ weder glück noch hayl in Germania.' StaN, *Kirchen und Ortschaften auf dem Lande*, no. 454. Tennenlohe. I am grateful to Dr Philip Broadhead for this reference. Dr Broadhead alludes to this statement in his article 'Self-Interest and Security: Relations between Nuremberg and its Territory in the Early Sixteenth Century', *German History*, 11 (1993), 17.
[167] LKAN, MKA, Spez. 500, fo. 58.
[168] LKAN, MKA, Spez. 500 (10 November 1589) (8 December 1589). See the similar conclusions in Karant-Nunn, 'Neoclericalism', p. 636.
[169] LKAN, MKA, Spez. 500 (18 November 1589).

not the pastor, Sumpffelder concluded, and he should stick to his office.[170] There was no room for two spheres of authority with antagonistic traditions of rule.

Quite rightly, the village elite viewed the arrival of a Lutheran pastor with some apprehension. There was good reason for this concern. As the Bayreuth visitation instructions made clear, each pastor was expected to draft a 'thorough report and testimony of all officials and councillors, both in the cities and in the countryside, and all the church-goers in the parish' and present a summary evaluation of their conduct to the visitors.[171] The secular officials resented that the pastor might use this leverage against them. The *Kastner* of Leutershausen railed at Johann Eberlin von Günzburg when the latter involved the Ansbach authorities in their local dispute. 'You are a rogue,' were his words to the pastor, 'you have brought the Ansbach *Kastner* here, you scoundrel, and cited me before the margrave's councillors.'[172] In Hechlingen, pastor Christoph Planck raised the ire of the village elite when he tried to infiltrate their 'rule and dynasty'. Some secular officials, in an effort to secure themselves against the pastor's intrusions, simply excluded the clergyman from any parish activities that might place their rule in jeopardy. Peter Meckel of Großhabersdorf recorded in 1586 how the *Richter* Wolf Fürst had taken the chest of documents from the church:

and without my knowledge, removed all letters from the church and taken them to their court. They then inspected the same, just as if they should be better and more readily informed on church secrets than the pastor. And although they now assert, that these are things for the most part relating to the court, this is no excuse. For they haven't had a court notary for four months; and up to now, all court-related matters have gone through the pastor's hands, and thus not kept from him.[173]

Wolf Fürst's reaction was just one type of defensive strategy utilized by the secular authorities to keep the Lutheran clergymen at bay.

There is no doubt that organised resistance was in the hands of a few men in the parish. The commune, the vast majority of the parishioners, played no role in the disputes. In part this is due to the structure of power in sixteenth-century rural society. The commune in Ansbach and Kulmbach did not have the claims to

[170] LKAN, MKA, Spez. 697, *Ettliche Artickul Jacoben Sumpffelters pfarherren zu Repperndorff, so ein Schultheyß Burgermeÿster, Gerichte und ein Gantze Gemeindt wider Ihn seines lebens halben clagt* (21 February 1581).

[171] LKAN, MSK, 157, *Bericht der Spetial Visitation, In der Süperintendentz Beÿrreuth A[nn]o 1572*, fo. 4 (my pagination).

[172] Schornbaum, 'Leutershausen bei Beginn der Reformationszeit', p. 23. Schornbaum may have been citing the words attributed to the *Amtmann* Wolf von Heßberg: 'Item, du Boßwicht hast mich verlogen vor den Rathen, hast den Castner von Onoltzbach herauß bracht.' LKAN, MKA, Spez. 500, fo. 49. Eberlin does not always make the distinction between the *Kastner* Veit Gattenhofer and the *Amtmann* Wolf von Heßberg clear.

[173] LKAN, MKA, Spez. 348 (6 June 1586).

rule warranting its intervention; and by the same token, the commune could neither contravene nor act independently of the higher secular officials. As Johann Conrad observed of his Leutershausen parishioners, they could not challenge the policy of the town officials: 'quite clearly the people [*Bürger*] can say nothing against the new official and the council [*den Neuen vogt und Senat*].' When they were consulted, Conrad continued, they were forced to confirm the findings of the council.[174]

But even in a situation where the commune, in theory, should have played a part, the bulk of the parishioners had no knowledge of events and no influence over the course of policy. The pastor faced the opposition of a few men, the ruling elite. In 1570, for instance, although the 'mayor, council, and entire parish of Langenzenn' submitted a letter of grievance against their pastor, the Ansbach examiners soon discovered that 'although the entire parish subscribed to the list of grievances, nevertheless only a minority had any knowledge of it'.[175] Christoph Planck made the same observation in 1574 when he was coming to terms with the letters of complaint against him submitted to the Ansbach authorities by the 'entire parish, complete and unanimous' of Hechlingen. Planck accused the two *Vierer*, Hans Büssel and Caspar Lengle, of falsifying the charges and then signing the document in the name of the commune without actually soliciting their approval. At most, Planck wrote, this was the work of a small collusion of village elite headed by Büssel and Lengle – 'twelve or fifteen people do not constitute an entire parish'. Planck claimed that the leaders of this conspiracy worked 'in darkness, in secret' to realise their aims. They never informed the commune of their actions, nor did they ever seek the commune's approval.[176] The testimony gathered by the Ansbach officials in a later inquiry revealed that Christoph Planck was right: the vast majority of the parishioners played no part in the grievances submitted in the name of the commune. As one witness testified, no one had asked them 'whether they stand by the parish or whether they want the pastor to fall'.[177] This type of underhand scheming frustrated the pastors. 'Why haven't they asked the entire parish and heard their say?' wondered pastor Paul Faber of Martinsheim, called to answer charges against his conduct drawn up by the mayor and court officials in his parish, but signed in the name of 'the entire parish'.[178] 'Neither he nor his neighbours were summoned [to endorse it]', answered Hans Kolb in the parish of Neudrossenfeld, when called to answer for the collective letter of complaint submitted against the pastor Kaspar Günther. The letter was commissioned without the commune's

---

[174] LKAN, MKA, Spez. 500 (8 December 1589): 'daselbst sind sie Instrucirt und verhetzt worden was sie reden sollen ut consentiant secu. So sind sie nit privatum vom H. Decano, ut decuisset (den sie eingenommen nit wenig) sonder plente Senatu eingelassen und verhört worden, und also deß senats klagen bestettigen müssen.'

[175] LKAN, MKA, Spez. 527, fo. 91.

[176] LKAN, MKA, Spez. 394, fos. 176, 239.

[177] LKAN, MKA, Spez. 394, fos. 221, 215–28.

[178] LKAN, MKA, Spez. 566, fo. 104.

knowledge and drafted by a Bayreuth scribe.[179] Throughout the century, despite the protests of the pastors, the secular officials evoked the name of the commune to endorse the intrigues of a ruling minority.

The confrontation between the pastor and the parish, and thus between the disciplinary aims of the Lutheran church and the moral licence of the rural parishioners, was played out at this level: the pastor versus a handful of secular officials. But it was more than just a battle of wills or personalities. No matter how resolved their opposition, local authorities could hope to accomplish little in the long term against a Lutheran pastorate supported by the territorial prince. In order for these men to be successful, if only transitorily, they had to undermine the pastor's credibility. On occasion, as noted above, this parish resistance was not only coercive enough to thwart the pastor's objectives: resistance to the pastor might even end with his dismissal. This is due to the strategy behind the parish defence. In Großhabersdorf, for instance, when it became apparent to the *Richter* Wolf Fürst in 1587 (one year after he removed the chest from the church) that pastor Peter Meckel intended to remain in the parish and interfere with his policies of rule, Fürst shifted the focus of his defence. The new concern was now Meckel's 'tyranny in the confessional'. Peter Meckel was cited before the Ansbach authorities as an unsuitable Lutheran pastor.[180] The village officials in Weimersheim, incensed by their pastor's stubborn resolve to burden the parish with novelties, compiled a list of his alleged failings, which 'to the best of our simple understanding is contrary to our princely grace's ordinance'. The list imputed the pastor's performance at mass, his pedagogical skills, and his residence record in the parish. They ended the draft by appealing for a new pastor.[181]

In Hechlingen, the attack against Christoph Planck's competence was even more calculated. Soon after his arrival in Hechlingen, Planck became involved in a quarrel with the village rulers over a plot of land in the parish and whether it should be tithed. This was an issue with a considerable pedigree: the plot of land had been contested in 1525, 1532, and 1556. On each occasion the parishioners defended their claims with reference to a contract awarded to them by margrave Albrecht Achilles in 1448. After 1574, however, as the tension between the pastor and the village officials flamed up, Planck's antagonists adopted a new strategy. Although the central issue was still the tithes, other themes now gradually entered the dialogue. The village leaders began to focus on Planck's failings as a Lutheran clergyman: he refused to extend the sacrament; he spent his time drinking with ne'er-do-wells; he denied absolution; and, most damaging of all, the principal task of the Lutheran pastor – the preaching of the Word –

---

[179] StaB, C3, 1223, fos. 145, 143–54. *Aussage Etlicher Personen in genumener Inquisition den Pfarrherr zu Drosenfeldt und seine Pfarrkhinder betreffent.*

[180] LKAN, MKA, Spez. 348 (1588).

[181] LKAN, MKA, Spez. 964, fos. 42–4.

was abused in his hands.[182] The charges against Planck are almost certainly false,[183] but there can be no doubt that whoever formulated the complaints against Planck was familiar with the expectations of the Lutheran church and knew that the charges would be damaging.[184] This was a deliberate rhetorical strategy. In Brandenburg-Ansbach-Kulmbach, throughout the latter decades of the sixteenth century, complaints against the clergymen started taking on similar definition: irrespective of the real issue under dispute the pastor was measured against the backdrop of the Lutheran faith and the expectations of his office. The ruling elite sought to justify its resistance with reference to the association of standards introduced by the Reformation, and yet it was the Reformation itself, and the strength of disciplinary purpose it inspired, that first induced the act of resistance from a tradition of rule under threat. In the fullest sense, pastor and local elite were at odds: both used the Lutheran faith, but for completely different ends.

An event like the Reformation, an episode of such deep importance for western history, is misrepresented when its reach is limited to the realm of faith alone. Concepts such as social disciplining and confessionalisation do justice to the broader implications of the Lutheran movement in Germany. Church did merge with state in Lutheran territories and the effect of this union spread to every corner of society. The desire to reform parish morality, for instance, became a concern of both church and state; as a consequence, methods of parish surveillance improved, while edicts and mandates governing behaviour grew in scope and complexity. But success was not inevitable. In the Lutheran margravate of Brandenburg-Ansbach-Kulmbach, a distinction must be made between the claims and injunctions of the authorities and the actual exercise of power. The Lutheran authorities were often unable to impose their disciplinary aims on the parishioners in the sixteenth century. The very men responsible for the execution of disciplinary measures at the local level presented active, and frequently successful, resistance to the local agents of Lutheran reform, the parish pastors. When the Reformation is examined at the level of its implementation, at the level where it became the flesh and blood reality of its abstract designs, it amounts to much less than what its founders envisioned. Perhaps the Reformation's place of purchase was the realm of thought.

---

[182] LKAN, MKA, Spez. 394, fos. 1, 10, 22–6, 60–9, 163–66, 208–212, 248 (copies of the contract: 50, 51, 94.) This land may have been part of the property sold to Hechlingen by Ludwig von Oettingen in 1367. See Robert Schuh, *Gunzenhausen* (Munich, 1979), p. 125.

[183] During the examination of the parishioners everyone save one man gave him a good witness and opposed a change of clergyman. According to his own report, not a single grievance had been forwarded against him in the visitations. Nor between 1576 and 1598 did the congregation of Schauernheim have anything bad to say about him in the Neustadt visitations after his transfer to this parish in 1576. StaN, *Ansbacher Neues Generalrepertorium*, no. 49, Rep. 103ᵉ, fos. 24, 52, 75, 84.

[184] Indeed, as one of the ringleaders had ripped nine pages out of the Hechlingen copy of the 1533 church ordinance, it is tempting to imagine them working away into the night, using the nine pages as a book of reference. LKAN, MKA , Spez. 394, fo. 236.

5

The acculturation of the parish mind

THE COMPLEXION OF RELIGIOUS REFORM

The lands of Franconia, Ansbach and Kulmbach included, had not been immune to religious innovation before the arrival of the Reformation.[1] Nor was the territory exempt from the suspect outgrowths of the religious revival common to other regions of the Empire in the sixteenth century. Anabaptism, for example, took root in Herzogenaurach, Erlangen, Uttenreuth, and Nuremberg (all located within the borders of Ansbach), where it had been planted and fertilised by the influential Anabaptist leader Hans Hut.[2] At first, margrave Georg was reluctant to prosecute the Anabaptists with too much vigour; he feared, as he expressed it in 1528, that surplus zeal in this matter might cause some of the true followers of Christ to fall under the blade.[3] Nevertheless, he did issue a mandate against Anabaptism that same year and continued to encourage the Ansbach council to remain vigilant and displace unwanted sects.[4] Total success, a territory-wide uprooting of deviant persuasions, was never a possibility, nor was it ever a strict necessity. Pockets of Anabaptist congregations remained well into the closing years of the century; visitations continued to unearth parishioners who were considered (or considered themselves) to be members of this forbidden sect. But their beliefs endured as a private confidence shared among socially harmless groupings tucked away in the rural parishes. Anabaptism did not present the margravial church with a real threat.[5]

[1] Hermann Haupt, *Die religiösen Sekten in Franken vor der Reformation* (Würzburg, 1882); Gerhard Schlesinger, *Die Hussiten in Franken* (Kulmbach, 1974), pp. 54–76.

[2] Günther Bauer, *Anfänge täuferischer Gemeindebildungen in Franken* (Munich, 1966); Werner O. Packull, *Mysticism and the Early South German-Austrian Anabaptist Movement 1525–1531* (Scottdale, 1977); Krauβold, *Geschichte der evangelischen Kirche*, p. 81; Lith, *Erläuterung der Reformationshistorie*, p. 231.

[3] StaB, C3 1225, (7 March 1528). Letter from Augsburg. Georg felt that the imperial orders to execute suspected Anabaptists without a hearing was 'zu vil scharpff'.

[4] StaN, *Ansbacher Religionsakten III*, Tom. 12, fo. 84. (1532). For the process in the parish of Schalkhausen, see Eberhard Teufel, 'Der Täuferprozeβ gegen Pfarrer Hechtlein in Schalkhausen bei Ansbach 1529–1530', *ZbKG*, 18 (1949), pp. 88–98; LKAN, MKA, Spez. 756. 1529ff.

[5] StaN, *Ansbacher Neues Generalrepertorium*, no. 49, rep. nr. 103^e, fo. 16. Hans Schöman of Ipsheim was accused in 1578 of being an Anabaptist 'wie er selbs bekennt'. The charge of Anabaptism was often only a blanket accusation against the parishioners who seemed to question the Eucharist. The pastor of Obernbreit confessed: 'das etliche personen nit allein ötwa in 10 Jaren nicht zum

Within its own borders, the principality was free of serious confessional antagonism: neither crypto-Calvinism, Zwinglianism, Counter-Reformation Catholicism, nor any sizeable followings of the more kindred theological offshoots, such as the followers of Matthias Flacius Illyricus, found voice in the margravate. The only other consolidated religious grouping was that of the Jews. Small cells of Jewish believers in Ansbach can be traced back to the year 1303. The margraves had granted the Jews special dispensations due to their usefulness as money lenders; even Georg the Pious allowed for them to reside in the margravate. Not until Georg Friedrich ordered the expulsion of the Jews in 1560 is it proper to speak of a campaign against the faith; and even after Georg Friedrich's 1560 resolution Jewish communities could, and did, endure – there was no pogrom, no mass exodus, no wave of persecution.[6] Protests against the Jews – as when parishioners submitted grievances against the Jewish community in Fürth – usually arose when the villagers thought their business dealings suspect or their behaviour somehow disrespectful of the Christian faith.[7] Mutual antagonism and shared hatred between Christians and Jews was, of course, a common state of affairs in early modern society, and it should come as no surprise that disputes between the townsfolk and the Jews in Fürth often ended in violent quarrels in the open streets. (The fracas between Hans Hübner of Wassertrüdingen, Georg Beuchel, and a Jewish couple, for instance, ended with the latter two suffering a physical assault.[8]) And yet in

---

Abentmal khumen, sunder sindt auch des Widertauffs verdechtig gewesen, doch nach besprechung des Pfarrers mit denselben personen, hat sich befunden, das sie oecolampadische bucherin gehabt'. LKAN, MKU, 8, Obernbreit (29 September 1581).

6   Siegfried Haenle, *Geschichte der Juden im ehemaligen Fürstenthum Ansbach* (Ansbach, 1867), pp. 8–21, 52–8.

7   StaN, 16a B-Laden Lade 191 no. 4 (17 October 1564). Although the jurisdiction of Fürth was disputed between Ansbach and Nuremberg, the complaints were sent to Ansbach because Georg Friedrich had subjects in Fürth (the pastor included). The Fürth pastor had received a harsh reprimand from the regional official of Cadolzburg for preaching against the Jews. Apparently he had said that the Jews should be killed like dogs, which prompted one man to try to kill a Jew (23 October 1564). This event gave rise to a correspondence between a senior member of the Jewish community and the pastor. The pastor denied the statement, and added that, in any case, the animosity between Christians and Jews predated their own quarrel. The pastor then took issue with the (alleged) insults poured down on the Fürth Christians by the local Jews – that Mary was a whore and that Christ had deceived his followers. The pastor ended the letter with the claim that he knew well what the Jews were up to: 'Du sollst mich, Mein Jud, für kein Find ansehen, sonder wissen, das mir ewer judische anschlag, list, dück, leben gebett, wandel, alles wolbekandt ist...' (13 October 1564). The Jewish community wrote a response (15 October 1564) asking to be left in peace, but this was not to be. In 1567 an inquisition was mounted investigating the fate of some stolen goods. *Außzug was in kurtzen Jarn den Burgern alhie gestoln und under die Juden gein Furth versetzt ist worden 1567*. In a later defence (*Requisition der Juden zu Fürt 1571*), the Jewish comunity, as they had done earlier, justified their actions with reference to the rights granted to them by the Emperor and the local lord (in this instance the dean of the Bamberg cathedral). StaN, 16a B-Laden Lade 191, no. 6.

8   *An Ihro Römisch-Kayserliche auch in Germanien und zu Jerusalem Königliche Majestät in Akten und Rechten Bestgegründete Ausführung der seit Jahrhunderten zwischen dem Hochstifft und der Domprobstey Bamberg, dann dem hochfürstlichen Hauße Brandenburg-Onolzbach über die Vogtheyliche Obrigkeit in der Hofmark Fürth* (1778), vol. 1, pp. 69–78, 73.

Fürth, and elsewhere, the Jewish settlements persisted and even prospered. In Unterlaimbach, Oberhochstatt, Schornweisach, Ühlfeld, Weidenberg, and Gerhardshofen, to name but a few parishes, there were Jewish settlements secure enough to have schools and synagogues.[9] The Reformation did not displace the Jewish communities.

Aside from these small clusters of deviant faiths, religious life in Ansbach and Kulmbach was uniformly Lutheran in inspiration. Georg the Pious, as his successor Georg Friedrich, always deferred to the religious counsel of Wittenberg. The district reports for the pending Augsburg Diet, drawn together in 1530 to represent the religious opinion of the Brandenburg-Ansbach-Kulmbach clergy (fifty reports in all), were strongly Lutheran in tone. References were made to Johannes Brenz, Philipp Melanchthon, Andreas Osiander, Lazarus Sprengler, Johannes Bugenhagen, Urbanus Rhegius, as well as the Ansbach theologians Andreas Althamer and Johann Rurer, but the final authority was always Martin Luther.[10] Although the church ordinance of 1533 was the work of Andreas Osiander and Johannes Brenz, and although both men, especially Osiander, had their differences with Luther, the work was in essence true to Lutheranism.[11]

In so far as the theological innovations introduced by Luther formed a consolidated school of thought before the Formula of Concord, the leading clergy in the margravate can be termed orthodox Lutherans. Andreas Althamer was an active supporter of Luther in the early 1520s; he had been persecuted for his evangelical beliefs as early as 1524 and later wrote a number of pamphlets in defence of the faith as well as a popular catechism.[12] Johann Rurer, perhaps the

---

[9] StaN, *Ansbacher Neues Generalrepertorium*, no. 49, rep. nr. 103°, fo. 95 (Leimbach 1583), fo. 68 Obernhochstatt (21 September 1582), fo. 73 Gerhardtshofen (25 September 1582), fo. 152; Unterleimbach 1588: 'vom Junckern wird ein Juden Schul doselbst vergunstiget, aber kein Christen Schul gehalten.', fo. 137 (Ultfeld 1587); StaB, C2 1823 Weidenwerk (20 September 1592); LKAN, MKN, 92a, Schornweisach (3 July 1606).

[10] The reports are analysed in Schneider, *Gutachten evangelischer Theologen.*

[11] In the 1520s, Melanchthon approved of the theological work of Osiander. The disagreements that arose in the early years were mostly over textual interpretation, such as Osiander's analysis of the book of Daniel, his interest in the Talmud and the Old Testament, and his astrological musings. Osiander ultimately fell foul of the theologians with his theory of salvation in the 1550s. Gottfried Seebaß, *Das reformatorische Werk des Andreas Osiander* (Nuremberg, 1964). Johannes Brenz had a great influence upon margrave Georg the Pious and thus the evolution of the faith in Ansbach. Some of his ideas about the use of the monasteries and fasts were considered suspect, but he was in agreement with Luther in important theological matters. Friedrich Wilhelm Kantzenbach, 'Johannes Brenz und die Reformation in Franken', *ZbKG*, 31 (1962), 148–68. The Wittenberg theologians approved the 1533 ordinance (though they did have some reservations about the use of the ban). Seebaß and Müller, *Andreas Osiander D. Ä. Gesamtausgabe* (1983), vol. 5, pp. 38–42.

[12] Althamer's early pamphlet literature was concerned with convincing the parishioners of the truth of the evangelical faith and dissuading them from opting for 'radical' alternatives such as Anabaptism. In *Anzey/gu[n]g Warumb/Got die Wellt so lang/hab lassen irrhen* (Nuremberg, 1526), Althamer claimed that man's ignorance of God's Word had blinded him to the truth. He published a Latin sermon against 'false Christians' in 1526, but this did not appear until 1533 in German as *Die Epistel/S. Jacobs/Mit newer ausle/gung/Andree Althamers/wie sie gepredigt worden/zu Onoltzbach*

most active clergyman during the first decade of reform in Ansbach, honoured Luther's ideas when drawing up his report for Augsburg in 1530. Rurer, like Althamer, also wrote a pamphlet designed to win souls to the new faith.[13] Georg Karg, the man most responsible for the outer form the church assumed in mid-century, was prone to wander from the narrow path of orthodoxy at times, falling prey to charges of Anabaptism and Calvinism (in his support of Melanchthon); but Karg was always willing to submit himself to the judgement of Wittenberg.[14]

Theological dissension among the lesser clergy was rare. On occasion a pastor or a schoolmaster might be cited before the consistory due to suspect beliefs. Adam Unfug of Geißlingen called Christ a liar and wondered aloud 'whether a thing might be impossible for God'.[15] Benedict Thalman of Hechlingen, a schoolmaster who fell suspect of 'sacramentarian, Zwinglian, and Calvinist' leanings, managed to defend himself with reference to the works of Johannes Brenz.[16] At the other extreme, the young Heinrich Brehm, a student from Hof studying at Wittenberg, refused to sign the Torgau articles in 1574 for fear that this might contradict the works of Luther and Melanchthon and by implication the body of Ansbach beliefs.[17] Rather than compromise the purity of his faith, the pastor of Münchsteinach confessed to the visitor he would rather not go to heaven if Matthias Flacius Illyricus were there.[18] These and similar statements remind us that the local clergy might stray from the path of orthodoxy on occasion, just as they might observe Lutheranism with stern inflexibility, but such a show of hands paints an uneven picture. Perhaps the most faithful guide to the principality's religious complexion, and the most telling testimony to emerge from the archival materials, is the silence, the absence of theological dissent at the parish level. Neither Ansbach nor Kulmbach was home to confessional infighting; the margravate was uniformly Lutheran in inspiration, and uniquely Lutheran in form.

(Wittenberg, 1533). Works of a theological nature in support of the faith would include *Von der/ Erbsund das sye der/Christen kynder gleich als/wol verdamb als der/heyden* (1527) wherein Althamer stressed the essential notion of the Lutheran faith ('Die gerechtikeit gottes kumpt durch den glauben in Jesum Christum, zu allen und auf alle die da glauben') and *Von dem/Hochwirdigen/ Sacrament des leibs und/blut unnsers herrn Jesu/Christi, wider die irrigen/geyster, so unns das na/ chtmal des herrns/zünichtigen* (Nuremberg, 1521), which is a strict Lutheran interpretation of the Lord's Supper.

13 Schneider, *Gutachten evangelischer Theologen*, pp. 31–4. Rurer's pamphlet *Christliche unterrichtung eins/Pfarhern an seinen herrn, ein fur/sten des heyligen Reychs*... (1526) was a defence of Lutheranism – 'Das ist, der glaub macht alleyn frum oder gerecht vor Got.'

14 Weiss, *Vom notwendigen Verstand*, pp. 22–8; Wilke, *Georg Karg*, pp. 55–68. Karg had been placed in jail in Wittenberg as a student on charges of Anabaptism. *D. Martin Luthers Werke* (Weimar, 1914) *Tischreden*, 3, nos. 3699 & 3713; *Briefwechsel*, 8 (1938), 179–84.

15 LKAN, MDU, (24 May 1628–4 August 1628).

16 LKAN, MKA, Spez. 394. fos. 253–4 (29 March 1575). Given that the parish was Hechlingen, the charges should be viewed with some suspicion.

17 StaB C2 1834, fos. 1–5.

18 StaN, *Ansbacher Neues Generalrepertorium*, no. 49, rep. nr. 103ᵉ, fo. 128.

Education

After Luther's death, in an effort the preserve the purity of his teachings, Ansbach sided with the followers of Melanchthon. As in other Protestant lands, this gave rise to theological unease among some clergy; the Eucharist controversy in particular stimulated disputes in Ansbach.[19] But Luther's teachings, imparted through the work of Melanchthon, remained in force. When the Protestant powers drew up the Formula of Concord, Ansbach shied away from the project at first because it seemed to eclipse Melanchthon's stress on the Gospel and the doctrine of justification. Ultimately, with promised dispensations, the theologians signed and the Formula of Concord was introduced.[20] By the end of the century the list of approved theological texts included Luther's catechisms, the Confession of Augsburg, the *Corpus Doctrinae* of Melanchthon, the Schmalkaldic articles, the Formula of Concord, and the 1533 church ordinance. The memory of Martin Luther became sacred; clergymen termed him a 'holy man' and a 'prophet'. In 1589 the visitors of Hof took note that a recently deceased pastor had been born on 18 February 1546, 'therefore the death [date] of Saint Luther'.[21]

The principality was Lutheran throughout the sixteenth century; it did not suffer forced conversions, recatholicisation, or the fragmentation of the faith from within due to contending beliefs. From 1528 to the death of Georg Friedrich in 1603 (and beyond) the aim remained consistent: to meld the beliefs of the parishioners into a single faith. To this purpose a religion such as Lutheranism, a religion reliant less upon gesture, ritual, or performance than the force of spoken language (so 'contemplative and immaterial a religious practice', to cite the words of Montaigne) needed an arena for the transmission of ideas. Two obvious forums existed and were used: the school and the pulpit.

EDUCATION

In 1978 Gerald Strauss published *Luther's House of Learning*, a book which has since become a standard reference point in any debate about the impact of the

---

19 Karl Schornbaum, 'Philippisten und Gnesiolutheraner in Brandenburg-Ansbach', *Beiträge zür bayerischen Kirchengeschichte*, 18 (1912), 97–110. Throughout the century the Kulmbach and Bayreuth clergy were less divisive over the matter of the Lord's Supper (and truer to Luther) than were the clergy of Ansbach. For instance, in 1565 they approved without hesitation the Württemberg draft relating to the mass: 'nämlich, daß im heiligen Abendmahl Christi mit dem Brot der wehre natürliche Leib Christi am Kreuz für uns in den Tod gegeben und im Wein sein heiliges Blut für uns vergossen gegenwärtig und wahrhaftig ausgeteilt und genossen werden...'. Karl Schornbaum, 'Die Brandenburgischen Theologen und das Maulbronner Gespräch 1564', *Zeitschrift für Kirchengeschichte*, 34 (1913), 382.

20 Though not without some opposition. LKAN, MKA, Spez. 564. fos. 75–85. For the theological subtleties see Karl Schornbaum, 'Die Einführung der Konkordienformel in der Markgrafschaft Brandenburg', *ZbKG*, 5 (1930), 176–209.

21 StaB, C2 1833 Statement of theologians 1567; StaB, C2 1827 Münchberg (15 October 1589). On the cult of Luther see Scribner, *Popular Culture and Popular Movements*, pp. 301–22, 323–53.

Reformation (or, as Strauss phrased it, the 'success or failure').[22] Strauss viewed the Reformation as an educational experiment. In his words:

It embarked on a conscious and, for the first time, remarkably systematic endeavour to develop in the young new and better impulses, to implant inclinations in consonance with the reformers' religious and civic ideals, to fashion dispositions in which Christian ideas of right thought and action could take root, and to shape personalities capable of turning the young into new men – into the human elements of a Christian society that would live by evangelical principles.[23]

Strauss examined the principles of late-medieval pedagogy, the concepts of learning, native perceptions of childhood and youth, the place of the family, the goals of the reformers, the means by which reform was to be accomplished, and its association with religion. According to Strauss's findings, the reformers' aims were only superficially realised: 'A century of Protestantism had brought about little or no change in the common religious conscience and the ways in which ordinary men and women conducted their lives.'[24] In view of its initial goals, the pedagogical reformation was a failure.

Are Strauss's conclusions valid for Brandenburg-Ansbach-Kulmbach? In the following section the relationship between the Reformation and parish education will be examined. Education is to be understood in an empirical sense: the growth of schools, the emergence of the educators, the tools of indoctrination, the results in the parish. Possible reasons for the type of failure described by Strauss will be addressed in a later section; here the sole intention is to identify the media used by the clergy to impart the principles of the faith and to chart their development.[25]

In October 1531 Althamer, Rurer, and the pastor Simon Schneeweiß sent a list of complaints to Georg the Pious. According to their draft, the school in Ansbach was poorly run, haphazardly maintained, and nearly empty. People would not send their children to class since they believed that 'man does not need any more priests, doctors, Masters of the Arts, Bachelors of the Arts, or scholars for secular or spiritual rule, because there is no more need of popish monks or mass

---

22 Gerald Strauss, *Luther's House of Learning: Indoctrination of the Young in the German Reformation* (London, 1978); Gerald Strauss, 'Success and Failure in the German Reformation', *Past and Present*, 67 (1975), pp. 30–63. Strauss's book has met with criticism. See James Kittelson, 'Successes and Failures in the German Reformation: The Report from Strasbourg', *ARG*, 73 (1982), pp. 153–74; James Kittelson, 'Visitations and Popular Religious Culture: Further Reports from Strasbourg', in Kyle C. Sessions and Phillip N. Bebb (eds.), *Pietas and Societas: New Trends in Social History* (Kirksville, 1985), pp. 89–102; Mark U. Edwards, 'Lutheran Pedagogy in Reformation Germany', *History of Education Quarterly*, 21 (1981), pp. 471–7; Scott H. Hendrix, 'Luther's Impact on the Sixteenth Century', *Sixteenth Century Journal*, 1 (1985), 3–14.
23 Strauss, *Luther's House of Learning*, p. 2.
24 Strauss, *Luther's House of Learning*, p. 299.
25 For the history of education in Franconia, see M. Liedtke (ed.), *Handbuch der Geschichte des bayerischen Bildungswesens*, vol. 1, *Geschichte der Schule in Bayern. Von den Anfängen bis 1800* (Bad Heilbrunn, 1991).

priests'.[26] The Reformation seems to have given rise to this idea, for a decline in student numbers affected all of Lutheran Germany.[27] 'Wherever Lutheranism has taken root', sighed Erasmus, 'learning perishes'.[28] In part this was due to the emphasis the reformers placed on self-education. Luther himself stressed the intensely personal nature of a proper religious education in the 1520s, making the *pater familias* 'bishops in their own homes'. This was a comforting vision, but it soon became apparent that household teaching methods would not suffice. Reformers began to draft comprehensive church and school ordinances relocating the task of religious education back in the classroom, and thus under the auspices of the secular elite.[29] This was perhaps a reluctant concession for the reformers – from the family to the ruler (though the patriarchal ruler). Althamer maintained the metaphor of 'proper household' in his catechism of 1528, though by that date he was advising the margravial clergy on its use. Schooling became more and more systematised and ordered as the state and the church authorities worked in close alliance.

In Ansbach the drive to reform the schools began as soon as Georg the Pious arrived in the principality. On 3 December 1528 the major clergy of the principality gathered in Ansbach and addressed the problems confronting education. Writing in private, yet voicing a common concern, the pastor Adam Weiß of Crailsheim advised the margrave to ensure that the schools and the educators were suitable, not only suitable enough to communicate the basic academic skills, but to impart the fear of God in the young.[30] Funding for the educational reform, it was generally agreed, could be shouldered by the Catholic legacy. 'So that the common youth are raised without impediment to the honour of God and Your Princely Grace [Georg the Pious], as well as being of service to the land' the clergy earmarked the wealth from the vacant foundations and monasteries for educational purposes. Wary at first, the margrave approached Johannes Brenz for advice, who suggested putting the monasteries into the service of the state church. Luther, in contrast, when sounded out in the same matter, advised against Brenz's counsel and told the margrave to let the monasteries atrophy with time. Instead of resurrecting Catholic monuments, Luther encouraged the spread of more Latin schools, and, he added: 'Thirdly [I advise] that in all cities and small towns (*flecken*) good children's schools be established from which those competent enough for the higher schools can be chosen ... for with time when the common man sees that their sons can become

26 StaN, *Ansbacher Religionsakten III*, Tom. XI, fo. 296.
27 Martin Luther, *An die Ratsherren aller Städte deutschen Landes das sie christliche Schulen aufrichten und halten sollen* (1524). 'Auf's erste erfahren wir jetzt in deutschen Landen durch und durch, wie man allenthalben die Schulen zergehen läßt.'
28 Erasmus to Willibald Pirckheimer. Cited in Notker Hammerstein, 'Universitäten und Reformation', *Historische Zeitschrift*, 258 (1994), 339.
29 Strauss, *Luther's House of Learning*, pp. 2–19.
30 StaN, *Ansbacher Religionsakten III*, Tom. XI, fo. 42.

pastors, preachers, or other officials, they will once again place them in the schools.'[31]

The margrave reacted to this advice. In 1528 the Ansbach Gymnasium was established using funds from Dr Johann Pfotel's 1504 endowment. In Hof (1528) the Latin school was improved with the use of foundation wealth, thoroughly reformed in 1546, and by 1549 there were 383 students. Similar reforms were undertaken in the Latin schools of Kulmbach, Kitzingen, Uffenheim, Langenzenn, Gunzenhausen, Creglingen, and Leutershausen.[32] In Kulmbach, the Lyceum was improved using the wealth from an Augustinian monastery (though it suffered destruction in 1553 during Albrecht's wars and was not further rebuilt until 1567).[33] In 1530 the school in Wunsiedel was reformed by the town council, an office of schoolmaster emerged in its own right (separate from the *Stadtschreiber*), and by 1566 there were three instructors in the Latin school in addition to a German school and a school for girls.[34]

Most of this educational reform did not take hold until mid-century. Wunsiedel and Kulmbach, like the other above-mentioned institutions, were already home to large Latin schools. Smaller establishments suffered when the Catholic endowments ran dry; and in actual fact the number of Latin schools overall decreased. In place of the smaller Latin schools, run by local monasteries or foundations, large town and city schools emerged. The prerequisites for an education became more stringent, conditions more restrictive, funding less attainable, and overall numbers fell. The percentage of Ansbach students attending universities declined; student numbers were lower, as access to schools grew more difficult.[35] Luther was correct to prophesy that the monasteries would slowly atrophy over time, but more than just the regular clergy was bound up with their decline.

Educational reform was not a real possibility until mid-century. The church and education were inseparable developments; they worked on each other in a mutual field of influence. The mid-century reform of the Ansbach church under Georg Friedrich also ushered in a period of educational innovation. The synodal ordinance of 1556 ordered that, in addition to the monastery schools, many of which should be resurrected along the lines of the Saxon model, reform should reach to the parishes: 'not only in the cities, but rather in the larger villages schools should be established and ... properly maintained'. Where there was no schoolmaster, the sexton, chaplain, or (in the last resort) the pastor should instruct

[31] Jordan, *Reformation und gelehrte Bildung*, vol. 1, pp. 101–12; Johann Paul Reinhard, *Beyträge zu der Historie Frankenlandes und der angränzenden Gegenden* (Bayreuth, 1760), part 1, pp. 134–6.

[32] Jordan, *Reformation und gelehrte Bildung*, pp. 312–14.

[33] Franz Pietsch, 'Geschichte der Gelehrten Bildung in Kulmbach', *Schriften für Heimatforschung und Kulturpflege in Ostfranken*, 33 (1974), 53–5.

[34] Elisabeth Ponader, 'Lateinschule und Deutsche Schule in Wunsiedel von den Anfängen bis zum großen Stadtbrand 1731', *Archiv für Geschichte von Oberfranken*, 68 (1988), 55–60.

[35] Jordan, *Reformation und gelehrte Bildung*, pp. 329–40.

the children in his stead.[36] The parish clergy were instructed to keep a watch over the schools; superintendents monitored the chapter, 'so that not only in the cities, but rather in the villages as well the schools are maintained with industry and the youth educated in the proper subjects [*in gueten Kunsten*] and raised in virtue'.[37] The visitation instructions admonished the margravial officials to inspect the schools on a regular basis, and with the 1594 consistorial ordinance the margrave extended the scope of his intervention to include the installation and examination of all schoolmasters, so that no 'false teaching' should be broadcast. All educational affairs were henceforth centralised in the consistory.[38]

The educational requirements and expectations of a schoolmaster would vary according to the status of the school, the location, and the needs of the parish. In many Latin schools, Wunsiedel for example, the curriculum was no different from the pre-Reformation agenda: Latin grammar, with the exempla of Cato, Aesop, Terence, Cicero, or Virgil as the exercise texts. The instructions for the schoolmaster of Gunzenhausen (1580) – in a working day from 6:00 am to 10:00, and then from 12:00 to 3:00 pm – referred to the grammar books of Melanchthon and the text of Cicero for the study of Rhetoric, Aesop's fables for the writing exercises.[39] But as there was no single school ordinance published in Ansbach until 1692, there is little point in deducing the quality of the Ansbach educator from the course descriptions.[40] Moreover, the majority of the schools to be dealt with in this study were smaller, village schools – German schools – which taught only the basics of language and the catechism. The tasks expected of the German schoolmaster, often concurrently the sexton, should not be compared with the tasks of his Latin school confrères. The expectations of the schoolmaster/sexton of Lehengütingen, Hans Rümmel, for instance, ranged from safeguarding the church books, visitation of the sick, sounding and maintenance of the church bell, stocking of baptismal water, teaching the children to read, write, sing, and pray in the school for five hours (summer and winter), watching over the church, to leading a virtuous life.[41] In addition to his projected duties, the schoolmaster often doubled as the town scribe.[42]

For his troubles the village schoolmaster received a salary both in currency and

---

[36] Hermann Jordan and Christian Bürckstümmer, *Reformation und gelehrte Bildung in der Mark-grafschaft Ansbach-Bayreuth* (Erlangen, 1922), vol. 2, pp. 6–7; Simon, *Evangelische Kirchen-geschichte Bayerns*, p. 312.

[37] Jordan and Bürckstümmer, *Reformation und gelehrte Bildung*, vol. 2, p. 8.

[38] Jordan and Bürckstümmer, *Reformation und gelehrte Bildung*, vol. 2, p. 40.

[39] LKAN, MDG, 71, fo. 119–21.

[40] Pietsch, 'Geschichte der Gelehrten Bildung', p. 55.

[41] LKAN, MDF, 203, unpaginated loose leaf.

[42] A position which required its own set of skills, if the parishioners of Kaubenheim are to be believed. In 1578 their schoolmaster applied for the post, but they refused to accept him because he was not up to the job: 'darein so viel tagwerck nutzung gehören, als tag im Jar sind, darüber nit ein jeden zu trauen, gehört auch ein wichtiger kopff darzu, der beÿm schulmeister nit zu befinden'. StaN, *Ansbacher Neues Generalrepertorium*, no. 49, rep. nr. 103ᵉ, fo. 26.

kind. No single amount was stipulated in any chapter; the cash income might vary from fifty gulden to twelve, or to nothing at all if the income was harvested in kind alone.[43] In 1551 the Ansbach council approved a yearly salary of thirty gulden for the schoolmaster of Langenzenn, to be amassed from a neighbouring foundation, and raised it to fifty gulden in 1552.[44] Fifty gulden was a considerable income relative to many of the parishioners (and indeed the pastors themselves), but a surfeit of money was rarely the schoolmaster's lot. Salaries were more likely to be only ten or twenty gulden, spread out unevenly in the calendar year, often forcing the schoolmaster to go from house to house to collect his weekly sums and his maintenance in kind (*laib brot und weihnacht küchen*). The cost of sending a child to school was often beyond the means of the parishioners (so they claimed); even the meagre quarterly fee could not be met.[45] Schoolmasters were obliged to take on other jobs, most frequently the office of town scribe (*Markschreiber*) or whatever work would come their way. 'With the sextons, or schoolmasters, the situation is such', wrote the Kulmbach visitors in 1572. 'Their upkeep is mean and wretched; [they] must earn more than just that of their church office from trade and labour.'[46]

In light of the precarious state of their maintenance, it is little wonder that the quality of the sixteenth-century village schoolmaster varied from parish to parish. If the visitation returns can be believed (even marginally) some schools in Ansbach and Kulmbach were home to grossly incompetent and violent men. And yet at the same time there were men like the 'old schoolmaster' of Muggendorf who constructed a small schoolhouse for the village youth from his own wealth.[47] Ability is difficult to quantify, and it seems senseless (though well within the bounds of possibility) to compile a list of village schoolmasters and search for a median. A study of the schoolmaster in office, at work, out of work, and in need of support, offers more insight on the standards of village education.

A state of poverty was ubiquitous, not just poverty in income, but poverty in housing, poverty of security, poverty of status. The problems besetting the clergymen were shared by the schoolmasters and usually amplified. Many parishes did not have a schoolhouse; instead the church was used, the pastor's house, the schoolmaster's house, or perhaps a communal building. Independent classrooms, no more than small barns, suffered from wet and cold. Even the schoolmasters of Nuremberg had cause to complain about the quality of the buildings.[48] Because the housing was poor and the income was low, it was not likely that the office of

43 Rudolf Herold, 'Zur Geschichte der Schwarzenberger Pfarreien', *Beiträge zur bayerischen Kirchengeschichte*, 5 (1899), 75–90.
44 LKAN, MDLz, 666, nos. 17 & 18.
45 StaN, *Ansbacher Neues Generalrepertorium*, no. 49, rep. nr. 103e, fo. 80 (4 November 1582).
46 LKAN, MSK, 157 *Bericht der Spezial Visitation, In der Süperintendentz Bëyrreuth A[nn]o 1572*, fo. 9 (my pagination.)
47 LKAN, MSK, 157. Muggendorf (20 February 1559).
48 StaN, 16a B–Laden Akten, Lade 205, no. 10 (9 January 1527).

schoolmaster would attract especially competent men. In the large market town of Gunzenhausen the council recognised that the low salary was the reason 'no schoolmaster, especially one who is learned and industrious, can stay here for long'.[49] The schoolmaster was often forced to supplement his income by doubling as a scribe for the local secular authorities or the neighbouring nobility. The proliferation of his duties could force him to neglect the children, especially if he worked as a scribe for the town council.

'In fact this complaint is everywhere', noted the Kulmbach visitors in 1578, 'that council business is hindering the schoolmasters in their school office and the children [as a result] are being neglected. There is a great need for the schoolmaster and the clerk to be separate and distinct offices and [also] for their maintenance to be sorted out by particular people.'[50]

Counted among the many alternative employments assumed by the schoolmasters were the office of sexton, the overseeing of forest and pastures, book binding, copying, singing, and healing (*wundartzeneÿ*).

In spite of their precarious standing, perhaps because of it, parish educators exercised a degree of freedom and immunity which left many of the margrave's clergy believing they were 'lords unto themselves'.[51] Often the local authorities, whether a margravial official, a nobleman, or the village commune, claimed power of appointment, thereby circumventing the pastor's judgment altogether.[52] In the larger towns, such as Bayreuth, the council presented the schoolmaster without even consulting the pastor. In this matter, as in so many others, the Reformation encountered the weight and defiance of tradition. The secular powers' involvement in the affairs of local education was a process underway well before the arrival of the Reformation.[53] Decades of such liberties emboldened Wolf von Wirsberg in Lanzendorf, who upheld his right to appoint the schoolmaster and the right to judge the quality of the man in office. 'If we found failings, we should go and tell him', was what he said to the visitors.[54] Local customs were hard to eradicate. Over the course of the century the

49   LKAN, MDG, 71, fo. 88 (1579).
50   LKAN, MSK, 157, Rehaü 1578.
51   LKAN, MSK, 157, *Bericht der Spetial Visitation, In der Süperintendentz Bëyrreuth A[nn]o 1572*, fo. 8 (my pagination). '...das solche schulmeister, und Merrkschreiber nichts auf Ire verordente pastores geben, sondern enzihen sich ires gehorsam allerdinge, und seind *domini per se*.'
52   In Kaübenheim the *Gemeinde* dismissed the schoolmaster in his absence and appointed another without consulting the authorities. StaN, *Ansbacher Neues Generalrepertorium*, no. 49, rep. nr. 103^e, fo. 105 (1584). The ever-industrious community of Hechlingen first approached the count of Oettingen in 1544 with a demand for a schoolmaster. (The parish was disputed between Oettingen and Ansbach. See Hofmann, *Gunzenhausen-Weissenburg*, p. 38.) Their petitions were repeated in 1549, 1556, and 1565, and on each occasion they forwarded their own choice. LKAN, MKA, Spez. 394, fos. 45–58, 138–9, 143.
53   Rudolf Endres, 'Das Schulwesen in Franken im ausgehenden Mittelalter', in Bernd Moeller, Hans Patze and Karl Stackmann (eds.), *Studien zum städischen Bildungswesen des späten Mittelalters und der frühen Neuzeit* (Göttingen, 1983), pp. 173–214.
54   LKAN, MSK, 157, Lanzendorf 1592. The liberty exercised by the nobility was a common problem.

territorial church made inroads, but progress was slow. In Roth am Sand, for instance, after the council had presented the schoolmaster in 1556, 1565, 1571, and 1575, the consistory demanded that he be made subject to examination before appointment. The council resisted; another man was selected in 1582 without first appearing before the consistory. And yet in the end the councillors of Roth were forced to give way. With the publication of the 1594 consistorial ordinance, all local powers of presentation were centralised in Ansbach and Kulmbach. The margrave demanded that each schoolmaster be presented for examination, approbation, and confirmation before appointment.[55]

At the level of the parish the reform of the schooling system was slow to take shape. Often the secular authorities obstructed the efforts made by the local clergymen. In the parish of Ahornberg, to offer an example, the pastor appointed a schoolmaster in 1584 without involving the council. The local secular authorities thought that the pastor – 'in this matter, as in others' – had gone too far and took their case to a neighbouring official. The village officials were angered that the appointment took place without the foreknowledge of the *Kastner*, council, or parishioners, though it had always been the custom to involve the village in the appointment of a schoolmaster. The neighbouring official, to whom the parishioners had directed their grievance, was uncertain whether the pastor had the right of appointment and whether the secular officials had the right to intervene, so he sought the advice of the margrave.[56] An inquisition (30 March 1584) confirmed the allegations of the secular officials: they had not been consulted over the dismissal of the old schoolmaster. Above all, it seems to have angered the *Kastner*, who penned a letter expressing his discontent. If there were something wrong with the schoolmaster, he wrote, the pastor should have consulted the local authorities. For the old schoolmaster, Hans Fischer, had sworn an oath to the council and, more significantly, to the *Kastner* himself.[57]

Aurelius Streitberger, the superintendent of Hof, drew up a report of the Ahornberg conflict for the general superintendent.[58] The contours of the dispute now began to take shape. Hans Fischer, the report read, was a lazy, violent man, whose name had cropped up before in the visitations. Indeed, both the pastor and Fischer had appeared before Streitberger in February, where it was agreed that Fischer would leave the parish while a candidate for the vacant school office was forwarded to the consistory. As the consistory had

---

55 Jordan and Bürckstümmer, *Reformation und gelehrte Bildung*, vol. 2, pp. 37–8.
56 StaB, C2 1858 (31 March 1584).
57 StaB, C2 1858 (30 March 1584);

> allein weil der hanß fischer schulmeister, mihr, so wol auch einem Erbarn Ratht, Ambts halben, Mit aidt und pflichten verwandt und zugethan, Sollte der offtgedachtes herr pfarrer E.E. bericht haben, das er unß auch mit aidt und pflichten unterworffen...

58 StaB, C2 1858 (3 April 1584).

approved the translation, the pastor's actions had not been independent – as the secular officials claimed – but rather in answer to the directives of the Kulmbach consistory. Streitberger considered the quarrel in Ahornberg in essence a power struggle between the local *Kastner* and the church. Was the schoolmaster subject to the secular or the ecclesiastical officials? Streitberger did not dwell long on the problem: the schoolmaster was subject to the church. And he advised the general superintendent (his father) that since so many local officials 'would fain rule the churches, the pulpits, and the schools with their impertinent wisdom' the dispute had to be settled in favour of the consistory, so that the local officials 'in this and other places, may learn and experience how far in such cases their office extends'.[59] Fischer was dismissed; the *Kastner's* designs to be 'suffragan superintendent or indeed archbishop' were foiled.[60] But as the events in Ahornberg illustrate, the reform of education often met stiff resistance at the parish level.

A competent schoolmaster in every parish was of course a paramount goal of the reformers. This was a noble ideal, but suitable instruction could only be effective if the children went to school, and the evidence exposes truancy as a common offence. In the summer months in particular, during the harvest season, the children worked in the fields. 'The parishioners do not want to let their children go to the schoolmaster to learn their ABCs'.[61] It was more profitable for the parents to harness the energy of their offspring at home, and that is by and large what they did. Having said this, however, it would be wrong to place all of the blame on the parents. Children disliked school and contrived ways to avoid it. The youth of Gunzenhausen, with a German and a Latin school to choose from, juggled between the two:

The German school in Gunzenhausen is ruining the Latin school, for as soon as it comes to the point where the boys have to learn [Latin] declension and conjugation and things become a little tougher, they all run off to the German school. And when they grow listless

59 StaB, C2 1858, (3 April 1584):

  das nicht allein die bestellung dieser offt angeregter schuldienst der alberaith gemachten ordnung nach ins werckh gezogen werde, sondern auch die Castner, Voigt und andere Regimentspersonen an den und andern örthen erfarhen und lernen mögen, wie weit sich in sollichen fellen Ihr ambt erstrecket...

60 StaB, C2 1858 (8 April 1584). The general superintendent doubted the verity of the *Kastner's* earlier inquisition:

  [The *Kastner*], der in disen neun dörffern der Superattendenten Suffraganeus oder gar Ertzbischoff sein will, umb Rath gefragt haben, das nun zwen einige bawern aufs einem einigen dorff das umbstossen sollen, was die andern alle beschlossen, ist vielleicht ein newes Castnerisch Recht...

  Also it was suggested by the pastor in his defence (*Andtwort deß Pfarrers zu Ahornberg uff der Gemeinde außsag wegen deß Schulmeisters*) that the majority of the villagers had nothing to do with the affair.

61 StaN, *Ansbacher Neues Generalrepertorium*, no. 49, rep. nr. 103ᵉ, fo. 33.

in the German school, they return to the Latin school. All of this makes the school officials weary and fed up. Therefore it would be good if the boys went to the Latin school and the girls alone were sent to the German schools.[62]

Poor attendance and missed classes remained a problem for the reformers throughout the century. Parish children would go to school in the winter months, in the absence of a harvest, in search of a warm hearth, and wait for the thaw. Came the spring, the schools were nearly empty. Small wonder the pastor of Merkendorf saw little hope in a long-term educational programme. 'For when they spend eight days in the school', he wrote, 'soon they stay away and forget what they had learned before.'[63]

And yet despite the picture painted by these poor reports, the Reformation did make some inroads in the quality of higher education on offer. During the reorganisation of the external church under Georg Friedrich the educational superstructure was constitutionally altered for the better. The Latin schools were reformed, the number of scholarships increased, and the system was centralised, so that each schoolmaster (in theory) had to answer to the consistory. The margrave's officials kept a closer watch on the type of people teaching in the villages.[64] In those parishes lacking a schoolmaster, the visitors instructed the pastors themselves or the sextons to assume the duty of education.[65] The officials were directed to round up the capable students in their districts and send them to the Latin schools. In 1581 the number of boys at Heilsbronn was increased from 36 to 100.[66] Even in some of the smaller parishes, such as Roβtal, student numbers, were 'increasing, praise God, ever longer, ever more.'[67]

But Roβtal's success was the exception. Educational reform in Brandenburg-Ansbach-Kulmbach was nascent; the educational improvements envisioned by the reformers did not reach fruition during the sixteenth century. The reformers did not have the concrete educational system at their disposal capable of endowing the rural populace with a lasting knowledge of the Lutheran faith. Village schools were few and inadequate; educators were untutored, underfed, helpless when earnest, unchecked when careless. The schooling system in the villages at the end

---

[62] LKAN, MDG, 71, fo. 74 (1578). During the early 1520s and the Peasants' War, occasional soundings for cross-gender education 'so that both the male and the female sex, created equal by God, may the better know the laws and faith' were aired, but education seems to have remained a male preserve. Scott and Scribner (eds.), *The German Peasants' War*, p. 177; Susan C. Karant-Nunn, 'The Reality of Early Lutheran Education. The Electoral District of Saxony – a Case Study', *Lutherjahrbuch*, 57 (1990), 137–42.

[63] LKAN, MDG, 71, fo. 142.

[64] In 1601 Ansbach dispatched a notice to Leutershausen relating to the foreign teachers discovered in the chapter. This was repeated in 1611, with the additional warning that no schoolmaster should be assumed without prior consultation with the superintendent. LKAN, MDL, 93 (22 September 1601); (13 September 1611).

[65] LKAN, MDL, 93 (13 August 1566).

[66] LKAN, MDLz, 671 (22 September 1581).

[67] LKAN, MDLz, 701, nos. 25–6.

of the sixteenth century was little better than it had been in the late-medieval period.[68] Granted, some progress had been made. By 1633 the consistory was mounting a serious effort to standardise the quality of the village schoolmasters.[69] But given the spirit that saw the birth of the 1533 church ordinance and the scale of reform it envisioned, many clergymen may have viewed this 1633 ruling as one hundred years too late.

THE CATECHISM

Appended to the 1533 church ordinance was a lengthy treatise written by Andreas Osiander which served as a summary of the faith – the catechism. The word 'catechism', as Althamer explained in his own such work, is derived from the Greek, meaning to repeat, to respond, to echo. The Humanists, and the reformers after them, shared in the belief that learning was essentially a mechanical activity; constant study of proper ideas would nurture the memory, which in turn would aid the faculty of cognition and thus the intellect. The catechism, in its standardised format of question and answer, its terse, central tenets of the faith unfolding in rhythmic sequence, was the ideal mnemonic tool. Lutheran thinkers soon realised the value of these disposable booklets. A catechism, observed Johannes Brenz, is 'a short synopsis of all of Scripture, containing for us everything necessary for true and eternal salvation ... so that the catechism can really be termed "a small Bible".'[70] In most Lutheran regions, elementary religious education was communicated through the catechism. In Württemberg the Bible itself was not used by the students until (the equivalent of) the fifth or sixth form. Up to that stage the children learned of the faith through the catechisms.[71]

The clergy of Brandenburg-Ansbach-Kulmbach were among the first in Germany to publish catechisms. Andreas Althamer (aided to some extent by Johann Rurer) published a catechism in 1528, which was reprinted in 1529. That same year Kaspar Löner drew up a catechism for the children in Hof, and it was soon used in the other parishes of Kulmbach. Once Luther's larger and smaller catechisms appeared, they quickly became the standard texts in the principality. But other works circulated as well. In addition to Osiander's 1533 catechism, Brenz's own work found an audience, and Rurer's Ansbach successor, Jakob

---

[68] Compare Karl August Hugo Burkhardt, *Geschichte der sächsischen Kirchen- und Schulvisitationen von 1524 bis 1545* (Darmstadt, 1981), pp. 41, 52, 140, 317; Hans Georg Kirchhoff, 'Kirchspiels- und Küsterschulen in der Reformationszeit. Das niedere Schulwesen im Spiegel von Visitations-berichten des 16. Jahrhunderts', in Klaus Goebel (ed.), *Luther in der Schule* (Bochum, 1985), pp. 127–47.

[69] Jordan and Bürckstümmer, *Reformation und gelehrte Bildung*, vol. 2, p. 71.

[70] Cited in Christoph Weismann, *Eine kleine Biblia* (Stuttgart, 1985), p. 10.

[71] Strauss, *Luther's House of Learning*, pp. 74–84, 151–72; Gerald Strauss, 'Lutheranism and Literacy: A Reassessment', in Kaspar von Greyerz (ed.), *Religion and Society in Early Modern Europe 1500–1800* (London, 1984), p. 114.

Stratner, penned a *Katechismus oder Kinderlehre* in 1539, as did the later Ansbach clergyman Georg Karg. In fact Karg was commissioned to draft his catechism by the margrave. Karg's work was completed in 1557, and while it was later questioned by Brenz, it soon enjoyed great popularity.[72]

Without a doubt the most common complaints to emerge from the visitation returns related to the poor performance of the catechumens.[73] The visitors of Konradsreuth (to select a representative example) lamented: 'among all of the children ... we have not found one who knew the catechism and its short interpretation.'[74] Most of the children refused to go to the session, so it is no surprise they learned so little. The pastor of Unterlaimbach estimated that of the 150 children in his parish, perhaps twenty attended catechism sessions. Nor could the pastor expect the older parishioners to enforce attendance; the adults were regularly cited as the worst culprits. When admonished to attend, older villagers, such as Linhardt Böchner of Wernsbach, dismissed the catechism as playing no practical role in their lives; work was more important than the catechism.[75] In terms of attendance, the parishioners of the outlying hamlets were the arch-offenders. When reprimanded by the visitors for their truancy, they answered that they just followed the example of those in the cities: reform the cities first, and they would follow suit.[76] The rural parishioners did not feel that the catechism session was crucial for their salvation. Far more important for the travails of daily life was tending the fields, working the crops, minding the animals, or taking part in social events. Even as a handbook of discipline for the young, the catechism found few supporters. The parents did not consider the catechism a useful way of controlling the children. As an official of Leutershausen rationalised: Christ could

---

[72] Gerhard Müller, 'Die Reformation im Fürstentum Brandenburg-Ansbach/Kulmbach', *ZbKG*, 48 (1979), 10–11; Karl Schornbaum, 'Zur Geschichte des Katechismus im Fürstenthum Brandenburg-Ansbach', *ZbKG*, 9 (1934), 149–52; Johann Michael Reu, 'Zur katechetischen Literatur Bayerns im 16. Jahrhundert', *Beiträge zur bayerischen Kirchengeschichte*, 13/14 (1907/8), 122–49, 127–36; Karl Schornbaum, 'Zur Geschichte des Kargschen Katechismus', *Beiträge zur bayerischen Kirchengeschichte*, 31 (1925), 111–13; Kolde, *Andreas Althamer*, pp. 46–8; Weiss, *Vom notwendigen Verstand*, pp. 143–73.

[73] LKAN, MDG, 71, fo. 14 (1567). For example:

> Es ist auch aller pastorn ein gemaine klag, uber den unfleiß irer pfarkinder, der mehrerthail des poffels, achtet sich keiner predigt, kummen nit zw den tractation catechismi, schicken ire kinder nit darzu, die klain kinder lauffen auff der gassen, was erwachsten ist, laufft zu den dentzen, und auff die kirchweihen, und bleibt also die welt immer das welt [sic]...

[74] LKAN, MDH, V, 1a, Konradsreuth (12 October 1572). A similar conclusion was expressed by the visitors of Koditz that same year: 'In der offentlichen verhör würd auch an diesem ort beÿ der Jügen groser unvleiß vermerket, und schir kein kind gefunden, das seinen Catechismum mit der auslegung herte hersagen konnen'.

[75] StaN, *Ansbacher Neues Generalrepertorium*, no. 49, rep. nr. 103[e], fo. 160; LKAN, MKA, 998, *Von gemeinen Gebrechen so in der pfarr Wernsbach befunden werden* (*c*.1578): 'Es were Ihme in seiner Narung und Haushaltung merers dann an diesem gelegen, er konte es nit thun.'

[76] LKAN, MDG, 71, fo. 14 (1567): 'sie thun, wie die in die stetten, man soll die stethischen zuvor reformieren, und alsdann wöllen sie auch volgen.'

not convert the Pharisees, 'therefore other people can not better themselves by learning from him'.[77]

The response to the catechetical experiment was poor. The reality of the endeavour to impart the principles of the Lutheran faith through the catechism was much less than the ideal, and the early aspirations remained a ghostly rhetoric of reform which never took shape. In this matter, more than any other, a clear voice is sounded in the textual remains: it is a voice of sadness, frustration, and despair. 'Oh, that I had water enough in my head, and my eyes were springs, that I might mourn, day and night, for the great sins of the people'.[78]

THE PULPIT

Like the task of education, wherein a parishioner became the recipient of religious beliefs in a one-way flow of information, the sermon also allowed the religious authorities to broadcast the fundamentals of the Lutheran faith without (in theory) suffering the exchange or traffic of alternative ideas. For the Lutherans, a sermon from Holy Writ was more than just a rhetorical exercise: Scripture revealed the word of God; the promise of Christ was present in the New Testament. And while the Word had no efficacy of itself, its proclamation could work salvation within the individual. For where there is belief (strengthened by Scripture), there is the Spirit.[79] As the pastor of Mainstockheim phrased it in 1580: 'For it does not say, thus I teach, thus I speak; rather, thus teaches God's Word, so speaks the Lord'.[80]

The Word was fundamental to the spread of the Lutheran faith, and it follows that the frequency of sermons remained a primary concern throughout the sixteenth century. Each of the visitation commissions was instructed to inquire into the quality of the preaching, as well as the number of services given in the course of a week. Of course, the frequency of sermons in a given parish could vary; different schedules were followed for different locations, according to the size and the needs of the parish. In Feuchtwangen, a large town, there might be sermons three or four days of the week. In the smaller villages a single Sunday sermon might have been the norm. The Ansbach theologians stipulated at the 1556 congress that at least one sermon should be held each week, either a chapter from the Bible or a piece out of Veit Dietrich's summary, while on Sunday and Holy Days a more comprehensive service should be performed, which might take its cues from the 1533 church ordinance.[81] The weekly sermon usually fell on Wednesday.

---

[77] LKAN, MKA, Spez. 500 (8 December 1589).
[78] LKAN, MSK, 157, *Beschwerung und Ergernus* from Hof (1578). Point 4.
[79] Klaus Haendler, *Wort und Glaube bei Melanchthon*. (Gütersloh, 1968), pp. 161–85.
[80] LKAN, MKA, Spez. 564, fo. 100.
[81] Karl Schornbaum, 'Zum gottesdienstlichen Leben Feuchtwangens im 16. Jahrhundert', *Siona*, 31 (1906), 207–8; Sehling, p. 336.

Like his medieval predecessor, the Lutheran clergyman had a mass of preaching aids at his disposal. The clergymen of Ansbach also had the 1533 church ordinance as a guide. But it would seem that the Ansbach pastors sometimes shaped their sermons to appeal, or at least to relate, to the native understanding of their audience. Pastors might convey the essence of Lutheran belief in metaphors and analogies. At times this worked against the pastor's intention, as a sermon could be interpreted in very personal terms. An earthy discourse could offend as well as entertain.[82] But in general it was a useful means of getting across a message. Many of the popular preachers in the 1520s attracted crowds through such means, and later clergymen followed suit.[83] A copy of the 1533 church ordinance, now housed in the Schwabach church archive, is covered in marginalia (in sixteenth-century hand) building upon the common prayers and thanksgivings written into the text. The crux of Lutheran belief, the role of Jesus Christ as redeemer, is constantly stressed; but it is interesting how this idea is strengthened with reference to God the protector and Christ as intermediary. The prayers ask that they might be granted 'friendly, Christian, blessed rule in this land'; that God might protect 'the fruit of the earth'; that God might redeem them from 'all error, sickness ... imprisonment, pestilence, and from all ill will'. In short, the pastor made sure that the common prayers sought the safeguard (*schutz und schirm*) of God. This is language that a subject of the margrave would readily understand.[84]

It is difficult to assess the preaching standards of the parish clergy. Complaints from the parishioners were few. If a pastor was cited before the authorities on account of his sermons it was usually due to the use he made of the pulpit (i.e. as a platform for accusation – *Neidt predigten*), his weak voice, or old age, rather than suspect beliefs or heretical ramblings.[85] The vast majority of pastors would have fulfilled the basic preaching requirements without calling attention to themselves. A survey of twelve villages, taken from the 1592 Wunsiedel visitation returns, would suggest that the parishioners could expect a full sermon two days of the

---

[82] For instance the quarrel between the mayor and the pastor of Marktleuten (1586). The mayor was personally offended by the pastor's scriptural parables, as he thought the pastor was referring to him. 'Zeiget [the mayor] an der pfarrer hett offentlich gepredigt und gesagt: Wenn du gleich ein gantze gaβen heuser hettest, so hastu es doch mit schinderey und dieberey, deβen muste er sich annemen, weil sonst keiner im Marck der die heuser aneinder ... Der pfarrer sagte, Er hette Ihn nit genent, sonder hette in gemeyn geredt Es were uff Landt ein Bauer der hette auch zwen höffe oder heuser aneinander.' In 1592 the parishioners again reported on the pastor's 'Neidt predigten'. StaB, C2 1830, fo. 7; C2 1831, fo. 11.

[83] Otto Erhard, 'Johannes Schwanhausen, der Reformator Bambergs', *Beiträge zur bayerischen Kirchengeschichte* (1897), p. 7–9.

[84] I would like to thank Herbert Spachmüller for allowing me to view the ordinance. Scribbling prayers along the edge of the 1533 church ordinance seems to have been a fairly common practice. See Hans-Joachim König, 'Die Crailsheimer Originalausgabe der Brandenburg-Nürnberger Kirchenordnung von 1533', *Blätter für Württembergische Kirchengeschichte*, 88 (1988), 68–77.

[85] LKAN, MSK, 157, Helmbrecht (1 November 1586). The parishioners asked that their pastor speak with them before he made accusations from the pulpit.

week. Some parishes, in contrast, had no weekly sermon at all. The pastor of
Marktleuten let the weekly sermon fall in the summer; Schönwald relied upon a
neighbouring chaplain for Sundays and holidays (as did Bernstein); the pastor of
Thierstein 'only preached on holidays, and did not hold a weekly sermon'; and the
pastors of Thiersheim and Schirnding neglected the midweek sermon as well.[86]

It is doubtful whether the quality of the pastor's sermons was a major concern
for the parishioners. Although the focus of the early evangelical movement was
Scripture and the salvation-inducing pure Word of God, disrespect for the parish
sermon continued throughout the century. As early as 1531 Georg the Pious was
issuing mandates to stop the 'contempt, derision, ridicule [*belachen*], blasphemy,
and abuse' poured on the Word and the servants of the church.[87] Poor church
attendance was an oft-cited offence in the visitation returns; it was referred to as
the 'common complaint' of the clergymen. And it remained a common complaint
'everywhere' until 1611 and beyond.[88] When encouraged by the visitors to hold a
weekday sermon, the pastors pointed out the fruitlessness of such an ideal, for the
churches would be empty. In Mark Selb (1586) the incumbent reckoned on three
or four people, at most, attending the weekday sermon; and there was little hope
for improvement, since the local officials had not been for a whole year.[89] In the
face of such lassitude (or perhaps resistance) many towns must have opted for a
precaution similar to Kulmbach's 1572 effort: the council ordered the gates closed
during the sermons. Unless they had special dispensation (*sundere ehaft*), no one
was allowed in or out of the city.[90]

Nor did the Sabbath command greater reverence. When there was work in the
fields, few parishioners attended the weekend service. The pastor of Wonsees
observed in 1578 that, during the months when the crops had to be tended and
gathered, very few parishioners attended the service. The adults kept the children
away from the church so they could work in the fields.[91] Indeed, it was just these
days of prayer and reverence that might be set aside by the peasants for the
purpose of catching up on work. Violation of the Sabbath was not viewed by the
peasants as a sin.[92] Traditional customs and occupations were enjoyed on Sundays

---

[86] StaB, C2 1831, 1592 *passim*.
[87] StaB, C3, 49, fo. 14 (28 February 1531).
[88] LKAN, MDU, 8, Sickershausen (29 September 1575); 'Pastor hat die gemeine klag das
nachlessigkeit sey in der horung gottlichs worts...' LKAN, MDG, 71, fo. 169; Gunzenhausen
1611: 'Also ist auch uberal klag fur gefallen wegen der verächten des worts und der hoch wirdigen
sacramenten...'
[89] StaB, C2 1830, fo. 8.
[90] LKAN, MSK, 157, *General* (compiled 4 June 1573), fo. 2. (my pagination).
[91] LKAN, MSK, 133, Wonsees 1578.
[92] LKAN, MSK, 157, *Bericht der Spetial Visitation, In der Süperintendentz Beÿrreuth A[nn]o 1572*,
fo. 5 (my pagination.):

   Und haben die leutt schier auf keine andere zeitt mehr zuthun und zuarbeitten als eben auf diese
   tage, und was der gemeine Man die gantze wochen, nit khan ausrichten, das will er auf den Son
   und Feÿertage sparen.

and Holy Days as on any other days of the week; the sale and purchasing of goods, baking, reaping, cutting, gathering in groups, berry picking, beer drinking, dancing, brewing, collecting wood, walking, or travelling to neighbouring parishes figured on weekends as well as weekdays. The service itself was often preceded by secular business in the church.[93] If a Holy Day fell on a weekday invested by local significance, the sacred gave way to the profane. In Hof the visitors noted how the failure to honour the Sabbath was no longer considered a sin. The parishioners would go about their business on Sundays and Holy Days without a thought about the church.[94] In Brandenburg-Ansbach-Kulmbach, a sermon from the book of God was not enough in itself to guarantee an audience.

Lutheranism was not going to convert the peasantry with words, at least not during the first century of reform. This was not due to a lack of effort on the part of the pastors. The parishioners had no excuse at their disposal, so claimed the clergymen of Schwabach and Roth: if they wished to learn of the faith, the opportunities were myriad. 'But whoever does not want to learn the Word of God will not be forced to do so by a visitation; rather, as experience teaches, he will become even more stubborn.'[95] If Lutheranism were to make inroads, it had to force itself upon the parishioners; it had to be the only alternative in the field of religious action. And if it could not effect this through the spoken word of God, or through the written word of God, then it would have to set itself up as the sole champion of God, the sole custodian of his grace and favour, and the lone tributary of his power. It would have to limit access to the divine; it would have to discredit its rivals; it would have to erase the medieval Catholic church from the popular memory.

THE DISENCHANTMENT OF THE CHURCH

Martin Luther reduced the number of sacraments from seven to two: baptism and the Eucharist remained. This left the medieval church – which Keith Thomas has termed a 'repository of supernatural power' – bereft of key claims to sacral favour. Luther and his followers recognised that the sacraments, and their lesser kin the sacramentals, were not only symbols of supernatural power, but crucial supports in

---

The author added: 'wie dan diese beschwerungen, fast an allen Örtten befunden, und die arme Kirchendiener Mundtlich und in schriften mit seuftzen geklagen'; LKAN, MSK, 157, *Casendorff: Gravamina von dem Pfarrer daselbst in der Visitation furgebracht* (1592), 'die Verbrechüng des Sabbaths auch ungestrafft bleibt, wirdt sie auch für keine sundt mehr geachtet...'

[93] LKAN, MDG, 71, Gunzenhausen fo. 13 (31 October 1567):

In der Kirchen, gehe es unrichtig mit viln dingen zw, dan alles so ein rath oder gemain zuverkundigen, zuverbieten, und zuverkauffen hatt, das schreiet der büttel, in der Kirchen vor der predigt...' The margrave issued a mandate against this practice in 1533. *Corpus Constitutionum Brandenburgico-Culmbacensium*, (1746), p. 115.

[94] StaB, C2 1827 (1589) fo. 13.

[95] StaN, Ansbacher Oberamtsakten 1105ᵃ (Oberamt Schwabach), no. 195 (3 September 1571.)

the medieval structure of belief. If Lutheranism were to win souls from Catholicism, it had to discredit the sacraments; it had to drain them of their traditional significance and make them symbols of Lutheran belief. The dialogue between the Lutheran church and the religious beliefs of the rural parishioner revolved in large part around the role played by the sacraments and the sacramentals.[96]

Of the seven sacraments recognised by the Catholic church (confirmation, marriage, extreme unction, holy orders, penance, baptism, and the Eucharist), the most difficult to distance from the popular mind were naturally those with a prominent place in the medieval cycle of worship: baptism, confirmation, penance, the mass, and rites of separation. For the community of believers, these sacraments were recurring, frequently at their disposal, and familiar conduits of sacred power. If the Catholic church was, so to speak, a reservoir of sacral wealth, the fountainhead of divine favour, Lutheranism had to stem the flow, or at least redirect the current, so that the new church had greater control. In what follows, Lutheranism's influence on the popular perception of three of these sacraments will be assessed: penance, baptism, and the Eucharist.

Confession was central to the medieval cycle of worship. The Christian believer viewed the sacrament as a spiritual pilgrimage from grace to sin, sin to confession, absolution, and satisfaction (penance), and then back to grace. Confession enabled the individual Christian to receive the grace of God while at the same time it restored the wayward sinner to the communal fold. The Catholic church took great pains to ensure that it was administered properly. After the Fourth Lateran Council (1215), at which time annual confession became church law, a type of literary genre was born as theologians began to compile manuals for the parish priests to ensure that they administered the sacrament in the appropriate manner. These summas for confessors categorised the many possible sins and then suggested the appropriate penance. Many of these summas began to approach the subject of sin in a 'massive, encyclopedic way', prompting some scholars to see the confessional manual as a form of social control. For contemporaries, Luther among them, the medieval confessional was primarily seen as a means of spiritual control, a way of dictating and oppressing the religious conscience in the service of the Catholic faith.[97]

---

[96] Thomas, *Religion and the Decline of Magic*, pp. 27–57.
[97] The reference to the confessional as a form of social control is taken from Thomas N. Tentler, *Sin and Confession on the Eve of the Reformation* (Princeton, 1977); Thomas N. Tentler, 'The Summa for Confessors as an Instrument of Social Control', in Charles Trinkaus and Heiko A. Oberman, *The Pursuit of Holiness in Late Medieval and Renaissance Religion* (Leiden, 1974), pp. 103–25; Cameron, *The European Reformation*, pp. 80–3. Steven Ozment has argued that the appeal of Protestantism lay in its attack on the confessional and the psychologically burdensome demands of the Catholic Church. Ozment, *The Reformation in the Cities* (1975). Tentler and Ozment do not agree on the extent to which the sacrament of penance worked in answer to the summas and how much the sacrament was 'tempered by a more sober sense' of what could be expected. Ozment, *The Age of Reform*, pp. 218–19. Ozment's thesis has also been challenged by Lawrence G. Duggan, 'Fear and Confession on the Eve of the Reformation', *ARG*, 75 (1984), 153–75.

The Lutheran assault on the Catholic practice of confession must be understood within the context of Luther's theology. There is no doubt that the early reformers reacted against the tyranny (as they saw it) exercised by the Catholic confessors.[98] But Luther did not believe that the sinfulness of man could ever be fully revealed; man was both sinner and saved, absolution could not wash the sins away. Only Christ could infuse man with grace, regardless of the amount of remorse or contrition on the part of the sinner. Luther thus presented the medieval notion of penance with two fundamental objections: first, absolution is unconditional, and requires nothing for its validity beyond Christ's sacrifice; and second, absolution cannot be 'achieved': it only works if the sinner has true belief.[99] The practical corollaries of this position included a move to divest the former sacrament of penance of its urgency and necessity. Confession no longer impinged upon salvation. The actual act of absolution was no longer afforded the same 'magical' efficacy it had enjoyed in the Catholic church, and this worked against the medieval parishioner's tendency to view the efficacy of the confessional as automatic. For on the eve of the Reformation most parishioners viewed the process of confession, absolution and penance as an 'automatic' means of acquiring God's grace. 'The doctors might enunciate that, without contrition and the resolute intention to sin no more, confession was invalid and the sacrament a sacrilege, but the people, even if such theories penetrated down to them, paid little heed so long as the parish priest or his vicar was willing to mutter the magic formula over them and admit them to the paschal communion.'[100] The Lutheran notion of confession deprived the act of its 'magical' potency; instead of automatically receiving grace, the Protestant confessor could do no more than reveal to God his or her remorse – the rest was in God's hands. The parishioners were expected to realise the gravity of their sins in the confession and the reasons why they should fear God. Confession became a forum for soul-searching with no guaranteed or immediate reward. It was no longer a perfunctory or automatic rite.

In Brandenburg-Ansbach-Kulmbach the confessional, as a result, assumed a new significance. Confession became a form of private counsel (*ratforschung*) with the clergyman.[101] It was left to the individual to come to terms with his own sin; the act of absolution itself did not effect grace. Indeed, true penance was nothing more than 'to bear sorrow for acknowledged sins, to fear God's wrath, and to seek

---

98 Ozment, *The Reformation in the Cities*, p. 50: 'The first Protestants attacked the medieval church for demanding too much, not too little, from laymen and clergymen, and for making religion psychologically and socially burdensome, not for taking it too lightly.' The 1533 church ordinance also read: 'Und damit sich das volk soliches anzeigens [pre-communion confession] dester weniger beschwere, sollen sie die pfarherr und prediger erinnern, wie ein groβe bürde sie vorhin an der erzwungen beicht getragen haben...'. Sehling, p. 185.
99 Tentler, *Sin and Confession*, pp. 352–60.
100 Henry Charles Lea, *A History of Auricular Confession and Indulgences in the Latin Church* (London, 1896), vol. II, p. 415.
101 Schülin, *Fränkische Reformations Geschichte*, p. 43.

comfort'.[102] And yet, although the Lutherans shifted the focus of confession from the automatic efficacy of absolution to the private state of contrition and penance, it was still very much regulated and facilitated by the clergyman. Private confession was encouraged by Luther, and the idea found its way into the 1533 Brandenburg-Nuremberg church ordinance.[103] The pastor could demand that each communicant confess before the reception of the sacrament. Lutheran pastors thus had the power to use the confessional as a means of controlling their flocks. (This power prompted some reformers to fear that it might be used oppressively, like 'a new Papacy'.[104]) Unlike their Catholic predecessors, however, the Lutheran pastors did not act as intermediaries of salvation. Only faith could secure God's grace.

The Lutherans thus desacralised the act of penance and instituted a practice of confession whose efficacy was reliant upon the faith of the penitent. To ensure that the parishioners understood the importance of confession, it was made a prerequisite for the reception of the Lord's Supper (a practice not too far removed from the 'forced confession' of its Catholic predecessors). The Lutheran church wanted to invest the act of confession with renewed meaning, and it took steps to legislate this change. Is it possible to appraise the success of this venture? Is it possible to determine whether the average parishioner complied with the demands of the Lutheran form of penance? Since the historian cannot probe the minds of the dead, we must rely upon the few textual fragments relating to confessional practice and behaviour. Taken as a whole, the fragments would suggest that the mechanistic ritual of confession, wherein the parishioners attended confession in search of automatic absolution, maintained a strong hold.

The few references relating to confession would suggest that it had failed to become the forum of soul-searching the reformers envisioned. People were reluctant to discuss their sins in detail with the confessor. To a large extent confession remained a token obligation infused with sacramental significance. The parishioners felt uneasy whenever they were denied access to confession in times of urgency. One of the charges brought against pastor Peter Hochmuter in 1596 related to his refusal to grant absolution to a peasant woman near the throes of childbirth.[105] The peasants still sought the protective agencies of the rite of absolution. When Peter Meckel was accused of a reign of 'tyranny in the confessional', his great offence was his refusal to grant absolution.[106] In most

---

102 Sehling, p. 128.
103 Private confession was maintained, and in 1592 general confession was added. Simon, *Evangelische Kirchengeschichte Bayerns*, p. 309.
104 StaN, *Ansbacher Religionsakten III*, Tom. XI, fo. 460; Ozment, *The Reformation in the Cities*, pp. 151ff.
105 LKAN, MDH, XX, 3, *Interrogatoria darauf Hans Friederichen Rabensteiners zu Döla...* (1596), points 5–7.
106 LKAN, MKA, Spez. 348 (11 March 1588). *Summarische Relation* (c.1588/9).

cases absolution was the ultimate aim; the clergyman was still seen as performing the function of mediator between the grace of God and man. A woman in Trumsdorf, for instance, thought it very humorous that she had been allowed to attend communion, even though she had withheld her sins from the confessional beforehand. In her eyes the pastor was the dupe, not only because he granted her communion while she was in a (self-perceived) unfit state, but also because she had been able to outwit him in his office as the custodian of salvation.[107]

The Lutheran idea of private confession, wherein each parishioner was taken in turn after the ringing of the church bells (usually midday Saturday or the day before a Holy Day), though instituted, did not take uniform hold. Parishioners continued to overrun the churches on Sundays and Holy Days demanding confession and absolution just as they had done in the late-medieval era.[108] Of course, confessional practice varied with the convictions of the local clergymen; unlike the sacramentals, the parishioners needed the pastor for the desired effect. But it appears that wherever private confession was not strictly enforced, the Catholic practice persisted. Confession *en masse* in the parish of Kairlindach was not challenged by the Lutheran authorities until the year 1583. Three years later the pastor of Lenkersheim was reminded to separate his flock in the confessional, rather than hear them in groups (*gregatim*). The problem facing the clergymen, such as the pastor of Weißdorf, was that the penitents descended upon them at the same time, Sundays and Holy Days.[109] The idea of sacramental absolution, gained automatically and perfunctorily on days infused with significance, was still common in the minds of seventeenth-century Ansbach parishioners.[110]

The sacrament of baptism, on the other hand, enjoyed an ambiguous status. The Lutherans preserved baptism as a sacrament instituted by God; it was a sign of his promise. Unlike the Catholic idea of the efficacy of baptism, however, which temporarily set the Christian free from original sin, Luther believed that baptism, like the Word, conveyed the promise of salvation through the grace of

---

[107] LKAN, MSK, 157, Drümbsdorff 1592:

> Ist nach begangener unzucht zum H. Abendmal gangen und vom pfarrer und Diacono nit erkandt worden, als sie aber den Calicem empfangen ist sie mit Lachen erschottert davon gangen, welches als es pfarrer gesehen, hat er sie nach verrichtem Ambt in die sacristen fordern lassen und ursach warumb sie also gelacht, von Ir zu wissen begert hat sie zurantwort geben, Sie haben Irs so wol lachen mögen das sie weder pfarrer noch caplon gekennt und sie also ohne abbietung der kirchen zugelassen haben.'

[108] Wilhelm Kneule, 'Beichte, Konfirmation und Kirchenzucht in der ehemaligen Markgrafschaft Brandenburg-Bayreuth-Kulmbach 1533–1810', *ZbKG*, 37 (1968), 109–14, 109; LKAN, MSK, 133, Lehenthal (18 December 1583); LKAN, MKH, V, 1a, fo. 45; StaB, C2 1831, fo. 7 (1592).

[109] StaN, *Ansbacher Neues Generalrepertorium*, no. 49, rep. nr. 103^c, fos. 99, 121; LKAN, MDH, V, 1a, Weißdorf (8 October 1572).

[110] Hans-Christoph Rublack, 'Lutherische Beichte und Sozialdisziplinierung', *ARG*, 84, (1993), 127–55.

God. This promise was valid for a lifetime.[111] The Lutheran reformers tried to deemphasise the popular notion of baptism erasing sin, expelling demons from the wailing child, and 'purifying' and protecting the soul of the infant. As might be expected, this notion was slow to take hold. Trust in the apotropaic efficacy of the Catholic rite weighed heavily in the minds of the parishioners, some of whom bore their infants to Catholic parishes for the rite, though they might attend a Protestant service.[112] For some parishioners, baptism was central to the spiritual and physical welfare of a young child. Midwives were frequently reprimanded for baptising the children before they were even born.[113] And yet, without understating the importance of the baptismal ritual, stubborn dependence on pre-Reformation baptismal rites was not a recurrent problem for the Lutheran pastors. If anything, the parishioners had a rather lax attitude toward baptism, a humour summed up by the noblewoman of Lanzendorf:

On one occasion as she lay in childbed, her husband away from home in Prague, she let her child lay unbaptised for fourteen days. And although she had been reminded of the danger by many good-hearted people, she answered with these words: What difference does it make? It will be just the same child afterwards that it was before.[114]

The sacrament of baptism was viewed as necessary for salvation by some parishioners, and held in small regard by others.

For the laity, the logic ruling the occasion of baptism was primarily social. In the example given above, the woman's reference to her husband's absence is significant, for she waited on his return before baptising the child. In the rite of baptism, the child was not only freed from the hold of the Devil, but accepted into the extended family of the living, incorporated into the community of Christians through the institution of godparenthood.[115] Reception of the child into a suitable kindred, one that might replace the child's own natural family and preserve its place in the Christian fold, weighed first and foremost on the minds of the parents. To have appropriate godparents at the ready was second only in importance to the miracle of a successful birth. As the clergyman of Neudrossenfeld pointed out, parishioners would ask for a baptismal service only after they had secured a godfather.[116] This could be a source of tension between the clergyman and the parishioners. The 1533 church ordinance made it clear that

---

[111] In the words of Althamer: 'Weyl nun Gott den Tauff hat selbs eingesetzt, bevolhen, geheyliget durch sein wort, so müß mir der Tauff dienen zu abweschung der Sünd, von des worts wegen, und nit darumb des es wasser ist, sunder das es Gott also geheyssen hat'. In *Von der/Erbsund das sye der/Christen kynder gleich als/wol verdamb als der/heyden* (1527). Paul Althaus *The Theology of Martin Luther*, trans. Robert C. Schultz (Philadelphia, 1966), pp. 353–74.

[112] LKAN, MDG, 71, fo. 142 (1583).

[113] LKAN, MDU, 8, *Relation Visitation* (1565), fo. 5 (my pagination). The 1536 visitation had formulated a quite comprehensive list of questions directed at the midwives. Sehling, pp. 320–1.

[114] LKAN, MSK, 157, Lanzendorf 1592.

[115] Bossy, *Christianity in the West*, pp. 14–19.

[116] LKAN, MSK, 157, Drosenfeld 1573.

pastors were to admit only 'understanding' godparents to baptism, but this was not always possible, for once a choice had been made, it was difficult for the pastor to change the parishioners' minds. In Schornweisach, to offer an example, Contz Lantz had decided on Contz Salmen as the godfather. Since the pastor thought Contz Salmen was not suitable, he recommended another man. Contz Lantz was relatively flexible, willing at first to hear the pastor out, but his wife would have none of it: 'Early Good Friday he came to me', recounted the pastor, 'in threatening dress [*mit wehr und Rockh*] before the window and said his wife would not suffer another godfather (save this Salmen).'[117] To make matters worse for the local clergy, godfathers were often residents of a foreign parish, where the child might be taken and baptised if the proposed godparents were refused. The child became a member of the Christian community when it found its place by kith and kin, the *compaternitas*. If godparents could not be found, children were sometimes buried unbaptised.[118] The problem facing the Lutheran authorities was less to alter the sacral immediacy attributed to the baptism ceremony than to foster such an attitude.

The sacrality of the baptismal rite was less ritualistic than symbolic. During the medieval period the magical aspect of the sacrament had suffused to the blessed objects held in preparation for the rite. In the minds of contemporaries, childbirth represented a spiritual danger and required such protection. The strength of this belief is borne out by the practice of churching the women after the birth, separating them from the faithful for six weeks as a ritual of purification. Churching persisted in Protestant lands regardless of the prohibitions. Well into the eighteenth century women who had just given birth (*Sechswocherin*) were considered people of unusual powers in Ansbach.[119]

Of primary importance for the Lutheran authorities was the task of disenchanting the powers attributed to the baptismal sacramentals: the water, the salt, the oil.[120] This crusade was mounted in vain. Parishioners continued to believe in the charged and unique qualities of baptismal water. Blessed water was sometimes mixed in with the horse feed to act as a remedy for illness (or as a general protective measure). One pastor reported (in near disbelief) how three women of Weidelbach had taken water from the church font and added it to their food and drink in order to induce a pregnancy. As late as 1594 the consistorial ordinance was instructing the clergy to watch out for this type of practice, 'since in many

---

[117] LKAN, MSN, 92ᵃ (4 April 1602). (This letter must have been incorrectly dated, since the pastor was not in the parish until 1604, and the superintendent Simon Menzel was not in office until 1606.)

[118] LKAN, MSK, 133, Seibelsdorf (11 December 1583); StaB, C2 1831, fo. 3 (1592).

[119] R. W. Scribner, 'The Impact of the Reformation on Daily Life', in *Mensch und Objekt im Mittelalter und in der frühen Neuzeit. Leben-Alltag-Kultur* (Vienna, 1990), pp. 331–4. The 1533 church ordinance warned against the practice. Sehling, p. 177; 'Aberglauben des gemeinen Volks im Anspachischen,' *Journal von und für Deutschland*, 3 (1789), 180, 250.

[120] Sehling, p. 174; Thomas, *Religion and the Decline of Magic*, pp. 40–2.

places, remaining from the Catholic superstition, the sexton sells the leftover baptismal water ... which is then later used for magic'.[121] Similar parasitical beliefs were attached to the Eucharist.[122] More than any other issue, communion and the doctrine of transubstantiation became a 'bone of contention' among the Protestants and remained a moot point throughout the century. Luther disagreed with the Catholic definition of transubstantiation, but he did not deny the presence of Christ's body and blood during the act of consecration. Luther settled the matter with his doctrine of ubiquity and his belief that two 'realities' were present at the altar at the same time. Thus the Eucharist itself was not disenchanted by the Reformation. What the reformers did try to effect, however, was a privileged control of the sacrament, and a drive to distance the Eucharist from the hold of popular magic.

Johan Huizinga's now classic work *The Waning of the Middle Ages* argued that medieval piety was hypersensual. Subsequent works seem to agree, and scholars have since made it clear that the celebration of the mass was one of the most visually significant religious gestures of the age. Central to the ritual of communion was the elevation of the host, and it was this act above all that was held in awe by the parishioners. The actual perception of the host, 'the sacramental gaze', was such a crucial gesture it assumed a merit of its own; it became something of a good work, as if the people were participating in a liturgical action. Even those who later rejected the notion of Real Presence had an inbred fear of the elevated host.[123] To help guard against this superstition, select reformers tried to abolish the elevation altogether. Martin Möglin of Kitzingen wrote against the common beliefs associated with the elevation of the host in 1529: 'That it is enough in itself to view and adore the reverent host as it is raised in the mass, and once such idolatry has occurred, everyone runs from the church, secure in the opinion that they have done what is right and honoured the Holy Sacrament with the appropriate humble reverence'.[124] No mention was made of the abolishment of the elevation in the 1533 ordinance; in fact, the Ansbach council recommended the practice continue as before. Elevation may have fallen into disuse in the later

---

[121] StaB, C2 1831, fo. 10 (1592); LKAN, MKA, Spez. 1015 (3 March 1580); Sehling, p. 391; StaN, *Ansbacher Neues Generalrepertorium*, no. 49, rep. nr. 103^e, fo. 115 (1584).

[122] On the popular beliefs surrounding the mass, see Adolf Franz, *Die Messe im deutschen Mittelalter* (Darmstadt, 1963), pp. 73–114; Miri Rubin, *Corpus Christi. The Eucharist in Late Medieval Culture* (Cambridge, 1994), pp. 288–346; Thomas, *Religion and the Decline of Magic*, 38–40.

[123] Peter Browe, 'Die Elevation in der Messe', *Jahrbuch für Liturgiewissenschaft*, 9 (1929), 20–66; Bob Scribner, 'Popular Piety and Modes of Visual Perception in Late-Medieval and Reformation Germany', *The Journal of Religious History*, 15 (1989), 448–69; Rubin, *Corpus Christi*, pp. 49–82; Eamon Duffy, *The Stripping of the Altars* (London, 1992), pp. 95–107; Parishioners in the Upper Palatinate who were thought to be Zwinglians or Anabaptists refused to watch the elevation: 'They don't want to look at it, they hold their hats in front.' Cited in Trevor Russell Johnson, 'The Recatholicisation of the Upper Palatinate (1621–circa 1700)', PhD thesis Cambridge University, 1991, pp. 189–90.

[124] StaN, *Ansbacher Religionsakten III*, Tom. XI, fo. 344. *Eyn geschrifft des heyligen Sacraments yn der mess auffheben, und zum teyl, anbetten belanngend 1529.*

years, and Georg Karg certainly called for its abolition, but scattered examples of the elevation of the host during communion exist for the later decades and it is doubtful that there was a uniform pattern in any superintendency.[125] In any case, downplaying the act of consecration or limiting access to the 'sacramental gaze' did not alter the popular perception of the host as an object of wonder.

In the middle ages it was commonly believed that the consecrated host possessed magical qualities. Hosts could ward off all manner of ills and impart desperately needed benefits. As love potions and protective amulets, talismans sewn into clothing, tucked away in a pouch, or as a crushed and powdered remedy taken bodily to guard against illness, these consecrated wafers were tangible symbols, and workable elements, of divine power.[126] Lutheranism did not suspend these beliefs, nor reduce the popular need for this tangible proof of God's favour. The parishioners still viewed the host with awe and considered it the receptacle of preternatural powers. Clergymen were occasionally held under suspicion if they used normal bread for the mass. Pastor Peter Hochmuter was cited by the parishioners (during an inquisition in 1596) for once letting the host fall to the floor, in addition to distributing unworthy wafers (*zerbrochene oblat*). Magical remedies continued to include the host as part of a potion or displayed independently in the form of an amulet on the neck of an ox.[127] It retained a mystique of strange properties. In 1591 the visitors of Altheim were told that:

if one goes to the Lord's Supper and takes the host ... out of one's mouth and steps on it or sticks it with a knife, blood will flow. If the host is put in a bucket of water, and if the water is sprinkled or poured to earth, it will poison the ground.[128]

Parishioners viewed the host with wonder and awe, an object endowed with powers capable of responding to their needs; it was never sheltered from the popular imagination by the Lutherans. Catholic and Protestant parishioners alike manipulated the powers of the Eucharist. (Some parishioners did not even recognise a difference between the two forms of communion.)[129] The host, elevated and viewed, carried, swallowed or otherwise borne, remained an object

---

[125] LKAN, MDLz, 666, no. 9; LKAN, MDU, 3, fo. 18; Löhe, *Erinnerungen*, pp. 153, 155.

[126] Peter Browe, 'Die Eucharistie als Zaubermittel im Mittelalter', *Archiv für Kulturgeschichte*, 20 (1930), 134–54; StaN, *Ansbacher Religionsakten III*, Tom. II (*c*.1525), no. 19, fo. 75: 'man gieng gantz spötlich mit dem sacrament umb, einer [trieg] es in der tasch, der ander im bueß, der dritte im Ermel etc. ...'

[127] LKAN, MKA, Spez. 724. fos. 60–2 (*c*.1530); LKAN, MDH, XX, 3, 4 June 1596 Inquisition. Ninth and fourteenth witnesses. fos. 32, 34; Theodor Hampe, *Crime and Punishment in Germany*, trans. Malcolm Letts (London, 1929), p. 106. The 1594 consistorial ordinance warned against using residual hosts for magic. Sehling, p. 391.

[128] StaN, *Ansbacher Neues Generalrepertorium*, no. 49, rep. nr. 103ᵉ, fo. 235.

[129] LKAN, MDG, 71, fo. 122 (1581): 'Hans Emerer, begert vom pfarrer das sacrament des leibs und bluts zuempfangen, will doch vom Bapstumb nit abstehn, sagt es sei das Bapstümb wie das Lutherthumb er wiß kain underschaidt zwischen baiden...'; Scribner, 'The Impact of the Reformation on Daily Life', pp. 324–5.

invested with magical power, and would be found among the belongings of any Ansbach or Kulmbach wisewoman worth her (blessed) salt.

The consecrated host was a sacrament; it was effective *ex opere operato* - independent of the disposition of its handler. Sacramentals, in contrast, had to be blessed by a clergyman, and were dependent (in theory) upon the disposition of the user. Since any blessed object might be a sacramental, the list of possibilities was long – herbs, images, salt, bread, altars, candles, water, vestments.[130] In spite of the great variety of possible objects, however, Lutheranism in Ansbach made the most headway against the cult of the sacramentals – or so it would seem, given that the references to the abuse or overuse of this practice are few (which would follow, since the number of religious objects had diminished and the sacred space had been confined to the church). But the lack of references to the continued use of sacramentals does not necessarily mean that the rationale behind them was discredited. In essence, the trust in objects thought to have a unique and direct relationship with the divine endured.

The persistent belief in sacramentals was most forcefully borne out by those blessed objects which physically survived, church bells for instance. The village church usually had a consecrated bell, sometimes baptised and named, which was rung during periods of crisis or inclement weather in the trust that its apotropaic powers would be enough to ward off danger. Lutheran attempts to abolish the practice met with resistance. As the Kulmbach visitors observed in 1586: 'Although the ringing of weather bells has been abolished in the General Visitation, it still persists in many cities, villages, and parishes'. Throughout the century local sextons were paid to toll the bells to deflect inclement weather.[131] In Neudrossenfeld (1591) the church tower was hit by lightening; the cause, so claimed the parishioners, came down to the pastor's refusal for the blessed and baptised bell to be used as a sonorous weather-vane.[132] Not only did the ringing of church bells continue in Kulmbach, but the practice was widespread enough for church bells to be sounded in a different fashion from parish to parish:

in many places, all the bells are rung continuously one after the other without stopping just as long as the weather persists. In other places, all the bells are rung at the beginning, but then they continue with only one bell (while the others are silenced); and if the weather does not let up, the bells are then rung again as they were at the beginning, without slacking or stopping...[133]

---

[130] Adolf Franz, *Die kirchlichen Benediktionen im Mittelalter* (Freiburg, 1909); Scribner, *Popular Culture and Popular Movements*, pp. 5–8.

[131] LKAN, MSK, 157, *Acta Visitationis in der Culmbacher Superintendentz 1586*, fo. 5 (my pagination); Kramer, *Volksleben im Fürstentum Ansbach*, p. 185.

[132] Karl-Sigismund Kramer, 'Protestantisches in der Volkskultur Frankens. Konfessionelle Rivalität und Nachbarschaft', *Hessische Blätter für Volkskunde*, 60 (1969), 82; also cited in Scribner, 'The Impact of the Reformation on Daily Life', p. 327.

[133] LKAN, MSK, 157, *Generalia* (1592), fos. 1–2 (my pagination.)

The visitor considered it a 'Catholic superstition' and hoped, in good Lutheran fashion, that the ringing of bells would rather serve to remind people of prayer. Meanwhile, beneath the belfry, objects adored for their proximity to the divine were in the very nave of the church: pictures, images, paintings. A belief in the inculcatory effects of pictures is common to most religions, and Christianity was no exception.[134] Throughout the Middle Ages pictures and images of saints, the Virgin Mary above all, were held as sacred objects; they were considered reserves of sacrality. The Lutheran authorities fought against this belief. Pictures and images in themselves were adiaphora, but when prayers were directed at the image, it was idolatry.[135] The reformers realised they could not effect a change in the popular religious mentality overnight; the most they could do was to teach the villagers that pictures were aids to worship, not ends, and remove the more offensive images from the parish churches. The parishioners were slow to learn. In 1567 the Gunzenhausen visitors compiled a report for Ansbach in which they asserted 'there is very little difference between these churches and the popish churches', adding that the banners, candles, and 'countless dreadful idols' served no pious purpose, but rather facilitated idolatry. In short, the visitors concluded, the parishes had not been purged of the Catholic superstitions (*die alte larven des Bapstumbs*).[136]

Not only did the idea persist that a visual image was a window onto the sacral realm, but pictures and statues were often thought to dispense special protective powers susceptible to the active solicitation of the faithful. In the parish of Ühlfeld (1582),

there is an altar in one spot in the church with a picture of Mary and the baby Jesus. When their churching has come to an end, the women [*sechswocherin*] are in the habit of visiting the church with a number of their neighbours and bearing their child from one altar to the next. When they finally arrive before the picture of Mary, they begin to suckle the child. According to this superstition, the length of time the child drinks from the mother is the same length of time it can stay under water without drowning.[137]

---

[134] David Freedberg, *The Power of Images: Studies in the History and Theory of Response* (London, 1989).

[135] Sehling, p. 134. Often the visitors solved the problem by removing the picture and putting a crucifix in its place. Nuremberg did the same thing. See Gerhard Hirschmann, 'The Second Nürnberg Church Visitation', in Buck and Zophy (eds.), *The Social History of the Reformation*, p. 366

[136] When the visitor wished to do away with the images he fell suspect of iconoclasm: 'werde ich bezichtiget, das ich ein bildstumer sëy'. LKAN, MDG, 71, fo. 14. Compare Bugenhagen's measured advice: Wolf-Dieter Hauschild (ed.), *Lübecker Kirchenordnung von Johannes Bugenhagen 1531*. (Lübeck, 1981), p. 144. These images and altars were still there in 1568 (one of which, entitled 'Heaven', was a holdover from the Corpus Christi processions) and attracted people from foreign parishes.

[137] StaN, *Ansbacher Neues Generalrepertorium*, no. 49, rep. nr. 103ᵉ, fo. 69. A similar practice was observed in some Nuremberg parishes. Dannenbauer, *ZbKG*, 7 (1932), 236–7. The Virgin Mary was the most popular image, but other saints were also honoured. In Weidenbach there was a picture of Saint George (LKAN, MDG, 71, fo. 86, 1579); in Wirsberg a picture of Saint Leonhard (LKAN, MSK, 157, Wirsberg, 17 November 1558); and in Seibeldsdorf they were reputed to have numerous 'götzen' in the church (LKAN, MSK, 157, Seubelsdorf 1573). For the

A pregnant woman of Wallmersbach had a related ritual. According to the sexton Endres Mauer she asked to be let in the church to do penance (*sie heth ein pues zu thun*). Upon her return, she told him that if he saw an inverted picture, he should leave it in place until the third day. At first he found nothing, and then in the belfry he discovered an inverted crucifix (presumably an image). The woman returned before the three days were up and told him he could remove it. Her penance, it seems, was done.[138] When pressed to answer, the parishioners, like the schoolmaster of Schwand, claimed they did such things to honour God. That is an unbefitting honour, said the pastor of Schwand in reply, for one should always appeal directly to God; there is no need for intermediaries.[139]

Despite the reformers' earlier assurance that pictures and images did not threaten salvation, a 'free matter' the pastors might let stand, neither party – the higher clergy or the parishioners – seem to have been able to compromise in practice. The example of Langenzenn is illustrative. In 1553 the clergyman Christoph Kyfer wrote to Ansbach of how in this church

There is still a hideous idol ... an unsightly image. Teaching and preaching, up to this point, have not been able to remove it from its place in the hearts of the common man. Indeed now, more and more, the idol is being honoured and adored by them ... people from foreign places make their way there to seek the help of the idol.

When Kyfer confronted a woman and pleaded with her to leave off her false devotion before the picture, she prolonged her silent reverence without pause and would not turn to face the clergyman. Parishioners continued to gather there, leaving wax dolls and chickens.[140] When Georg Karg heard of this, he referred to the image (an image of the Virgin) as a 'black devil', honoured by high and low estate, seducing the parishioners and turning their thoughts away from God. He ordered that it be reduced to ashes. It is unlikely that the events in Langenzenn surprised the Ansbach superintendent. All the churches in the principality, according to Karg's estimate, were 'full of altars and pictures'.[141] Like blessed water, like the host, like the array of sacramentals spawned by the medieval church, the image was seen as a vehicle of sacred power. The Reformation did not overthrow these charms.

The very charms themselves were invested with the belief in a supernatural power fundamental to the livelihood of the Protestant church. Take, for example,

idea that popular piety might appropriate particular saints in certain locales, see Donald Weinstein and Rudolph M. Bell, *Saints and Society* (London, 1982); William A. Christian, Jr, *Local Religion in Sixteenth-Century Spain* (Princeton, 1989).

[138] LKAN, MKA, Spez. 941. fo. 6. (no date. *c*.1528–49). She was later punished for her 'zauberey'.
[139] LKAN, MDS, 171, *Gravamina Beschwernus des Jonae Pfitzingern Pfarr[er] zu Schwandt wider den Schulmeister und Meßner daselbsten* (1614). 'Das sei Gott ein schlechte Ehre, man soll Gott anruffen...'
[140] For the type of objects being offered, see Lenz Kriss-Rettenbeck, *Ex Voto: Zeichen Bild und Abbild im christlichen Votivbrauchtum* (Zürich, 1972), p. 60.
[141] Above paragraph taken from LKAN, MKA, Spez. 527, fos. 33–6.

spells, blessings, and incantations. While in theory the distinction between a spell and a prayer is that the former claims an automatic efficacy and the latter relies upon the will of God, this division was blurred in practice. Nor was this a lay perversion of ecclesiastical finery. Eamon Duffy's words are worth quoting in full:

it would be a mistake to see even these 'magical' prayers as standing altogether outside the framework of the official worship and teaching of the Church. The world-view they enshrined, in which humanity was beleaguered by hostile troops of devils seeking the destruction of body and soul, and to which the appropriate and guaranteed antidote was the incantatory or manual invocation of the cross or names of Christ, is not a construct of the folk imagination. Such ideas were built into the very structure of the liturgy, and formed the focus for some of its most solemn and popularly accessible moments.[142]

Sixteenth-century charms regularly called upon the power of Christ, God, or the Trinity to help those in need. Not only was Christ called upon, but He played an active role in the fulfilment of the wish. Equally, the peasantry frequently entreated Christ and Mary in spells and verses to overcome illness, to protect the crops or the animals, and to secure the welfare of the parish.[143] There is no doubt that spells and incantations were thought to possess a power of themselves, especially core verses rhymed in succession.[144] But the language, the words that are used in a spell, the references, the significations – these things must have meaning as well. Throughout the sixteenth century the parishioners of Ansbach and Kulmbach believed that an appeal to Christ, to Mary, to the Father, or indeed to the godhead, would elicit a response. The church was tapped for its sacral protection, as it had been for centuries.

The popular belief in the powers of the divine – that they could be harnessed for earthly ends – ran counter to the Protestant insistence on man's impotency and his inability to do anything to tempt God's favour. God had created the world, once blessed, and his work could not be manipulated to serve human ends.

---

[142] Duffy, *The Stripping of the Altars*, p. 279.

[143] LKAN, MSK, 157, Nemersdorf (8 October 1584): 'Christ gieng auff Erden, Es wolt ein wetter werden, Er hueb auff sein gebeneden hand, Er segnet das wetter uber den wilden wald, Das weder leut noch viehe mag schaden tragen, Noch der lieben frücht auff dem feldt.' The introductory formula 'Christ ging auff Erden' or 'Unser Herr Jesus ging über/durchs Land' was common. See Irmgard Hampp, *Beschwörung, Segen, Gebet: Untersuchungen zum Zauberspruch aus dem Bereich der Volksheilkunde* (Stuttgart, 1961), pp. 238–41. Compare the spells unearthed by the Nuremberg authorities: Heinz Dannenbauer, 'Die Nürnberger Landgeistlichen bis zur zweiten Kirchenvisitation', *ZbKG*, 4 (1929), 236–7.

[144] Such as the *Wurmackersegen*, which generally preserved the core text and added requests appropriate to the situation. Manfred Geier, 'Die magische Kraft der Poesie. Zur Geschichte, Struktur und Funktion des Zauberspruchs', *Deutsche Vierteljahrsschrift für Literaturwissenschaft und Geistesgeschichte*, 3 (1982), 369. A similar verse was recorded by the visitors in Neudrossenfeld (LKAN, 157, Drosenfeld 26 October 1579/80). Other examples are in Hampp, *Beschwörung, Segen, Gebet*, pp. 241–2. The English equivalent would seem to be 'Tetter, tetter, thou hast nine brothers/God bless the flesh and preserve the bone/Perish thou tetter and thou be gone/In the name of the father...' Maria Brie, 'Der germanische, insbesondere der englische Zauberspruch', *Mitteilungen der Schlesischen Gesellschaft für Volkskunde*, 16 (1906), p. 17.

The disenchantment of the church

The Lutherans closed up the church like a monstrance. People like Katherina in the parish of Stübach, a woman who carried grain into the church on Good Friday to preserve her pigs from death, were told 'never to do it again'. People like Friedrich Fischer of Baudenbach, a man who nailed INRI on his threshold in the hope that it might help his bodily pains, were brought before the visitors and admonished to put away these relics of medieval belief. As the Baudenbach pastor said to two of Friedrich's fellow parishioners, such things were done in contempt of God. Some parishioners would not succumb to the pressure of the pastor so easily. In Hetzelsdorf (1592) the outlying peasantry devised a courier system for blessed parcels, sending their herbs to the Catholic parish of Bretfeld where they were consecrated. 'And though they are punished by the pastor for this', said the visitor, 'nothing helps.' Still other people, like Barthel Seitz of Rüdisbron, resented the intrusions of the clergy and told them as much. Barthel reminded his pastor in 1589 that he would not make the final journey for them, either to heaven or to hell, so he should leave them in peace.[145] But if the Protestant mission included a campaign to disenchant the church, a campaign to free parish piety from its belief in the power of the sacraments and the sacramentals, then it could not leave the people in peace. For the people remained true to their medieval traditions.

The Lutheran reform did not desacralise or 'disenchant' the church during the course of the sixteenth century. This point has been made most convincingly in the work of R. W. Scribner, who has shown in a series of articles that the Protestant world was no less convinced that a supernatural force could intervene in the profane world at any time than the Catholic, the only difference being 'it did not do so at human behest and could not automatically be commanded'.[146] This latter observation refers to a fine point of theological judgement which, while of central importance to Lutheran doctrine, was not enough to dissuade the people from believing in a sacred power which could be utilised for private use. For the average parishioner, the Lutheran religion did not represent a fundamental alternative to the Catholic faith. The sacramentals were not made redundant; popular trust in a realm of sacral power, of which the church and its related paraphernalia was both a reservoir and a pathway, persisted.[147] Thus for the historian assessing the 'impact' of Reformation thought on the parish mind during the first century of reform, the most useful strategy is less one of

---

145 StaN, *Ansbacher Neues Generalrepertorium*, no. 49, rep. nr. 103°, fos. 66, 94, 155; LKAN, MSK, 157, Hetzelsdorf 1592.

146 Robert W. Scribner, 'The Reformation, Popular Magic and the "Disenchantment of the World"', *Journal of Interdisciplinary History*, 23 (1993), 475–94; Bob Scribner, 'Magic and the Formation of Protestant Popular Culture in Germany', unpublished MS, 1992, forthcoming; Scribner, *Popular Culture and Popular Movements*, pp. 1–16; Scribner, 'The Impact of the Reformation on Daily Life'.

147 Compare Ernst Walter Zeeden, *Kleine Reformationsgeschichte von Baden-Durlach und Kurpfalz* (Karlsruhe, 1956), pp. 43–8; Ernst Walter Zeeden, *Konfessionsbildung. Studien zur Reformation, Gegenreformation und katholischen Reform* (Stuttgart, 1985), pp. 154–60.

contrasting two starkly separate worlds of understanding than sketching a compendium of beliefs, and then determining whether this realm of popular belief could be manipulated in praxis – and if it was, identifying the process. It would follow from this that the question to ask is not whether religion could accommodate the parishioner, but whether the parishioner could accommodate the church.

POPULAR BELIEFS AND THE REFORMATION

In 1589 the pastor Jacob Graeter gave an extended sermon to his parishioners in Schwäbisch Hall entitled (to cite the preamble) *Hexen oder Unholden Predigten*.[148] Graeter spoke on the subjects of magic and witchcraft. The words 'witch', 'magic', 'fiend', or 'sorcerer' were laden with significance for the sixteenth-century mind and Graeter used them to advantage. But it is doubtful whether the average parishioner induced the range of meaning implied by the clergyman: 'What we say here of sorcerers should also be understood of magicians, necromancers, purveyors of black magic, soothsayers, crystalball readers, and others of the Devil's brood.'[149] The sermon equated magic with trust in the Devil. Graeter's homily was intended to make an impression on his audience; he warned against the wiles of the Evil One, and how easily man may forswear his belief in Christ and fall prey to Satan's promised 'mountain of Gold'.

In recent years historians of early modern Europe have concerned themselves more and more with the reception and appropriation of the ideas in sermons like *Hexen oder Unholden Predigten*, rather than the subtleties of their invention. This has necessitated a study of popular culture, which has problems of its own. Representations of popular culture were often distorted or manipulated as they were set down by the observer. Written accounts of the thoughts and behaviour of the parish populace are not transparent windows on the past. In response to this textual bias, historians have begun to focus on the mediating process itself, the world view of the author, the flow of cultural influences, and the contact between traditions of thought. And yet this concern with the transmission and mediation of traditions has not abolished the dichotomy familiar to most studies of early modern culture: Two cultural traditions did exist in this period, and to distinguish between a 'great' and a 'little' tradition does not necessarily deny the fact that the relationship was fluid or that one tradition shaped or modified its counterpart. Popular culture was part of a wider context of beliefs; it was not fixed and uniform, impervious to influence. But the culture of the people was clearly

---

[148] A condensed version of the following appears in Trevor Johnson and R.W. Scribner (eds.), *Popular Religion in Germany and Central Europe, 1400–1800* (London, forthcoming). I would like to thank Macmillan Press for allowing me to reprint this material.

[149] Jacob Graeter, *Hexen oder Vnholden Predigten. Darinnen zu zweyen vnderschiedlichen Predigten, auff das kürtzest vnnd ordenlichest angezeigt würdt, was in disen allgemeinen Landtklagen, vber die Hexen und Vnholden, von selbigen warhafftig vnnd Gott seeliglich zuhalten* (Tübingen, 1589), p. Dii[r].

separate from the culture of the church or the culture of the court. The notion of a two-tiered cultural world does not belie the realities of the age.[150]

With this emphasis on cross-cultural interaction in mind, the following will address two aspects of popular culture and the sixteenth-century Reformation movement. The first section will portray manifestations of popular culture, the type of activity Graeter termed 'crystalball seeing', soothsaying, fortune telling, and magic. What was the nature of popular belief? What was the association between popular beliefs – or the trust in magic – and traditional parish religion? The second section will examine the relationship between the Reformation and this tradition of local beliefs. Did the Lutheran authorities undertake a reform of popular culture? If they did, how profound was its influence and how resonant was its effect?

The study of late medieval lay religiosity has usually privileged the canonical forms and objects of worship for its speculations on the degree of Christian conviction. There is no doubt that the late Middle Ages was a period of intense devotion. The number of foundations, masses, images, and relics increased, the cult of the saints diversified, the concern with salvation and damnation found a more desperate and socially stratified voice, and the laity began to create opportunities of their own to get in contact with the divine.[151] Popular worship centred on Christ, Mary, and the saints – in particular and in general – to avoid God's wrath and ensure that the community of Christian souls remained in his trust.

And yet, this reliance on the medieval church, its saints, and its sacraments and sacramentals did not necessarily exhaust the outlets and vehicles of popular devotion. Parishioners often created means of their own to get in touch with the divine, some of which were institutionalised – guilds, lay brotherhoods, chantry priests – some of which were personal, practical, pragmatic, 'superstitious', and more akin to magic than religious devotion. Parish religion on the eve of the Reformation was essentially apotropaic in character, concerned with prevention and protection, and therefore not antithetical to the rationale behind recourse to magic. Given the sweep of popular religiosity, it is difficult to draw firm boundaries between what was religious and what was 'superstitious' in practice.

---

[150] Roger Chartier, *Cultural History: Between Practices and Representations*, trans. Lydia G. Cochrane (Oxford, 1988); Burke, *Popular Culture in Early Modern Europe*; Bob Scribner, 'Is a History of Popular Culture Possible?' *History of European Ideas*, 10 (1989), pp. 175–91; Michel Vovelle, *Ideologies and Mentalities*, trans. Eamon O' Flaherty (Oxford, 1990), pp. 81–113.

[151] Johan Huizinga, *The Waning of the Middle Ages* (New York, 1984); Jacques Toussert, *Le Sentiment religieux en Flandre à la fin du moyen-âge* (Paris, 1963); Etienne Delaruelle, *L'Eglise au Temps du Grand Schisme et de la Crise Conciliaire* (1378–1449) (Paris, 1964); L. Veit, *Volksfrommes Brauchtum und Kirche im deutschen Mittelalter* (Freiburg, 1936); Rosalind and Christopher Brooke, *Popular Religion in the Middle Ages* (London, 1984); Bernd Moeller, 'Religious Life in Germany on the Eve of the Reformation', in Gerald Strauss (ed.), *Pre-Reformation Germany* (London, 1972), pp. 13–42; and also the observations in Raoul Manselli, *La Religion Populaire au Moyen Age* (Montreal, 1975).

'Religion' and 'magic' were not strict categories in the average parishioner's mind.[152]

In a similar sense, just as there is a danger in supposing that canonical forms of worship were the only forms of worship, there is an equivalent danger in assuming that this seeming *immense appétit du divin* expressed a pure and homogeneous form of religiosity. Late-medieval and early-modern parishes were home to many opponents of the faith, and others who were simply religiously indifferent. A headcount of mass foundations so~ 'imes overlooks the fact that sceptics and earthly saints might share the same ₅e streets.[153]

Some parishioners in Ansbach and Kulmbach left explicit reminders that they did not cower before the church and its agents; they were quite willing to face life and its many mysteries without clerical assistance. In the case of Linhardt Megel, the reason was elementary: he thought himself to be God, consigned by a cabal of power-hungry potentates to labour on earth. (Of course, this also explains his prolonged absence from the Lord's Supper, and it is hard to find fault with his aversion to self-ingestion.)[154] In a neighbouring parish, a servant shrugged off the threat of damnation with reference to his 'good warm hell' at home in the service of his master. He then stood up and left the sermon. Dorothea Hofman claimed that 'when she dies, man may place her where he will; she doesn't care' (*sie frag nichts darnach*). Gabriel Grosinger of Kirchleus gave a similar answer: he wanted to be buried beneath a tree in his backyard and cared little for a Christian burial.[155] Why should they observe a particular practice in death, reasoned a man in Gunzenhausen, for who can bring the bones of the dead back to life?[156]

An indifferent or quarrelsome parishioner might challenge the very powers of the faith. The pastor cannot help him get to heaven, observed a man in Unterlaimbach, so why should he pay him such great respect?[157] A villager in the superintendency of Gunzenhausen even questioned the clergyman's role as a dispenser of the sacraments, since he could perform this service himself.[158] Some

---

[152] Richard van Dülmen, 'Volksfrömmigkeit und konfessionelles Christentum im 16. und 17. Jahrhundert', in Wolfgang Schieder (ed.), *Volksreligiosität in der modernen Sozialgeschichte* (Göttingen, 1986), p. 20.

[153] The most famous sixteenth-century village sceptic is now the Frulian miller Menocchio. See Carlo Ginzburg, *The Cheese and the Worms* (London, 1982).

[154] StaN, *Ansbacher Neues Generalrepertorium*, no. 49, rep. nr. 103ᵉ, fo. 17: 'Linhard Megel ein zimlich alter Mann, gibt fur, er seÿ gott, und seÿ das sacrament selbst, darumb ers nit empfehet'; fo. 25: 'Linhardt Megel ein alter man zu Bernhaim [Burgbernheim], sagt er seÿ selbst Gott, wünscht Im in den himel nicht, denn die Obersten im Himel haben Ime des sein genomen, darumb er sich mit arbeit auf erden weren muβ.'

[155] StaN, *Ansbacher Neues Generalrepertorium*, no. 49, rep. nr. 103ᵉ, fos. 82, 116; LKAN, MSK, 157, Kirchleüs 1580.

[156] LKAN, MDG, 71, fo. 170–1 (1619). A man cited as an 'Epicurer': 'do sehet Ihr wie es mit uns zugehet, wer Reit der reit, wer leut der leut, das diese bein sollen wider lebendig werde, glaub Ich nicht, darumb thu Ihme ein jeder guttes weil er lebt.'

[157] StaN, *Ansbacher Neues Generalrepertorium*, no. 49, rep. nr. 103ᵉ, fo. 139.

[158] LKAN, MDG, 71, fo. 85 (1579).

parishioners, like the *artzt und empiricus* Hans Pfall of Goldkronach, went so far as to follow the 'laws of nature' above those of the church.[159] In response to the question 'Who is Christ?', Michael Mair of Auernheim returned rather agnostically: 'How can he know something, which in his entire life he has not seen with his eyes?'[160] But this type of deliberate deviance was not always the essential motivation. For Klaus Ubelein and his wife, religion came with the territory. Although he was subject to the visitation in Baudenbach, he actually lived on a property near Bamberg which required that he remain Catholic. 'If he could sell his land however', observed the visitor, 'he is quite willing to give himself to the Lutheran faith.'[161]

The statements and behaviour cited above, viewed from the perspective of a sixteenth-century Lutheran clergyman, were equivalent to atheism. Atheism in the sixteenth century meant no more than a disposition to entertain the possibility that no single religion was necessarily privileged or that the universe might be subject to forces additional to those reserved for God.[162] Some people were willing to do without the church (in its entirety) in their efforts to come to terms with the world. Rather than view such people as radicals, they should, perhaps, be seen as the norm, as conservatives secure in a wider context of beliefs allowing for them to depreciate the official faith. The parishioners of Ansbach and Kulmbach have left scattered reminders or traces of behaviour which, seen as a whole, betray such a tradition of beliefs. This tradition was not a native alternative to the Lutheran faith, but antecedent and paramount to it, and the context of thought in which religion found meaning.

In 1581 the pastor of Berg, Andreas Schaller, a Wittenberg-educated clergyman described in 1560 as 'pious and industrious', was brought before the chancellery officials. The charge against him was as follows: his wife, together with her maid, had sought aid from a wisewoman in the parish of Baiergrün. The main concern for the Lutheran officials was Schaller's traffic with this woman, which looked bad for the clerical estate (for it was well-known [*ein gemein geschreÿ*] in the parish). Schaller faced the interrogations of Johann Moninger, a doctor and archivist in Kulmbach, together with the assembled clergy.[163] After an impassioned session,

---

[159] LKAN, MSK, 157, Goldkronach 1580: 'Hans Pfall ein artzt und empiricus ist 8 Jar da gewesen, unsern [sic] Gnedigen Herschafft unterworffen, ein wunderlicher mensch, hat sich vor der zeit wen er in der Visitation erfordert worden, allerlei seltzamer red vernemen lassen und unter andern auch dieser, Er lasse sich nit anders machen, Er empfahe das abendmal wen es sein andacht gebe, wen er schier gar verzweiveln wolle, wolle ers wol empfahen, Er halte das gesetz der Natur.'

[160] LKAN, MDG, 71, fo. 5 (1567). 'Einer mit namen Michel Mair, als er gefragt wurdt, wer Christus were, gab er antwort, wie er es wissen künth, so er in sein leben lang doch mit augen nit gesehen hab.'

[161] StaN, *Ansbacher Neues Generalrepertorium*, no. 49, rep. nr 103ᵉ, fo. 60.

[162] On atheism in this period, the standard work is still Lucien Febvre, *Le Problème de l'incroyance au XVIᵉ siècle: la religion de Rabelais* (Paris, 1942).

[163] On Moninger, see Otto Clemen, 'Joh. Moninger, Poet, Historiker, Arzt, Apotheker und Archivar', *ZbKG*, 13 (1938), 215–23.

the pastor of Selbitz coaxed a confession from Schaller: it was true, his wife had visited the Baiergrün woman, purchased herbs (*kreutter*), and fed them to the cattle. But it had all occurred without his knowledge, or so claimed Schaller. Doctor Moninger was not convinced. If Schaller knew of this woman in Baiergrün, why had he not reported her to the authorities? Moninger, twenty-one years in the service of the margrave, was certainly right: it was Schaller's clerical duty to report repeated offenders of the faith to the visitation commission. The doctor's ambitions, however, were unrealistic. It would take more than the efforts of a single pastor to banish the wisewoman of Baiergrün.[164]

For many years the pastor of Kirchleus, Pancratius Feindtel, had been instructing his parishioners to place their trust and hope 'in no one else than solely in the true eternal and omniscient God.' But in practice the opposite was happening. In times of pressing need, Feindtel wrote, many of his parishioners sought help and salvation not (as instructed) with God in Heaven, but rather from a woman in Baiergrün. 'They hold such people in their hearts as a God.'[165] Recourse to the Baiergrün wisewoman was wide-spread. In the 1580s alone, parishioners from Schauenstein, Bischofsgrün, Stammbach, Harsdorf, Hof, Münchberg, Selbitz, Köditz, Berg, and Kirchleus were cited as making the trek (or 'pilgrimage') to Baiergrün – a thirty-five mile radius. And when they got there, who did they find? Reports vary. Pancratius mentioned a woman and a man. The visitor of Hof simply mentioned 'a woman in Baiergrün'. The Schauenstein pastor cited two women: one, Margaretha Hohenberger, who was the main offender; the other, the wife of a soldier who had died in France. And the pastor added: 'to the one, no less than to the other, a great pilgrimage has emerged'.[166]

Parishioners sought the help of the wisewoman in times of illness, when they needed to seek remedies to ill-fortune, to procure abortions, to recover stolen goods, or to learn of the future. As the Hof visitor made clear, many people believed 'that the woman of Baiergrün can advise and help with all kinds of bodily afflictions; therefore, as at other places, without doubt there are many here as well who seek her counsel and advice.'[167] In Kulmbach a clergyman remarked on how she was consulted not only 'during the sickness of men and

---

[164] LKAN, MDH, XX, 2, nos. 1–4 (1581):

> Nun ist aber zu Baÿerngrun Im Ampt Schauenstein eine Zauber vettel, wonhafft, welche sich nicht allein von Urinis (ea reverentia zu reden) villeicht durch Cristallen zu Judicirn und Artzney zugeben, sundern auch von gestolnen und verlornnen dingen. Auch von verzauberniß und (wie es der gemainen Mann Pflegt zunennen) vorgethenen sachen responsa und oracula pÿthonica zugeben Angemoset derhalben auch zu ir ein lange Zeitt hero, ein unglaublich groß gelauff, von nahe und ferne gewesen, und leider noch ist Und derowegen vil Clag in den Visitationis fürkommen, Aber gleichwol noch biß hero nicht ohne viler gotsfuerchtiger leutt seufftzen, unabgeschafft geblieben.

[165] LKAN, MSK, 352 (28 January 1584).
[166] LKAN, MSK, 157, Schauenstein 1580 *Querelae pastoris*.
[167] StaB, C2 1827, fo. 11 (1589).

animals' but often persuaded to visit many parishes (*an vil Ende geholet*) in the hope she could bring remedies to their door. Such a house-call was a relative luxury; most people would have been faced with the situation confronting an official of Köditz. When his son fell sick in 1587, he rushed him to Baiergrün to seek aid, but the child died on the journey.[168] There was no scarcity of soothsayers and wisewomen in the parishes of Ansbach and Kulmbach, nor a paucity of home remedies, so the popularity of Margaretha Hohenberger of Baiergrün must have been well-earned. As late as 1603 Margaretha Vießman, answering to the charge that she was a soothsayer, confessed to inheriting her crystal ball (*Cristallen*) from her aunt, and her aunt in turn had received it from 'the woman of Baiergrün'.[169]

There seems to have been a fairly comprehensive network of practitioners of popular magic in the parishes of Kulmbach (cunning people, soothsayers, white witches, etc.) singled out as effective in their craft. It was difficult for the visitors to root them out, for, as the superintendent of another Lutheran principality remarked, they often befriended one another in a fellowship of silence.[170] And yet the source materials do offer examples of people similar to Margaretha Hohenberger of Baiergrün. The superintendent of Hof referred to two people in the district of Hof who were suspected of purveying magical remedies. They had a crystal ball and seventy-two species of herb at their disposal.[171] The visitation protocols listed a cunning man in Dottenheim, another in Unternesselbach, Hans Scheffer in Heidenheim, Michael Igel of Thuisbrunn, a woman (*Sägensprecherin*) in Equarhofen, another in Pfofeld, the cunning woman (*weis fraw*) near Würzburg, the soothsayer of Absberg, the soothsayer of Plech (whose reputation was widespread), a woman in Münchberg, the barber's wife in Aha, and the shepherdess near Köditz, who blessed the people and their children in times of illness.[172] These are just some names that failed to escape detection. No doubt the visitor of Hof was correct in assuming that these 'Devil's vermin' worked in secret in many parishes.[173]

The same Hof visitor made another observation worth note: not only were the 'simple, superstitious people' in the countryside flocking to the cunning people in

---

168 StaB, C2 1827, fo. 108 (1589).
169 StaB, C2 3240 (16 February 1603).
170 F. Spanuth, 'Die Grubenhagenische Kirchenvisitation von 1579 durch Superintendent Schellhammer', *Jahrbuch der Gesellschaft für niedersächsische Kirchengeschichte*, 52 (1954), 117. On soothsayers in general: Willem de Blécourt, 'Witch Doctors, Soothsayers and Priests. On Cunning Folk in European Historiography and Tradition', *Social History*, 19 (1994), 285–303.
171 LKAN, MSK, 157, *Beschwerung und Ergernus* (1578), point 2. They claimed that they had learned it from the Jews.
172 StaN, *Ansbacher Neues Generalrepertorium*, no. 49, rep. nr. 103ᵉ, fo. 16, 59; LKAN, MDU, 8, Equarhofen 1587; Walmersbach 1573. LKAN, MDG, 71, fo. 37, 43, 45; LKAN, MSK, 157, *Bericht der spetial Visitation, In der Süperintendentz Beÿrreuth A[nn]o 1572*, fo. 14 (my pagination); *Executio Visitationis Anno 1574 vorrichtett*, fo. 2 (my pagination). StaB, C2 1827, fo. 147.
173 LKAN, MSK, 157, *Beschwerung und Ergernus*, (1578), point 2.

droves, but the prominent (*fürnembsten*) city burghers also held 'everything they say, advise, or do' as correct:

'Last summer', wrote the pastor of Weißdorf in 1576, 'Junker Hans Eitel of Sparneck housed a public magician at his Weißdorf estate, maintaining him for a long time, and letting him soothsay for him and other people. And when the pastor, as befits his office, preached against it (which annoyed the magician or soothsayer) he not only abused [the pastor] horribly, but threatened to harm him. And all of this was heard and tolerated by the said Hans Eitel of Sparneck.'[174]

Noble women sought the services of the Köditz shepherdess. In 1569 a noble-woman sent her maid to the sexton's wife in Birk (a soothsayer) bearing considerable gifts.[175] Barbara Fleißmann, resident of Kulmbach and wife of Johann Thomas Fleißmann, a man on familiar terms with Imperial counsellors, was herself accused of dealings in magic. She denied the charge, referring instead to her German books of astronomy, and asked that she be treated lightly 'on account of her good name and lineage'.[176]

Perhaps even more surprising than the involvement of the secular elite in the practice is the number of clergymen associated with the magical arts. Doctor Moninger's doubts about pastor Schaller's (non)relationship with the Baiergrün wisewoman were not necessarily ill-placed. The pastor of Windsfeld, Georg Schneider, promised the Absberg soothsayer one thaler for her services after an infamous drinking bout. In Oberferrieden, the clergyman's wife was also accused of treating with cunning people to heal her husband's illness, going so far as to invite them into the house. Pastor Kaspar Günther of Neudrossenfeld was valued for his talents with herbs, but he had to be careful lest he fall suspect of alchemy. For the clergy, there was a fine line between indulgence of popular magic and abetting unwanted and unlawful superstitions. Clerical reactions were correspondingly varied. Faced with the suspicion of the consistory, the incumbent in Kairlindach decided to throw all of his suspect books into a fire.[177]

In view of the fact that recourse to prophesy, soothsaying, divining, adjurations, blessings, protective healing, or any other form of 'magic' was outlawed by both the ecclesiastical and the secular authorities, it needs to be explained why these popular remedies remained so dominant, and just what it was they were thought to accomplish. A contemporary scholar has concluded that popular magic was 'undoubtedly a form of cultural practice concerned with mastering the exigencies of material and daily life, and specifically the processes of production and reproduction, the maintenance of physical and spiritual well-being, the preserva-

[174] StaB, C2 1826, fo. 4.
[175] StaB, C2 3235, fo. 5.
[176] StaB, 3237, (28 February 1592).
[177] LKAN, MDG, 71, fo. 43. (1572); LKAN, MDS, 122, T.1 (3 March 1575); StaB, 1223, fo. 149 (1568); StaN, *Ansbacher Neues Generalrepertorium*, no. 49, rep. nr 103ᵉ, fo. 61.

tion of property, and the management of social relations.'[178] This definition chimes with the comments of contemporaries. A return from Neudrossenfeld (1575) offers a summary:

Magic and recourse to soothsayers have become very common on account of [the frequency of] theft; and it follows from this that many use magic in times of illness, and bring these soothsayers to themselves. These same people [*teuffels banner*] teach the parishioners many kinds of unpleasant arts for the cattle's food and health; many times they make innocent people suspect, and show how they can cause people to die.[179]

Other clergy, in their assessments of the purpose of magic, included the desire to recover stolen goods, to locate a lost person, to bewitch or correct the mind of an acquaintance, to still pain, to deaden remorse, to purge melancholy, to liven the crops, to tempt the weather, to save the life of a child, or to catch a thief. The function of popular magic was to answer those urgent needs of the parishioner insoluble in any other way. The common denominator was the need. In a pre-industrial society, this might apply to the most basic situations and desires confronting man.[180] The sheer reach of its claims reveals magic's centrality in the parishioners' lives.

Having finished a wash, with it hanging near the Neberschmidt's stairwell in the city of Kulmbach, Barbara von Lichtenstein's maid Margaretha Röslein heard the voice of her mistress and returned home. When she later went back to fetch the wash, it was gone. Margaretha asked the lady of the house, but she knew nothing; 'She was with her mother and did not see it.' Nor did the other neighbours know the whereabouts of the wash. Margaretha was forced to tell her

---

[178] Scribner, 'Magic and the Formation of Protestant Popular Culture', p. 1.

[179] LKAN, MSK, 157, Drosenfeld (8 September 1575).

[180] Take, for example, the lack of rudimentary medical services available to the sixteenth-century Ansbach subject. Quite aside from the primitive state of the science in this period (which in itself was enough to kill most people), the parishioners' problems were compounded by the undersupply of legitimate doctors. Gunzenhausen had no doctors, nor did Ansbach ('zw Onoltzpach [Ansbach] kainen medicum oder leibs artzt'). Many parishioners might have experienced the same problems as the pastor of Mitteldachstetten. When his sight began to fade, he approached some eyedoctors in Nuremberg (*schidtartzt und oculist*), paid them a great sum of money, and then suffered further damage. Undaunted, he later sought the services of a man in Ansbach and his sight was momentarily restored. But it did not last, and in the end he spent thrity gulden in a fruitless venture. LKAN, MKA, Spez. 600 (31 December 1599). In Bayreuth, the situation was a bit better. A *Stadtphysikat* began in Bayreuth in the sixteenth century. And indeed by the 1550s some doctors were so specialised they were known to treat specific diseases (ie: a *Franzosenartzt, Augenartzt*). Although the city had something of a history of medical practitioners, the margravial physician Dr. Moninger's nearby residence and later intervention in a dispute between an *Apotheker* and a *Gewürzkrämer* must have helped to establish order. Helmut Haas, 'Hygiene und Prophylaxe und Oberfranken in Mittelalter und Neuzeit', *Archiv für Geschichte von Oberfranken*, 61 (1981), 59–81; Horst Fischer, 'Die Apothekenanfänge in Bayreuth und die Entwicklung des Apothekenrechts in der Markgrafschaft bis um 1800', *Archiv für Geschichte von Oberfranken*, 57/8 (1978), 187–271; Dr. Andräas, 'Beiträge zu einer Geschichte des Gesundheits- und Medicinalwesens der Stadt und des Fürstenthums Bayreuth', *Archiv für Geschichte und Alterthumskunde von Oberfranken*, 15 (1882), 1–132.

noble patron, who answered in a threatening tone 'that in no way does she wish to be without such things'. Upset, and worried over the prospect of having to replace the wash herself, Margaretha went in tears to her friend Else Fischer and told Else of her plight. Else was sympathetic and stopped in at the von Lichtenstein household later that day with the following advice:

she was with the old sexton's wife Frau Hübner, who told her that the maid should neither fret nor cry. Many people used to come to her former husband, the sexton, for the nails that had been removed from the coffins. These objects are then used whenever someone has lost something ... the nail should be hammered into the place where the lost goods had been left, and the thief who has purloined the goods will bring them back to the same place.

Margaretha was reluctant to follow this advice and put it off until morning. When she awoke, despite cautions from other women in the household ('*Mädchen, if I were in your place, I wouldn't do it*') the noblewoman's insistence prompted her to carry out the deed. Using the nail she had asked Else to get from the sexton the day before (at a cost of fourteen pfennig), Margaretha returned to the Neberschmidt's house and apprised them of her plans. Lorenz Neberschmidt was not averse to the idea; in fact he let her use his hammer. So Margaretha set the nail in place, driving it into the wood 'in the name of the Evil One [*böesenfeindts*]'. And then it took effect.[181]

The most immediate effect was the subsequent arrest of Margaretha, Else, Katherina, the former sexton's wife, and even Lorenz Neberschmidt and the current sexton Hans Hainolt.[182] Katherina confessed to telling Else that 'when such a nail is taken and placed or nailed in the spot where something was lost, the lost item must be brought back'. But, she added, she did not recommend it, nor did she ever do it herself; it was simply common knowledge (*gemeinen reden*) often mentioned by her former husband.[183] Katherina's testimony did not incorporate the Devil's name as part of the formula, though both Else and Margaretha considered it crucial enough for inclusion. Lorenz Neberschmidt specifically denied any knowledge of Margaretha's intention to use the Devil's name. When he heard of it, he suddenly remembered a related occurrence:

He admits that his wife had been sick even before the maid hammered in the nail. After this had taken place, however, his wife was visited with such bodily discomfort she could not have a normal bowel movement. The nail alone is held responsible.[184]

---

[181] StaB, C2 3236, fos. 5–8; 'des Magdlein Außsag' (10 May 1587).

[182] Sextons, given their proximity to the church and the gravesite, were often cited as brokers of illicit 'magical' objects, whether the sacramentals or small objects, such as hair or nails, taken from a corpse. The 1594 consistorial ordinance specifically mentioned the sexton (*mesner*) when it issued orders against the selling of the sacramentals for magical ends. Sehling, p. 391.

[183] StaB, C2 3236, fo. 9 (10 May 1587).

[184] StaB, C2 3236, fo. 15 (15 May 1587). The authorities later responded to this charge (furthered in a letter by the Neberschmidt woman, 8 July 1587) that it was a case of 'Malefitz' and was thus out of their hands (fos. 22–5).

The sexton Hans Hainolt, as if prescribing a remedy for the ailing Neberschmidt, added that such a nail, fashioned to form a ring, also worked against body aches (*das Reissen*). In the end there were as many stories as tongues, and yet, though they could not agree upon Margaretha's intent, her culpability, or the particular affects the nail might have, they all agreed on one thing: the magic created a reaction of some kind, a reaction that could scarcely be held in check or confidently predicted.

The outcome of this case is not recorded, but for the investigating authorities nothing about it would have been especially novel. Coffin nails and wood, bones from the grave or the corpse itself – anything to do with the dead – were seen as receptacles of supernatural power.[185] Georg Carl Lamprecht 'obtained [a] piece of skull and other bones from the dog-killer at Kitzingen, who told him that they were good for shots if hung about the neck'.[186] In Heidenheim the local wiseman was well-known for his bundles of coffin splinters taken from the graves of children. Skulls were often used for similarly arcane ends, whether to prophecy, cast, to cure animals, or to work magic.[187] Nor would the notion of catching a thief in this manner have raised many eyebrows. The year before Margaretha was placed under arrest, some parishioners in Buchheim, having recently suffered a robbery, buried the hat and the walking stick of the thief (conveniently left behind) in the hope that 'as soon as these objects began to rot, so too would the thief dry up until he died'.[188] Of course, in this instance the objects had a special significance, as they were once the property of the assumed victim. But clothing might be used in other ways. The women of Casendorf were wont to secure their husbands' underclothes to the horn of a sick cow. Once released, the cow would then wander to the source of its bewitchment. In a similar manner, Kunigund Rethin threw her husband's underclothing in a pot to work her magic.[189]

Other means were used for different ends. Abortions were thought to be effected with herbs and potions. 'Aye, harr harr', soothed Magdelena Schefflin's lover, if she were to take the remedy he prescribed, place it in some warm beer, the child would be aborted. More prudent women used magic to render men impotent beforehand.[190] Roots and herbs were used to relieve pains and illness. Like the wife of pastor Schaller, the majority of patrons approached a cunning person for roots or plants, or some sort of concoction 'with herbs and natural

---

[185] On the superstitions surrounding death and the act of burial in Protestant Germany, see H. Höhn, 'Mitteilungen über volkstümliche Überlieferungen in Württemberg. Sitte und Brauch bei Tod und Begräbnis', *Württembergische Jahrbücher für Statistik und Landeskunde*, 2 (1913), 307–57.

[186] Hampe, *Crime and Punishment*, p. 111. Unfortunately for Lamprecht's dog, he tested this theory.

[187] LKAN, MDG, 71, fos. 84; 190; StaB, C2 3235, fo. 5 (1569).

[188] LKAN, MDU, 8, No. 155, Buchheim 1586.

[189] LKAN, MSK, 157, *Casendorff: Gravamina von dem Pfarrer daselbst in der Visitation furgebracht* (1592); StaB, C2 3238, *Warhaffte Articuli Positionales, Fraw Regina Streitbergerin wittib zu Culmbach contra Künigund Rethin doselbsten* (1594).

[190] StaB, C2 1814, *Acta* 1583; StaN, *Ansbacher Neues Generalrepertorium*, no. 49, rep. nr 103ᵉ, fo. 12.

things' believed to serve the desired purpose.[191] Slips of paper with random words or letters on them (like INRI) were held to work magic, though it might be the case, as in Unternesselbach, that the bearer 'cannot read a single letter'.[192] In the parish of Lehenthal a soothsayer blessed the children with a pitchfork (*mistgabel*). Along the same lines, the Baiergrün wisewoman once advised that a change of straw (possibly from the bedding), with the old straw thrown on the manure pile and stamped underfoot, would remedy a child's ailing limbs.[193] Inanimate objects could thus work as conduits of supernatural power. The universe was electric with unseen energies ripe to assist, and perhaps to harm. When the city of Kulmbach feared contagion in 1587, they remembered the burning sack Benedict Preußern had thrown through his window late one night and left to spark and smoulder in the city streets.[194]

If the world were alive, teeming with a great chain of corresponding objects of power, it is little wonder that some people claimed to have a window on its workings. Margaretha Vießman was often consulted as a soothsayer because she had a crystal ball 'in which she can fathom hidden and secret things ... and what has been stolen or secretly borne off, she can learn its shape and bring it back'.[195] Katherina Hoser, the sexton's wife in Birk, had a crystal ball or *Wetterstein* in which events and cures were revealed to her. When a maid approached her asking whether 'a woman big in body' was pregnant, Katherina responded by looking into her stone. (See following section.) Literate people like Barbara Fleißmann placed their trust in almanacs and books of astrology.[196] (Though this habit of referring to published works was not necessarily confined to an elite readership. The pastor Georg Caesius of Burgbernheim is thought to have published a *practica* almost every year between 1570 and 1604.[197] The Wallmersbach pastor Johann Schülin, famous for his popular prognostications and almanacs, estimated that thousands of his calendars had been printed. This admission did not hold him in good stead with the margrave.[198])

In general, popular beliefs in Ansbach and Kulmbach, in so far as they are

---

[191] StaB, C2 3240 (16 February 1603).
[192] StaN, *Ansbacher Neues Generalrepertorium*, no. 49, rep. nr 103ᵉ, fo. 123.
[193] LKAN, MSK, 157, Lehenthal 1592; Schaüenstein (4 November 1579/80) The word used is 'stro', which could denote straw or perhaps thatch.
[194] StaB, C2 3238 (16 August 1587). Benedict was able to exonerate himself.
[195] StaB, C2 3240 (16 February 1603).
[196] StaB, C2 3237 (28 February 1592). Answer 7.
[197] Robin Bruce Barnes, *Prophecy and Gnosis: Apocalypticism in the Wake of the Lutheran Reformation* (Stanford, 1988), pp. 155, 299, no. 26.
[198] Pastor Schülin's curious prognostications were examined by the Ansbach clergyman Michael Stiber. In the end he was told to forgo the calendars and spend time reading 'more useful and necessary books' like the Bible. See LKAN, MKA, Spez. 942. *Wallmersbach Miscellanea: Kalendarium des Pfarrers Johann Schülein 1588–91.* But this judgement may have been a bit unfair. In 1586/7 it was recorded that Schülin had sent '24 gulden gen Wittenberg M. Johan Rühlein Bibliopolae vor 2. Jarn fur Bücher unkosten' and he owed thirty gulden to the Crailsheim council for his studies. LKAN, MDU, 12, fo. 48a.

preserved in the source materials, correspond to the popular practices common to medieval and modern Europe.[199] Some talents – healing for instance, or the power to foresee – might be the preserve of local cunning people and soothsayers, but recourse to popular magic remained an overarching means by which the average parishioner could deal with the exigencies of sixteenth-century parish life. According to a Kulmbach official in 1592, not a single day passed in his district without a complaint about magic coming to his notice.[200] The Reformation did not cleanse Ansbach and Kulmbach of popular magic and its practitioners, despite the fact that it was a conscious goal of the movement and its leaders. Lutheranism did not seduce a people into betraying their traditions of belief. Such popular beliefs, and the 'superstitions' attendant upon them, were the manifestations of a parish mentality which remained unchanged throughout the first century of reform.

Pastor Korneffer of Merkendorf, to his immense displeasure, discovered the popularity of magic first hand. As he informed the neighbouring abbot of Heilsbronn, he had continued to lecture against forbidden beliefs, hoping that the Word of God would be enough to purge his parishioners' hearts of this sin. But the soothsayer of Absberg remained a dominant figure for the Merkendorfers and crucial in their lives. Korneffer referred the matter to the authorities, and an investigation followed (28 December 1571). In total, eleven people were singled out as having been in contact with the woman. The testimony of Hans Winebrecht speaks of her popularity and the effect of her presence on the faith:

I had the wise woman come and stay with me last Friday to help me with my horses (one of which is once again ailing). Several of my fellow townsmen came to my house to seek her counsel. In doing so, we neglected the catechism session (amongst other things) and boozed and whooped it up during the church service, as has happened in other places ...

The woman offered Hans and his friends her remedies, usually a blessing invoking the powers of God, and she received four thaler and a loaf of bread in return. Upon hearing of this report, the Ansbach council dispatched a statement ordering the offending parties to spend three days in the tower, with the threat of more serious punishments should they repeat the offence. If the wise woman were ever encountered, she was to be placed under arrest.[201]

For the Lutheran clergy, it seemed that their preaching was in vain. Pastors repeatedly gave sermons on the evils of magic, the wiles of the Devil, and (more to the point) why it was a sin to trust in powers other than those of Christ. But the

---

[199] Thomas, *Religion and the Decline of Magic*, pp. 209–332; Richard van Dülmen, *Kultur und Alltag in der Frühen Neuzeit* (Munich, 1994), vol. 3, pp. 55–96; Richard Kieckhefer, *Magic in the Middle Ages* (Cambridge, 1990); Valerie I. J. Flint, *The Rise of Magic in Early Medieval Europe* (Oxford, 1991); Richard Cavendish, *A History of Magic* (New York, 1977); Lynn Thorndike, *The History of Magic and Experimental Science* (New York, 1934), vol. 4, pp. 274–307.

[200] StaB, C2 3238, fo. 9–10 (4 May 1592).

[201] Georg Muck, *Geschichte von Kloster Heilsbronn von der Urzeit bis zur Neuzeit* (Nördlingen, 1879), vol. 2, pp. 55–62, 57.

people would not surrender their beliefs.[202] In the final decades of the century, it was not uncommon for the higher clergy in Kulmbach and Bayreuth to refer to this stubbornness as *Sicherheit* – denoting security, certainty, confidence, a trust in alternative powers, and all at religion's expense. The physician and demonologist Johann Weyer (1515–1588) thought the root cause of such 'foolish work of the Devil' was just this lack of belief in Christ, an *Unglaubigkeit der Menschen*, (admittedly, he adds, less widespread in lands where the Gospel was preached), which left man predisposed to favour magic (and thus Satan) over the salvation-inducing faith in Christ.[203] No compromise was brooked between religion and magic; the superstitious man, as Weyer wrote, was a man without faith. 'It is startling to hear', concluded the Ansbach council in 1569, 'that despite the pure preaching of the efficacious and salvation-inducing word of God, people should be found who are dependent upon magic and superstitious things'.[204] Recourse to magic, as the 1533 church ordinance observed, remained a panacea for the 'simple peasants' whose weak powers of reasoning could not think of any other explanation for the strange or unusual.[205]

Two different world views were at crossroads. The clergy, whose plangent forecasts are scattered throughout the protocol of the visitation returns, saw the continuance of magical beliefs as a refusal to join the Christian fold. The outcome of this stubbornness could only be the damnation of the individual soul, God's wrath, and the destruction of the principality (not necessarily in that order). Frequent references were made to 'Sodom and Gomorra' and other Old Testament examples of divine anger. In part this was just rhetorical style, and yet it was also reflective of a cast of mind imbued with the notion that popular culture and religion were natural enemies. The sheer weight of references to soothsayers, forecasters, wisewomen, and other magical remedies owes much to the fact that it was uppermost in the clerical mind. For the religious authorities, magic was a crime against the faith.

In contrast, the parishioners did not order the world in such systematic terms.[206] Fundamental to all forms of popular beliefs was the notion that a power

---

[202] As late as 1705 the margrave was dispatching mandates against 'Segensprechen und andere aberglaubische Dinge' – though by this late date, as the research into witchcraft has evidenced, there was also a concern with the 'Satanischen Wesen' of such practices. *Von Gottes Gnaden/Wir Wilhelm Fride/rich, Marggraff zu Branden/burg, in Preussen ... Onolzbach den 2. Martii Anno 1705* in LKAN, MDS, 29.

[203] Johann Wierus (Weyer), *De Lamiis: Von Teuffelsgespenst Zauberern und Gifftbereytern...*(Frankfurt, 1586), pp. 17–18, 22, 33; *Von verzeuberungen, verblendungen, auch sonst viel und mancherley gepler des Teuffels und seines gantzen Heer...*(Basel, 1565), p. 302. On Weyer, see Rudolph van Nahl, *Zauberglaube und Hexenwahn im Gebiet von Rhein und Maas* (Bonn, 1983), pp. 37–78. Van Nahl doubts that Weyer was Protestant, despite the claims of some scholars.

[204] StaB, C2 3235, fo. 82.

[205] Sehling, p. 160.

[206] See the observations and the literature in Stanley Jeyaraja Tambiah, *Magic, Science, Religion, and the Scope of Rationality* (Cambridge, 1990); Daniel Lawrence O'Keefe, *Stolen Lightning: The Social Theory of Magic* (Oxford, 1982); Peter Winch, 'Understanding a Primitive Society',

could be conjured, harnessed, and then applied to specific tasks. 'Magic', observed Marcel Mauss, 'is essentially the art of doing things.'[207] The notion of return without effort, or effect without deliberate cause, is alien to a mode of thought which views the world as a fretwork of correspondences, each acting on the others all the way down the chain. For the popular mind, as the discussion of sacraments and sacramentals has suggested, religion was understood in the same terms: ritual devotion plus hallowed object equals desired effect. Even the relationship between the worshipper and the object of worship (as scholars have described it) was of a contractual nature. The peasants offered their devotion to a heavenly overlord (*Bauerngott*) or a particular saint, expecting a gesture or act of reciprocation in return. The sacred – in so far as it was qualified by the parishioner – was ordered in answer to a profane logic, a logic of mutuality.[208] Caspar Eÿsenman of Adelshofen summed up this attitude: 'He had prayed once before, but our Lord God did not offer him anything in return, so he will no longer recite the Ten Commandments or the Lord's Prayer'.[209] Magic was of the same nature: all the examples above demonstrate that the parishioner undertook certain tasks in a fixed sequence and expected a corresponding result. The distinction between magic and religion, so clear to educated men like Johann Weyer, was blurred in the parish mind. There were no unbridgeable spacial or mental borders separating the sacred from the profane. The supernatural was everywhere.

Thus it was left to the Lutheran authorities to mark the boundaries between popular magic and religion, and in doing so, the reformers not only drafted a catalogue of forbidden beliefs, unprecedented in its intimacy, they also asked the parishioners to betray their deepest convictions.[210] Historians have labelled this process 'the reform of popular culture' or the 'acculturation of the rural world'. Unlike earlier medieval attempts at reform, which were sporadic, localised, hampered by primitive networks of communication and law enforcement, both the sixteenth-century Protestant and the Catholic drives to enforce a unified faith

---

American Philosophical Quarterly, 1 (1924), 307–24; J. D. Y. Peel, 'Understanding Alien Belief Systems', *The British Journal of Sociology*, 20 (1969), 69–84; and also the introduction by C. Scott Littleton in Lucien Lévy-Bruhl, *How Natives Think*, trans. Lilian A. Clare (Princeton, 1985).

[207] Marcel Mauss, *A General Theory of Magic*, trans. Robert Brain (London, 1972), p. 141.

[208] Scribner, *Popular Culture and Popular Movements*, p. 13 (citing Max Rumpf); William A. Christian Jr., *Apparitions in Late Medieval and Renaissance Spain* (Princeton, 1981), p. 22: '[Apparitions] were charters for relationships between the village and the natural world'; William A. Christian Jr., *Local Religion in Sixteenth Century Spain*.

[209] LKAN, MDU, 8, no. 152 Adelshofen 1573. 'Caspar Eÿsenman ein Epicurischer man sagt Er hab hevor ein mal gebeth, unser her Gott hab Ihm noch nichts dafur geben, Betet weder 10 gebot noch vater unser mehr.' Other examples include: LKAN, MDG, 71, Drosenfeld (26 October 1579/80). 'Caspar Albert sein Bruder ist in 6 Jaren nit darzugangen [to communion]. gibt fur er habs ein mal empfangen hab darnach ein bain gebrochen.'; StaB, C2 1830, fo. 8. 'Jacob Zeidler in zweien iharen [had not attended communion], gebe fur so er mit seinem weib nicht were zu deß herrn Abentmal gangen so were ihm sein son nicht gestorben.'

[210] Richard van Dülmen, 'Volksfrömmigkeit und konfessionelles Christentum im 16. und 17. Jahrhundert', p. 26.

were founded on a much more systematic and articulate programme. Robert Muchembled views the emergence of the modern state as the essential engine behind this process. The intrusion of the state, going so far as to effect a 'destructuration' of the traditional social context, shattered the relative peace enjoyed by the practitioners of popular beliefs.[211] Other historians see the process as a more static intellectualisation: the process of reform, in this instance the Counter-Reformation, represents the actual 'Christianization' of the rural masses through indoctrination.[212] These are sibling ideas of the more general view of confessionalisation, and the multifaceted influences seen as engendered or accelerated by the Reformation (or Counter-Reformation) movement.[213] Here, for our purposes, the consequences may be seen as twofold: the extension of the state's reach to the realm of parish practice and the subsequent indoctrination of the faith.

There is no doubt that the Reformation in Brandenburg-Ansbach-Kulmbach presented the broad stratum of popular beliefs with a threat. And although, as has been implied above, the first century of reform did not eradicate these beliefs, there is reason to believe some parishioners felt themselves under siege. In 1536, with the second visitation, the visitors were instructed to examine the midwives to determine whether the women were employing 'superstitious charms and words' in order to facilitate birth. By 1578 such concern had extended beyond this traditional subsection of the village population (known for their suspect remedies) to include the specialists of popular magic (*zauberer, segensprecher, wahrsager*) or indeed any member of the parish suspect in the eyes of his or her more orthodox neighbours.[214] Secular injunctions followed suit. The 1516 Brandenburg Criminal Court Ordinance called for an investigation of the type of magic used by the defendant (*mit was wortten oder wercken*) and whether the magic could be reworked. In 1582, when it was reissued, the same section – *So der Gefragte Zauberey bekennet* – was appended with the order: 'So should also be asked: From whom such magic was learned, how it came to be known, whether such magic has been used against more people, and whom, and what harm occurred as a result.'[215] Hopeful of banishing the Baiergrün wisewoman, the Hof superintendent ordered an investigation into the type of magic she was using along with the type of people who were seeking her advice. And he broadened the investigation to include all of the parishes in his chapter. 'Otherwise it could well be that

---

211 Robert Muchembled, *Popular Culture and Elite Culture in France 1400–1750*, trans. Lydia Cochrane (London, 1985); Robert Muchembled, 'The Witches of Cambrésis: the Acculturation of the Rural World in the Sixteenth and Seventeenth Centuries', in James Obelkevich (ed.), *Religion and the People, 800–1700* (Chapel Hill, 1979), pp. 221–76.

212 Jean Delumeau, *Le catholicisme entre Luther et Voltaire* (Paris, 1971).

213 See Richard van Dülmen, 'Reformation und Neuzeit. Ein Versuch', *Zeitschrift für historische Forschung*, 14 (1987), 1–25.

214 Sehling, pp. 321, 352.

215 Copy of the *Brandenburgische Halßgerichtsordnung* (1516) in StaN, *Ansbacher Generalakten*, 23. 1582 edition in *Corpus Constitutionum Brandenburgico-Culmbacensium* (1748), pp. 27–8.

charmers and witches and similar people are secretly in the parish. Thus the strictest observance should be kept.'[216]

The Lutheran clergy worked in more subtle ways as well. Protestant demonology placed greater weight on the theological implications of recourse to magic. To use magic was to submit to the temptations of the Devil. Lutheran authors stressed that demonic agency could only work within the limits determined by the divine; unpleasant events were 'allowed' by God to test the faith of the people.[217] 'So that He tests the pious and Godfearing in their faith, whether they remain steadfast in misery as well as bliss.'[218] Two corollaries followed: first, to trust in magic was to abandon faith; second, all forms of magic necessarily implied the intervention of the Devil. Protestant pastors began to focus on the episodes of daily life and see the Devil at every turn.

'One hears daily', wrote the Ansbach clergyman Andreas Althamer, 'of the hideous deeds effected by the Devil. There many thousands are struck dead; there a ship goes down with many people beneath the sea; there a land perishes, a city, a village; there someone stabs himself; there someone hangs himself; there someone drowns himself; there someone loses his head ...[219]

Common and uncommon misfortunes previously countered with and explained by recourse to the realm of popular beliefs were now invested with the notion of diabolism. Scholars speak of the 'theologisation' of traditional folklore.[220] Magic, misfortune, and the mysterious were attributed to the Devil and his tireless allies: witches, sorcerers, soothsayers, and cunning men.

The parishioners grew wary of recourse to magic, but not because the 'reform of popular culture' convinced the peasantry it was wrong in principle; rather, they soon began to recognise that the forbidden practice of magic (*Zauberei*) – now strongly equated with the Devil – might elicit the attention of the authorities. Very few people were safe from accusation. Practitioners of blessings and spells were brought before the clergy on a regular basis and told to abandon their crafts. Often they replied that 'they did not know it was wrong' along with the promise 'to abstain from such things'. Other parishioners, realising that they were dabbling in forbidden matters, either defended their actions (with a reference to the

---

[216] StaB, C2 1827, fo. 11 Hof (8, 9, 10 December 1589).

[217] Stuart Clark, 'Protestant Demonology: Sin, Superstition, and Society (*c*.1520–*c*.1630)', in Bengt Ankarloo and Gustav Henningsen (eds.), *Early Modern Witchcraft. Centres and Peripheries* (Oxford, 1990), pp. 45–81.

[218] Reinhardus Lutz, *Wahrhaftigge Zeitung* (1571), p. Bi^r. 'Erstlich, darmit er die fromen und Gottsfürchtigen in ihrem Glauben probier, ob sie gleich so wol in trübsal als glückseligkeit bestendig bleiben wollen.'

[219] Andreas Althamer, *Eyn Predig von dem Teüffel, das er alles Unglück in der Welt anrichte* (Nuremberg, 1532), Aiii.

[220] Charles Zika, 'The Devil's Hoodwink: Seeing and Believing in the World of Sixteenth-Century Witchcraft', in Charles Zika (ed.), *No Gods Except Me. Orthodoxy and Religious Practice in Europe* (Melbourne, 1991), pp. 153–98.

'natural' powers of their herbs) or distanced themselves from the clergy. The old soothsayer in Dottenheim simply refused to enter the church. The shepherd of Mönchsondheim did not attend communion 'on account of his blessing'.[221] Sixteenth-century parishioners understood that the church represented a real menace to the autonomy of their beliefs. 'Say nothing to the clergymen [*Pfaffen*]', was how a Franconian shepherd, learned in the craft, advised his clients, 'don't confess and don't take communion, otherwise [my] art will not help.'[222] But the church would not go away, and so the people were forced to take shelter from the threat.

The 'reform of popular culture' in the sixteenth century thus induced an unprecedented process of dissimulation.[223] Feeling themselves under attack, the parishioners began to look for ways to deflect the threat without abandoning their beliefs or implicating themselves. In many ways this was a 'functional' or a social process, with a scapegoat, such as a witch, bearing the brunt of transition. The strategy is analogous to the dissimulation exercised by sixteenth-century scholars who, when addressing contentious issues, would take shelter in the ambiguity of their writing and look for scapegoats in their texts.[224] The range of dissimulation was no less complex at the parish level. Historians have noted for some time that the static model of popular versus elite culture (to use two applicable terms) and the emergence of the latter at the expense of the former is too simplistic.[225] As Carlo Ginzburg has recently demonstrated in his work on the witches' sabbath, many conceptual inheritances from the early-modern period might be seen as 'the hybrid result of a conflict between folk culture and learned culture'.[226] A similar hybrid of popular and elite culture proved the legacy of the Reformation. Parish beliefs were not passively erased by the encroaching state: popular culture adapted to the religious environment in order to survive.

In what follows, it is neither feasible nor presumed that, in a study situated in a single century in a single land, one can assess the impact of the Reformation on

---

[221] StaN, *Ansbacher Neues Generalrepertorium*, no. 49, rep. nr 103ᵉ, fos. 16, 55, 120; LKAN, MSK, 157, Lentzendorff (11 October 1586); LKAN, MSK, Untersteinach 1599; StaB, C2 1827, fo. 31 (1589); LKAN, MDL, Kirchberg 16 Oktober 1594; LKAN, MDU, 8, Münchsentheim (20 September 1571).

[222] Fritz Heeger, 'Volksmedizinisches aus fränkischen Hexenprozeßakten', *Mainfränkisches Jahrbuch für Geschichte und Kunst*, 9 (1957), 204.

[223] Magical practices had always been explicitly condemned by the church. As Valerie I. J. Flint has demonstrated in *The Rise of Magic in Early Medieval Europe*, the interplay between the church and medieval parish culture was intimate enough for a exchange between the two traditions to take place. The result was a strain of 'tolerated' magical beliefs. But the type of surveillance introduced by the Reformation was more comprehensive than the medieval system and accelerated and facilitated intervention at the parish level.

[224] See Perez Zagorin, *Ways of Lying: Dissimulation, Persecution and Conformity in Early Modern Europe* (London, 1990).

[225] Scribner, 'Is a History of Popular Culture Possible?' pp. 178–81.

[226] Carlo Ginzburg, *Ecstasies: Deciphering the Witches' Sabbath*, trans. Raymond Rosenthal (London, 1990), p. 11.

the popular mind with any real authority. All that can be said with certainty is that in Brandenburg-Ansbach-Kulmbach the Reformation did not purge the parishes of popular magic. The actual influence of the Reformation is a more complex matter and deserves a broader study. Nevertheless, by using materials which amplify the conflict between traditional parish culture and the church, it is possible to illustrate aspects of the initial impact of the reform movement on the parishioner's expressed beliefs. The most detailed accounts of this process are found in trials against witchcraft; and one of the most detailed witchcraft trials of sixteenth-century Brandenburg-Ansbach-Kulmbach was the process against the sexton's wife of Birk, Katherina Hoser.

THE IMPRINT OF PROTESTANTISM

In the face of the emerging Lutheran church, no one was more at threat, especially as the sixteenth century passed into the seventeenth, than the noted wisewoman, the sorcerer, or, as she came to be categorised, the witch. Compared to the neighbouring dioceses of Bamberg and Würzburg, Brandenburg-Ansbach-Kulmbach prosecuted a relatively small number of women, but the principality was not immune to the 'witch-craze' sweeping through the Empire during this period, even if it kept its fear in relative check. The laws against maleficent magic were extracted from the *Bambergensis* and, as embodied in the 1582 reissuing under Georg Friedrich, called for punishment equivalent to that for heresy: death by fire. (Magic without harmful intent was to be punished 'according to the circumstances of the case'.) Thus the authorities did have the legal writ to try suspected witches and burn them at the stake, though the occasions appear to have been few.

Nevertheless, the threat of witchcraft was serious enough to encourage the margrave to assemble his leading secular and ecclesiastical authorities at Heilsbronn in 1591 to discuss the matter. During this gathering, the titular abbot Adam Francisci drafted his *Generalinstruktion von den Trutten*, wherein a call to arms against the 'curse' of witchcraft was sounded. Relying for the most part on the Old Testament, Francisci argued for the increased prosecution of such people, 'big or small', and entreated the margrave to warn his subjects to stay clear of the magical arts. In that same year, twenty-two witches were executed in Bayreuth.[227] As this campaign suggests, and as events in other territories demonstrate, the late sixteenth and early seventeenth century marked the apogee of the campaign against witchcraft; and yet the glut of trials was in part only a belated affirmation of steps already taken, if only on a smaller scale. In Kulmbach, processes against the village witch began many years before.

On 7 April 1569 Georg Nürnberger, an official in Creußen, informed the

---

[227] Friedrich Merzbacher, *D⸱ Hexenprozesse in Franken* (Munich, 1957), pp. 44–6; Wolfgang Behringer (ed.), *Hexen und Hexenprozesse* (Munich, 1988), pp. 223–4, 347–9.

Kulmbach council that Katherina Hoser, wife of the Birk sexton Bastian Hoser, had been cited before the authorities due to the suspicion that she was a soothsayer.[228] She had already been summoned before the clergy on one occasion, where she was told to renounce her 'superstitions' and surrender her soothsaying stone (*wetterstein*) to the superintendent.[229] And indeed, this is what Katherina did. But she did not hold fast to her promise to abstain and was again taken into custody. In fact, if the report of the clergyman Nikolaus Friederich is correct, Katherina was somewhat audacious on her return to the parish. At the local inn, she is alleged to have boasted: 'recently she had overcome nine clergymen at the chaplain's house in Creuβen. She could overcome other people as well.' Kunigund Streber, as she sat cutting fabric, explained to Katherina how she had heard of the confiscation of her stone. To this, Katherina rather cheekily replied: 'as you might have guessed'.[230] But this boldness did little to help her case, and she was forced to answer to the clergy.

Katherina had earned a considerable reputation as a wisewoman, or soothsayer, and she was frequently consulted by the neighbouring parishioners in times of crisis. A maid from Goldkronach, for example, was sent to Birk by her noble patron (bearing gifts) in the hope that Katherina could fathom if a woman friend, big in body, was expecting. 'She wants to see', explained the maid, 'whether or not it is a child.' After a quick look into her stone, Katherina declared that, although it looked like a child, it was not. On another occasion a neighbour asked what could be done with her sick cow. Katherina suggested the use of a skull, from which the animal should sip its water. She purveyed a multitude of remedies for humans as well. Hansen Hoffner's wife, 'swollen and sick' in body, was told she was ill from too much cold water and a cure was prescribed. Other women were advised to smear themselves in wine. Hans Grebner, suffering from gout, was once blessed by Katherina; in fact Katherina underwent a four-week diet of wine in place of water to ensure the cure would take effect.[231] She could also probe less manifest mysteries. She had a necklace of shiny stones used to discern 'what was sin and what not' in a manner comparable to *ein priester in den Buch*.[232] And she could locate lost people – or such was the hope of Barbara Rauben, who was upset over the disappearance of her husband and turned to Katherina for help.[233]

---

[228] Aside from the occasional mention, the only large-scale treatment of this case known to me is by Karl Lory, 'Hexenprozesse im Gebiete des ehemaligen Markgrafenlandes', in *Festgabe Karl Theodor von Heigel* (Munich, 1903), pp. 290–304. The following analysis is based upon the archive materials, StaB, C2, 3235.

[229] StaB, C2, 3235, fos. 1–4 (7 April 1569).

[230] StaB, C2, 3235, fos. 5–6 (5 April 1569).

[231] StaB, C2, 3235, fos. 5–6, 19–20. The verse she employed is transcribed on fo. 20. It ends with the line: 'Das seÿ dir Hans zur Bueβ getzeldt, Im namen vatters, sohn und des hailigen gaist. Amen.'

[232] StaB, C2, 3235, fo. 6: 'daran etliche gleisende stain gehangen sein, am hals gehenckt, hatt kirchnerin die angegrieffen und gesagen, in diesen steinen kons sie baβ sehen, was sünd oder nicht sünd seÿ, dan ein priester in den Büch.'

[233] StaB, C2, 3235, fos. 7–8.

There is no clear indication as to how Katherina's activities first came to the attention of the authorities. The diversity of her clientele, coupled with the breadth of her expertise – hinted at by the types of problems brought her way – would suggest it was not difficult for the clergy to find her. In later inquisitions, the examiners often coloured a factual statement with the prologue: 'Since she is held to be (*beschrait*) a soothsayer and sorcerer in Creußen and other surrounding places'. But it may have been the case that social tensions gave rise to the accusation. Often the village witch had close ties with her accusers, or at least there was usually a more intimate connection – beyond the supposed act of maleficent magic – between the victim and the witness sufficient to account for witchcraft accusations.[234] Later testimony from Katherina herself singled out Barbara Rauben, who turned to her after Katherina's meeting with the clergy in Creußen.

In the process of consulting three different soothsayers over the whereabouts of her husband, Barbara Rauben received three different answers: 'The first had said, he lies under the town hall in a well; the second, he lies in a storage room [*Kemmath*]; the third, he lies in a cellar and old wall.' Finally, desperately, she turned to Katherina, who in turn informed her (with some misgiving) that she could indeed see Contz Rauben in her weatherstone: he was at the house of Georg Prebitzer settling an account with the maid. Then, said Katherina, he disappeared: 'He must have used magic, so that she could no longer see him in the stone.'[235] But she could see other things in the stone, in particular the vision of Barbara Rauben hitting her husband with a kitchen spoon. She also claimed that Contz, as he would not appear in the stone, might be dead by his own hand. What was worse, she added, he may have been spirited away by the Devil. In any case, were Katherina to see him, she assured Barbara that she would inform the town officials. No doubt all of these unwanted images caused a rift between Katherina and Barbara, for soon after the latter's visit, Katherina began to cry.

When her daughter and husband asked her what was wrong, she said to them that she had seen in her stone, that because she had recently promised the gathered clergy at Creußen she would no longer soothsay, she fears now that Barbara Rauben would betray her, and that they would have cause to place her under arrest.[236]

In this instance her prophecy was correct.

Georg Nürnberger was instructed by the Kulmbach councillors to interrogate the now incarcerated Katherina using a résumé of questions sent to him for that purpose.[237] Katherina Hoser's period of imprisonment, the number of hearings to

---

[234] For rural witchcraft in Germany, see Walter Rummel, *Bauern, Herren und Hexen* (Göttingen, 1991), pp. 259–315; Eva Labouvie, *Zauberei und Hexenwerk* (Frankfurt, 1991), pp. 57–94, 202–19.

[235] StaB, C2, 3235, fo. 10. 'Es muste der Rau ein Kunst gebraucht haben, das sie Ihn in Ihrn stein nit ferner sehen konnen'.

[236] StaB, C2, 3235, fos. 10–12; 11.

[237] StaB, C2, 3235, fos. 15–16 (15 April 1569).

which she was subjected, the questions put before her, and the torture used to elicit the wanted response, were in part a consequence of the 'learned' stereotype of the witch which beset continental Europe in the sixteenth century. The learned notion of witchcraft focused on the pact with Satan and the nocturnal Sabbaths; the necessary liaison between demonic forces and the manipulation of the environment was the logic behind the clerical interrogations.[238] Katherina insisted at the outset that she did not exercise maleficent magic, she did not harm people or animals, and, more significantly, she denied the accusation, as couched in the questions, that she was in fellowship with the Devil and had inherited her talents under his tutelage. Rather, Katherina said she found the stone under the grass on a hillock and 'perhaps God had given this luck to her'. She was able to see in the stone the cure for her ailing father, for she was a 'Sabbath daughter' (*guldes suntags kindt*).[239] Unmoved, the authorities thought she was hiding the truth, so the trial continued, though now with the application of torture to loosen her tongue.

The questions drawn up for the first interrogation (12 April 1569) and sent to Georg Nürnberger were true to the logic of the learned view of the witch, taking for granted the demonic pact and thus tautologically worded, always trying to uncover the particulars and the motives of the covenant. This notion appears to have worked its way into Katherina's fears. She began to speak of devils, and she soon realised that she was considered suspect, even dangerous, by the church. One night in April, while Katherina was in jail, (according to a story she told the wife of a Creußen official [*Statknechtin*]), some tiny black devils appeared in her stone and told her that the clergy were on their way to see her. Katherina asked the woman whether it was true. 'And when the woman answered yes', recounted Justus Bloch, the Bayreuth superintendent, '[Katherina] had responded that she knew it well, for the little black men had said it to her.'[240] Justus Bloch had indeed been informed of this case by the authorities, who feared that Katherina's actions (and perhaps denials) occurred 'from the blinding of the Evil One, [who] can easily seduce the poor women'. Bloch was ordered to travel to Creußen along with other clergy in order to interrogate her.[241]

During Bloch's first session with Katherina, she spoke of her maltreatment at the hands of her demons in her cell.[242] It is clear at this stage that Katherina was suffering from her exposure to torture and was willing to confess to Bloch's accusations just to escape the pain. After Bloch's repeated insistence that 'such could not happen without a pact with the Devil' she succumbed to his charges: 'That she spoke with the Devil; that the arts which she knew were promised by him; and that he had asked

---

[238] See Brian Levack, *The Witch-hunt in Early Modern Europe* (London, 1987), pp. 25–62, 93–115; Richard Kieckhefer, *European Witch Trials* (London, 1976), pp. 73–92.

[239] StaB, C2, 3235, Questions fos. 13–14; Answers fos. 17–22.

[240] StaB, C2, 3235, fo. 29.

[241] StaB, C2, 3235, fos. 27–8 (19 April 1569): 'so achten wir doch das solches aus verblendung des bosen feindts ... [der] ... die armen weibs personen leichtlich verfuren kahn...'

[242] Lory, 'Hexenprozesse', p. 292.

her to be his, which she also agreed to.'[243] She also revealed how the Devil forbade her to attend communion or pray. Her only reservation was raised when it was suggested that the man who appeared to her in the stone had a cloven foot (*Geißfuß*). Bloch, however, had no such uncertainty. 'We knew full well beforehand that it was the Devil', he wrote, 'were he to have these or any other feet.'[244] Finally, on the Thursday sitting, after persistent questioning intent on exposing her dealings with the 'Evil One', Katherina looked into her stone as she sat in the presence of Bloch, the pastors of Creußen and Gesees, the city scribe, and Georg Nürnberger, and her spirit broke. The scribe recorded her reaction:

When she looked in the stone she began to shake, shiver, and grow pale. She threw the stone away on the table and cried: 'Ah, Margaretha, he has a cloven foot! I want my life long never to look in the stone again. Oh, Oh, that God in Heaven should be merciful, I am a conjurer of demons [*Teufels bannerin*].'[245]

Bloch tried to console the woman in his own way: 'You see Katherina, as you did not know you were in league with the Devil, we had to convince you with your own art'.[246] Katherina confessed to a confederacy with the Devil; all the other implications of the demonological stereotype followed in train.

It is worth stressing the extent to which Katherina was manipulated, both physically and mentally, to extract her confessions. A letter from the Kulmbach council (4 May 1569) advised the executioner to be wary of too much torture, since she was weak in body.[247] But this did not exempt her from bouts of torture (*Taumenstockh und Zugkh*). The executioner was once reprimanded for leaving Katherina strapped to the rack for several hours while he drank wine at the inn.[248] Such torture, combined with the unremitting references to the Devil in the interrogations, the leading questions and the learned sophistries – all of this forced Katherina to admit to anything she was asked. But when she had recovered, and when it seemed safe to recant, she denied her previous statements. In a letter signed Katherina Adlerin (her maiden name) she 'revoked and retracted' all she had confessed about her relations with the Devil. Her words were, she claimed, the product of torture.[249] She could not bear the betrayal of her conscience and

---

243   StaB, C2, 3235, fo. 30.
244   StaB, C2, 3235, fo. 31.
245   StaB, C2, 3235, fo. 38.
246   StaB, C2, 3235, fo. 38. 'Sihe Katherina hastu nicht gewust das du Eine Teufels bannerin bist gewesen, mußen wir dich mit deiner kunst selbs uberweisen.'
247   StaB, C2, 3235, fos. 43–4.
248   StaB, C2, 3235, fo. 60. In Franconia, a session of torture was to last no longer than half an hour. Merzbacher (1957), p. 118.
249   StaB, C2, 3235, fos. 54–5:

Nachdem ich umb schweres vordachts willen, durch einem burger Georg Brebitzern zu Creussen gefenglichen eingetzogen, nit allein sieben wochen lang Ihnnen gelegen, Sondern mit Schwehrer hefftiger tortr und peinligkeit durch denn [Nachrichter] befraget worden, das ich also [umbesümner] weiß, umb des grosen schmertzen bekenndt und angeitzeigt, wie das ich mit dem Bösenfeindt, hete vormischung gepfleget...

sought shelter in the exoneration of a higher power: 'Oh, woe my poor soul,' cried Katherina one night from her cell, 'a holy angel from Heaven has come and whispered in my ear and said I have not answered correctly. It is not true and I do myself a wrong. I should recant'.[250]

It would be overambitious, not to say methodologically suspect, to abstract from this isolated case of supposed witchcraft laws governing the interchange of ideas. Having said this, however, the subject of witchcraft in the early modern period is hardly suffering from a poverty of research, and there is nothing especially unusual about this case.[251] The trial of Katherina Hoser does not speak in a vacuum. Although a witchcraft trial was a specific event following a predetermined logic, in many ways it was no more than the process of reform situated and accelerated, with a 'popular' offender and an 'elite' jury. As Serge Gruzinski has written, in similar circumstances though a different context, individual experience alone, the particular evidence of epochal change, is our only true guide to grand historical movements.[252] The process against Katherina Hoser can be used to illustrate the relationship between the Lutheran church and parish beliefs in the sixteenth century. In what follows, the trial of Katherina Hoser will be analysed to illustrate the effect of elite thought on the popular mentality; questions and answers will be analysed to show the response of a parishioner faced with the learned stereotype of the witch and the gradual sedimentation of this notion in her mind.

Central to the concerns of the inquisitors was the provenance of the stone. Question two of the 15 April examination made clear their intention to know: 'From whom she received the stone which she used for her magic.' Under a small lot of grass on a hillock in the village where she was born was her original answer. She found the stone at a propitious moment, as her father was quite ill; and she was able to see in the stone the reason for his misfortune along with the possible cure.[253] When pressed, she claimed that God had given her the luck to discover the stone. As a later deposition read, 'such was given to her by God, and not from the Devil'. By May, following her subsequent recantation, the story changed, but essentially it was true to her original claim that she came upon the stone in all innocence. A woman named Anna Hörlin had given her a stone, in addition to a verse used to conjure its powers, many years before.[254] But she rejected all hints of association with the Devil.

[250] StaB, C2, 3235, fos. 56–7.
[251] On witchcraft, see the comments and literature in Eva Labouvie, *Zauberei und Hexenwerk;* Norman Cohn, *Europe's Inner Demons* (London, 1975); Kieckhefer, *European Witch Trials;* Gábor Klaniczay, *The Uses of Supernatural Power*, trans. Susan Singerman (Oxford, 1990), pp. 151–67, 230–31.
[252] Serge Gruzinski, *Man-Gods in the Mexican Highlands*, trans. Eileen Corrigan (Stanford, 1989), p. 5.
[253] StaB, C2, 3235, fo. 11. The illness was attributed to a small parcel of goods, perhaps an amulet, purposefully buried in the yard and affecting her father by its proximity. This was a common form of harmful magic (*defixionum tabellae*).
[254] StaB, C2, 3235, fo. 46.

After the initial April interrogations, the application of torture, and the recurrent impression of the demonological theme, Katherina changed her story. She confessed to visitations by 'little black devils' in her Creuβen cell. And, more significantly, when told it was impossible for her to have discovered the stone unaided, without danger to her soul, Katherina answered: 'At first there was a small dark man who appeared and said she should lift the grass. She would find the stone there.' When asked who she thought this man was, she answered that: 'she did not know, [and] does not think it the Devil, but rather God'.[255] As she told Bloch and the pastor of Gesees, this diminutive man had advised her: 'Look under the tuft of grass beside where you sit, there is a stone. Grab it, and you will see what your father has, where he got it, and how he can be cured.'[256] For Bloch, this was clearly the Devil; it was not possible that this little man would have appeared to her 'without explicit confederation or union with Satan'.

When this tiny devil reappeared, he was no longer external to the stone, working as an advocate, but in the stone, part of the stone. A report of her statement, drawn up by a secular official (27 April 1569), continues her story about the discovery of the stone on the hillock: 'In which stone, a small black man [*Menlein*] stood, who had a body, and hands, like any other man.' She added that she did not know whether he had a cloven foot (since she had not looked), nor whether 'such black man was the Devil ... she does not know'. And she denied the (implicit) accusation of having conjured the man to the stone. He had been there when she found it.[257] Katherina now attributed her powers of foretelling and prophecy to the man in the stone. It was at this stage that Bloch forced her to look at the man's feet, and they were, as everyone expected, cloven. 'She had not considered that this man was a devil', is how the report was worded. 'She had thought it was God.'

In the final version, the presence of God was altogether resigned and Satan himself took full stage, thus replacing the little black demon. In a later report (5 May 1569), written by the secular authorities, and subsequent to a bout of torture, Katherina spoke of the Devil's appearance. In 1563, on her way to Creuβen, 'at first a small dark man had come toward her, and he grew ever longer and ever bigger until finally he was as big as her husband. This was the Devil.'[258] Here, quite literally, the figure of Satan evolves from the smaller demon and approaches her on numerous occasions, with 'black clothing, dark and big like her husband' and seduces her into a covenant. Katherina confirms the learned stereotype: She agreed 'to be his'; she had sexual relations with him, finding his body of 'a really cold nature'; he promised to teach her maleficent magic, how to harm people and animals; and he admonished her to stay clear of the church. Moreover, he takes

---

[255] StaB, C2, 3235, fos. 29–30.
[256] StaB, C2, 3235, fo. 40.
[257] StaB, C2, 3235, fos. 34–5.
[258] StaB, C2, 3235, fo. 47.

pains to protect her from the clergy. He warned against a trip to Creußen, where he believed she would be imprisoned, tortured, and burned; and when his forecast was partially realised, he visited her in her cell, offering to free her from the chains and 'fly out through the window' into the night air. Katherina looked to God (she claimed) and his power was undone. She then looked to her captors for guidance.

Modern historiography is still coming to grips with the concept of *mentalité* and the grounds for assuming a uniformity of thought when a multiplicity is, historically, more the norm.[259] Some scholars, most notably anthropologists, have moved away from a 'history of ideas' approach to the past – which isolates certain intellectual trends for analysis – to investigations of how ideas were actually used, how they were reproduced and modified, and what sort of factors might influence their composition, transmission, and codification.[260] An approach of this nature, more concerned with ideas in context than the study of ideas through time, seems most suited to an investigation of the effect of Lutheran thought on the rural populace. The reform of popular culture was a long-term fluid process; it included the birth of some ideas and the conflation of others. Rather than simply substituting one belief system for another, one vernacular *mentalité* for a more learned alternative, the effect of the reform of popular culture on the parishioner might be seen as more dynamic, more of an exchange. The case of Katherina Hoser lends itself to just such an investigation. While her confession was told in different drafts at different times, and the narrative was not so ordered as it is represented above, a gradual variation in the story does unfold, and it does so around the object of scrutiny: Katherina's stone.

At the beginning of her testimony, Katherina claims she found her stone by chance, rather good chance, and when this is doubted it becomes a moment of chance, she suggests, engineered by God. Under further scrutiny, and further accusations that the powers of the stone must implicate its user with the Devil, Katherina distances herself from its discovery and instead surrenders herself to the clerical notion that she was entrapped in a realm of (demonic) power in strict opposition to the church. The idea is at first still alien; the demon must cajole her, trick her, dupe her into discovering the stone. But Katherina does not yet think she acted improperly and the stone is still a neutral object. With time, however, the stone itself takes on the substance of the learned accusations: it becomes the property of the Devil, and indeed the Devil (or perhaps a minion) resides within it. The world of the forbidden, the prohibited, a world in strict opposition to

---

259 See Roger Chartier, 'Intellectual History or Sociocultural History? The French Trajectories', in Dominick LaCapra and Steven L. Kaplan (eds.), *Modern European Intellectual History* (London, 1982), pp. 13–46; Peter Burke, 'Strengths and Weaknesses of the History of Mentalities', *History of European Ideas*, 75 (1986), 439–51.

260 For example: Fredrik Barth, *Cosmologies in the Making: A Generative Approach to Cultural Variation in Inner New Guinea* (Cambridge, 1987); G. E. R. Lloyd, *Demystifying Mentalities* (Cambridge, 1990).

sanctioned Lutheran beliefs, is seen in microcosm, and it dwells in Katherina's stone. Once this is conceded, the full implications can no longer be denied, and Katherina confesses to a confederacy with the Devil. The demon in the stone grows to full size, meets her at times she can remember, assumes the likeness of her husband, wears clothes she can describe, and she is – literally – seduced. Katherina now imagines herself in a world created by the clergy.[261]

Scholars have traced a similar process at work in the conquered lands of Mesoamerica. Christianity was only assimilated (and never completely) through a gradual acculturation. In the first instance, alien concepts – such as an omnipotent, benevolent God – were only adopted in so far as they could be embodied in the religious system. The Devil, for example, was overlaid upon those gods with malevolent characteristics, and thus a degree of syncretism took place; following this, the knowledge of prehispanic religion ebbed, and the Devil assumed a more 'European' significance; finally the old religion evaporated almost completely, leaving nothing but 'disjointed structural residues' and the devils of old shorn of their former meanings. Such a 'slide toward Christianity', viewed over the course of centuries, not only divested Indian beliefs of their original significance, but by the eighteenth century popular (Indian) piety went so far as to express itself through the written word, and so order was imposed upon a world of heterogeneous beliefs.[262] This process of acculturation is similar to the model suggested by the Hoser trial: in both examples people were not converted, beliefs were not abandoned; aspects of popular belief were simply invested with different values until the original context of thought was shattered.

Unlike the reform of morality, which relied upon the imposition of restraint and the displays of power, the Lutheran campaign against popular beliefs found its forum in the parish mind. As has been demonstrated above, the Reformation did not eradicate recourse to magic; but with the threat of punishment ever present, the parishioners gradually integrated the ideas of the church and began to consider their own beliefs in relation to the ideas of the 'elite'. Rather than consider their tradition of thought as at odds with the church, the parishioners first assimilated the idea of demonic intervention to explain away their reasons for recourse to popular magic. It was only later, when popular magic could not avoid the brush of diabolism, when each rite or gesture had a corresponding tie with the

---

[261] Compare Carlo Ginzburg, *The Night Battles* (London, 1985).

[262] Gruzinski, *Man-Gods in the Mexican Highlands*; Fernando Cervantes, 'The Devil in Colonial Mexico: Cultural Interaction and Intellectual Change (1521–1767)', PhD thesis, Cambridge University, 1989, pp. 52–97; Nathan Wachtel, *The Vision of the Vanquished: The Spanish Conquest of Peru through Indian Eyes 1530–1570*, trans. Ben and Siân Reynolds (Sussex, 1977), pp. 150–65; Amos Megged, 'Conversion and Identity in Early Colonial Perspectives: Friars and Indians in Mesoamerica 1545–1670', PhD thesis, Cambridge University 1988, pp. 153–89. On the notion of religious syncretism in general, see Charles Stewart and Rosalind Shaw (eds.), *Syncretism/Antisyncretism. The Politics of Religious Synthesis* (London, 1994).

Devil, that magic and religion could no longer be held in separation.[263] Popular beliefs were slowly invested with a changing set of values as the parish mind was drawn into a more systematic context of thought. This is not the erasure of one tradition of beliefs by another, but its gradual distortion. By the seventeenth century, there is reason to talk of 'Protestant forms of magic', as this process of reconfiguration occurred.[264]

The very practice of investigation, the rules and logic of inquiry, forced order on the eclectic world of popular beliefs. Again the witchcraft trial is the archetype of the process. In seventeenth-century Franconia, each trial pursued an equivalent end: to discover where the magic was learned – whether from the Devil or one of his brood – how it was facilitated, with what words or things, how many other people were implicated, and what reasons led a soul to witchcraft.[265] The authorities were in search of tidy answers to sorted questions and they forced the parishioners to organise their thoughts. 'It is not appropriate or fitting to answer here "it must have been" "it must have been",' was how the inquisitors advised their victims, 'rather you should just answer yes or no.'[266]

For the parishioners, in the face of this reforming threat, the most immediate defensive reaction was that of social accusation. In the search for a first cause, for the source of the magic, the parishioners turned to one another in order to deflect the attention of the authorities. In the case of Katherina Hoser, the final days of her inquisition unearthed hitherto unmentioned names and thus broadened the reach of the investigation. But it is likely that over the course of time select practices were signally discredited or considered suspect, and so the parishioners were then forced to view certain forms of magic in relation to others. Gradually a template of order emerged – from the forbidden to the allowable – and the worlds of magic and religion were given firm boundaries. This is a process which demands a long-term investigation in order to prove the point, but a glimpse at events in sixteenth-century Brandenburg-Ansbach-Kulmbach would suggest that a start had been made. The Reformation did not put an end to the variety of parish culture, but it was the death knell for private beliefs.

---

[263] Compare Labouvie, who speaks of a *Verteufelung* of popular tradition, though she suggests that certain categories (such as good and bad magic) were already in place before the church began to invest them with connotations of diabolism. Labouvie, pp. 27–41.

[264] Scribner, 'Magic and the Formation of Protestant Popular Culture.'

[265] Dr. Jäger, 'Geschichte des Hexenbrennens in Franken im siebzehnten Jahrhundert aus Original-Prozeß-Akten', *Archiv des historischen Vereins für den Untermainkreis*, 2 (1834), 10–12.

[266] Heinrich Heppe (ed.), *Soldan's Geschichte der Hexenprozesse* (Stuttgart, 1880), vol. 2, p. 128, no. 2.

Conclusions

In 1530, while at the Diet of Augsburg as one of Ansbach's theological advisors, the Crailsheim pastor Adam Weiß recorded a dream in his diary.[1] Weiß presented the enigmatic 'dream of a certain townsman', whose vision of an ecclesiastical council was juxtaposed with the violent rages of Leo. Whether this is an allusion to pope Leo X is difficult to say; although the outcome of the dream, wherein Leo was finally overcome by 'the old man who seemed to be sleeping', is certainly redolent of Luther's early contest with and final victory over Catholic efforts to suppress him. For ultimately, as evangelical pastors like Weiß were wont to point out, no setback would be so great as to prevent the triumph of God's word and the emergence of the Lutheran faith. And yet, for all their words of comfort, many reformers were also quick to admit that the Reformation had been slow to take root. Reform had not worked its way into the rural parishes; the Lutheran faith had not been embraced by the subject population. There seemed to be just as much opposition to religious change at the parish level as there was on the imperial stage. All of their efforts seemed in vain. Little wonder pious men like Adam Weiß were suffering nightmares. For as this work has demonstrated, the Reformation in the rural parishes did not live up to the reformers' early expectations.

The evangelical faith was not introduced into the parishes at once; in the early years, pockets of resistance were matched against enclaves of reform. Only with the intervention of the margrave was real direction offered and a modicum of religious uniformity introduced. The Reformation in the countryside, in contrast to events in the urban centres, could not rely upon popular (lay) support for its evolution. The parishes did not have the power to introduce independent reform measures without provoking the margrave or arousing resistance. Moreover, many parish clergymen saw themselves as bound in obedience to their patrons and were reluctant to accept the new faith without leave. But this does not mean that the evangelical movement was lacking in popular support. This notion of obedience, inherent in the relations of power between ruler and ruled in early modern Germany (encapsulated in the German word *Herrschaft*), was also fundamental to the parishioners' reception of the faith. The villagers demanded

---

[1] Adam Weiß, *Diarium* (Schwabach, 1743), pp. 690–1.

the word of God, for it had been granted to them by the margrave, it was their right as his subjects, and it was the clergyman's duty to act in response to the margrave's will. Moreover, it was the will of God, their own divine overlord (*Bauerngott*) – no less bound in the matrix of reciprocity forging their world view – and they desired to hear His voice. If the parishioners' understanding of the faith was superficial, their interest non-theological, this did not lessen their interest.

Out of the reforming passions unleashed by the evangelical movement in the 1520s the margraves eventually created a Lutheran church. In the first decade of reform, the secular authorities, acting on the orders of the margraves, monitored events in the parishes. Later they were joined by adjunct clergymen. This type of church rule soon proved ineffective, and in mid-century Georg Karg and margrave Georg Friedrich constructed a more proficient system of ecclesiastical governance using the examples provided by Saxony and Württemberg. The land was divided into superintendencies, while a hierarchy of ecclesiastical and secular officials worked within these divisions under the watchful eyes of the margrave. The church itself grew into a more efficient institution: Marriage courts were established, a consistory was created, synodal articles were issued, visitation commissions patrolled the parishes in the autumn of each year and sent their reports back to Ansbach. The process was slow, and it suffered its share of setbacks, but by the end of the century the margrave was at the head of an ecclesiastical institution completely under his charge. With its network of officials and its sophisticated administrative reach there could be little doubt that the villager would ultimately have to come to terms with the intrusion.

The intrusion of the Lutheran clergyman, if less systematic, was a more intimate and immediate style of trespass. In many ways the Lutheran pastor was *the* innovation of the Reformation; the men themselves were frequently different in kind from their Catholic predecessors. The clergy became better educated and more willing and able to fulfil the tasks expected of them, whether that meant the preaching of the Gospel, the dispatch of their sacerdotal duties, the policing of moral transgressions, or the education of the young. In the eyes of the higher clergy, the parishes were staffed with competent men. In the eyes of the villagers, however, the Lutheran pastor made an impact at another level. The clergy were not prized for their theological acuity, nor admired as proselytisers, but rather resented as disturbers of the peace. With the disappearance of many pre-Reformation sources of income the Lutheran clergyman was forced to look for new ways to support himself once in office, and this disrupted the status quo of parish life. The parishioners often felt threatened by the new demands placed upon the parish and its people by these (frequently married) men of God and the margrave. As chapter 3 demonstrated, the villager experienced the Reformation, via the Lutheran clergyman, as the disruption of parish norms, the violation of custom, the disregard for communal rights, the challenge of local power, the

Conclusions

planting of fear, or the imposition of unwanted scrutiny. For the Reformation made the most progress at this level: the Lutheran church was able to stock the parishes with competent clergymen and it was able to provide for their upkeep, even though the reform of clerical maintenance often met with stiff resistance at the parish level. But in all of this the villagers did not oppose the Reformation, nor a reformed clergy, nor did they seem to take notice that these men were the vanguards of a new faith. The parishioners' field of vision did not extend beyond the horizons of their community, beyond custom, usage, and traditional expectation. Anticlericalism was the voice of parish custom vented against the practical innovations of reform.

Although the Reformation movement was as much concerned with how the parishioners acted as what they believed, the Lutheran authorities in Brandenburg-Ansbach-Kulmbach failed to implement the strict moral code they preached. Confessionalisation, social disciplining, 'the reform of popular culture' – these are useful labels to describe a programme of rule, a rhetoric or policy of control which emerged with a vigour in tandem with sixteenth-century religious change. There is little doubt that the parishioner became an object of unprecedented scrutiny; customs, morals, and local diversions occupied the attentions of the authorities as never before. But there is also little doubt that village life in Ansbach and Kulmbach was not markedly altered, in spite of this increased surveillance. The moral licence of the rural inhabitant suffered very few limitations. Popular culture and the many pastimes routine to parish life continued without intermission. Public rituals subject to the control of both church and state (baptism, marriage, the Lord's Supper) could not be wrested from their traditional contexts or controlled by the Lutheran authorities. Reform could not force its way into the workings of village life. Village leaders and local officials were negligent of the most elementary duties of discipline and punishment. At the same time, the Lutheran pastor found himself unable to work his way into the local systems of discipline, punishment, control, and governance. The traditional monopoly of rule enjoyed by the local elite remained an obstacle to the pastor's efforts to introduce stricter disciplinary measures. What is more, once they recognised what a threat the Lutheran pastor was to their local liberties, the ruling elite began to look for ways to discredit the clergyman and weaken his status in the parish. Conflicts provoked by the clergyman's efforts to introduce stricter disciplinary measures were soon transmuted into quarrels between pastor and parish over local rights, thus providing the village officials with a plausible defence in the face of the pastor's increasing intervention. A dialogue emerged, created by the process embodied in the idea of confessionalisation, between the local officials and the emerging territorial church: the village rulers looked for ways to stave off the intrusions of the Lutheran pastor. This dialogue, this practical and rhetorical strategy, changed over time, so that by the closing years of the century the Lutheran church was opposed by a defence of village custom and rule markedly

Conclusions

Lutheran in tone. This was one effect among many as the church and state fused their energies in the sixteenth century; it does not counter the idea of confessionalisation or social disciplining, but if the parishioner remains the object of concern, it does introduce a new complexity to these concepts.

Above all, the Reformation might be seen as a massive campaign of indoctrination, an unyielding drive to purge the parishes of the residues of Catholicism and the delusions of popular beliefs. Brandenburg-Ansbach-Kulmbach was a Lutheran principality, and, like other Protestant states, placed its trust in the strengths of education and the sober appeal of the church sermon. But the reform of schooling, while it was improved under the auspices of the Lutheran margraves, remained for the most part an urban event. In the rural parishes, school attendance was low, the quality of the schoolmasters was generally poor, their upkeep was meagre, their duties too many, and the practical oversight of parish education remained in the hands of the local rulers. The church sermon and the catechism session, where they were honoured, were unpersuasive, unattended, and most parishioners did not benefit, or wish to benefit, from the Word. Recognising these problems quite early on, the reformers realised they would have to administer a 'traumatic shock' to the mental outlook of the rural parishioners, erasing the old (with force, if necessary) and bringing in the new. But the Reformation's drive to erase the Catholic church from the parish memory was not successful: The local church remained a receptacle of the sacred, the sacraments were worked as reservoirs of automatic sacrality, the sacramentals manipulated as conduits of divine power. The belief system of the rural parishioner, in short, was not disenchanted in answer to Lutheran demands. Nor were the parishes purged of popular beliefs, such as magic, soothsaying, charming, or astrology – these and similar practices remained staples of daily life. Although the Reformation launched a crusade against popular beliefs, it failed to cleanse the parishes of these unwanted, ungodly practices. And yet, in so far as it can be perceived at this distance, there was a change in the way people perceived the powers inherent in the natural world. With the attack against magic in full swing, and the threat of prosecution ever present in the parish mind, there is reason to suspect that the parishioner began to view the world in the terms created by the Lutheran church. Like Katherina Hoser, guided by a foreign logic and pressed by a very real risk of correction, the villager began to invest traditional practices with alien values.

What place has this interpretation in the traditional understanding of the Reformation movement? Seen from nearly half-a-millennium's distance, the Reformation seems a sudden upheaval. Inspired by their Humanist forerunners, Lutheran reformers renounced the Catholic church, its teachings, its soteriology, and created another in its place – and not just a church and not just a theology, but another religious history of man. The implications were profound: uncompromising, as Luther himself was uncompromising, Reformation theology repudiated the teachings of the Catholic church, and with it centuries of belief and tradition;

Conclusions

unforgiving in its anticlericalism, wherever the Lutheran faith took hold the Catholic church was dismantled, its administration restructured, its clergy retrained or rejected; unmistakably urban in character, the Reformation transformed the early modern city and the lifestyle of its inhabitants; unavoidably authoritarian at its core, Lutheran theology was soon manipulated by the territorial princes to sanction an increased encroachment of the state into the moral and religious lives of its subjects. There was national and regional diversity, but in the span of a few decades, Europe was irreversibly transformed, irreversibly biconfessional.[2]

And yet, as this book has demonstrated, most of this reform and development left the sixteenth-century rural parishioners untouched and their habits unchanged. Neither the ideas, nor the implications of the ideas, filtered down to the parish to any substantial degree. For as the Lutheran authorities knew only too well, the customs, beliefs, and traditions of rural society were deeply entrenched; they offered a much more 'drastic' challenge to the Lutheran authorities than the relatively flexible and accommodating outlook of their urban counterparts.[3] Thus the Reformation in the countryside, from its very outset, was less compromising than the type of reform movement common to the cities. The margrave dictated the course of reform without paying heed to the wishes of his subjects; mandates and ordinances poured off the presses defining the parameters of godly thought and behaviour; the margrave's higher officials, secular and spiritual alike, worked to enforce the will of the territorial church. But in all of this the parishioners were not passive participants in a massive reforming campaign. The Reformation in the countryside was not just a stand-off between two opposing world-views, a static acculturation. In the realm of ideas, a gradual syncretism took place; in the realm of church and parish relations, there was a gradual transformation in the exercise and understanding of power. The Reformation did work its way into the rural culture of Ansbach and Kulmbach, but not in the form its supporters envisioned and not with the effects they had hoped for. Like the old man in the dream of Adam Weiβ, the Reformation was a long time waking.

[2] See the contributions in Andrew Pettegree, (ed.), *The Early Reformation in Europe* (Cambridge, 1992).

[3] See Scribner's observations in Bob Scribner, Roy Porter, Mikulás Teich (eds.), *The Reformation in National Context* (Cambridge, 1994), pp. 221–2.

Bibliography

Abel, W. *Agrarkrisen und Agrarkonjunktur.* Hamburg, 1966.

Abray, L. J. *The People's Reformation. Magistrates, Clergy, and Commons in Strasbourg 1500–1594* Oxford, 1985.

Adam, P. *La vie paroissiale en France au XIVe siécle.* Paris, 1964.

Althaus, P. *The Theology of Martin Luther,* trans. Robert C. Schultz. Philadelphia, 1966.

Arnold, K. 'Die Stadt Kitzingen im Bauernkrieg', *Mainfränkisches Jahrbuch,* 27 (1975), 11–50.

'Dorfweistümer in Franken', *Zeitschrift für bayerische Landesgeschichte,* 38 (1975), 819–76.

Axtmann, R. ' "Police" and the Formation of the Modern State', *German History,* 10 (1992), 39–61.

Bader, K. S. *Dorfgenossenschaft und Dorfgemeinde* Weimar, 1962.

Bahl, H., W. O. Keller, and K. Löffler, 'Ansbachs wirtschaftliche Situation in der zweiten Hälfte des 16. Jahrhunderts und die Almosenordnung von 1581', in *Ansbach – 750 Jahre Stadt.* Ansbach, 1971, pp. 65–83.

Bakhtin, M. *Rabelais and His World,* trans. Helene Iswolsky. Bloomington, 1984.

Barth, F. *Cosmologies in the Making: A Generative Approach to Cultural Variation in Inner New Guinea.* Cambridge, 1987.

Bauer, G. *Anfänge täuferischer Gemeindebildungen in Franken.* Munich, 1966.

Bayer, A. 'Pfarrei und Kirche St Johannis zu Ansbach im Mittelalter', *Jahresbericht des historischen Vereins für Mittelfranken,* 67 (1931/32), 37–52.

St. Gumberts Kloster & Stift in Ansbach. Munich, 1948.

Beauroy, J., M. Bertrand and E. T. Gargan (eds.). *The Wolf and the Lamb: Popular Culture in France.* Saratoga, 1977.

Beck, P. 'Zwei Hexenprozesse aus dem Fränkische', *Jahresbericht des historischen Vereins von Mittlefranken,* 43 (1889), 7–25.

Blauert, A. and G. Schwerhoff (eds.), *Mit den Waffen der Justiz.* Frankfurt, 1993.

Blickle, P. *Die Revolution von 1525.* 2nd edn. Munich, 1983.

Blickle, P. *Gemeindereformation, Die Menschen des 16. Jahrhunderts auf dem Weg zum Heil.* Munich, 1987.

'The "Peasant War" as the Revolution of the Common Man-Theses', in B. Scribner and G. Benecke, *The German Peasant War of 1525 – New Viewpoints.* London, 1979, pp. 19–23.

Blickle, P. (ed.). *Zügange zur bäuerlichen Reformation.* Zurich, 1987.

Bog, I. *Dorfgemeinde Freiheit und Unfreiheit in Franken.* Stuttgart, 1956.

Bibliography

Böhme, F. M. *Geschichte des Tanzes in Deutschland.* Hildesheim, 1967.

Boles, S. K. 'The Economic Position of Lutheran Pastors in Ernestine Thuringia 1521–1555', *Archiv für Reformationsgeschichte*, 63 (1972), 94–125.

Bossert, G. *Beiträge zur Geschichte der Reformation in Franken.* 1880/1882.

'Die Anfänge der Reformation in Berolzheim,' *Blätter für bayerische Kirchengeschichte*, 2 (1887), 17–20.

'Die ersten Schritte zur Neuordnung der Kapitel in der Markgrafschaft Brandenburg-Ansbach 1528 ff', *Blätter für bayerische Kirchengeschichte*, 3 (1887), pp. 33–8.

'Zur Geschichte Kitzingens im ersten Jahrzehnt der Reformation,' *Blätter für bayerische Kirchengeschichte*, 1 (1887/88), 190–2.

Bossert, G. and E. F. H. Medicus. 'Die Brandenburg-Nürnbergische Kirchenvisitation vom Jahre 1528', *Beiträge zur bayerischen Kirchengeschichte*, (1887).

'Das Examen der Pfarrer bei der Kirchenvisitation in der Markgrafshaft Brandenburg-Ansbach im Jahre 1528', *Jahresbericht des historischen Vereins für Mittelfranken*, 43 (1889).

Bossy, J. 'The Mass as a Social Institution', *Past and Present*, 100 (1983), 29–61.

Christianity in the West 1400–1700. Oxford, 1987.

Brandmüller, W. 'Dr. Joh. Winhart, der letzte katholische Stiftsprediger in Ansbach', *Würzburger Diözesangeschichtsblätter*, 18 (1957), 125–47.

Brecht, M. 'Herkunft und Ausbildung der protestantischen Geistlichen des Herzogtums Württemberg im 16. Jahrhundert', *Zeitschrift für Kirchengeschichte*, 80 (1969), 163–75.

Brecht, M. and H. Ehmer, *Südwestdeutsche Reformationsgeschichte.* Stuttgart, 1984.

Brooke, C. N. L. *The Medieval Idea of Marriage.* Oxford, 1989.

Brooke, R. and C. *Popular Religion in the Middle Ages.* London, 1984.

Browe, P. 'Die Elevation in der Messe', *Jahrbuch für Liturgiewissenschaft*, 9 (1929), 20–66.

'Die Eucharistie als Zaubermittel im Mittelalter', *Archiv für Kulturgeschichte*, 20 (1930), 134–54.

Buck, L. P. 'Opposition to Tithes in the Peasants' Revolt: A Case Study of Nuremberg in 1524', *Sixteenth Century Journal*, 4 (1973), 11–22.

Bültner, E. 'Der Krieg des Markgrafen Albrecht Alcibiades in Franken 1552–1555', *Archiv für Geschichte von Oberfranken*, 23 (1908), 1–164.

Burke, P. *Popular Culture in Early Modern Europe.* London, 1978.

'Strengths and Weaknesses of the History of Mentalities', *History of European Ideas*, 75 (1986), 439–51.

The Historical Anthropology of Early Modern Italy. Cambridge, 1987.

Büttner. *Materialien zur Ansbachischen Geschichte, Topographie und Rechtsverfassung.* Ansbach, 1807.

Cameron, E. *The European Reformation.* Oxford, 1991.

Chartier, R. 'Intellectual History or Sociocultural History? The French Trajectories,' in D. LaCapra and S. L. Kaplan, *Modern European Intellectual History.* London, 1982, pp. 13–46.

The Cultural Uses of Print in Early Modern France, trans. L. G. Cochrane. Princeton, 1987.

Cultural History: Between Practices and Representations, trans. Lydia G. Cochrane. Oxford, 1988.

Bibliography

Christian Jr., W. A. *Apparitions in Late Medieval and Renaissance Spain*. Princeton, 1981.
Local Religion in Sixteenth-Century Spain. Princeton, 1989.

Clark, S. 'Protestant Demonology: Sin, Superstition, and Society (*c*.1520–1630) in B. Ankarloo and G. Henningsen (eds.), *Early Modern Witchcraft. Centres and Peripheries*. Oxford, 1990, pp. 45–81.

Clauβ, D. H. 'Kirchenvisitation des 16. Jahrhunderts im Dekanat Neustadt a. A.', *Zeitschrift für bayerische Kirchengeschichte*, 9 (1934), 152–64.

Clauβ, H. *Die Einführung der Reformation in Schwabach 1521–1530*. Leipzig, 1917.

Clauβ, L. 'Aus Gunzenhäuser Visitationsakten des 16. Jahrhunderts', *Beiträge zur bayerischen Kirchengeschichte*, 3 (1925), pp. 101–10.

Cohn, H. 'Anticlericalism in the German Peasants' War', *Past & Present*, 83 (1979), 3–31.

Cohn, N. *Europe's Inner Demons*. London, 1975.

Conrad, F. *Reformation in der bäuerlichen Gesellschaft. Zur Rezeption reformatorischer Theologie im Elsass*. Stuttgart, 1984.
'Die" bäuerliche" Reformation. Die Reformationstheologie auf dem Land am Beispiel des Unterelsaβ', in P. Blickle, A. Lindt & A. Schindler (eds.), *Zwingli und Europa. Referate und Protokoll des Internationalen Kongresses aus Anlaβ des 500. Geburtstags von Huldrych Zwingli*. Zurich, 1985, pp. 137–50.

Constable, G. 'Resistance to Tithes in the Middle Ages', *The Journal of Ecclesiastical History*, 13 (1962), 172–85.

Dannenbauer, H. 'Entstehung des Territoriums der Reichsstadt Nürnberg', *Arbeiten zur deutschen Rechts- und Verfassungsgeschichte*, 7 (1928),1–258.

Davis, N. Z. *Society and Culture in Early Modern France*. London, 1975.

Delumeau, J. *Catholicism between Luther and Voltaire: A New View of the Counter-Reformation*. London, 1977.

Devos, R. and B. Grosperrin, *La Savoie de la Réforme á la Révolution française*. Rennes, 1985.

Dieterich, H. *Das protestantische Eherecht in Deutschland bis Mitte des 17 Jahrhunderts*. Munich, 1970.

Dollinger, R. 'Evangelische Kirchendisziplin in den fränkischen Kirchen', *Zeitschrift für bayerische Kirchengeschichte*, 14 (1939).

Dorfmüller, T. H. 'Aeltere kirchliche Geschichte von Culmbach', *Archiv für Geschichte und Alterthumskunde des Ober-Main-Kreises*, 1 (1831), 7–45.

Drews, P. *Der evangelische Geistliche in der deutschen Vergangenheit*. Jena, 1910.

Duby, G. *Medieval Marriage*, trans. E. Forster. London, 1978.

Duffy, E. *The Stripping of the Altars*. London, 1992.

Duggan, L. G. 'Fear and Confession on the Eve of the Reformation', *Archiv für Reformationsgeschichte*, 75 (1984), 153–75.

Dülmen, R. van. *Die Entstehung des frühneuzeitlichen Europa 1550–1648*. Frankfurt, 1982.
'Volksfrömmigkeit und Konfessionelles Christentum im 16. und 17. Jahrhundert', in Wolfgang Schieder (ed.), *Volksreligiosität in der modernen Sozialgeschichte*. Göttingen, 1986, pp. 14–30.
Reformation als Revolution. Frankfurt, 1987.
'Reformation und Neuzeit. Ein Versuch,' *Zeitschrift für historische Forschung*, 14 (1987), 1–25.

Bibliography

Theatre of Horror. Crime and Punishment in Early Modern Germany, trans. Elisabeth Neu. Oxford, 1990.

Dülmen, R. van, (ed.), *Dynamik der Tradition*. Frankfurt, 1992.

Dykema, P. A. and H. A. Oberman (eds.). *Anticlericalism in Late Medieval and Early Modern Europe*. Leiden, 1993

Eckstein, E. *Geschichte der Juden im Markgraftum Bayreuth*. Bayreuth, 1907.

Edwards, M. U. 'Lutheran Pedagogy in Reformation Germany', *History of Education Quarterly*, 21 (1981), 471–7

Elton, G. R. *Reformation Europe 1517–1559*. London, 1986.

Endres, R. 'Zur wirtschaftlichen und sozialen Lage in Franken vor dem Dreißigjährigen Krieg', *Jahrbuch für fränkische Landesforschung*, 28 (1968), 5–52.

'Probleme des Bauernkriegs im Hochstift Bamberg', *Jahrbuch für fränkische Landesforschung*, 31 (1971), 91–138.

'Der Bauernkrieg in Franken', *Blätter für deutsche Landesgeschichte*, 109 (1973), 31–68.

'Absolutistische Entwicklungen in fränkischen Territorien im Spiegel der Dorfordnungen', *Jahrbuch für Regionalgeschichte*, 16 (1989), 81–93.

'Stadt- und Landgemeinde in Franken', in P. Blickle (ed.), *Landgemeinde und Stadtgemeinde in Mitteleuropa*. Munich, 1991, pp. 101–17.

Estes, J. M. *Christian Magistrate and the State Church: The Reforming Career of Johannes Brenz*. London, 1982.

Febvre, L. *The Problem of Unbelief in the Sixteenth Century*, trans. B. Gottlieb. London, 1982.

Fischer, J. B. *Geschichte und ausführliche Beschreibung der Markgräflich – Brandenburg Haupt – und Residenz – Stadt Anspach, oder Onolzbach, und deren Merkwürdigkeiten...'.* Ansbach, 1786.

Stätistische und topographische Beschreibung des Burggraftums Nürnberg unterhalb des Gebürgs; oder des Fürstentums Brandenburg-Anspach. Ansbach, 1790.

Flint, V. I. J. *The Rise of Magic in Early Medieval Europe*. Oxford, 1991.

Forster, M. R. *The Counter-Reformation in the Villages*. Ithaca, 1992.

Foucault, M. *Discipline and Punish*, trans. Alan Sheriden New York, 1979.

Franz, A. *Die kirchlichen Benediktionen im Mittelalter*. Freiburg, 1909.

Die Messe im deutschen Mittelalter. Darmstadt, 1963.

Franz, G. *Der Deutsche Bauernkrieg*. Darmstatt, 1977.

Freedberg, D. *The Power of Images: Studies in the History and Theory of Response*. London, 1989.

Fuhrmann, Rosi. 'Glaube, Kirche und Recht – Ländliche Pfarreien im deutschen Spätmittelalter', *Tel Aviver Jahrbuch für deutsche Geschichte*, 22 (1993), 153–206.

Galpern, A. N. *The Religion of the People in Sixteenth-Century Champagne*. London, 1976.

Genicot, L. *Rural Communities in the Medieval West*. London, 1990.

Georgii, Ja. F. *Nachricht von der Stadt und dem Markgrafthum Ansbach, Nebst einigen zu solcher gehörigen Urkunden*. Frankfurt, 1732.

Gestrich, A. 'Protestant Religion, the State and the Suppression of Traditional Youth Culture in Southwest Germany', *History of European Ideas*, 11 (1989), 629–35.

Ginzburg, C. *The Cheese and the Worms*, trans. John and Anne Tedeschi. London, 1982.

The Night Battles, trans. John and Anne Tedeschi. London, 1985.

Bibliography

Ecstasies: Deciphering the Witches' Sabbath, trans. R. Rosenthal. London, 1990.

Goertz, H. J. 'Aufstand gegen den Priester. Antiklerikalismus und reformatorische Bewegung', in P. Blickle (ed.), *Bauer, Reich und Reformation*. Stuttgart, 1982, pp. 182–209.

Pfaffenhaß und groß Geschrei. Die reformatorischen Bewegungen in Deutschland 1517–1529. Munich, 1987.

'Träume, Offenbarungen und Visionen in der Reformation', in R. Postel and F. Kopitzsch (eds.), *Reformation und Revolution: Beiträge zum politischen Wandel und den sozialen Kräften am Beginn der Neuzeit*. Stuttgart, 1989, pp. 171–92.

Goody, J. *The Development of the Family and Marriage in Europe*. Cambridge, 1983.

Gordon, B. *Clerical Discipline and the Rural Reformation. The Synod in Zürich, 1532–1580*. Bern, 1992.

Gottlieb, B. 'The Meaning of Clandestine Marriage', in R. Wheaton and T. K. Hareven (eds.), *Family and Sexuality in French History*. Philadelphia, 1980.

Götz, J. B. *Die Glaubensspaltung im Gebiete der Markgrafschaft Ansbach-Kulmbach in den Jahren 1520–1535*. Freiburg, 1907.

Gravenhorst, F. W. *Markgraf Georg Friedrich 1557–1603*. Kulmach, 1966.

Grimm, H. *Lazarus Spengler, a Lay Leader of the Reformation*. Columbus, 1978.

Grossen, J. M. *Burg und Marggräflichbrandenburgische Kriegshistorie der löblichen Fürstenthümer Kulmbach und Ansbach*. Bayreuth, 1748.

Grünenwald, E. 'Das Porträt des Kanzlers Georg Vogler (1550+) [mit einem Beitrag von Wilhelm Engel]', *Mainfränkishes Jahrbuch für Geschichte und Kunst*, 2 (1950), 130–5.

Gruzinski, S. *Man-Gods in the Mexican Highlands*, trans. E. Corrigan. Stanford, 1989.

Gurevich, A. *Categories of Medieval Culture*. London, 1985.

Medieval Popular Culture: Problems of Belief and Perception. Cambridge, 1990.

Gürsching, H. 'Die Entstehung des Ansbacher Konsistoriums', *Zeitschrift für bayerische Kirchengeschichte*, 4 (1929), 13–48.

Haendler, K. *Wort und Glaube bei Melanchthon*. Gütersloh, 1968.

Haenle, S. *Geschichte der Juden im ehemaligen Fürstenthum Ansbach*. Ansbach, 1867.

Hagelstange, A. *Süddeutsches Bauernleben im Mittelalter*. Leipzig, 1898.

Hampe, T. *Crime and Punishment in Germany*, trans. M. Letts. London, 1929.

Hartung, F. 'Die Literatur über die Reformationsgeschichte der Markgrafschaft Ansbach-Kulmbach', *Beiträge zur bayerischen Kirchengeschichte*, 14 (1908), 79–96.

Hasel, K. 'Die Entwicklung von Waldeigentum und Waldnutzung im späten Mittelalter als Ursache für die Entstehung des Bauernkriegs', *Allgemeine Forst- und Jagdzeitung*, 138 (1967), 141–50.

Haupt, Hermann. *Die religiösen Sekten in Franken vor der Reformation*. Würzburg, 1882.

Hausmann, G. 'Das Bemühen des Ansbacher Konsistoriums um kirchliche Ordnung und reine Lehre im Zeitalter der Orthodoxie', *Zeitschrift für bayerische Kirchengeschichte*, 59 (1990), 69–103.

Heckel, M. *Deutschland im konfessionalen Zeitalter*. Göttingen, 1983.

Heeger, F. 'Volksmedizinisches aus fränkischen Hexenprozeßakten', *Mainfränkisches Jahrbuch für Geschichte und Kunst*, 9 (1957), 194–206.

Helmholz, R. H. *Marriage Litigation in Medieval England*. Cambridge, 1974.

Bibliography

Hendrix, S. H. 'Luther's Impact on the Sixteenth Century', *Sixteenth Century Journal*, 1 (1985), 3–14.

Herding, O. 'Die politische Landesbeschreibung in der Markgrafschaft Ansbach', *Jahrbuch für Frankische Landesforschung*, 4 (1938), 26–56.

Herold, R. *Ein Stück Kirchengeschichte. Geschichte des Dekanates Uffenheim.* Gütersloh, 1891.

Herrmann, E. *Geschichte der Stadt Kulmbach.* Kulmbach, 1985.

Hirsch, J. 'Über die erste allgemeine Kirchenvisitation im Fürstentum Culmbach (Bayreuth), besonders zur Zeit der Reformation', *Archiv für Geschichte von Oberfranken*, 8 (1860), 6–18.

Hirschmann, G. 'Die zweite Nürnberger Kirchenvisitation', *Zeitschrift für bayerische Kirchengeschichte*, 32 (1963), 111–32.

Hofmann, H. H. 'Freibauern, Freidörfer, Schutz und Schirm im Fürstentum Ansbach. Studien zur Genesis der Staatlichkeit in Franken', *Zeitschrift für bayerische Landesgeschichte*, 23 (1960), 195–327.

'Bauer und Herrschaft in Franken', in G. Franz (ed.), *Deutsches Bauerntum im Mittelalter.* Stuttgart, 1976, pp. 424–464.

Hofmann, M. 'Die Dorfverfassung im Obermaingebiet', *Jahrbuch für fränkische Landesforschung*, 6/7 (1941), 140–96

Höhn, H. 'Mitteilungen über volkstümliche Überlieferungen in Württemberg. Sitte und Brauch bei Tod und Begräbnis', *Württembergische Jahrbücher für Statistik und Landeskunde*, 2 (1913), 307–57.

Holle, J. W. 'Georg Friedrich, Markgraf von Ansbach und Bayreuth 1557 – 1603', *Archiv für Geschichte und Altertumskunde von Oberfranken*, 7 (1857), 1–28.

Höss, I. 'The Lutheran Church of the Reformation: Problems of Its Formation and Organization in the Middle and North German Territories', in L. P. Buck and J. W. Zophy (eds.), *The Social History of the Reformation.* Columbus, 1972., pp. 317–39

Hsia, R. Po-Chai. *Social Discipline in the Reformation. Central Europe 1550–1750.* London, 1989.

Hsia, R. Po-Chai (ed.). *The German People and the Reformation.* Ithaca, 1988.

Huizinga, J. *The Waning of the Middle Ages.* New York, 1984.

Jacobi, F. *Urgeschichte der Stadt und des ehemaligen Fürstenthums Ansbach, zugleich aelteste Geschichte der meisten Pfarreien, Schlosser, Burgen, Staedte und Doerfer im Mittelfranken.* Ansbach, 1868.

Jäger, C. 'Markgraf Kasimir und der Bauernkrieg in den südlichen Grenzämtern des Fürstentums unterhalb des Gebirgs', *Mitteilungen des Vereins für Geschichte der Stadt Nürnberg*, 9 (1892), 17–164.

Jäger, D. 'Geschichte des Hexenbrennens in Franken im siebzehnten Jahrhundert aus Original-Prozeß-Akten', *Archiv des historischen Vereins für den Untermainkreis*, 2 (1834), 1–72.

Jegel, A. 'Die landständische Verfassung in den ehemaligen Fürstenthumern Ansbach-Bayreuth', *Archiv für Geschichte und Altertumskunde von Oberfranken*, 25 (1912/13), 1–52/1–106.

Jordan, H. *Reformation und gelehrte Bildung in der Markgrafschaft Ansbach-Bayreuth.*

Bibliography

Leipzig, 1917. Volume 1; Hermann Jordan and Christian Bürckstümmer. Erlangen, 1922 Volume Two.

Kanter, E. W. *Markgraf Albrecht Achilles von Brandenburg*. Berlin, 1911.

Kantzenbach, F. W. 'Johannes Brenz und die Reformation in Franken', *Zeitschrift für bayerische Kirchengeschichte*, 31 (1962), pp. 148–68.

Karant-Nunn, S. C. *Luther's Pastors: The Reformation in the Ernestine Countryside.* Philadelphia, 1979.

'Neoclericalism and Anticlericalism in Saxony, 1555–1675', *The Journal of Interdisciplinary History*, 24 1994, 615–37.

Kieckhefer, R. *Magic in the Middle Ages.* Cambridge, 1990.

Kittelson, J. 'Successes and Failures in the German Reformation: The Report from Strasbourg', *Archiv für Reformationsgeschichte*, 73 (1982), 153–74.

'Visitations and Popular Religious Culture: Further Reports from Strasbourg', in K. C. Sessions and P. N. Bebb (eds.), *Pietas and Societas: New Trends in Reformation Social History.* Kirksville, 1985, pp. 89–102.

Klaniczay, G. *The Uses of Supernatural Power*, trans. S. Singerman. Oxford, 1990.

Klaus, B. 'Soziale Herkunft und theologische Bildung lutherischer Pfarrer der reformatorischen Frühzeit', *Zeitschrift für Kirchengeschichte*, 80 (1969), 22–49.

Kneitz, O. *Albrecht Alcibiades, Markgraf von Kulmbach.* Kulmbach, 1951.

Kneule, W. 'Beichte, Konfirmation und Kirchenzucht in der ehemaligen Markgrafschaft Brandenburg-Bayreuth-Kulmbach 1533–1810', *Zeitschrift für bayerische Kirchengeschichte*, 37 (1968), 101–92.

Kirchengeschichte der Stadt Bayreuth. Neustadt/Aisch, 1971.

Kolde, G. 'Zur Brandenburgish-Nürnburgischen Kirchenvisitation 1528', *Beiträge für bayerische Kirchengeschichte*, 19 (1913), 275–81.

Kolde, T. *Andreas Althamer, der Humanist und Reformator in Brandenburg-Ansbach.* Erlangen, 1895.

Kramer, K. S. *Die Nachbarschaft als bäuerliche Gemeinschaft.* Munich, 1954.

'Würzburger Volk im 16. Jahrhundert', *Mainfränkisches Jahrbuch für Geschichte und Kunst*, 7 (1955), 143–70

Bauern und Bürger im nachmittelalterlichen Unterfranken. Würzburg, 1957.

Volksleben im Fürstentum Ansbach und seinen Nachbargebieten 1500–1800. Würzburg, 1961.

'Protestantisches in der Volkskultur Frankens. Konfessionelle Rivalität und Nachbarschaft', *Hessische Blätter für Volkskunde*, 60 (1969), 77–92.

Kraußold, L. *Geschichte der evangelischen Kirche im ehemaligen Fürstenthum Bayreuth.* Erlangen, 1860.

Kriss-Rettenbeck, L. *Ex Voto: Zeichen Bild und Abbild im christlichen Votivbrauchtum.* Zurich, 1972.

Krodel, G. G. 'State and Church in Brandenburg-Ansbach-Kulmbach 1524–1526', *Studies in Medieval and Renaissance History*, 5 (1968), 141–213.

Kuhr, G. 'Der katholische Pfarrer Johannes Mendel und die Anfänge der Reformation in Ansbach', in *Festgabe Matthias Simon: Zeitschrift für bayerische Kirchengeschichte*, 32 (1963), 74–82.

Labouvie, E. *Zauberei und Hexenwerk.* Frankfurt, 1991.

Bibliography

Lang, K. H. *Neuere Geschichte des Furstentums Baireuth.* 3 vols. Nuremberg, 1798/1801.

Lang, P. T. 'Konfessionsbildung als Forschungsfeld', *Historisches Jahrbuch,* 100 (1980), 479–93.

'Würfel, Wein und Wettersegen – Klerus und Gläubige im Bistum Eichstätt am Vorabend der Reformation', in V. Press and D. Stievermann (eds.), *Martin Luther: Probleme seiner Zeit.* Stuttgart, 1986, pp. 219–43.

Langbein, J. H. *Persecuting Crime in the Renaissance.* Cambridge, 1974.

Lea, H. C. *A History of Auricular Confession and Indulgences in the Latin Church.* London, 1896, vol. 2.

Levack, B. *The Witch-hunt in Early Modern Europe.* London, 1987.

Lévy-Bruhl, L. *How Natives Think,* trans. L. A. Clare. Princeton, 1985.

Liermann, H. 'Protestant Endowment Law in the Franconian Church Ordinances', in Jonathan W. Zophy and Lawrence P. Buck (eds.), *The Social History of the Reformation.* Ohio, 1972, pp. 340–54.

Lippert, *Die 400 jährige Reformation im Markgrafentum Bayreuth.* Bayreuth, 1928.

Lith, J. W. von der. *Erläuterung der Reformationshistorie vom 1524 bis zum 28 Jahr Christi incl. aus dem Hoch–Fürstlich. Brandenburg–Onoltzbachischen Archiv an das Licht gebracht.* Schwabach, 1733.

Lloyd, G. E. R. *Demystifying Mentalities.* Cambridge, 1990.

Löhe, W. *Erinnerungen aus der Reformationsgeschichte von Franken, insonderheit der Stadt und dem Burggraftum Nürnberg ober und unterhalb des Gebirgs.* Nuremberg, 1847.

Lohse, B. *Martin Luther.* Munich, 1983.

Looshorn, J. *Die Geschichte des Bisthums Bamberg.* Bamberg, 1903.

Lory, K. 'Hexenprozesse im Gebiete des ehemaligen Markgrafenlandes', in *Festgabe Karl Theodor von Heigel.* München, 1903, pp. 290–304.

Machilek, F. 'Margraf Friedrich von Brandenbur–Ansbach, Domprobst zu Würzburg 1497–1536', *Fränkische Lebensbilder,* 11 (1984), 101–39.

Manselli, R. *La religion populaire au Moyen Age.* Montreal, 1975.

Maurer, W. *Die Kirche und ihr Recht.* Eds. G. Müller and G. Seebaß. Tübingen, 1976.

Mauss, M. *A General Theory of Magic,* trans. R. Brain, London, 1972.

Medick, H. 'Village Spinning Bees: Sexual Culture and Free Time among Rural Youth in Early Modern Germany', in D. Sabean and H. Medick (eds.), *Interest and Emotion: Essays on the Study of Family and Kinship.* Cambridge, 1984, pp. 317–39.

Medicus, E. F. H. *Geschichte der evangelischen Kirche im Königreiche Bayern.* Erlangen, 1863.

'Die brandenburg-nürnbergische Kirchenvisitation vom Jahre 1528', *Blätter für bayerische Kirchengeschichte,* 4 (1888), 59–4.

Merzbacher, F. *Die Hexenprozesse in Franken.* Munich, 1970.

Meyer, C. 'Aktenstücke zur Geschichte des Interims im Fürtentum Brandenburg-Ansbach', *Jahresbericht des historischen Vereins für Mittlefranken,* 40 (1880), 29–53.

Meyer, J. *Die Einführung der Reformation in Franken.* Ansbach, 1893.

Moeller, B. *Deutschland im Zeitalter der Reformation.* Göttingen, 1981.

Monter, W. *Ritual, Myth and Magic in Early Modern Europe.* London, 1983.

Moxey, K. *Peasants, Warriors and Wives.* London, 1989.

Muchembled, R. 'The Witches of Cambrésis: The Acculturation of the Rural World in the

Bibliography

Sixteenth and Seventeenth Centuries', in J. Obelkevich (ed.), *Religion and the People, 800–1700*. Chapel Hill, 1979, pp. 221–76.

Popular Culture and Elite Culture in France 1400–1750, trans. L. Cochrane. London, 1985.

Muck, G. *Beiträge zur Geschichte von Kloster Heilsbronn*. Ansbach, 1859.

Geschichte von Kloster Heilsbronn von der Urzeit bis zur Neuzeit. Nördlingen, 1879, Vol. 2.

Müller, G. 'Verfassungs- und Verwaltungsgeschichte der sächsischen Landeskirche', *Beiträge zur Sächsischen Kirchengeschichte*, 9 (1894), 1–272.

Müller, G. 'Die Reformation im Fürstentum Brandenburg-Ansbach/Kulmbach', *Zeitschrift für bayerische Kirchengeschichte*, 48 (1979), 3–18.

Müller G. and G. Seebaß (eds.), *Andreas Osiander D. Ä. Gesamtausgabe*. Gütersloh, 1979–.

Müller, K. 'Die Anfänge der Konsistorialverfassung im lutherischen Deutschland', *Historische Zeitschrift*, 3 (1909), 1–30.

Müller, K. 'Markgraf Georg von Brandenburg-Ansbach-Jägerndorf. Eine Gestalt aus der fränkischen und schliesischen Reformationszeit', *Jahrbuch für schliesische Kirche und Kirchengeschichte*, 34 (1955), 1–30.

Müller, U. *Die ständische Vertretung in den fränkischen Markgraftümern in der ersten Hälfte des 16. Jahrhunderts*. Neustadt a.d. Aisch, 1984.

'Markgraf Georg der Fromme. Ein protestantischer Landesherr im 16. Jahrhundert, *Jahrbuch für fränkische Landesforschung*, 45 (1985), 107–23.

Münch, P. *Zucht und Ordnung. Reformierte Kirchenverfassungen im 16. und 17. Jahrhundert*. Stuttgart, 1978.

Nahl, R. van. *Zauberglaube und Hexenwahn im Gebiet von Rhein und Maas*. Bonn, 1983.

Neubauer, H. J. 'Der Bau der großen Bastei hinter der Veste 1538–1545. Ein Beitrag zur Geschichte der Nürnberger Stadt Befestigung und zu den Auseinandersetzungen mit Markgraf Georg dem Frommen von Brandenburg-Ansbach,' *Mitteilungen des Vereins für Geschichte der Stadt Nürnberg*, 69 (1982), 196–263.

Nischan, B. *Prince, People, and Confession. The Second Reformation in Brandenburg*. Philadelphia, 1994.

Nobbe, H. 'Das Superintendentenamt, seine Stellung und Aufgabe nach den evangelischen Kirchenordnungen des 16. Jahrhunderts', *Zeitschrift für Kirchengeschichte*, 14 (1894), 404–29.

Oberman, H. A. *Luther: Mensch zwischen Gott und Teufel*. Munich, 1986.

Oestreich, G. *Strukturprobleme der frühen Neuzeit*. Berlin, 1980.

Neostoicism and the Early Modern State. Cambridge, 1982.

O'Keefe, D. L. *Stolen Lightning: The Social Theory of Magic*. Oxford, 1982.

Ozment, S. *The Reformation in the Cities*. London, 1975.

The Age of Reform. London, 1980.

When Fathers Ruled. London, 1983.

Protestants. The Birth of a Revolution. London, 1993.

Packull, W. O. *Mysticism and the Early South German–Austrian Anabaptist Movement 1525–1531*. Scottdale, 1977.

Peel, D. Y. 'Understanding Alien Belief Systems', *The British Journal of Sociology*, 20 (1969), 69–84.

Peters, C. '"Der Teufel sieht mich hier nicht gern...' Die Zwölf Briefe Johann Eberlins

Bibliography

von Günzburg aus seiner Zeit als Pfarrverweser in Leutershausen (1530–1533)', *Zeitschrift für bayerische Kirchengeschichte*, 59 (1990), 23–68.

Petersohn, J. 'Staatskunst und Politik des Markgrafen Georg Friedrich von Brandenburg-Ansbach und Bayreuth', *Zeitschrift für bayerische Landesgeschichte*, 24 (1961), 229–76.

Pettegree, Andrew (ed.). *The Early Reformation in Europe*. Cambridge, 1992.

Pfeiffer, G. 'Der Aufstieg der Reichsstadt Nürnberg im 13. Jahrhundert', *Mitteilungen des Vereins für Geschichte der Stadt Nürnberg*, 44 (1953).

Pietsch, F. 'Geschichte der Gelehrten Bildung in Kulmbach', *Schriften für Heimatforschung und Kulturpflege in Ostfranken*, 33 (1974).

Pohl, H. *Hexenglaube und Hexenverfolgung im Kurfürstentum-Mainz. Ein Beitrag zur Hexenfrage im 16. und beginnenden 17. Jahrhundert*. Stuttgart, 1988.

Ponader, E. 'Lateinschule und Deutsche Schule in Wunsiedel von den Anfängen bis zum großen Stadtbrand 1731', *Archiv für Geschichte von Oberfranken*, 68 (1988), 55–60.

Reicke, E. *Der Lehrer in der deutschen Vergangenheit*. Leipzig, 1901.

Reinhard, J. P. *Beyträge zu der Historie Frankenlandes und der angränzenden Gegenden*. Bayreuth, 1760, Part 1.

Reinhard, W. 'Zwang zur Konfessionalisierung? Prolegomena zu einer Theorie des konfessionellen Zeitalters', *Zeitschrift für historische Forschung*, 10 (1983), 257–78.

Reu, M. 'Zur katechetischen Literatur Bayerns im 16 Jahrhundert', *Beiträge zur bayerischen Kirchengeschichte*, 13/14 (1907/1908), 122–49, 127–36.

Richter, L. *Geschichte der evangelischen Kirchenverfassung in Deutschland*. Leipzig, 1851

Robisheaux, T. 'Peasants and Pastors: Rural Youth Control and the Reformation in Hohenlohe, 1540–1680', *Social History*, 6 (1981), 281–300.

Rural Society and the Search for Order in Early Modern Germany. Cambridge, 1989.

Roper, L. "Going to Church and Street": Weddings in Reformation Augsburg', *Past and Present*, 106 (1985), 62–101.

Rubin, Miri. *Corpus Christi. The Eucharist in Late Medieval Culture*. Cambridge, 1991.

Rublack, H. C. 'Reformatorische Bewegungen in Würzburg und Bamberg', in B. Moeller (ed.), *Stadt und Kirche im 16. Jahrhundert*. Gütersloh, 1978, pp. 109–24.

Rublack, H. C. (ed.). *Die lutherische Konfessionalisierung in Deutschland*. Gütersloh, 1992.

Rublack, H. C. and D. Demandt *Stadt und Kirche in Kitzingen*. Stuttgart, 1978.

Rummel, W. *Bauern, Herren und Hexen*. Göttingen, 1991.

Rütte, H. von. 'Von der spätmittelalterlichen Frömmigkeit zum reformierten Glauben. Kontinuität und Bruch in der Religionspraxis der Bauern', H. von Rütte (ed.), *Itinera*, 8 (1988), 33–44.

Sabean, D. W. *Power in the Blood*. Cambridge, 1984.

Safley, T. M. 'Marriage Litigation in the Diocese of Constance 1551–1620', *Sixteenth Century Journal*, 12 (1981), 61–78.

Let No Man Put Asunder. Kirksville, 1984.

Sahlins, M. *Islands of History*. London, 1985.

Scheible, H. (ed.). *Das Widerstandsrecht als Problem der deutschen Protestanten 1523–1546*. Gütersloh, 1969.

Scherzer, W. 'Die Dorfverfassung der Gemeinden im Bereich des ehemaligen Hochstifts Würzburg', *Jahrbuch für fränkische Landesforschung*, 36 (1976), 37–64.

Schilling, H. 'Reformierte Kirchenzucht als Sozialdisziplinierung? Die Tätigkeit des

Bibliography

Emder Presbyteriums in den Jahren 1557–1562', in W. Ehbrecht and H. Schilling (eds.), *Niederlande und Nordwestdeutschland*. Cologne, 1983, pp. 261–327.

'"History of Crime" or "History of Sin"? Some Reflections on the Social History of Early Modern Church Discipline', in E. Kouri and T. Scott (eds.), *Politics and Society in Reformation Europe*. London, 1987, pp. 289–310.

'Die Konfessionalisierung im Reich. Religiöser und gesellschaftlicher Wandel in Deutschland zwischen 1555 und 1620', *Historische Zeitschrift*, 246 (1988), 1–45.

'Sündenzucht und frühneuzeitliche Sozialdisziplinierung. Die calvinistische, presbyteriale Kirchenzucht in Emden vom 16. bis 19. Jahrhundert', in G. Schmidt (ed.), *Stände und Gesellschaft im Alten Reich*. Stuttgart, 1989, pp. 265–302.

Religion, Political Culture and the Emergence of Early Modern Society, trans. Stephen G. Burnett. Leiden, 1992.

Schlesinger, G. *Die Hussiten in Franken*. Kulmbach, 1974.

Schmidt, H. R. *Reichstädte, Reich und Reformation*. Stuttgart, 1986.

Konfessionalisierung im 16. Jahrhundert. Munich, 1992.

Schneider, B. *Gutachten evangelischer Theologen des Fürstentums Brandenburg-Ansbach/Kulmbach zur Vorbereitung des Augsburger Reichstags von 1530*. Munich, 1987.

Schoenberger, C. G. 'The Development of the Lutheran Theory of Resistance 1523–1530', *Sixteenth Century Journal*, 8 (1977), 61–76.

Schornbaum, K. *Die Stellung des Markgrafen Kasimir von Brandenburg zur reformatorischen Bewegung in den Jahren 1524–1527*. Nuremberg, 1900.

'Zur religiösen Haltung der Stadt Ansbach in den ersten Jahren der Reformation', *Beiträge zur bayerischen Kirchengeschichte*, 7 (1901), 146–66, 193–214.

'Wann wurde in Ansbach der erste evangelische Gottesdienst gehalten?, *Zeitschrift für bayerische Kirchengeschichte*, 9 (1903), 26–9.

'Zur Klostersäkularisation des Markgrafen Kasimir', *Beiträge zur bayerischen Kirchengeschichte*, 10 (1904), 129–40.

'Das Testament des Georg Vogler', *Beiträge für bayerische Kirchengeschichte*, 11, (1905), 268–74.

'Leutershausen bei Beginn der Reformationszeit und das Ende Eberlins von Günzburg,' *Beiträge zur bayerischen Kirchengeschichte*, 11 (1905), 5–34, 78–92.

'Zum gottesdienstlichen Leben Feuchtwangens im 16. Jahrhundert', *Siona*, 31 (1906), 207–13.

'Die Säkularisation des Klosters Solnhofen', *Beiträge für bayerische Kirchengeschichte*, 12 (1906), 212–25.

Zur Politik des Markgrafen Georg von Brandenburg vom Beginne seiner selbständigen Regierung bis zum Nürnberger Anstand 1528–1532. Munich, 1906.

'Zur zweiten brandenburgischen Kirchenvisitation 1536', *Jahresbericht des historischen Vereins für Mittelfranken*, 53 (1906), 1–22.

'Das Interim im Markgraftum Brandenburg-Ansbach. *Beiträge für bayerische Kirchengeschichte*, 14, (1908), 1–27, 49–79, 101–26.

'Pfarrbesoldungen im 16. Jahrhundert', *Beiträge zur bayerischen Kirchengeschichte*, 14 (1908), 42–5.

'Die Säkularisation des Klosters Wülzburg', *Sammelblatt des historischen Vereins Eichstätt*, 24 (1909), 1–18.

Bibliography

'Die Geistlichen der Markgraftschaft Brandenburg-Ansbach von ca. 1520–1578', *Beiträge zur bayerischen Kirchengeschichte*, 16 & 17 (1910/11), 85–92, 137–9, 183–91, 231–6.

'Philippisten und Gnesiolutheraner in Brandenburg-Ansbach', *Beiträge zur bayerischen Kirchengeschichte*, 18 (1912), pp. 97–110.

'Die brandenburgischen Theologen und das Maulbronner Gespräch 1564', *Zeitschrift für Kirchengeschichte*, 34 (1913), 378–94, 491–513.

'Die Bündnisbestrebungen der deutschen evangelischen Fürsten und Markgraf Georg Friedrich von Brandenburg-Ansbach 1566–1570', *Zeitschrift für bayersiche Kirchengeschichte*, 38 (1920), 262–82.

'Die Ansbacher Synode 1556', *Beiträge zur bayerischen Kirchengeschichte*, 27 (1921), 1–11, 33–43, 106–18, 151–66.

'Die brandenburgisch-nürnbergische Norma doctrinae 1573', *Archiv für Reformationsgeschichte*, 19 & 20 (1922/23), 161–93, 5–37, 102–26.

'Markgraf Georg Friedrich von Brandenburg und die evanglischen Stände Deutschlands 1570–75', *Archiv für Reformationsgeschichte*, 22 (1925), 269–300.

'Zur Geschichte des Kargschen Katechismus', *Beiträge zur bayerischen Kirchengeschichte*, 31 (1925), 111–13.

Aktenstücke zur ersten Brandenburgischen Kirchenvisitation 1528. Munich, 1928.

'Die zweite Unterschreibung der Formula Concordiae in der Markgrafschaft Brandenburg', *Zeitschrift für bayerische Kirchengeschichte*, 4 (1929), 240–55.

'Die Einführung der Konkordienformel in der Markgrafschaft Brandenburg', *Zeitschrift für bayerische Kirchengeschichte*, 5 (1930), 176–209.

'Zur Reformationsgeschichte im Bayreuther Oberland', *Zeitschrift für bayerische Kirchengeschichte*, 6 (1931), 203–6.

'Zur Geschichte des Katechismus im Fürstentum Brandenburg-Ansbach. *Zeitschrift für bayerische Kirchengeschichte*, 9 (1934), 149–52.

'Geilsheim in der Reformationszeit', *Zeitschrift für bayerische Kirchengeschichte*, 22 (1953), 173–82.

Schubert, E. 'Gegenreformationen in Franken', *Jahrbuch für fränkische Landesforschung*, 28 (1968), 275–307.

'Protestantisches Bürgertum in Würzburg am Vorabend der Gegenreformation', *Zeitschrift für bayerische Kirchengeschichte*, 40 (1971), 69–82.

Schuhmann, G. *Die Markgrafen von Brandenburg Ansbach. Eine Bilddokumentation zur Geschichte der Hohenzollern in Franken*. Ansbach, 1980.

Schülin, J. H. *Leben und Geschichte des weyland Durchlauchtigsten Marggraff Georgens, zugenannt des Frommen*. Frankfurt, 1729.

Schulze, W. 'Gerhard Oestreichs Begriff "Sozialdisziplinierung in der Frühen Neuzeit",' *Zeitschrift für historische Forschung*, 14 (1987), 265–302.

Schwanhäusser, G. *Das Gesetzgebungsrecht der evangelischen Kirche unter dem Einfluß des landesherrlichen Kirchenregiments im 16. Jahrhundert*. Munich, 1967.

Scott, J. C. *Weapons of the Weak. Everyday Forms of Peasant Resistance*. London, 1985.

'Resistance without Protest and without Organization: Peasant Opposition to the Islamic Zakat and the Christian Tithe', *Comparative Studies in Society and History*, 29 (1987,) 417–52.

Domination and the Arts of Resistance: Hidden Transcripts. London, 1990.

Bibliography

Scott, T. 'The Peasants' War: A Historiographical Review', *The Historical Journal*, 22 (1979), Part 1: pp. 693–720; Part 2: pp. 953–74.

Scribner, R. W. *Popular Culture and Popular Movements in Reformation Germany*. London, 1987.

The German Reformation. London, 1987.

'Police and the Territorial State in Sixteenth-Century Württemberg', in E. Kouri and T. Scott (eds.), *Politics and Society in Reformation Europe*. London, (1987), pp. 103–20.

'Popular Piety and Modes of Visual Perception in Late Medieval and Reformation Germany', *The Journal of Religious History*, 4 (1989), 448–69.

'Is a History of Popular Culture Possible?' *History of European Ideas*, 10 (1989), 175–91.

'The Impact of the Reformation on Daily Life', in *Mensch und Objekt im Mittelalter und in der frühen Neuzeit. Leben-Alltag-Kultur*. Vienna, 1990, pp. 315–43.

'Pastoral Care and the Reformation in Germany', in J. Kirk (ed.), *Humanism and Reform: The Church in Europe, England and Scotland, 1400–1643*. Oxford, 1991.

'Magic and the Formation of Protestant Popular Culture in Germany' unpublished MS, forthcoming 1992.

'The Reformation, Popular Magic and the "Disenchantment of the World"', *Journal of Interdisciplinary History*, 23 (1993), 475–94.

Scribner, R. W., R. Porter and M. Teich (eds.). *The Reformation in National Context*. Cambridge, 1994.

Seebaß, G. *Das reformatorische Werk des Andreas Osiander*. Nuremberg, 1964.

Seyboth, R. 'Die Reichspolitik Markgraf Kasimirs von Ansbach-Kulmbach 1498–1527', *Zeitschrift für bayerische Landesgeschichte*, 50 (1987), 63–108.

'Markgraf Georg von Ansbach-Kulmbach und die Reichspolitik', *Jahrbuch für fränkische Landesforschung*, 47 (1987), 35–81.

'Markgraf Georg Friedrich d Ä. von Brandenburg-Ansbach-Kulmbach (1556–1603) als Reichsfürst', *Zeitschrift für bayerische Landesgeschichte*, 53 (1990), 659–79.

Sicken, B. 'Landesherrliche Einnahmen und Territorialstruktur. Die Fürstentümer Ansbach und Kulmbach zu Beginn der Neuzeit', *Jahrbuch für fränkische Landesforschung*, 42 (1982), 153–248.

Simon, M. *Bayreuthisches Pfarrerbuch. Die Evangelisch-Lutherische Geistlichkeit des Fürstentums Kulmbach-Bayreuth (1528/29–1810)*. Munich, 1930/32.

Evangelische Kirchengeschichte Bayerns. Nuremberg, 1952.

Ansbachisches Pfarrerbuch. Die Evangelisch-Lutherische Geistlichkeit des Fürstentums Brandenburg-Ansbach 1528–1806. Nuremberg, 1955/57.

'Zur Visitation der Nürnberger Landpfarreien im Jahre 1528', *Zeitschrift für bayerische Kirchengeschichte*, 35 (1966), 7–41.

Simpson, J. 'The Local Legend: A Product of Popular Culture', *Rural History*, 2, 1 (1991), 25–35.

Skalweit, S. *Reich und Reformation*. Berlin, 1967.

Spindler, Max (ed.). *Handbuch der Bayerischen Geschichte*. Munich, 1971, Vol. 3.

Sprung, W. 'Zehnten und Zehntrecht um Nürnberg', *Mitteilungen des Vereins für Geschichte der Stadt Nürnberg*, 55 (1968), 1–71.

Stahl, F. J. *Der Protestantismus als politisches Princip*. Berlin, 1853.

Bibliography

Stieber, G. *Historische und Topographische Nachricht von dem Fürstenthum Brandenburg-Onolzbach, aus zuverläßigen archivalischen Documenten, und andern glaubwürdigen Schrifften verfaßet.* Schwabach, 1761.

Stillfried, R. G. *Kloster Heilbronn. Ein Beitrag zu den Hohenzollerischen Forschungen.* Berlin, 1877.

Strauss, G. 'Success and Failure in the German Reformation', *Past and Present*, 67 (1975), 30–63.

Luther's House of Learning. Indoctrination of the Young in the German Reformation. London, 1978.

Strebel, J. S. *Franconia Illustrata, oder Versuch zur Erläuterung der Historie von Franken.* Schwabach, 1761.

Tentler, T. N. 'The Summa for Confessors as an Instrument of Social Control', in C. Trinkaus and H. A. Oberman, *The Pursuit of Holiness in Late Medieval and Renaissance Religion.* Leiden, 1974, pp. 103–25.

Sin and Confession on the Eve of the Reformation. Princeton, 1977.

Theibault, J. 'Community and *Herrschaft* in the Seventeenth-Century German Village', *The Journal of Modern History*, 64 (1992), 1–21.

Thomas, K. V. *Religion and the Decline of Magic.* London, 1985.

Thorndike, L. *The History of Magic and Experimental Science.* New York, 1934, Vol. 4.

Tittmann, C. A. *Geschichte der deutschen Strafgesetze.* Leipzig, 1832.

Tolley, B. *Pastors and Parishioners in Württemberg during the Late Reformation, 1581–1621.* Stanford, 1995.

Toussaert, J. *Le Sentiment religieux en Flandre à la fin du moyen-âge.* Paris, 1963.

Veit, L. *Volksfrommes Brauchtum und Kirche im deutschen Mittelalter.* Freiburg, 1936.

Vice, R. L. 'Vineyards, Vinedressers, and the Peasants' War in Franconia,' *Archiv für Reformationsgeschichte*, 79 (1988), 138–57.

Vocke, W. 'Ueber das Steuerwesen im 16. und 17. Jahrhundert, Ein Beitrag zur Finanzgeschichte des Fürstenthums Brandenburg-Ansbach', *Jahresbericht des historischen Vereins für Mittelfranken*, 34 (1866), 39–62.

Vogler, B. *Le clergé protestant Rhénan au siècle de la Réforme (1555–1619).* Paris, 1976.

'Die Entstehung der protestantischen Volksfrömmigkeit in der rheinischen Pfalz zwischen 1555 und 1619', *Archiv für Reformationsgeschichte*, 72 (1981), 158–95.

Vogtherr, F. 'Die Verfassung der evangelish-lutherischen Kirche in den ehemaligen Furstentümern Ansbach und Bayreuth' *Beiträge zur bayerischen Kirchengeschichte*, 2 (1896), 209–21, 269–87.

Geschichte der Stadt Ansbach. Ansbach, 1927.

Vovelle, M. *Ideologies and Mentalities*, trans. E. O' Flaherty. London, 1990.

Wachtel, N. *The Vision of the Vanquished: The Spanish Conquest of Peru through Indian Eyes 1530–1570*, trans. B. and S. Reynolds. London, 1977.

Wasserschleben, H. *Das landesherrliche Kirchenregiment.* Berlin, 1872.

Weinstein, D. and R. M. Bell, *Saints and Society.* London, 1982.

Weismann, C. *Eine kleine Biblia.* Stuttgart, 1985.

Weiss, H. M. *Vom notwendigen Verstand der Lehre.* Neustadt a.d. Aisch, 1991.

Westermayer, H. *Die Brandenburgisch-Nürnbergische Kirchenvisitation und Kirchenordnung 1528–1533.* Erlangen, 1894.

Bibliography

Wilke, G. *Georg Karg Parsimonius, sein Katechismus und sein doppelter Lehrstreit.* Scheinfeld, 1904

Winch, P. 'Understanding a Primitive Society', *American Philosophical Quarterly*, 1 (1924), 307–24.

Wolf, E. *Ordnung der Kirchen.* Frankfurt, 1961.

Wunder, H. 'Serfdom in Later Medieval and Early Modern Germany', in Aston et al (eds.), *Social Relations and Ideas. Essays in Honour of R. H. Hilton.* Cambridge, 1983.

Die bäuerliche Gemeinde in Deutschland. Göttingen, 1986.

'Die ländliche Gemeinde als Strukturprinzip der spätmittelalterlich-frühneuzeitlichen Geschichte Europas', in P. Blickle (ed.), *Landgemeinde und Stadtgemeinde in Mitteleuropa.* Munich, 1991, pp. 385–402.

Zagorin, P. *Ways of Lying: Dissimulation, Persecution and Conformity in Early Modern Europe.* London, 1990.

Zeeden, E. W. *Konfessionsbildung: Studien zur Reformation, Gegenreformation und katholischen Reform.* Stuttgart, 1985.

Zeeden, E. W. and P. T. Lang (eds.), *Kirche und Visitation: Beiträge zur Erforschung des frühneuzeitlichen Visitationswesens in Europa.* Stuttgart, 1984.

Ziegler, W. 'Territorium und Reformation. Überlegungen und Fragen', *Historisches Jahrbuch*, 110 (1990), 52–75.

Zika, C. 'Hosts, Processions and Pilgrimages: Controlling the Sacred in Fifteenth-Century Germany', *Past and Present*, 118 (1988), 25–64.

Index

Index

church ordinance of 1533, 30–2, 33, 41, 50, 56, 68, 71, 91, 120, 147, 157, 159, 165, 167, 169, 188
church services, 22–3, 27, 28, 30, 42
church wardens, 90, 97, 98
churching, 168
clergy, appointment of, 68–70; expectations of, 67–8; examination of, 70–1; standard of, 71–6; theological belief of, 74–5, 145–7, 191; pre-Reformation, 66–7; maintenance of, 84–92, 94–5, 97–101; relationship to *Gemeinde*, 76–82, 92–101, 132–42; as preachers, 160–1
common chest, 90; in Kitzingen, 11, 38; in Schwabach, 12, 38
Communal Reformation, *see Gemeindereformation*
confession, 80–1, 163–6
confessionalisation, concept of, 103–4, 190
Conrad, Franziska, 34, 37–8
Conrad, Johann, 37, 134–5, 138, 140
consistory, evolution of, 54–9, 121; in Ansbach, 57–9; in Kulmbach, 57; ordinance (1594), 58–9, 90, 98, 106, 151, 154, 168
Counter-Reformation, 15, 103, 144, 190
Crailsheim, 15, 86; chapter of, 52
Cranach, Lucas, The Younger, 102
Creglingen, 61, 150

dances, 108, 111, 112
Dannreuther, Johann, 54
Decker, Johann, 78–9
Dietrich, Hans, 22–3
Dietrich, Veit, 159
Dinkelsbühl, 133
discipline, measures imposed, 64–5, 102, 105, 106–8; regulation of, 109–18; failure of, 54, 109–18, 122–3, 126–8, 137–42, *passim*
district officials, 27, 48, 49, 52, 68, 70, 105–6, 114, 129–30, 135
Döberlein, Erhard, 87
Döhlau, parish of, 79
Dorsch, Johann, 12
Duffy, Eamon, 174

Eberhardt, Paul, 122
Ebner, Hieronymous, 8
Ebrach, monastery of, 11–12
Echter, Julius, 15
Eck, Johann (Kulmbach pastor), 15
Eck, Johann, 33, 35
education, reform of schools, 147–57; curriculum, 151; *see also* schools; schoolmasters
Eichstätt, bishop of, 26, 29, 43, 68–9
Elevation, 51, 169–70; *see also* Eucharist
Endres, Rudolf, 44
Erasmus of Rotterdam, 66–7, 149

Ernst, Contz, 123
Eucharist, 23, 30, 35, 147, 162, 169–71; *see also* Lord's Supper
Evangelical Movement, *see* Gospel

Faßnacht, Sebastian, 96
Feindtel, Pancratius, 118, 180
Fenstern, 123–4
Ferdinand, Archduke of Austria, 20, 29
Feuchtwangen, Lutheranism in, 22–3; chapter of, 52
Feudalism, in Franconia, 44
Feyelmayer, Johann, 12
Fischart, Johann, 112
Fischer, Else, 184–5
Fischer, Friedrich, 175
Fischer, Hans, 154–5
Flacius Illyricus, Matthias, 74–5, 144, 146
Fleißmann, Barbara, 182
Folk Healers, network of, 181; remedies, 183–7; clientele, 181–2, 193–202; *see also* magic; wisewomen; Hoser, Katherina
Formula of Concord, 145, 147
Francisci, Adam, 193
Franck, Hans, 45
Freudenbach parish of, 39, 40
Fröschlein, Johann, 69
Fürst, Wolf, 139, 141

Gattenhofer, Veit, 135
Geilsheim, parish of, 25–6, 37, 39, 40–1
Gemeinde, 128–30; political composition of, 129–32, 139–41; power relations, 132–42
Gemeindereformation concept of, 3, 7, 34, 37–8, 45, 46
Gemeindeversammlung, 131
Gennep, Arnold van, 123–4
Georg Friedrich, margrave of Ansbach, 5, 111, 116, 150; contributions to Lutheran church, 51–4; and schools, 150–1
Georg the Pious, margrave of Ansbach, 5, 24, 40, 56, 89, 91, 105, 112, 120–1, 124, 148–9; reaction to Reformation, 26–32, 60, 161; and Schools, 148–50; death of, 50
Gericht, 130
Ginzburg, Carlo, 192
Glantz, David, 71
Gnodstad, parish of, 41
Gospel, dissemination of, 35–6; demand for, 1, 16–17, 18–20, 37–43; preaching of, 14, 22–4, 35, 67–8, 159–60; relation to *Gemeinde*, 37–43; *see also* Lutheranism; sermons
Graeter, Jacob, 176, 177
Großhabersdorf, parish of, 139, 141
Grunzinski, Serge, 198
Guilds, in Schwabach, 11

224

Index

Index

Index

CAMBRIDGE STUDIES IN EARLY MODERN HISTORY

Series list

War, State and Society in Württemberg, 1677–1793
PETER H. WILSON
From Madrid to Purgatory: The Art and Craft of Dying in Sixteenth-Century Spain
CARLOS M. N. EIRE
The Reformation and Rural Society: The Parishes of Brandenburg-Ansbach-Kulmbach, 1528–1603
C. SCOTT DIXON
Labour, Science and Technology in France, 1500–1620
HENRY HELLER

Titles available in paperback marked with an asterisk*

The following titles are now out of print:
French Finances, 1770–1795: From Business to Bureaucracy
J. F. BOSHER
Chronicle into History: an Essay in the Interpretation of History in Florentine Fourteenth-Century Chronicles
LOUIS GREEN
France and the Estates General of 1614
J. MICHAEL HAYDEN
Reform and Revolution in Mainz, 1743–1803
T. C. W. BLANNING
Altopascio: a Study in Tuscan Society 1587–1784
FRANK MCARDLE
Gunpowder and Galleys: Changing Technology and Mediterranean Warfare at Sea in the Sixteenth Century
JOHN FRANCIS GUILMARTIN JR.
The State, War and Peace: Spanish Political Thought in the Renaissance 1516–1559
J. A. FERNÁNDEZ-SANTAMARIA
Calvinist Preaching and Iconoclasm in the Netherlands, 1544–1569
PHYLLIS MACK CREW
The Kingdom of Valencia in the Seventeenth Century
JAMES CASEY
Filippo Strozzi and the Medici: Favor and Finance in Sixteenth-Century Florence and Rome
MELISSA MERIAM BULLARD
Rouen during the Wars of Religion
PHILIP BENEDICT
The Emperor and his Chancellor: A Study of the Imperial Chancellery under Gattinara
JOHN M. HEADLEY
The Military Organisation of a Renaissance State: Venice c. 1400–1617
M. E. MALLETT AND J. R. HALE
Neostoicism and the Early Modern State
GERHARD OESTREICH
Prussian Society and the German Order: An Aristocratic Corporation in Crisis c. 1410–1466
MICHAEL BURLEIGH

Series list

The Changing Face of Empire: Charles V, Philip II and Habsburg Authority, 1551–1559
M. J. RODRÍGUEZ-SALGADO
Turning Swiss: Cities and Empire 1450–1550
THOMAS A. BRADY JR

231

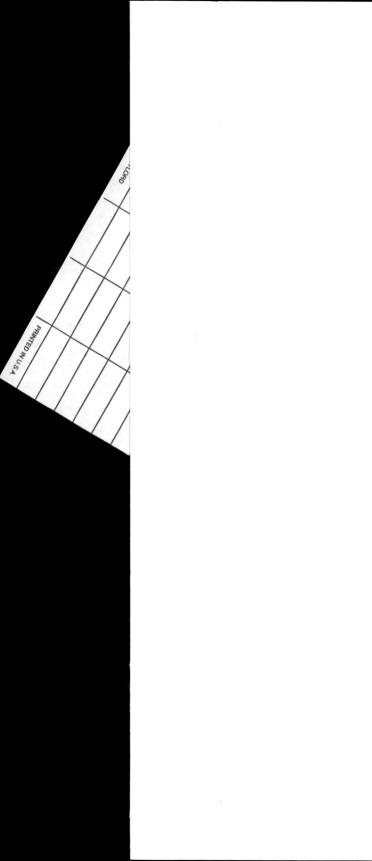

Light All Around Us

Sources of Light

Daniel Nunn

www.raintreepublishers.co.uk
Visit our website to find out more information about Raintree books.

To order:
☎ Phone 0845 6044371
🖹 Fax +44 (0) 1865 312263
✉ Email myorders@raintreepublishers.co.uk

Customers from outside the UK please telephone +44 1865 312262

Raintree is an imprint of Capstone Global Library Limited, a company incorporated in England and Wales having its registered office at 7 Pilgrim Street, London, EC4V 6LB – Registered company number: 6695582

Edited by Dan Nunn, Rebecca Rissman, and Siân Smith
Designed by Marcus Bell
Picture research by Tracy Cummins
Production by Victoria Fitzgerald
Originated by Capstone Global Library Ltd
Printed and bound in China by Leo Paper Products Ltd

ISBN 978 1 406 23812 9 (hardback)
16 15 14 13 12
10 9 8 7 6 5 4 3 2 1

ISBN 978 1 406 23816 7 (paperback)
17 16 15 14 13
10 9 8 7 6 5 4 3 2 1

British Library Cataloguing in Publication Data
Nunn, Daniel.
    Sources of light. -- (Light all around us)
    1. Light sources--Juvenile literature.
    I. Title II. Series
    535-dc23

Acknowledgements
The author and publisher are grateful to the following for permission to reproduce copyright material: Getty Images pp.4 (Comstock), 5 (Bruce Laurance), 12 (Fabrice Lerouge), 14 (Holger Leue), 17, 23d (Science Faction/William Radcliffe); istockphoto p.13 (© digitalskillet); Shutterstock pp.6 (© photobank.ch), 7 (© Amma Cat), 8a (© Elenamiv), 8b (© a123luha), 8c (© Rido), 9a (© R-O-M-A), 9c (© Valentina R.), 9d (© Coprid), 10 (© Hydromet), 11 (© Kapu1), 15 (© John Wollwerth), 16 (© Zinaida), 18 (© Rovenko Design), 19 (© mark cinotti), 20 (© fairy_tale), 21 (© greenland), 21 (© dedi), 22a (© Triff), 22b (© windu), 22c (© Susan Montgomery), 22d (© Vadim Ponomarenko), 22e (© Mike Flippo), 22f (© Luminis), 23a (© mark cinotti), 23b (© Zinaida), 23c (© Kapu1).

Cover photograph of a girl with a lantern by a lake reproduced with permission of Corbis (© Don Mason). Back cover photograph of different light sources in a room reproduced with permission of Shutterstock (Amma Cat).

We would like to thank David Harrison, Nancy Harris, Dee Reid, and Diana Bentley for their assistance in the preparation of this book.

Every effort has been made to contact copyright holders of material reproduced in this book. Any omissions will be rectified in subsequent printings if notice is given to the publisher.